CLARENCE JORDAN

A Radical Pilgrimage in Scorn of the Consequences

Clarence Jordan, outside the First United Methodist Church in
Americus, Georgia, August 24, 1969.

CLARENCE JORDAN

A Radical Pilgrimage in

Scorn of the Consequences

Frederick L. Downing

MERCER UNIVERSITY PRESS | *Macon, Georgia*
2017

MERCER
UNIVERSITY PRESS

Endowed by
TOM WATSON BROWN
and
THE WATSON-BROWN FOUNDATION, INC.

MUP/ H943

ISBN   978-0-88146-632-4
Cataloging-in-Publication Data is available from the Library of Congress

Faith is not belief in spite of evidence

but a life in scorn of the consequences.

—Clarence Jordan

To

Amy and John David

who know about service in the fields of the Lord

Contents

Foreword

Fred Downing has spent his academic life thus far reflecting on how to write "religious biography" in a compelling and faithful way. His published biography of Elie Wiesel was an effective experiment for his work. Now, concerning Clarence Jordan, he has mobilized his mature learning in a "religious biography" that is disciplined, discerning, and imaginative. The outcome of his work is a treasure of a book that preserves the "dangerous memory" of Jordan as a passionate Christian with intrepid integrity who took on the principalities and powers embodied in US racism.

Downing has understood two major points concerning such religious biography. First he understands that close attention must be paid to family origins that largely determine the trajectory of the life that is to be lived. Second, he understands that such a narrative must not be a day-by-day account of a reported life, but must reflect on decisive turns so that the dramatic force of the life becomes available to the reader. On both counts Downing has succeeded in remarkable ways.

On the first point concerning family origins Downing sees that Clarence Jordan was from the outset "morally precocious," being schooled by a mother deeply committed to Jesus. Her way of "schooling" was to love Clarence inordinately so that he came to know he was peculiarly and particularly "chosen" for a life work that would link him to Jesus. His precociousness was "moral" so that he early on saw the conflictual dimension of conventional social relationships. Indeed, he saw so acutely that at one point as a youngster he rebuked even his own father. The anchoring faith of his mother continued to be decisive for him.

On a second point of the pivotal turns in Jordan's life, Downing is clear and perceptive. Among these decisive turns we may especially notice three of them. First, as a college student at the University of Georgia Jordan attended a series of conferences at the Blue Ridge Conference Center of the YMCA. These conferences brought him into contact with headliner radical Christian social witnesses that propelled his awareness in new and daring directions. One specific outcome of his new consciousness was his decisive renunciation of his ROTC involvement that he sensed to be a contradiction of his gospel faith.

Second, in his commitment to "incarnational evangelism," after a stint in Louisville (after seminary) that featured racial upheaval, Jordan bought the property near Americus, Georgia in 1942 that was to become Koinonia Farm. (He got "koinonia" from reading the Book of Acts.) The farm was an experiment in racial cooperation that conflicted in profound ways with the white population of the community. From the beginning Jordan and his community faced aggressive and dangerous hostility from the community. Jordan saw that the hostility was in the service of the maintenance of a plantation mentality that would sustain a plantation economy of cheap Black labor.

The dramatic turn in that long season of hostility was the expulsion of Jordan and his wife from the Rehoboth Baptist Church where they had been active participants. The church acted in fear that Jordan would bring his Black friends and neighbors into the church. This expulsion marked Jordan deeply and cast him as an "ex-Baptist." This dramatic displacement opened him to a large vista of radical faith and drove him to more intense reflection on his own faith identity. But it also profoundly disoriented him from his long-term identity.

The twenty years of contested life at Koinonia Farm led Jordan to deep disappointment about his agricultural experiment. But it also led him to larger dreams beyond that farm community. Thus a third maker was his new friendship with Millard Fuller out of which came the vision for "Habitat for Humanity" that Jordan understood to be both a critique of and an alternative to capitalism that is deeply enmeshed in racism.

In his later years, out of his painful pondering of his faith and life Jordan came to see that the "religion of the cross" was in deep contradiction to "the American Dream." (Clearly he had remained faithful to the trajectory on which his mother had set him). Jordan's discernment of this contradiction is more recently fleshed out by Ta-Nehisi Coates (*Between the World and Me*) who sees that "The Dream" is a white vision of being "masters of the galaxy" that depends on Black subservience. Jordan would resonate completely with Coates's characterization of "the Dream."

Over the long sweep of his vexing experiment Jordan emerges as a prophetic figure that Downing compares to Jeremiah in his capacity for grief, honesty, and hope. Jordan practices both prophetic critique of a capitalist racist regime and prophetic alternative that is constituted by a practice of neighborliness. Downing shows Jordan to be situated in a world occupied on the one hand by W.E.B. Du Bois, Dietrich Bonhoeffer, and Will Campbell, and on the other hand by George Wallace and W. A. Criswell, the Baptist titan from Dallas. The distinctive mark of Jordan in this cast of characters is the way in which he acted in costly and dangerous ways that embodied the cross; he walked he talk!

Downing has rendered us a great and judicious service by his compelling research. It is crucial that Jordan in all his daring courage should be remembered. Downing assures us that this singular saint of gospel obedience will not be forgotten.

Walter Brueggemann
Columbia Theological Seminary
June 12, 2017

Preface

Clarence Leonard Jordan was born in the West Central Georgia town of Talbotton in the early years of the twentieth century, and his life was spent attempting to confront what W. E. B. Du Bois called the "Negro Problem"—the story of those millions "who are America's dark heritage from slavery and the slave-trade."[1] He lived out his adult life on an interracial farm he called "Koinonia" in Southwest Georgia near Americus, not far from the Civil War site of Andersonville Prison and just a few miles from Plains, the home of Jimmy Carter. Jordan's pilgrimage was radical and he embodied a profound critique of region and religion. Because of the impact of Jordan's life on the culture, by the early 1980s—less than fourteen years after his death—he was being hailed as a "Southern Saint."[2]

Despite the early consensus that Jordan was an extraordinary religious person, almost fifty years after his death there is yet to be a study of his life that attempts to chart the nature and dimensions of that radical pilgrimage. How is it that Clarence Jordan went so far beyond his church and his culture? In her work, Tracy Elaine K'Meyer gives the accepted view on the origin of Jordan's radical Christianity: his experience as a twelve-year-old young person rebelling against the church in the context of his awareness of the Georgia chain gang. Then she goes on to say, "Chance [sic] are, Jordan was not really this self-aware as a teenager. The stories about Jordan's childhood are glimpses of his character seen in retrospect through the lens of his later work."[3]

Likewise, Charles Marsh speculates, "It is not at all clear why certain white children form early impressions of racial inequities and feel moved to correct them." Marsh goes on to say, "Perhaps their sensitivity is the result of feeling different themselves...." With eloquent prose, Marsh writes that Jordan's acceptance of this burden "was a slow turning composed of a series of numerous early impressions of race framed by high standards of holiness and a sensitivity to the maternal face of poverty."[4] This study will seek to chart that "slow turning"—the spiritual periodicity and genetic epistemology of Clarence Jordan—to understand the origin of Jordan's religious journey and his acceptance of the burden of racial justice in a new way, by utilizing the heretofore unused corpus of letters that Jordan shared with his mother, interviews with family and friends, and the theories of figures like Erikson, Fowler, Capps, and Brueggemann.

This is, therefore, not a traditional biography. But it does employ a method and philosophical underpinning that is becoming more commonplace. David Mariniss has employed a similar perspective in his studies of Bill Clinton and Barack Obama. Mariniss recently noted the importance of the study of childhood in the life of important historical figures. Mariniss argued that what shapes and influences later life comes early—hence the valid argument for the study of the early years. This "religious biography" of Clarence Jordan employs a similar strategy. Importance is given to the early years, which are seen as a foundation for adulthood. The poet Wordsworth said it first: "The child is father of the man." From this perspective, the challenge of this study is to ask how Clarence, the child, is the father of Jordan, the man. What crucial and formative experiences and influences come early in Clarence's life? Is there a life theme that emerges in childhood, and if so, how is it played out in adulthood? How does this life theme relate to his special project, Koinonia? I will argue that Mariniss is right—that what shaped Jordan, the man, came early. Because of this argument, the reader will find a more detailed portrayal of Jordan's childhood than one might anticipate.

When Clarence Jordan died in 1969 at the age of 57, I was a senior at the university. To a large extent, Jordan's life and work were in the backwater of the drama of cataclysmic change that was the 1960s. I first heard of him and his work in 1974 while doing graduate study in New Orleans. Some few years later in the late 1970s, I began to teach in a humanities program in a small liberal arts college in central Louisiana, which had been Will Campbell's introduction to the collegiate life. By then, Jordan was a legendary figure known by many for his radical faith and Christian idealism. About that time, I first met Will Campbell, who had become a friend of Jordan's, and like Jordan, a Baptist dissident. It was in Louisiana that I first began to read two other Georgians: Martin Luther King, Jr., Flannery O'Connor, and a third figure who eventually came to Georgia—a young scholar by the name of Walter Brueggemann.

It was Brueggemann's book, *The Prophetic Imagination*, that in time greatly influenced my own understanding of religion and culture, and which I will use in this book to help describe the life and work of Clarence Jordan.

My understanding of "religious biography" began to develop in Princeton, where I met three professors who would prove to be influential in my later work. They were James Loder, Donald Capps, and James Fowler. It was James Loder who introduced me to the work of Erik Erikson and the field of religion and personality. I was particularly drawn to Erikson's focus on the historical-critical view of biography, and especially his portrayal of *homo religiosus*, the religious genius whose conflicted life is joined in struggle with an entire people.[5] I followed that initial tutorial with study with Donald Capps and James Fowler. Donald Capps had argued in an early article that Erik Erikson "allowed his narrative to take on a religious tonality consistent with the life experiences and...the psychological conflicts of his subjects." The narration through the reconstruction of events became the point at which the psychology and religious life of the individual converge.[6] In this way, Erikson had succeeded, Capps argued, in establishing a new genre, which Capps called "religious biography." James Fowler wrote a few years later that Erikson's work seemed to mark "a major turn toward treating matters of religion and faith as non-reducible, central dimensions of human personality."[7]

After the time of study in Princeton, I went to Emory where I continued to study with Fowler and others, especially Robert Detweiler, whose focus was literary theory. In time, I saw a linkage between the psychosocial dynamics of Erikson's theory and the genetic epistemology of James Fowler. Both emphasized the journey inherent in spiritual periodicy—the growth and development of the individual through time. In addition, Fowler, like Erikson, seemed to focus on the religious genius with his characterization of "universalizing" faith for a few rare individuals. Consequently, I extended Donald Capps's definition of "religious biography" to include the theory of James Fowler, along with that of Erikson. While in Atlanta at Emory University, I formulated a research agenda to test this methodology. The agenda included the study of three figures from the perspective of religious biography: Martin Luther King, Jr., Elie Wiesel, and Clarence L. Jordan. The studies on King and Wiesel have been completed, and this work on Jordan is the final of the trilogy.[8] Fowler was deeply interested in the study of Clarence Jordan, and as a gracious mentor, Donald Capps would have welcomed the volume and added his own penetrating reading. Both Capps and Fowler died within months of each other in 2015.

Any writing project on Clarence Jordan has its own set of special problems. Clarence Jordan was an amazingly sensitive individual who was able to go beyond tribe and culture in a manner few others have attained. It is, therefore, difficult to read and write about Jordan without being changed by the drama and essential truths that his life reveals. To follow and describe that journey, one must enter into the struggle and come to terms with his Jacob-like wrestling match with the issues of race, war, and religion. Many of Jordan's biographers have seen him to be a prophetic figure. Abraham Heschel pointed out the difficulty of working with such prophetic figures: "Reading the words of the prophets is a strain on the emotions, wrenching one's conscience from the state of suspended animation."[9] But, if Jordan was a prophetic figure, he tended to embody a journey into darkness and suffering accompanied by an extraordinary level of commitment and faithfulness.[10] And, like the prophets, Jordan tended to embody the nature and character of *homo religiosus*, which in part means that the complexity of Clarence Jordan's story is that his life became intertwined with that of his entire region, and eventually his nation. In time, after his death, Jordan would become known as a "saint," a model for the rebuilding of the region and country.

As the story of his life continued in the collective memory of those who shared his ideals—primarily through Habitat for Humanity and the various efforts of those who wrote and spoke about him—he became in some measure the voice of the voiceless, the cry of the plundered poor of his time, but also the call of a prophet to his region to come to terms with its history and tragic past. Clarence's story, as Charles Marsh puts it, was "an exercise in repentance, reconciliation, and costly discipleship."[11] But it was more. Inasmuch as recent years have seen the "Southernization" of the nation, the narrative of Clarence Jordan has become a parable of an entire land seeking redemption. After years of "elective" warfare undermining military lessons learned in Vietnam and years of extreme greed, which have had devastating repercussions worldwide, some sensitive individuals in this country continue the search for the nation's soul.[12] Even in death, Clarence Jordan provides a model for rebuilding the land that he loved.

Notes

[1] W. E. B. Du Bois, *The Souls of Black Folk* (New York: Barnes and Noble Books, 1903, 2003) 83.

[2] Robert Parham, "A Reconciler from 'Dixie': Clarence Jordan," *The Baptist Peacemaker* (July 1983): 6.

[3] Tracy Elaine K'Meyer, *Interracialism and Christian Community in the Postwar South: The Story of Koinonia Farm* (Charlottesville: University of Virginia Press, 1997) 27.

[4] Charles Marsh, *The Beloved Community: How Faith Shapes Social Justice, from the Civil Rights Movement to Today* (New York: Basic Books, 2005) 57.

[5] See especially, Erik H. Erikson, *Gandhi's Truth: On the Origins of Militant Nonviolence* (New York: W.W. Norton & Company, Inc., 1969) 117–33.

[6] Donald Capps, "Psychohistory and Historical Genres: The Plight and Promise of Eriksonian Biography," in Peter Homans, ed., *Childhood and Selfhood* (Lewisburg: Bucknell University Press, 1978) 218.

[7] James W. Fowler in James W. Fowler and Robin W. Lovin et al., *Trajectories in Faith: Five Life Stories* (Nashville: Abingdon Press, 1980) 16.

[8] The books on King and Wiesel were also published by Mercer University Press.

[9] Abraham Joshua Heschel, *The Prophets* (New York: Harper & Row Publishers, 1962) 7.

[10] See Gerhard von Rad, *Old Testament Theology II* (New York: Harper & Row, Publishers, 1965) 204–206.

[11] Marsh, *The Beloved Community*, 84. The characterization of the prophetic voice in this paragraph is based on Heschel, *The Prophets*, 5.

[12] A consensus that developed after the Vietnam War—and lasted for at least twenty-five years—was that the U.S. could engage in warfare only as a last resort when there was a clear national interest, with a strong public support, and the hope of a quick, inexpensive resolution. See Harvard Sitikoff, "The Postwar Impact of Vietnam," in John Whiteclay Chambers, ed., *The Oxford Companion to American Military History* (New York: Oxford University Press, 1999). See also, John Egerton, *The Americanization of Dixie: the Southernization of America.* Egerton argues that the "Americanization of Dixie" and the "Southernization of America" are both part of a bi-directional process of homogenization that has been ongoing since the time of the Civil War. Though full of paradox and contradiction, this homogenization demonstrates a social process in which a nation

attempts to deal with fear, failure, and alienation. The thesis of the book is that the separate cultural regions of North and South have tended to imitate the worst aspects of each other by importing the vices but not the virtues. The end result of this cultural symbiotic relationship has been the creation of an increasingly weaker society devoid of moral and spiritual values. Therefore, more than 145 years after the Civil War, the nation still searches for a way to bring social mores closer to the founding principles of the country.

Introduction

In a tense, crowded room, the angry voices grew louder. A black man got up and stepped to the front of the room. Then he shouted: "Just like the whites kill a Negro for this, I am going to kill a white man." In dramatic fashion, as if scripted in a Shakespearean tragedy, a courageous young white man barely twenty-seven years of age stepped forward and confronted the anger of the crowd: "If a white man must die for this," he said in his distinctive Southern drawl, "…let it be me." As he laid his head down on the table, he proclaimed: "Do it now." The place was the so-called "Haymarket" region of the inner city of Louisville, Kentucky. The time was the late 1930s, and the name of the courageous young seminarian and student of the Greek New Testament was Clarence Leonard Jordan.[1]

How does a person so young—a brilliant and gifted humanitarian with so much to give and so much to live for—reach such a point that allows him to confront such anger seemingly without fear? Indeed, to offer himself in complete vulnerability as a scapegoat, as if seeking to atone for racial conflict now hundreds of years old in this country? This young man somehow grew up with a burden and a dream—in some way, he would reorder Southern society; he would have a part in bringing justice to a troubled land. In 1942, thirteen years before the beginning of the Civil Rights Movement in Montgomery, Clarence Jordan established an interracial farm in Southwest Georgia between Plains and Americus, and twenty-one miles south of the historic Civil War site of Andersonville Prison. In attempting to live out his dream of a reordered society, he would risk his own life and that of his own family—wife and children—and extended family in a hail of gunfire, explosions, and protracted boycotts. But Clarence Leonard Jordan had begun the demonstration plot in faith and would continue it because, for him, faith was a life lived in scorn of the consequences.

What Manner of Man: Biography in Context

In his seminal work, *The Souls of Black Folks*, W.E.B. Dubois describes the culture of South Georgia at the beginning of the twentieth-century. In elegant prose, Dubois argues that "the" issue of the twentieth-century is race. After examining reconstruction, the world of black education in rural Tennessee, and a critique of rising materialism in Atlanta, Dubois narrates a journey by segregated train 200 miles south of Atlanta to the region that he describes as the "Egypt of the Confederacy"—the famous Black Belt, where cotton remains king. His aim is to describe rural life in Georgia as representative of life in the Southern Black Belt. His assessment is that few African Americans are enjoying any economic success. The legal system of the day, when taken with tenant farming, ensures that the African American is only slightly removed from slavery. After mourning the loss of an infant son, Dubois poignantly reflects on whether or not that son were better off dead than to grow up in a world so dominated by the "color-line."[2]

In a recent study titled *Slavery by Another Name*, Douglas Blackmon extends Dubois's descriptive narrative and concludes that the white aristocracy of the Old South learned soon after emancipation that the economic engine of the region could not run without black Americans. So, consequently, the period between the Civil War and World War II became one of the most shameful but little-known periods in American history. Black Southerners were forced to labor against their will as the American dream was stolen from blacks in the South. Blacks were not slaves, but they were not free. Though the thirteenth amendment abolished slavery, it did so for all except those who commit a crime. Legislatures in the post-Civil War South quickly set up a system of laws that made it easy to imprison poor blacks. Among the range of such laws were the vagrancy statutes—if you could not prove you had a job, you could be arrested. Once arrested, one could be leased to large corporations, businesses, or farms. In this way the convict leasing system came into being.[3]

Clarence Jordan was born on the frontier awaiting the birth of a new South—nine years after Dubois's publication—and he would see the Georgia convict leasing system at work and get to know the prisoners in the camp at the Talbot County Jail, which was just behind his home.[4]

The screams in the night from this camp would be part of the poignant revelatory process that would change Jordan's life forever. Jordan's life is not well known, in part because he was a very humble man who did not seek publicity or fame. He was also a very spiritual man and the depth and contours of that religious character have not been perceived or portrayed. The type of religious biography done in this volume will seek to address that issue. One way to begin such a study is to attempt to put Clarence Jordan in a larger biographical and historical context. Jordan's life overlapped with two major international religious figures: Dietrich Bonhoeffer and Mohandas K. Gandhi. His life was also lived out in the context of three Southerners who are extremely well known and whose work helps us to understand Clarence Jordan better. These figures are: W.A. Criswell, Martin Luther King, Jr., and George C. Wallace.

Settin' the Woods on Fire: George Wallace and Clarence Jordan

"Settin' the Woods on Fire" is an old Southern expression. It is, in fact, a double *entendre*. It can be used as a metaphor for extraordinary and exemplary behavior or action. But, of course, it can also mean a form of disastrous and outrageous destructive behavior. George C. Wallace evoked this type of complex reaction from the American populous. He was seen by some as a champion of working-class values and by others as the embodiment of racism. Like Jordan, George Wallace was also born on the frontier of a new South. He, too, would be a protagonist in the unfolding story of civil rights in the 1960s. Like Jordan, he lived out his life on the edge of the famous Black Belt region, which Dubois described so poignantly. Wallace came to know the poverty of the region while very young. And, like Jordan, early on in his career he wanted to make a difference. He became a lawyer and a judge, and was a progressive figure who was first known as a liberal because of his fairness and commitment to justice for all races. Yet something happened in his first race for the governor's office in 1960 that changed the trajectory of his life. John Patterson, Wallace's opponent, played the race card against him and Wallace was beaten. Wallace then made what some have called a "Faustian" bargain. He vowed that no one would ever beat him again using race.[5]

Wallace turned to the right politically and began to advocate the cultural values of his region on race. Politically, George Wallace stood between Roosevelt's New Deal, with its Democratic majority in the Deep South, and the Reagan revolution, which began to mark a new era for the entire nation. It is clear in retrospect that no politician did more than George Wallace to set the tone and agenda of the historical civil rights era and that he had a major impact on the politics of the nation for the next twenty years. More than any other politician, Wallace anticipated the conservative groundswell that would remake American politics, putting Ronald Reagan in the White House and Newt Gingrich and his Republican majority in control of Congress. Put another way, the biography of George Wallace illuminates what John Egerton calls the "Southernization of America." His two presidential bids fired "the deep discontents of an embittered national political minority."[6] Wallace was truly "settin' the woods on fire" and left behind an essentially tragic legacy as Dan Carter rightly saw.[7]

Jordan and Wallace had an ironic relationship. Clarence Jordan could also be seen as "settin' the woods on fire." In the early years of his career, Jordan was a "rising star" among Baptists and was on the speakers' circuit to the best universities and some of the most important Baptist gatherings for young people, such as Ridgecrest. But he, like Wallace, eventually became the epitome of the "other" side and was seen by many leaders to have wasted his career.[8] Both Wallace and Jordan made crucial commitments early in life. In so doing, they would both take suffering upon themselves and their families. Wallace's move to the right would eventually lead to his campaigns for the presidency and made him the target of an assassin's bullet, which would paralyze him for the rest of his life. Jordan's commitment was to identify with the poor and disenfranchised, especially the blacks of his region. In time, he was not only voted out of his church, but his farm became the object of an intense boycott and attack from racist elements like the Ku Klux Klan and the White Citizens Council, some of the same elements that kept Wallace in power. Both Wallace and Jordan would eventually touch the American soul. Wallace, with his stand against integration and in his presidential bids, stirred anger and bitterness in the American electorate. Clarence Jordan profoundly changed the country through the program that eventually became "Habitat for Humanity," which began on Koinonia Farm. The tragic narrative of George Wallace's life was further shaped and measured, and given dimension, by his foundational work in implementing a strategy that could be described as the "Southernization of American Politics."[9] The work of Clarence Jordan challenged this American trajectory at the point of spiritual values. Jordan's life was a continuing dialogue with the culture that surrounded him, and sought to redefine that culture in a manner closer to his vision of the kingdom.[10]

Christ and Culture: W.A. Criswell and Clarence Jordan

One of the most important religious leaders in Jordan's native religion, the Southern Baptist Convention, was W.A. Criswell. The lives of Criswell and Jordan were so similar that they graduated from the same institution with the same degree—the Ph.D. in New Testament Greek from the Southern Baptist Seminary in Louisville. Both went on to hold unique views concerning the Bible and the church. They each held the Bible in high regard and both have been considered "fundamentalists." But Jordan was not a fundamentalist in any way that approached the historical movement of American fundamentalism.[11] Criswell wanted to see the Bible as the literal, inerrant word of God.[12] Jordan also held the Bible to be the word of God, but in some unique way he went beyond Criswell. In fact, some would say that Jordan took the Bible more seriously than did Criswell, who began and championed a "battle for the Bible" in the Southern Baptist Convention. Jordan also took the Bible literally but not in the sense of trying to defend its accuracy. Rather, Jordan, in a more provocative way, assumed that the Bible was personal and meant what it said.[13] Thus, for Jordan, the praxis orientation of the Bible was the crucial dimension. That is, he could not separate between his ideas about the Bible and the lived reality of biblical commitment, and because of that, one could call Jordan's reading "incarnational"—one must live the word and not just proclaim it to be divine reality. Jordan said, "A Christian is not one who believes the right creeds or says the right words....It's the one who does the will of the Father."[14]

Criswell and Jordan differed also on the nature of the church. Criswell became identified with a cultural view of the church—he was the churchman personified. He was pastor of the First Baptist Church of Dallas, Texas, for over fifty years, and became the leader of a movement that sought to disenfranchise all those who did not hold his view of the

Bible and church. Jordan, on the other hand, became a leader in a movement that sought to identify with the disenfranchised of American society, and was eventually excommunicated from his church because of that stance. From that day forward, Clarence Jordan remained an "ex-Baptist," while W.A. Criswell became a cultural icon, described by Bill Moyers as giving a "Criswellian soul" to the Southern Baptist Convention.[15]

Criswell not only epitomized the fundamentalist tradition among Baptists in his day, but his church was the heart of the Southern Baptist Convention, which was close to the soul of Southern culture. Under Criswell's leadership, the First Baptist Church of Dallas grew to 26,000 members and became the largest Southern Baptist church in the world. Criswell, like many Southern Baptists, tended to mirror the culture of the South. It is this dimension of religion tied to cultural values that allows Sam Hill to argue in *Religion and the Solid South* that Southern religion could be characterized as having a "god above God"—a set of cultural mores that were more cherished than the principles of biblical religion. For example, Criswell was initially critical of *Brown v. Board of Education* and he denounced the government's role in integration. In this sense, Criswell was protecting the status quo on race as he also did on issues of sexuality and gender.[16]

Despite much of his rhetoric, Criswell seemed to represent an assimilation of culture and cultural values—Christ in culture.[17] In contrast, Jordan seems to fit best in Niebuhr's mode of Christ transforming culture. In fact, Jordan should be listed with a small but influential group of Southern white churchmen who dissented from the status-quo Baptist politics and polity. While Southern Baptists generally were defenders of Southern society from the inception of the convention, these dissenters—like Jordan, Carlyle Marney, Will Campbell, and Martin England—took a far more progressive stance. They worked for civil rights, opposed the death penalty, worked for peace over against militarism, and typically took a praxis-oriented view toward matters of faith. One should not just talk about religion, but "do" it, instead. For example, in *The Substance of Faith*, Jordan challenges those churches who hold to a gnostic-like image of an exalted Jesus but fail to be obedient. Jordan later quoted in mocking fashion to say: "We'll worship the hind legs off of Jesus but we won't do a thing he says."[18]

As pastor of the largest Southern Baptist church in the world, who was also President of the Southern Baptist Convention on two occasions, Criswell became an icon or legendary figure and served as a model for many other Baptists. But he was not content to adhere to the historic Baptist principle of the separation of church and state. In 1976, Criswell addressed the presidential race from the pulpit and urged the election of Gerald Ford over against another Southern Baptist, Jimmy Carter.[19] In the 1980s, he supported Ronald Reagan and George Herbert Walker Bush. In so doing, he joined conservative religion and politics, and helped to push the country to the right. In his leadership role of the conservative resurgence among Baptists, which sought to disenfranchise those who disagreed with him, Criswell—like Wallace—seemed to stir anger and venom and direct it against those who were not like him.[20] To this end, one could say that, eventually, he wanted to give a Criswellian soul to the entire country. Criswell and the Southern Baptists became integral to the "Southernization of America." In the 1940s, Southern Baptists were mostly limited to the segregated South, but by the 1980s, they had churches in all fifty states and, through the conservative resurgence led by Criswell, Southern Baptists tried to remake the country in their own image. The 2000 election of George W. Bush, a conservative and Texan like Criswell, meant that Southern Baptists were largely successful in their efforts to reshape America.[21]

In marked contrast to Criswell's exclusivism, Clarence Jordan seemed to live his life for inclusivism. The theme of his life was "koinonia"—community. Clarence Jordan was so committed to the inclusion of the "other" that he was willing to endure the strictures of intentional community living. In that regard, Jordan never owned a home or a car because he so valued the inclusion of others in a community model. The terms of community living at Koinonia Farm were that the members did not own personal property or hold personal funds. The group voted on how the money was spent. Clarence eventually became a legend to those who valued inclusion beyond the shared cultural values of a region. But he became *persona non grata* in the Southern Baptist Convention, even at his alma mater in Louisville. Though Criswell and Jordan were in a graduate program together, Criswell could remember very little about Jordan.[22] Again, Criswell mirrored the stance of Southern culture and the Southern Baptist Convention.

Jordan was eventually excluded from the collective life and memory. He was not invited back to his own seminary until the very end of his life, and then only at the insistence of a longtime friend. Jordan, in contrast to Criswell, never endorsed a candidate for president. His attitude toward the government leaned more in the direction of the Anabaptists, which meant that he viewed governmental agencies with suspicion. This skeptical attitude was well-founded because Jordan was investigated by both the FBI and the GBI, as well as a Sumter County grand jury.[23] In addition, Jordan was far too humble to think in terms of spreading his influence in the way that Criswell did. He did not want such adulation. In fact, before he died, Jordan left instructions that he was to be buried in an unmarked grave.

Blessed Are the Peacemakers: Dietrich Bonhoeffer and Clarence Jordan

In the 1930s and early 1940s, Dietrich Bonhoeffer was a leader in the effort to fight the cultural captivity of the German church. He took an active role in working against the new national church (German Evangelical Church), which eventually came under the control of Adolf Hitler. Bonhoeffer's alternative was called the "Confessing Church," which was composed of about 5,000 pastors. In the end, however, most German Christians supported the Führer. Though originally a pacifist, Bonhoeffer eventually joined in an effort to overthrow Hitler. He was arrested on April 5, 1943, and hanged before the end of the war.

Jordan and Bonhoeffer held much in common in both the structure of their lives and in the content of theology. Both came from rather aristocratic families and attended elite institutions of higher education. Both had opportunities to take prominent positions that would have led to relative economic and professional security. Instead, the passion and strength of conviction led each to be engaged in efforts to change society. Seen from another angle, they chose to be identified with the suffering poor and powerless of their day, and to take up vocations that sought to bring redemption. Both Jordan and Bonhoeffer struggled with a popular institutional church, which neither could reconcile with his Christian vision. Both wanted the church to take a more prophetic stand on the ethical issues of the day, such as war and peace—and race. Both were pacifists and they thought that the culture deprived certain groups of their human rights. While Bonhoeffer struggled with Hitler, who became a kind of "god" above God, Jordan wrestled with the church as a cultural institution that had placed cultural mores in a position above the ethical and spiritual values of the religious tradition. Both Jordan and Bonhoeffer took a praxis-oriented view of the "Sermon on the Mount." Both worked to alleviate the cultural captivity of the church. Both understood the "cost of discipleship" and bore suffering with a contentment higher than happiness. In the end, both Jordan and Bonhoeffer, like Elie Wiesel, sought to resituate the divine-human encounter into a life of service, finding the divine in human relationships.[24]

It is clear that Bonhoeffer and Jordan lived on the frontiers of their time. They both came to see the world "from below." Each in his own time rejected the cultural forms that were raised above true religion. Both Bonhoeffer and Jordan called for the rejection of any form of cheap grace, and the acceptance of a radical discipleship. For Jordan, faith meant a life lived in scorn of the consequences, and for Bonhoeffer, the call to Christ was a call to die. As such, they both called for a new form of worldly Christianity and they were both on the forefront of a liberation theology.

The Quest for a Great Soul: Mohandas K. Gandhi, Martin Luther King, Jr., and Clarence Jordan

With very good reason, Mohandas K. Gandhi and Martin Luther King, Jr., are often considered two of the most important religious figures of the twentieth century. Though Clarence Jordan was also a person with a radical faith, he is not usually listed with them. And yet, all of them shared qualities of vision, character, and soul. Gandhi lived in an ashram with some 150 families. It was a microcosm of his view of the world. Inclusiveness, he thought, was the only way to save human beings from self-destruction. People must do more than tolerate one another—they must learn to respect and accept each other.[25] King's view of the "Beloved Community" was similar, and Clarence Jordan saw the intentional community of Koinonia as a "demonstration plot" where the faith would be lived out.

Martin Luther King, Jr., called Clarence Jordan "my friend, my mentor, and my inspiration." In fact, in his famous "I Have a Dream" speech at the March on Washington in 1963, Martin Luther King, Jr., could well have evoked the Clarence Jordan and Koinonia story when he said, "I have a dream that one day on the red hills of Georgia, the sons of former slaves and the sons of former slave-owners will be able to sit down together at the table of brotherhood." King and Jordan were both pastors raised in Georgia and they shared a commitment to racial reconciliation. They both saw the South as a place of deep faith—"Christ-haunted," as Flannery O'Connor called it—with special resources for building what King called the "Beloved Community," or what Jordan may have described as the "God Movement" or perhaps "koinonia." They were both committed to the idea that faith held the power to redeem the social order.[26] When Martin Luther King, Jr., thought of Clarence Jordan, he said, "Here was a son of the Old South, a white Baptist minister doing what we were just talking about doing. I went to Koinonia later to see it for myself and couldn't wait to leave because I was sure the Klan would show up and kill us both."[27]

Andrew Young echoed King's statement. "When we first heard about Clarence Jordan and Koinonia," he said, "we considered it too radical, too dangerous." Young went on to say that we were trying to get people the right to ride on a bus or shop in the local stores, "but here was Clarence—smack dab in the middle of Ku Klux Klan country—going for the whole loaf....Clarence put the rest of us to shame until we did something about it."[28]

It was 1942 when Clarence went to Sumter County, Georgia, to start Koinonia Farm. Martin Luther King, Jr., was in the seventh grade. This was twelve years before *Brown v. Board of Education* and thirteen years before the arrest of Rosa Parks and the beginning of the Montgomery Bus Boycott. This was the year Gandhi gave his famous "Quit India" speech, in which he called for the British to leave India. As Gandhi pursued his nonviolent fight to free India, Jordan would have heard of this grand attempt at the liberation of an entire nation and people.[29]

King learned of Gandhi when he was at Crozer Seminary, and was later greatly affected by Gandhi's theory of nonviolent resistance.

All three of these men grew up in very religious households, which left indelible imprints upon impressionable youths. They each had mothers or a grandmother who could be regarded as "saintly." They all grew up with a pervading sense of guilt and a compulsion to become the son of society, and in so doing change the world around them. In some unique fashion, all three of these young men grew up to share the common commitment to be a "rebel for a just cause," and all tended to have a praxis orientation toward religion. As Gandhi put it, there is an "unalterable law...God to be God must rule the heart and transform it."[30] For Jordan, the unalterable law was summed up in the Greek word "metanoia"—the demand in the preaching of Jesus that individuals change their entire way of thinking because "the new order of the spirit is impinging upon you." Put another way, "I'm calling you to a thing that demands a total change of your nature so that old things pass away."[31]

In life and in death, Gandhi, King, and Jordan identified with the poorest of the poor. Gandhi gave up Western clothes and dressed like the peasants of the rural countryside and ate very little. Jordan lived all of his adult life in an "intentional" community that kept a common purse, which meant that he had to ask the group if he could buy a new pair of shoes. He had one suit even though he traveled often to speak in public places like Yale University, or Union Seminary in New York City. King was also known for his "deacon-sober" suits and his frugal manner of living. Gandhi responded to the outbreaks of violence around him with depression and guilt, and sometimes went on hunger strikes to effect a different outcome. King was also very introspective and could be his own most severe critic. In the end, he only wanted to be remembered as a "drum major for justice." Likewise, Jordan also pushed deeper inside of himself—always searching for a Christ-like spirit—in the wake of his struggles with the violence of the boycott in 1957, and the continuing difficulties of the later years. While Gandhi, King, and Jordan were all charismatic individuals, they were also loved and hated by the people of their own times, and they all had the unique ability to bring forth feelings of shame as well as pride from people who knew them. In time, Gandhi was given the title "Mahatma"—great soul. It is also true that both King and Jordan had qualities of "great soul." All three of these great souls are, as Erikson described Gandhi, in the category of the "religious genius" or *homo religiosus*.[32]

The Legend of Greatness: Rereading and Rewriting Clarence Jordan

The story of Jordan's life is one of high drama in the fields of the Lord. It portrays a historic injustice; the element of conflict between an individual with extraordinary courage over against a cultural barrier of color; and the confrontation between two faiths—one of a religious genius and the other the faith of the ages and status quo. There are stories of suffering born in the manner of the most recognizable model in Western culture—that of the suffering Christ. That is, there was a "cruciform" nature to Jordan's thought and story. But there was also charisma, and an appeal to a tradition of transcendence. Already, by the early 1950s, Jordan had become something of a folk hero and a model for young and idealistic college students.[33] In retrospect, these days of heroic drama were the stuff of which legend would be made. As the years unfolded, Jordan came to take on an even more powerful and confrontational presence.[34] After death came to purge away the dross of human frailty from collective memory, Jordan began to take on the status of a hero—a saint—in Southern church tradition.[35]

The injustice done to African Americans by whites was great and ongoing. Southerners needed to remember those who had stood against such injustice and had sought to right the wrongs. Jordan's story was seemingly ready-made for mythic projection. Jordan himself was an authentic human being who did not "put on airs." Though he was basically a humble fellow, he had a lively sense of humor with a "country-boy charm." A part of Jordan's authenticity seemed to come from his deep roots in the rural, agrarian heartland and his commitment to the values shared with his family and church. And Jordan was not just rooted in the soil of the heartland; he also worked all his life doing hard physical labor as a farmer. He seemed to wear his blue jeans with pride before they became fashionable, and his attachment to the land and its sense of place seemed genuine. Yet, despite Jordan's authenticity, the memory screen that began to develop tended to distort the true image of the man, making it more difficult for readers to comprehend the man and the story in later years.

Few readers in the early twenty-first century will be able to understand life in the "Egypt of the Confederacy," as Dubois once described Georgia's Black Belt region in the early twentieth century. Neither can those readers approach the spectacle of the convict leasing system that Jordan encountered at the Talbot County Jail just behind his own home or begin to understand what a daring act Jordan's establishing of Koinonia Farm was in 1942, thirteen years before the beginning of the Montgomery Bus Boycott. By the same token, the reader tends to accept Jordan's own reading of his awakening toward racial justice. "The hero's coming to racial awareness amounts to a required topos of Southern liberal hagiography, and Jordan devotees know one story from his childhood. Jordan's tale, of hearing the groaning of a tortured prisoner and knowing that just hours before the warden who was supervising the tortured prisoner had been praising God in church...."[36] But 12-year-olds do not possess such understanding. How did Clarence Jordan come to an awakening of the issues surrounding racial justice? Yet there was some unrecognizable compulsion that pushed Jordan beyond some of the folk ways of Talbot County. What was it that propelled this young man rooted in the red clay dirt of Georgia to go so far beyond his family and his region that this favored son became the "black sheep" of the family, and a threat to the good folk of a town with the name of Americus?

As a young person learning about life in the microcosm of Talbot County, Clarence was awkward and shy. He preferred his sickly mother's stories above playing with his brothers in the yard. He grew up somewhat sheltered and privileged, especially by a mother who had lost an earlier child and wanted to love and protect Clarence. Consequently, he was known in the family as the favored one. Yet, for some reason, there was a spirit of antagonism in his earliest years and he grew up in something of a contentious mode—and because of countless arguments with his siblings, he was given the nickname "Grump." Nevertheless, he became sensitive to the environment around him, with a precocious ability to detect hypocrisy. While Jordan often spoke about his early awareness of contradictions between the teachings of the church and the actual practice of people around him, Joe Hendrix, who was a Talbot County native and an early observer of Jordan, said that he could not figure out how Clarence "came to be awakened." Hendrix saw "no line that leads from Talbot County to Koinonia."[37]

When Clarence went to Sumter County to begin his work at Koinonia, he did not start with the idea of the movement as an alternative to the church. He went there to join the community and, for a while, was able to be "the salt of the earth." But, in the crucible that was Sumter County in Southwest Georgia in the forties, fifties, and sixties, Clarence Jordan was pushed ever deeper into himself in order to remain faithful to his truest conception of the Christian life. The result was that Clarence was called upon to find ever more courageous forms of Christian commitment and living. The humble man whose primary commitment in life was to live out his faith was pushed to find new ways of expressing that faith, which by necessity became more and more radical.

As the years went by, Clarence found a way to integrate the various aspects of his personality. The shy, brooding figure gave way to a mature person who did not flinch or move away from confrontation or controversy. Thoughtful and deeply spiritual responses to the issues of the day came naturally. The maturing of the personality formed in the context of the struggles at Koinonia eventually yielded a figure who was a powerful presence.[38] Yet Clarence Jordan was a man of his times who faced all the frustrations and temptations of being human. How can one write about such an individual, showing his growth, development, and later heroic status?

From Americus to America: The Radical Challenge of Clarence Leonard Jordan

The thesis of this work is that Clarence Jordan, a white Southerner from Georgia, can now be portrayed as a pioneer on the frontier of the New South seeking the liberation of both the oppressed and the oppressor—as a poet-prophet calling for a new view of humanity and an alternative portrayal of God and the Bible at a historically crucial time.[39] A study of Jordan reveals that, like Martin Luther King, Jr., and Mohandas K. Gandhi, he was a *homo religiosus*—a religious innovator of the highest order—and that, eventually, his vision had universalizing characteristics. In life, Jordan attempted to be in dialogue with his culture, and in death his legacy is a "dangerous memory" subversive to the human tendency toward greed and the reckless disregard of the poor. Jordan's legend provides a strong iconoclastic dimension to collective memory and continues to call for alternative ways of being in a world where racism, militarism, and materialism continue to exist.

Reading the Life of Clarence Jordan:
  Auto/Biography and a Typology of the Life of Faith

The distinctive orientation of this volume is "religious biography," which seeks to employ a methodology that goes beyond hagiography and attempts to account for the interaction of the developing person with social and cultural forces, all while charting the relationship of childhood experiences and later struggles in adulthood. In this way, one can also look for spiritual periodicy—how one's life unfolds across the lifetime. From this orientation, one can ask: if Jordan is a generative religious figure—a *homo religiosus* seeking a new name for himself and a new way of being for the church, a poet-prophet on the border of a new South— then what is the nature and direction of his journey? Jordan held to a praxis-oriented view of faith. That is, the moral journey is tied to how one lives and can be found in the various expressions of the person across the lifetime. The spiritual pilgrimage of Clarence Jordan can be described in terms of different styles or periods of the way he lived through the years. But his life as a "lived word" becomes the most important statement, and it, too, can be seen from the perspective of pilgrimage with a focus on how Jordan envisions the world around him at each particular juncture or stage of the journey.[40]

The broad outline of Jordan's pilgrimage is evident from the descriptions given early on in his letters, in his books, and in the testimony of others. What is clear about Jordan's life taken as a whole is that the theme of his life is "koinonia"—community. A second theme is his iconoclastic vision and sense of identity with "Jesus the Rebel." There was a genuine core that appears again and again in the narrative of his life to challenge the culture and individuals within the culture. Consequently, there was a certain "over-against" quality to his whole life that may be related to the nickname "Grump" that he received as a young child.

The life story of Clarence Jordan has been told according to a certain literary pattern. The early days in Talbotton reflect the strong influence of his mother and the traditions of small-town life in West Georgia in the early years of the twentieth-century. The basic orientation continues at the University of Georgia in Athens, where a sense of confrontation builds in Jordan's life when his study of the "Sermon on the Mount" collides with the militarism of his ROTC experience at the end of his university career. This time of conflict leads to a period of disorientation, which yields to reorientation and a commitment to enter the ministry. The larger pattern of Jordan's life seems to suggest a movement of orientation, disorientation, and reorientation.[41]

After the collision with the militarism over against the "Sermon on the Mount," his faith takes a very reflective and iconoclastic turn. In Louisville, Jordan becomes increasingly involved in trying to find a way to address racial issues in the South. After the time in school in Louisville, Jordan returns to Georgia, where he establishes "Koinonia Farm" as a demonstration plot for the kingdom. His adult faith has to respond to excommunication from Rehoboth Baptist Church, which seems to push Jordan toward the church universal. He never joined another local church. Then the boycott from local businesses in Americus must have been experienced as a second cultural rejection, which pushed Jordan even further. In the 1960s, Jordan began to write the "Cotton Patch" translations, and finally, with Millard Fuller, he established Koinonia Partners and made plans for a realignment of the work at Koinonia. This initial framework guides the reader into the deeper levels of the story, the end result of which is the portrayal of enacted selfhood—a life lived for all the world to see—where Jordan identifies with the poor and continually searches for a way to make a difference and redefine the culture in a manner closer to his own sense of Christian vision.

Now, our task is to begin at the beginning—in the early years of Jordan's story. There in Jordan's hometown of Talbotton, we will begin to look for clues to the more complete story of this unlikely moral journey—clues to the "inner logic" of his life, his gifts—and, eventually, to ask how his life became interwoven with that of his generation. In so doing, we will on occasion have to follow a "disciplined subjectivity" as we search for ways especially to find glimpses of Clarence the child and, later, the young man prior to his having reached the status of a renowned figure. Those privileged glimpses may yield an enlarged construction of the figure behind the public face. To that quest we now turn.[42]

Chapter 1

Talbotton

The mother receives a child like an unstamped coin and stamps her own image on it.

—Clarence Leonard Jordan

Just six years after W.E.B. Dubois made his train ride from Atlanta to Southwest Georgia, another distinguished-looking African American came into Talbotton. It was a warm spring day in May 1909. A small crowd had gathered as usual to meet the 11:15 from Atlanta. The crowd in the town square was a bit surprised to find that the only passenger who got off the train was a well-dressed black man. Dubois had only recently declared "color" as the problem of the twentieth-century, and that the status of African Americans was much the same as it had been in slavery days. But this older fellow had the "air of prosperity" about him. His white, curly hair could be seen below the rim of a red derby hat. The stranger wore a black silk coat with seersucker pants. A gold watch hung from his red vest. It appeared from the response of the crowd that no one recognized or knew the elderly gentleman. After speaking with a station attendant, the older man began moving slowly down the street. As he walked with his cane, he appeared to be partially blind.[1]

The word went out that he had found his way to the home of William Carreker, who was thought to be well-to-do by local blacks. The old man, as the story goes, was a blind clergyman named Joseph Hardy. He soon became the center of attention in the black community at gatherings on the Carreker farm on Saturday nights and on Sundays. A prominent white planter, William Leonard, whose family had come south from Virginia, soon began to notice "an undercurrent of dissatisfaction" among the blacks who worked for him. When Leonard began to make inquiries about the matter, he found that Hardy—the stranger in town—was preaching to the blacks who gathered on the Carreker farm on the weekend about how they were "still living in slavery to the white man." They should break away and become free like him, the old man preached. If they were to do this, they, too, could wear nice clothes and have a gold watch.[2]

Leonard and many of the other large planters attended the Collinsworth Methodist Church. Before and after services, the planters began to meet to talk under the large oaks in the front of the church. They soon concluded that "the entire negro community was seething with insolence and an attitude unlike any they had encountered before." It was obvious to the planters that something had to be done; otherwise, they would have "an insurrection among the negroes." So, on June 19, 1909, the group met and rode to the Carreker home. They were on horseback armed with pistols. They arrived at the Carreker home shortly after sundown. They knocked on the door and William Leonard announced their "demands"—Hardy, the elderly preacher, was to be "thoroughly flogged" and then "made to leave the county."[3]

What happened next was that Carreker spoke to Leonard and asked that the group not hurt the old man, who didn't mean any harm. Leonard responded that the group had come to get "the voodoo preacher" and that they were not looking for "any more trouble." At that point, Leonard motioned to the group to advance. But, at that precise moment, a shotgun blast at close range dropped Leonard to the ground. The group behind Leonard—reportedly mostly young men and boys—quickly scattered. Leonard's riderless horse appeared back at his home the next morning. The word went through the community rapidly. Leonard's body was picked up and prepared for the funeral. By that afternoon, a large group of men from the surrounding counties had gathered at the Carreker home. The sheriff had come and deputized about fifty men, and they began to look for Carreker and Hardy.[4]

Hardy was found in a barn some two miles from the Carreker farm. He was beaten and bound, and then weighted down and thrown into Big Lazar Creek. Carreker was also hiding, but eventually turned himself in to the sheriff. He was placed in jail. Later that night, some of the fifty "deputies" came and took Carreker out of the cell and lynched him, leaving his body hanging from a utility pole near the Talbot County Courthouse. The *Atlanta Constitution* ran a series of stories detailing this episode in June 1909. The story of the lynching described the process as all being "done quietly and in perfect order."[5]

Fifty and sixty years later, the old men of the town would sit around the square in Talbotton and carry on the oral traditions of this and other lynchings in the area. Many of the first settlers who came to Talbotton, like the Leonards, were from Virginia and the Carolinas. They came looking for land on which to plant cotton. Many were already wealthy and brought their slaves with them. As Dubois's rich but poignant prose remembers: "Day after day the clank of chained feet marching from Virginia and Carolina to Georgia was heard in these rich swamps. Day after day the songs of the callous, the wail of the motherless, and the muttered curses of the wretched echoed from the Flint to the Chickasawhatchee."[6] In 1903, Dubois declared to the world what Carreker and the old preacher could not say by the light of day in Talbotton in 1909—this part of the South is the "Egypt of the Confederacy." It is "an armed camp for intimidating black folk."[7] Frank Jordan described Talbotton differently. "It's an old historic town with a lot of tradition."[8] Part of the tradition was, in fact, keeping the stories of intimidation alive. Robert Jordan sat in the town square and listened to the old men of Talbotton describe the killing of the old preacher and the lynching of Carreker sixty years after the events.[9] How did Clarence Jordan—born in 1912 with the middle name of "Leonard," for his Virginia ancestors—ever begin to envision a life beyond the "color bar," as Dubois called it?

Maude Marie Jossey Jordan: A Maternal Legacy

In his interview with P.D. East, Clarence seems to be aware of the dictum that has become commonplace in the psychological currency of the day. Wordsworth first gave poetic form to the idea—"the child is father of the man." David Mariniss, historian and biographer, recently paraphrased the idea in discussing his biography on Barack Obama: what shapes the life comes early. A corollary to this idea is that the developing faith of the child is greatly influenced by that first parental matrix. Thus, in order to learn about the adult life of a figure like Clarence Jordan, one must begin at the beginning with the most influential figures in his life— his parents—and ask what kind of world they created for him.

Maude Marie Jossey was like her husband, a native Georgian, but her ancestry went back to Virginia aristocracy. She, like William Marshal Leonard, was a descendant of the "prominent Van de Van Leonard clan," who came from Petersburg, Virginia.[10] Many of the men in her family fought in the Civil War. She was a member of the United Daughters of the Confederacy, and as Clarence remembered, she was "quite proud of the South, its traditions and its heritages."[11] Maude Jossey came from "a very well-to-do family" who, like everyone else in the South, lost everything in the Civil War and had to start over. She loved art and music and tended toward the "spiritual and idealistic" side of life. She was remembered by the Talbotton community as a "kind and thoughtful" person who was "a leader of Talbotton society" and active in the Baptist church.[12] Maude Jossey had experiences that were not common in Talbotton at the end of the nineteenth and the beginning of the twentieth-century. Her father, Frank Jossey, was appointed as a U.S. Treasury agent by President McKinley, and the family moved to the west, where they lived for a time in several large cities, including Portland, Oregon; Takoma, Washington; and Tucson, Arizona. When Frank Jossey died, Maude and her mother moved back to Talbotton.[13]

While the family lived in Tucson, Maude worked for a time as a teacher's aide at the historic San Xavier Mission, which was twelve miles from the Jossey home. She and another young woman who lived in Tucson would drive a horse and buggy out to the mission on Sunday afternoon and come back the next weekend. The mission was founded in 1692 by a Jesuit priest, Father Eusebio Francisco Kino. As he was traveling to California, Kino came upon a Pima Indian village near a stream in the Sonoran Desert, just south of what is today Tucson, Arizona. The villagers were receptive to his teachings and the mission work was begun. In the late 1760s, Charles III of Spain banned the Jesuits from work in Spanish lands. From that time on, the mission work in the region was taken over by the Franciscans. Though closed for a time, the school was reopened and remodeled in 1895. The generous and loving spirit required for working at the mission seemed to characterize Maude's life as mother to the Jordan family in Talbotton.

Maude Jossey met James Weaver Jordan on a trip back to Talbotton in the early 1900s. Maude Jossey had been engaged to a fellow in Arizona and had intended to live out west. But Jim Jordan changed her mind and she eventually came back to Georgia. The family kept the love letters that they shared. As the relationship progressed, the salutation changed in Maude's letters from "Dear Sir" to "Dear Mr. Jordan." A little further along, the greeting becomes "Dear Jim" and, finally, "My Darling Jim." One of Maude's niece's, Clara Spivey Periman, wrote about Maude shortly after her death in 1935 that she had a "God-given mother instinct," and that she had a "heart filled with love, love for her fellow man, love for birds and bees, and for flowers...and all things beautiful." According to her niece, Maude was a "champion of childhood," and she had a gentle touch, a soft voice, and tended toward noble deeds. Her acts of human kindness seemed to be innate, as was her desire never to inflict pain. Her sons remembered her as being very "tenderhearted." She especially hated guns, war, and fighting.[14] Her beloved father had been killed in an accident with a gun.[15] This portrayal of a warm and gentle personality is borne out by the letters that Maude and Clarence shared while she was alive.[16] Clarence Jordan was greatly influenced by his mother, Maude Jossey Jordan. In one of his early sermons, Jordan wrote that "the mother receives a child like an unstamped coin and stamps her own image on it."[17]

James Weaver Jordan: A Small-Town Tycoon

James Weaver Jordan, Clarence's father, was born in 1878. "The family lost everything they had in the Civil War," Frank Jordan recalled. Yet James Weaver Jordan was an exceptional individual and "very ambitious." Jordan went to school at the "old Farmers' Academy" in Talbot County and soon went to work at a mercantile company. After some years, he became a partner in the Farmers' Supply Company, where he developed the reputation for coming early and staying late.[18] With only a fifth-grade education, Jim Jordan became an influential businessman in Talbot County. Clarence later described his father as a small-town tycoon. He was a man of considerable energy and endowed with a strong work ethic, which also meant that he was often something of an "absent father" to his children just by virtue of the sheer workload that he took upon himself. Jim Jordan organized the Bank of Talbotton in 1906. He also owned the Jordan Supply Company and the Talbotton Milling

Company. Jordan owned and operated a large farm where he grew peaches and raised cattle. In addition, Jordan was a cotton broker. In time, he became a "highly respected citizen." In fact, so pronounced was Jim Jordan's involvement in the community and business life of Talbotton that the town became known as "Jordan city."[19] He was the mayor of Talbotton for several terms and was on the local schoolboard. If Maude Jossey was idealistic, Jim was realistic and pragmatic. The elder Jordan's ancestors had lived in the Talbot County area for generations.[20] Jim Jordan, like Maude Jossey, was a "deeply religious" person who was not just "involved" in the life of the local Baptist church—he was a "leader...all of his life." Jim Jordan held every office imaginable in Talbotton Baptist Church. He led in the construction and maintenance of the church building. Consequently, he took Clarence and the other children to church every week, and during the week, they often did "chores" around the church.[21] Jim Jordan's letters to Clarence reveal his father to be an articulate and thoughtful man who took his role of father seriously.[22]

The marriage of Maude Marie Jossey and James Weaver Jordan took place on Wednesday, June 25, 1903. The wedding took place at the Talbotton Methodist Church that evening at 8:30 P.M. The Reverend W.E. Mumford, uncle to Maude Marie, was a Methodist minister and came over from Macon to perform the service.[23] The wedding took place "in the presence of much of Talbotton and county society."[24] As was often the custom in the early years of the twentieth-century in America, the Jordans planned to have a large family. Ten children were born to Jim Jordan and Maude Jossey. Three of the ten would die in infancy and seven reached maturity: Frank Jossey, Cornelia, James Weaver, Jr., Clarence Leonard, George Leonard, Robert Henry, and John Harris.

The Jordan Home: An Enduring Legacy

The family remembered and testified that their mother and father "believed in doing things right and raising children right, so we always knew that they tried to teach us to do what was right."[25] Clarence Jordan knew that this family matrix influenced him—indeed, made a "profound impression" on him. "My father and mother taught me the fundamentals of decency and respect for other people," he said. One such fundamental cultivated in the children at an early age was that "color made no difference." In fact, Clarence noted that "they would punish me for insulting a Negro as badly as they would for a white person."[26] Another aspect of "doing things right" in the Jordan family was church attendance. Jim Jordan never missed a service at the Talbotton Baptist Church, and he made sure that the children, likewise, were faithful in attendance, including every revival meeting.[27]

Jim Jordan and Maude Jossey also created a family atmosphere of "moralistic expectation" with regard to conventional religious ideas. One such idea was remembering and honoring the Sabbath. In Southern Baptist life in the early days of the twentieth-century, Sunday became the Sabbath. In the Jordan family, as taught by their father, this meant "going to church in the morning and taking a long nap in the afternoon." In one of his sermons, Clarence remembers that the Jordan children were playing baseball on the front lawn one Sunday afternoon. They were "really whooping it up." Apparently, their playfulness awakened Jim Jordan from his traditional Sunday afternoon nap and he came out into the yard and said, "Don't you boys know this day is Sunday? If you're gonna play baseball, go out in [the] backyard."[28] Morality in the Jordan household had a sense of expectation of compliance with community mores. This sense of moralistic expectation is, on some level, internalized by the children and they begin to "police" themselves. In this manner, Clarence's older brother Buddy writes to him when he is a sophomore in high school and says, "Clarence, I think you are quite the stuff." And then Buddy goes on to say, "Frank and I are counting on you to hold up the name of Jordan. Let your motto be to take the name of Jordan just a little higher."[29]

Apparently, "doing things right" meant for Jim Jordan the building of an appropriate home for his bride and growing family. Three years after his marriage to Maude Jossey, Jim Jordan purchased a lot on Monroe Street from Mrs. G.T. Simpson. The lot extended uniformly toward the Talbot County Jail. The next year in 1907, Jordan built a large and stately home on the lot next to the plantation-style antebellum home owned by Mrs. G.T. Simpson. Jordan's new home "looked like money." There was a "lingering Victorian touch" to the architecture. It had a scroll sawed balustrade, turned posts and spandrels, all enclosing the wraparound verandah. The brick wall across the front and the wrought-iron gate gave the house a "baronial air." The home was a large one to match the size of the family. There were four bedrooms, a living room, a dining room, and a kitchen. Two double fireplaces provided heat for the front rooms of the house. Though it was a fine home by the standards of the day, it was a different time. There was no running water in the house. Water came from the well in the back. There was no electricity. The house was lit with kerosene lamps. There was no insulation, and the home tended to be hot in summer and cold in winter. The street in front of the house was unpaved and, hence, muddy when it rained, dusty when it did not. Horses and buggies frequented the road, though automobiles were soon to be popular. Despite the lack of the modern conveniences that would be available in the coming years, Jim Jordan was very detail-oriented and made the house a good place for his children to grow up. He watched carefully as the home was built by Beck and Durwood Allen.[30]

Clarence Leonard Jordan was born in this home July 29, 1912—five years after it was built. He was the fourth of seven children who survived infancy. In one of the most revealing interviews that Jordan ever gave, P.D. East came to Koinonia in the context of the severe boycott and had an extended conversation with Clarence. On one occasion, he asked Clarence, "What makes you tick?" Clarence responded that he did not know, perhaps his wife. Later, P.D. East asked Clarence, "How did you get this way? The why and wherefore. Why aren't you like the rest of us? Really capitalistic, whiskey-drinking, woman-chasing, hellraising, etc."[31] With characteristic and disarming freedom, Jordan came back: "How do you know that I'm not?" East would not play that game, and simply said to Jordan, "Tell me about it, will you?"[32]

At that point, Jordan said, "I don't think a person is ever sure what the many factors at work in his life are. There are many conditions that influence him. I can tell you some that I know influenced me." Then Clarence relates the "profound" impact of his family context, the teachings of his parents. At that point, Jordan began to relate another "factor in my life was that my home was located about 200 yards from a chain-gang camp." It was an "old-time Georgian chain gang…[where] terrible brutality…existed." Since the camp was on Clarence's way to and from school, he would spend a great deal of time over there—almost every day.

But there was another reason that he spent time there. One of Jim Jordan's best friends was in that jail, and he visited the man often and took Clarence with him. The man had murdered the superintendent of the county school system, who was having an affair with the man's wife. Jim Jordan thought the man was an "outstanding citizen" and that the murder was justifiable. So Clarence came to know the convict camp and the county jail at an early age. He told P.D. East that this was "my first awareness of the injustices to people because of race."[33]

The Root of Jordan's Radical Christianity

In the last interview that he gave, Clarence Jordan was once again asked about the origin of this radical movement—"why did you start the community at Koinonia?" Jordan immediately says, "I'd have to go way back to my boyhood to answer that." Then he describes how he was devoted to the church but came early to ask questions—serious questions. He returns to the story of the "old-fashioned chain gang" and how he made friends with the prisoners, most of them black. Jordan goes on to say that "they seemed more alive, more genuinely human than the people I met at church." He also met the warden of the chain gang, a Mr. MacDonald. Then Jordan describes how he had seen Mr. MacDonald in church singing in the choir. Mr. MacDonald had been carried away by the song "Love Lifted Me" on that hot August revival night in 1924. But, later that night, Clarence was awakened by the agonizing groans of a prisoner from the camp. The prisoner was being beaten. The whole episode "nearly tore me to pieces," Clarence said. Clarence also knew who was inflicting the pain—it was Mr. MacDonald, who, a few hours before, was "carried away" by "Love Lifted Me." Clarence went on to say, "That man's agony was mine...."[34]

Jordan's quest for justice led him to consider law, then agriculture, and finally, to the realization that there must be spiritual answers. This led him to the Southern Baptist Seminary in Louisville, Kentucky, where he earned a Ph.D. in Greek. While in Louisville, his work in the heart of the ghetto became a time of "spiritual awakening." There he discovered that many of the blacks in the Haymarket in downtown Louisville were refugees from Georgia and Alabama, where they had been forced to leave the farms. What Jordan saw was that "the city was grinding them up."

This new understanding gave new focus for Jordan. It drove him back to think about those areas and to ask whether the trend from the farms to the city could be reversed. This is how Jordan came to consider a farm like Koinonia as a demonstration plot in three of the areas where he thought the churches were "utterly failing": race, war, and materialism.[35]

Such was Clarence's explanation to Walden Howard. But how does a twelve-year-old become so empathetic that a prisoner's agony becomes his own? After tracing Jordan's retelling of these events, Tracy Elaine K'Meyer writes that Jordan has "packaged and explained his religious and racial awakening." She goes on to say, "Indeed, here was the root of his radical Christianity." But then K'Meyer writes, "Chance [*sic*] are, Jordan was not really this self-aware as a teenager. The stories about Jordan's childhood are glimpses of his character seen in retrospect through the lens of his later work."[36] She is, no doubt, correct that the stories are glimpses of his character seen in retrospect. But is the "chain-gang story" the root of Jordan's radical Christianity, or could there be an even earlier foundation? Are there hints in the Jordan narrative to an even more complex telling?

Chapter 2

"Grump"

Before you were born I consecrated you; I appointed you a prophet to the nations.

—Jeremiah ben Hilkiah

A Biographical Clue: Will Campbell's Call

In his magisterial telling of his own journey from innocence to experience, interwoven with community and social transformation, Will Campbell portrays in narrative form the beginning of religious experience and a call to vocation. Will's father was called "Preacher" by his peers because one day he came from the fields and announced that "he was going to be a preacher." But he had only a sixth-grade education and did not actually become a preacher, but was called by the name. Campbell also narrates how his great-grandmother married Preacher Baham, a successful farmer who could be heard praying in the fields. With such twin precedents, Will Campbell was "marked, or called at an early age….And…never questioned…[his] vocational future." And so, he became "the one marked early to be the preacher." Campbell was also "sickly." And, because of that, he was special. He was told by his mother that being special meant that if the family members were quarreling, he would be the one to bring the family together again. Campbell understood this to mean that he "would die early as punishment for the bickering of others who would thereafter live in peace and harmony." Campbell had an attack of double pneumonia when he was five and was "given up for dead." For nine days, he seemed to hover on the brink. But living through that near-death experience must have changed him and added to not only his sense of deference in the family, but also to the affirmation that he was the chosen one. That is, living through this near-death experience came to be a sign and seal of his special status and vocation. If indeed he lived when all expected him to die, then his life must be for a certain purpose and calling.[1]

Campbell's narrative emphasizes the birth of religious experience in the context of family—father, mother, and great-grandfather. The call came early, and Will Campbell was "set apart" in the context of the community that was the family. He became "special" early on, in part, through the interpretation and explanation of his mother. There was a near-death experience that seemed to validate the call. Having lived through pneumonia at a time when no one expected him to do so seemed to give assurance and validity to a religious reading and interpretation of his life.

Was there a similar experience in the early years of Clarence Jordan's life?

Consecrated Before Birth: Clarence Jordan as Chosen One

There is very little information on the early years of Clarence Jordan's life other than the typical stories that have found their way into the biographies and have through the years become a standard. The most oft-repeated narrative is the story of MacDonald, and the prisoner in the rack whose screams awaken Clarence. His remarkable sensitivity in this episode shows his precocious nature and the emerging conflict with his culture, but it is neither the origin of faith nor the beginning of a radical pilgrimage. In reflecting on this experience, Clarence said that the conflict between what he saw in the chain-gang camp and what he was learning in church caused a "fermentation" inside of his being that continued into adulthood. But, again, this is likely a memory screen, later experience projected onto an earlier event, which helps to give interpretation to his life.

His brothers remembered that Clarence developed an argumentative spirit early. As the middle child, Clarence "was sort of alone, in a way," Frank Jordan remembered. He developed a "contentious" mode that made him "just a little bit different" from the rest of us. He was given a room by himself because he "liked to argue a good bit."[2] His brothers and sister began to call him "Grump"—a nickname that continued until he was in high school.[3] His older brother Frank said that "we used to laugh and say that Clarence didn't care whether he was fighting up the line with me or down the line with John, just so he was arguing with some-body."[4] Clarence's sister Cornelia remembered that he "seemed a little bitter about the attitude of the family." From a fairly young age, Clarence seemed "frugal." He "just seemed to resent our having anything—meals or anything."[5] Once, when he was about 9 years old, a black delivery man came to the front door of the Jordan home, instead of the back door as was custom in the segregated South. Jim Jordan rebuked the man and put him in his place as deemed by the cultural code. Clarence, apparently embarrassed and angry over the incident, "scolded" his father. Yet, as powerful and poignant as these stories are, it is not likely that any of them are near the origin of Clarence's radical faith. These stories are important especially in the sense that they show the growth of the con-science—in fact, a precocious and severe one—which will push us to investigate how and why that happens so early in his young life. But these stories do not help us outline the nature and dimension of the earliest aspects of faith in the life of Clarence Jordan. However, there are two sources that have yet to be tapped that have promise to help us under-stand the early life of Clarence Jordan and his foundation of faith: the correspondence between Clarence and his mother while he was in Athens and Louisville; and the clues about an illness that he had, like Will Campbell, while he was in his preschool years.

A Mother's Interpretation of a Life:
Clarence as a Jeremiah/Jesus Figure

The correspondence between Maude Jossey Jordan and her son Clarence is extraordinarily revealing. Clarence wrote to his mother every Sunday when he was away. His mother responds with very caring letters. Her letters typically begin with the salutation "My Dear Son." She is always worried about his needs—health and safety. And, during the Depression years of the 1930s, she sends him as much money as she can. Maude Jossey is constantly telling Clarence of her love and devotion and how proud she is of him. She tells Clarence that she loves him more than the other children, which would tend to alienate him from the other siblings, though they would never admit to that even as adults.[6] In this sense, the family narrative replays biblical stories like that of Rebekah/Jacob and Jacob/Joseph and moves in the direction of a family romance.

In his sermon, "Jesus the Rebel," Clarence Jordan says that, in his childhood days when he was first learning to read the Bible, his mother gave him a Bible with pictures. He quickly came to the conclusion that Jesus looked like a woman. Indeed, he writes to his mother that her words are the words of God through an angel. The love of his mother is the love of God to him. In the last summer of her life, Maude Jossey writes a birthday letter to Clarence in Louisville. She begins, "My darling son…," and goes on to tell him how he has become their "pride and joy." Then she tells Clarence that his life has been a "benediction" to them throughout the years. At that point, Maude Jossey began to interpret Clarence's life: "I am quite sure that God placed His seal upon you and set you apart to do his bidding, even before you came into the world, for at a very tender age you loved to read the Bible and found for yourself a Savior's redeeming love." Once again she told Clarence of her love. She tells Clarence that the giving of your life to the kingdom's work has "drawn you closer to my heart than any of the other children." Then Maude Jossey goes on to explain, "You have always bestowed upon me such a wealth of love since early childhood that it is perfectly natural for me to love you more than I do the other children…."[7]

As Will Campbell's mother does for him, Clarence Jordan's mother interprets his life and affirms it as being vocational. Both Will and Clarence live through a life-threatening illness. And, having done so, each one must have sensed some new form of courage and purpose, if only in embryo. Like Will Campbell's mother, Maude Jossey tells Clarence that his life has been "set apart." And, like Will Campbell, Clarence must have sensed some "cruciform" nature to his mother's reading of the individual life. Maude Jossey tells Clarence that he has been called and set apart like the great biblical figures Jeremiah and Jesus, whose earthly years were said to be prefigured by God.

Maude Jossey Jordan and the Parental Matrix:
Clarence Jordan and the Origin of Childhood Faith

In the extraordinary corpus of letters shared with her son, Maude Jossey Jordan provides a stunning portrayal of her role as mother and the special relationship that she had with Clarence. This collection of letters allows one to construct a realistic portrayal of what that first parental matrix was like. And the words and images that Maude Jossey leaves behind in her letters to Clarence suggest what one would expect—that faith begins in the earliest years, and that the influences that shaped Clarence Jordan did come early. Clarence was, therefore, deeply influenced by Maude Jossey. He responds to the warm and caring spirit that his mother provides, and for a lifetime feels a strong bond of love with her that is so deep and pervasive, it appears to him as coming from God through an angel—though, as in all human relationships, there will be negative aspects and pressures in this parental matrix. It is clear that Clarence Jordan was marked for a lifetime by the way Maude Jossey Jordan welcomed him into the world and attempted to sustain him and his spirit as long as she lived. His first form of faith was deeply influenced by that first parental matrix. For a child like Clarence, to look into the welcoming face of the mother was tantamount to looking into the face of God.[8]

What we know about Clarence thus far is that he grew up in a richly traditional world of faith—both of his parents were formed and shaped by the Baptist piety of the South in the early twentieth-century. And, as with other young children, the rudiments of his religious life are traceable to this first basic world—the context of nurturing that takes place between the child and his primary caregivers. Clarence was, therefore, deeply influenced by both Maude Jossey and Jim Jordan. Through the process of identification with his parents as nurturers, Clarence learned imitative behavior and, in due course, to take on a sense of conscience. The type of faith characteristic of this early period in Clarence's life is, thus, intuitive and imitative. That is, based on the actions, examples, stories, and images presented by his parents and caregivers, Clarence learned to understand intuitively and, thereby, to feel the ultimate conditions of his universe. Based on that perception and imitation, Clarence began his journey of faith. Furthermore, the quality of relationships that he experienced in those early years continued to be with him as a factor throughout his life. The earliest years of his life were the most important in determining a direction in faith and morality. With imitative and intuitive skill, a child like Clarence would begin to envision the world. The remembered images of his parents eventually took on larger-than-life qualities. Clarence's first image of God was a simple blending of the perceived character of Maude Jossey and Jim Jordan.[9]

In his college years, Clarence would often write to his mother that she was an expression of God or God's love. On Mother's Day in 1931, Clarence wrote from Athens to his mother and said: "It seems to me that the terms 'God' and 'Mother' are closely allied. One is not complete without the other. I believe that Mother is only God come to earth and that in Heaven God will be Mother gone to Heaven." In closing that letter, Clarence described his mother as "the finest, gentlest, kindest, noblest, sweetest person who has ever set foot on this earth."[10] Two years later, Clarence wrote to his mother and told her that she was the "finest, sweetest angel" whom God was using to write to him.[11]

For a child like Clarence, the first years of life comprised a magical and heroic age. As a little human being, he was introduced daily to the mysteries of life, which became impressionable memories that affected him for a lifetime. The drama of life took on a mythic proportion, and the actors on the daily scene became heroes and god-like figures who, in fact, prefigured how he as a child built images of the divine. In the midst of such drama, Clarence began to contemplate an image of God. Ana-Maria Rizzuto's assessment is appropriate for the early years of life: "The child, like a little Dante, has to go through his own Divine Comedy until he and his God make peace with each other...."[12] What was Clarence's drama, and how did he make peace with God?

The Theme of a Lifetime: Abandonment and Community

What additional clues for understanding Jordan the man can be found in the years of Clarence the child? A first reading of Jordan's work might lead one to conclude that he was a typically religious child, who rebelled against the religion and culture of the South after the incident with the prison camp at age twelve. In fact, some have read his life in this way. But there are indications from his childhood of a more complex interpretation. Indeed, the childhood narrative of Clarence Jordan concerning his earliest years reveals a stunning story, with themes traceable throughout his life. The initial clue to understanding his first stage of life—and the theme he carries with him for a lifetime, influencing all other perspectives on living—is that of a sense of abandonment over against community.

Henlee Barnette, who knew Jordan well, said that the theme of his life was koinonia (community).[13] But the natural question that comes is: why this search and this theme? What provokes such a quest? Barnette is likely right—an individual life like that of Clarence Jordan may indeed be oriented around one particular theme.[14] But the story of Jordan's life seems to imply a complex theme of abandonment and a resulting quest for community. This, for Jordan, becomes a central life theme traceable from his earliest years until his death. The story of the establishment and founding of Koinonia is, then, the end result of a quest that begins in Clarence's earliest years and is seen already in embryo in the crisis of his preschool years. If indeed this is a correct analysis, Clarence Jordan and Will Campbell share a similar call and crisis experience. The message from Will's mother interpreting his life is also relevant for Clarence: You will "be the one to bring the family back together." The vicarious nature of Will's reading of his mother's words—"I would die early as punishment for the bickering of others"—is also relevant for Clarence.[15]

Clarence's First Crisis: Illness, Despair, and Melancholia

The issue of separation and abandonment actually first presents itself to a young child like Clarence in the very first year of life. A foundational sense of trust is gained by the child through the quality of interaction with the mother. Erikson theorizes that the foundational trust learned by the child from the daily and ritualized experience with the mother, caring for the child's every need, is the basis on which the child begins to create an image of God and a sense of faith. The quality of the child's exchange with the mother is experienced as a dialectic of "trust versus mistrust." One's sense of the world as trustworthy depends to some extent on the reliable and predictable quality generated by the nurture and care of the mother. By the same token, a lack of reliability generates some element of mistrust in the life of the child. Yet, in the process of relationship with the mother, the helpless and completely dependent child begins to experience the numinous. That is, this ritualization of experience—in which the mother greets the child with a special name with her unique tone, and lifts the child to her face—is very much like the encounter with the divine (the numinous experience) in the religious life. Such experiences help one to overcome the threat of separation and abandonment, which is the overwhelming fear of the first year of life for children.[16]

It is clear, especially from the letters that Clarence shared with his mother, that the quality of trust he carried with him from his earliest years was high and profound, and that the letters suggest something like an ongoing numinous experience shared between mother and child. If this is true, what was it that brought on the element of mistrust, and any hint of the great childhood fear of abandonment? Though it is clear that Maude Jossey had a rich and profound love for Clarence, there were factors in her life beyond her control. Born in 1879 and weighing only three pounds at birth, Maude Jossey was a very sickly person.[17] The birth of ten children no doubt took its toll on her body and spirit. She was prone to migraine headaches, which kept her in bed for two weeks on average per month. Though her commitment to Clarence was strong, there would have been many times in his first years that she would have been unavailable. Even as the "chosen" one, Clarence sometimes felt neglected. At a family gathering when he was a child, one of his brothers remembered that an aunt looked at Clarence, who was a bit unkempt, and said, "Clarence you have your left shoe on your right foot. You didn't put it on right." And Clarence as a little boy responded, "Well, Aunt Corrine, there wasn't anybody to look out for me. I just had to do the best I could."[18] What this story implies is that, as a young child about 5 years old, Clarence felt neglected. There was no one "to look out for me," he said.

The sense of a prehistoric core that emerges in the childhood narrative of Clarence Jordan is an affirmation of the warmth of love undergirding a sense of community balanced by an awareness that the precarious nature of life involves neglect—or, in more extreme terms, abandonment. The plan for Jim Jordan and Maude Jossey was a large family. So, soon after the birth of Clarence in 1912, they began to think of another child. The children tended to be about two years apart in age. So, when Clarence was in his second year of life, Maude Jossey became pregnant again. But a devastating thing happened. Maude Jossey's mother died. Maude Jossey was an only child and she took her mother's death hard. She grieved greatly. According to Cornelia Callier's memory and interpretation, Maude Jossey grieved so much over the loss of her mother that she lost this next child. That seemed to affect her relationship with Clarence. She was so afraid that she might lose Clarence that she doubled her efforts in caring for him, and the bond between mother and child became even closer. Yet, because Clarence was a young child reading his world intuitively, there would have been no way for Maude Jossey to disguise her grief. And the loss of the child would have meant more time absent from Clarence. The sense of neglect and fear of abandonment that Clarence felt as a child would have been very early and pervasive.

When he was about five years old, Clarence had scarlet fever. In the early days of the twentieth-century, this could be a life-threatening illness and it was contagious. Consequently, Clarence had to be quarantined. No one could be around him except his mother and nurse. The physical crisis led to an emotional and spiritual one. As he was recovering from the physical symptoms, Clarence felt very isolated, as if he were being shunned by his brothers and sisters. They were all sent to be with other relatives or friends. Clarence's older brother Frank remembered that, on one occasion, the brothers and sisters came over to see Clarence. Frank said, "I remember one time that we went over near to our home and they brought Clarence out on the porch and we saw him on the porch. A little kid, just almost dead…he looked so pitiful, just skin and bones."[19]

Clarence took the temporary loss of his siblings so personally that his father had to come and try to explain the situation and help Clarence know that his family had not abandoned him. Nonetheless, Clarence would be marked both physically and spiritually by this crisis. Physically, Clarence was severely ill and became very thin and emaciated, and seemed to hover near death for several weeks. The family understood the severity of the illness and that, in those days, nine out of ten children would have died with the disease. That's how close he came to dying as a child.[20] After he had gotten over scarlet fever, he had to learn to walk all over again. But, for a long time after, he must have wondered what had happened to his family. After this episode, Clarence, like Will Campbell, saw that his sickly nature continued to bring a certain deference and to contribute to the idea that in some way he was "special." On some unrecognizable level of being within Clarence and within the family, it is likely that living beyond the illness also contributed to the idea that he was fated to survive and have a life of some greater purpose that was not yet known. According to the watchful eye of Clarence's sister Cornelia, Maude Jossey "was always closer to him than any of the other children."[21]

The sister's description of Clarence's illness implies that Maude Jossey "had" to give extra attention to Clarence because of his illness. Since Maude Jossey was "sickly" herself, she would be even more sympathetic to Clarence. As a sickly child, Clarence could not be as active as his brothers and sister, so he would become a natural listener to his mother's stories. Having to stay inside also gave him an opportunity to watch his mother interact with the servants in a kind and loving way. His isolation also forced him to turn more to his mother for companionship. Despite the abundance of his mother's love, the absence of his parents and the loss of his siblings in the context of his illness push the emerging sense of "I" in these early stories about Clarence in the direction of a "melancholic 'I.'" He is a child who tends toward despair and melancholia. This sense will become more evident in the next era of his life.[22]

The fear of abandonment that Clarence experienced as a child seems to have been complicated by another factor: shame. The story about Aunt Corrine and the shoe on the wrong foot implies that at age five, Clarence had lost confidence in the trustworthy nature of his environment. There was, as he said to Aunt Corrine, no one "to look out for me." To be seen by an aunt with the wrong shoe on the wrong foot could be experienced as the exposure of one's vulnerability and as a sense of shame. But, perhaps more importantly, to be seen by one's siblings while one is near death, but at the same time to be abandoned by them, is also a profound sense of shame. In this case, Clarence is seen by his siblings and his father when he is at his most vulnerable point, and he feels abandoned by them, for which he also feels shame. Clarence would have felt shame as something like the "disapproving gaze" of his siblings and his father. Consequently, Clarence's sense of abandonment is further complicated by the sense of shame he experienced during his illness and the untrustworthy nature of his home environment. The birth of the

"Grump" personality for Clarence likely arises as a form of inner rage or defiance against those he feels is doing the shaming.[23]

The Abundant Love of the Mother—and No One
"To Look Out for Me"

The foundational image of the emerging faith of Clarence Jordan as a child seems to be the duality of the abundant and affirming love (of his mother) and the precarious absence of that love, leading to a sense of neglect and abandonment, pushing Clarence as a child to look for a sense of community with other members of the family. Unfortunately, his brothers and sister were gone because of the quarantine, and Jim Jordan was an "absent" father. In one sense, one could argue that Clarence's story does not appear unique. That is, all children experience the fear of abandonment. Such fears begin in children as young as 6 months old. But, for the child, the realization of this fear of abandonment is tantamount to the fear of death. Being helpless and virtually dependent on the parent, the child realizes that he or she is at the very mercy of the parent for survival itself. So this fear of abandonment, which dates to the first year of life, if not offset in the mind and psyche of the child with the care that leads to a deep and pervading sense of security, can lead to a primal element of fear and insecurity.[24]

These early stories about his childhood demonstrate that Clarence suffered with a strong sense of neglect and fear of abandonment. The theme of solidarity with the victim and the quest for a diverse human community, which manifests in Jordan's later years in the Haymarket of Louisville and at Koinonia, is an adult way to answer a central problem that emerges in its most personal form in his earliest childhood days. The larger theme of Jordan's life was a quest for "koinonia"—community to offset the devastating element of neglect/abandonment that had fallen upon the poorest of the poor.

At about the age of three or four, a young child like Clarence begins to find the courage to make the first tentative steps toward autonomous existence—that is, autonomous from the maternal matrix. Beginning at this point, the father has the opportunity to become the guardian of the child's autonomy. Assumable only by the father, this role of sponsorship allows something to pass from the father's bodily presence to the emerging selfhood of the child.[25] But what if the father is not there? What can a young child do?

Talbotton as Ultimate Environment:
  Clarence and Early Childhood Faith

In the early world of Clarence Jordan, Talbotton can be used as a metaphor for the Promised Land. The city itself became "Jordan city," but beyond that it was the natural landscape. In the earliest years of his life, it was the maternal matrix that was the milk and honey of his young existence. There was a time early in his life when his first ecological metaphor—his first way of making meaning intuitively sensed from the network of maternal mutuality—was nothing less than the sweetness and nurture of life. But the stories about Clarence also indicate an emerging ambivalence so that his first map of life includes feelings of absence, separation, and a feeling of abandonment. In his naturally egocentric view of the world, Clarence could not comprehend the loss that came his way. It is this infantile curse, visible already in his first ultimate environment, that will be projected forward in disguised form in his myth of becoming and will seek eventual transformation in adult deeds.[26] Is this, at least in part, the seedbed for the adult's later efforts to understand his then-larger history, the circumstances of dispossessed people, and his own efforts to bring comfort and liberation to oppressed and abandoned people everywhere?

In summary, young Clarence was a child with an abiding love for his mother, whose voice and presence were the image of divine reality, frustrated by the element of neglect caused by sickness and grief and a sense of abandonment that eventually extends to his siblings and absent father. This ongoing negative sense was intensified by the experience of scarlet fever and the fact that his siblings were by necessity taken out of the home while Clarence was quarantined. It is possible that his survival gave Clarence some innate but yet unrecognizable sense that, already as a child, he was fated to live, and that there must be purpose to his life. These factors together will eventually propel young Clarence toward a propensity for the religious journey. But his view of the world would be forever marked by this first period, which would become the foundation for his composition of the world. From this period comes what appears to be the central dialectic of his life: neglect/abandonment over against solidarity/community. It is this central theme, coming from his first years, that informs his writing and speaking, as well as his activism in causes for justice and peace.

Chapter 3

Gump: Becoming a Clown of God

Clarence was sort of alone in the family in a way. He was rather "contentious" and just a little bit different from the rest of us.

—Frank Jordan

The year 1917 was the beginning of a dramatic era for the United States. This was the year that the nation would enter World War I, which would be described as the "war to end all wars" and the war to "make the world safe for democracy." In other parts of the world, it was deemed the "Great War," with the recognition that it was the first worldwide war in the true sense of the word. The U.S. entered the war after Germany sank seven U.S. merchant ships and invited Mexico to join the Axis powers and attempt to recover Mexican lands in Texas, New Mexico, and Arizona.

Clarence would not know these realities, but as a young five-year-old, he struggled with a different conflict. Eventually, he would sue for his own "separate peace" on his own terms. But it was clear for now in the family in Talbotton that, for some reason, Clarence was growing up differently. As brother Frank remembered, Clarence was somehow "alone" in the family. The earliest and most lasting memories of Clarence by his siblings were that he was "contentious." Contending for what?…and why? His sister Cornelia wondered: maybe he had never quite gotten over the childhood experience of feeling left out, isolated, abandoned. Whatever the reason, young Clarence challenged, argued, and contended! So much so that his siblings agreed: "…he'd make a good lawyer." But Maude Jossey Jordan took a special interest in him. She gave him a Bible with pictures. She read to him often from the Bible, and Clarence began to learn a new story.[1]

Contending in School and Growing Up Just a Bit Differently

Clarence grew up with energy, a strong sense of competition, and a desire to be at the head of the group. When it was his turn to go to public school, like his siblings, he went to the Talbotton Public School where Jim Jordan was chairman of the school board. The building was large and impressive for a small town. It was a two-story building with columns on three sides. There was an extension on one side that the students called the "potato building," because it looked like a potato "curing house."[2] Clarence spent some of his early years in this building. Some of his teachers would have been "old-school." Brother George remembered that there were some tough teachers in the potato building. He, for example, had Miss Jessie Jameson in the second grade and later in the sixth. She would "crack heads" with a pencil for misbehavior. On one occasion, a student with the nickname "Little Brother" came up to Miss Jameson and said to her, "You gave me a zero and I don't think I deserve that grade." Miss Jameson said to him, "Well, Little Brother, I am sorry but that is the lowest grade that we have."[3]

Clarence's very first day in school was memorable for his brothers. Ironically, this young fellow, who later grew up to be a man known for peaceful ways, got into a fight with Joe Wells, a classmate in the first grade. As the story was remembered by his brother George, Clarence pulled Joe's long hair, but Joe could not pull Clarence's hair because he had a crew cut. So they ran all around the schoolyard fighting. Then Joe went home that night and told his father that he needed a crew cut so Clarence Jordan could not pull his hair any more. Throughout his school years, Clarence seemed always ready for a fight, but this was the only physical fight his brothers could remember. Though a born competitor at the ready for an encounter with his schoolmates, his verbal skills would usually win the day and turn the confrontation into a debate—a form of verbal and rational combat—which he would typically win.[4]

Because of his unorthodox ways and different views, some of his schoolmates gave him a nickname that was a play on a cartoon character. Some of the guys began to call Clarence "Gump," after the figure Andy Gump, who was the least heroic-looking of all the early comic characters.[5] Created in 1917, Andy was bombastic and gregarious, and typified the "ordinary citizen" or the mass of common folk who led uneventful lives. Though Clarence was intellectually near the top of his small class, some of his classmates may have so labeled him because of his eccentric ways that began in his family context. In retrospect, his classmates at the Talbotton Public School could not have been more wrong. Without a doubt, Clarence Jordan turned out to be the least Gump-like character— in terms of ordinariness—in all of Talbotton, and likely all of Georgia. And yet, there was a sense in which Clarence's peers saw something in his personality that would one day contribute to his genius. What was it?

Clarence as Gump: Becoming a Clown of God

When Frank Stagg first met Clarence Jordan when they were both in college, he thought that Clarence was a humorist because he told so many jokes.[6] There was a very lively nature to his personality—"a live-wire personality," as Dallas Lee described it—that enlivened his presence in a group. That lively nature seemed to stem from an element of brilliance combined with "country-boy" ways. But, over the years, he learned to use that combination very well. His jokes often had a "downhome" quality that could sometimes be described as even "corny." But Clarence could get away with it because, underneath the downhome qualities, there was such a sense of intelligence. Over time, Clarence learned to integrate his skills so that he eventually "communicated all over." His message came through in his tone of voice, in the gleam in his eyes, often through a stumbling but intentional misuse of language, and perhaps most of all, through his spirit.[7]

His schoolmates began to see this aspect of his being early on. His downhome ways and corny jokes likely sustained the use of the "Gump" nickname in Talbotton for a time. Clarence's brother George witnessed him on the playground at the school in Talbotton. Clarence was always a controversial character, George remembered. He was brilliant but often misunderstood by his classmates. If there was a group standing around, Clarence would come up and give some verbal assault or "crack" to "stir up the boys." George illustrated this aspect of Clarence's personality with a story from his schooldays. It was track season and the school was having a track meet. All the young men were interested in track. The high-school coaches had dug a pit for the broad-jump competition, and a group of eighteen young boys were standing around the end of the pit. Clarence came up to the group. The boys muttered to themselves, "Here comes ole Gump. Things will pick up now. He'll have something crazy to say." As Clarence heard the group talking about the broad-jump, he quickly told the crowd of boys, "I can broad-jump thirty-six feet." The disdainful reaction was quick: "What are you talking about?" Again, Clarence was quick to say, "I bet'cha I can." Eventually, the banter subsided and the crowd of eighteen boys crowded around the end of the pit called his bluff. "Let's see you do it," they said. Then Clarence took two long steps with his lanky legs and pointed to the ground with the eighteen pairs of shoes from the eighteen boys gathered round in the crowd, and said, "Give me the money. Two equals thirty-six." His two long steps had gone past eighteen boys gathered around the pit with their total of thirty-six "feet." The crowd hooted in laughter.[8]

Clarence learned early on in life to communicate with humor. It is very likely that he learned this communication style from his mother, who was a major influence in his earliest years. The women of Maude Jossey's day had to "submit," her daughter Cornelia recalled. They had to be at the "beck and call" of the husband. Cornelia remembered that her father was "bossy." Though Jim Jordan and Maude had an affectionate relationship, she was "cowed." Jim was constantly telling her what to do. If she was not "properly" dressed in his eyes, he would tell her to go change. The man, Cornelia said, was "lord and master" in those days. Yet Maude was "always telling a joke, laughing in spite of her illnesses."[9] Thus, in her communication style, Maude Jossey passed on to her son an age-old truth—that laughter is the ultimate act of criticism and resistance, for such laughter serves to unmask oppression and to create a social and emotional space for coping. Clarence would learn to emulate this model and use it again and again in his life, so that he took what may have originally been a title of derision and reshaped and transformed it into a mode of serving God.

The Legend of the Clown of God

It may be that when Maude Jossey worked at the historic San Xavier Mission south of Tucson, she heard the Franciscan priests tell an old Medieval legend about the "Clown of God," who learns to offer his talents as a gift to the Christ child. It may be that Maude Jossey used the story in her work with Indian children at the mission. The story has the power to captivate little children, and the story would have worked that way for the young Pima children and for Clarence. The story is about a young orphan named Giovanni. Despite a difficult life, Giovanni learned to juggle. So, early in his life, he was able to earn a bowl of soup by juggling fruit in front of customers at Signor Baptista's fruit stand in Sorrento, Italy. One day, a group of traveling actors come to town and he joins the troupe and tours with them, entertaining many people over time. His act involves the juggling of a series of colored balls, which look like a rainbow. A golden ball represents the Sun in the heavens. As Giovanni travels the country, he becomes famous but he always wears the face of a clown. Two monks tell him that his juggling "sings of the glory of God." He responds, "I only juggle to make people laugh...." After he grows old and begins to lose some of his skill, one day he drops the "Sun in the heavens" and people begin to ridicule him. Giovanni decides to give up juggling. Once again, Giovanni becomes a poor, homeless beggar. On a particularly cold and windy night, he seeks refuge in a church. While he sleeps, the people of the town come to offer gifts to Mary and the Christ child. When the crowds are gone, Giovanni sees that Mary and Jesus have sad and melancholy expressions. So he puts on his clown face and juggles once again for the baby Jesus. He performs better than ever. Giovanni puts all of his love and skill into the performance, yet he dies of a heart attack in the middle of his act. The priests who look on think that his juggling is a sacrilege, until they turn and look at the statue of Mary and the Christ child and see that now they are smiling.[10]

Clarence Jordan learned early on, perhaps from his mother's stories or by copying her coping strategy, that the life of faith sometimes participates in theater and performance, and that humor can be an important skill. Through the telling of humorous stories, one can critique the structures of power and create an emotional space where one can continue to cope. Perhaps, through the life and lifestyle of his mother, Clarence Jordan also learned that such performance could be an action pleasing to God. Whether innate or learned, the "Gump" aspect of his personality would serve Clarence well. Slowly, through the years, he would develop and hone the ability to react to difficult situations with a "disciplined subjectivity"—and creative spontaneity, such as his brother George remembered from the playground at the school in Talbotton. Clarence would learn the art of identifying with people in his audience. With disarming wit, sometimes self-deprecation that appeared to play the role of a lesser person, Clarence donned a mask that pointed to a deeper humanity.[11] In later years, Clarence will demonstrate that he will develop a certain "God-madness"—a quality of faith possessed by some others who perform for God.

The Generational Complex: Conscience and the Burden of Greatness

While it is clear that the "Gump" personality, with its penchant for humor, continued to live on in Clarence as he grew older, so did the "Grump" aspect of his being, with the tendency for serious criticism. The childhood stories about Clarence in his family context imply a precocious and severe sense of conscience. There was something in his life that compelled him to try to deal with, or compensate for, a "guilt of abundance." How does a child so young get such a precocious sense of guilt that he "resents" the family having food? How does a child of eight or nine, like Clarence, gain the capacity to judge the merits of his father's actions in speaking to a delivery man? To answer these questions, one must look for additional clues in Clarence's first world—his first images of faith, the beginning of his moral journey.[12]

Most would agree that the earliest years of life are foundational for the nature and direction of the moral journey. And further, it is the child's identification with the parents or other caregivers that in some way helps the child to take on a sense of conscience. Clarence's moral journey begins, however, with an overactive conscience, which suggests a precocious sense of guilt. Where does a child so young acquire such a sense of guilt? Is not the answer to be found in the process that is normal at this age—the process of identifying with the father?

Yet Clarence feels neglected. His mother is often sick and unavailable, and his father is absent. Cornelia describes the family matrix by saying that her father was so busy running the various businesses—the store, the bank, the farm—that "he didn't have time for children." In addition, since Maude Jossey was so often sick, Jim Jordan had to plan the meals and look after the servants and the nurse. His mode for dealing with the children was very "authoritarian." Cornelia says that he "would grab all of the children and spank them." She goes on to say, "That did something to me that I've hardly ever gotten over." In fact, Cornelia "had a hard time growing up and not being bitter." Because of her mother's sickness and the fact that she felt there was no one else to turn to, Cornelia grew up feeling like an "orphan." Clarence, for his part, was not close to his father.[13] When Clarence is twenty-one years old, he writes to his mother and says, "I am just beginning to really know my dad."[14] So, what does Clarence do about the age of five, when internally he begins to look for the image of the father to guide his emerging sense of autonomy—his first tentative steps away from the maternal matrix?

A child like Clarence will attempt to resolve the dilemma by identifying with a grandfather, or someone else who becomes a father figure. But this transaction, however, comes with a great price—a precocious conscience. That is, the child compensates for moving beyond parental authority at this young age by internalizing an extraordinary sense of guilt, which encourages the child to absolve himself by assuming responsibility for the pain of those around him. It is in this way that Clarence begins to be bitter toward the family attitude of abundance, and to resent that the family has anything. It also helps one understand how, at the age of eight or nine, Clarence can begin to judge his father's actions.

A mother who loves one child more than the other children in the family, as Maude Jossey did with Clarence, puts pressure on the favored child. But there may be an even larger perspective. In writing about Gandhi, Erikson noted that the Oedipal crisis is actually a part of a greater crisis, the "generational complex," for such conflicts are inherent in the way humans experience the larger issues of life in the "turnover of generations." Then Erikson theorized that it is likely that uncommon young men experience these conflicts, because they sense in themselves some aspect of "originality," which very early in life seems to point them beyond the competition with their individual fathers. Thus, the precocious and demanding conscience makes these young men—at a very young age—both feel and appear older than their peers, and perhaps their parents, who may reciprocate by regarding the child as a redeemer. So these young men grow up with a sense of obligation—grounded in a profound sense of guilt—to succeed and to create, whatever the cost. Such a dynamic prolongs the identity confusion in adolescence, and may later lead the young man to accept a whole body of people, perhaps humankind itself, as the object of his rescue.[15]

The Grandfather and the Reversal of the Generations:
  Clarence and Stories about His Maternal Grandfather

Clarence Jordan's story is testimony to the fact that, if a father is not physically and emotionally present to his child, the son will look for a father substitute. An important clue to understanding the early life of Clarence Jordan is to know that he was extremely close to his mother and that, when the other children got bored with Maude Jossey's stories and ran off to play, Clarence stayed and listened longer. Maude Jossey loved to tell stories about when she was young and lived out west in places like Seattle, Portland, Tacoma, and Tucson. But the older children had heard the stories before or simply got tired. They did not stay to hear the end of the stories. But Clarence did. "Clarence would always stay right with her and listen to her."[16]

What stories did Clarence hear? Apparently, Maude Jossey not only loved to relive her experience in the western U.S., but she also wanted to pass on the family legacy as she saw and understood it. So she told the stories about her parents and the exciting places they had been. Her mother was Clara L. Leonard, great-granddaughter of Van de Van Lennard, the Virginia plantation owner. Her father, and Clarence's maternal grandfather, was B. Frank Jossey, a U.S. Treasury agent who had received a presidential appointment to work in the western U.S. As a child, Maude Marie Jossey had lived an exciting life away from West Georgia, and as a young parent, she wanted to pass on the stories about that life to her children. No doubt she told stories about her work at the San Xavier Mission with the Tohono O'odham, who lived in the Sonoran Desert near Tucson, and how she and a friend rode twelve miles out into the desert twice a week.

The stories about her father and Clarence's grandfather, B. Frank Jossey, would have been wonderful—especially enlivened narratives about the man to whom Maude Marie was so devoted that she vowed never to marry as long as he was alive. Maude Marie's stories about her father would have portrayed him in the most positive manner. As a sensitive and spiritual person herself, Maude Marie would have seen her father as a person of strength and dedication, who not only loved his family and other people, but also sought to make a difference in the world. His life beyond Talbotton would have required a sense of competence and courage. His willingness to allow his daughter to work away from home in a somewhat dangerous area would require tolerance and risk-taking abilities, and perhaps above all, a commitment to the growth and development—and larger wellbeing—of his daughter. B. Frank Jossey would have been portrayed by his devoted daughter as a very strong model for her son. Her love for her father and Clarence would have meant that she wanted her father to live on in Clarence. And, for his part, Clarence would really identify with those stories—and with his grandfather—and he would have said to his mother, "Tell me another story about Grandfather." And, as Maude Jossey continued to tell the stories about Grandfather, he became what Erikson once called "one of the last representatives of a more homogeneous world."[17] And, as such a representative, the grandfather as seen in the stories of a devoted daughter served as a "provider of identity" for Clarence, who was an especially sensitive and responsive young boy.[18]

How does a young boy like Clarence attain such a sense of identification with a grandfather, and what does this have to do with Clarence's moral journey? In brief, this propensity to identify with the grandparent can bring on what Ernest Jones called the "reversal of the generations," the ability of the child to substitute a grandparent for a parent—and, in the process, to become, in a child's eyes, the parent of a parent. Likewise, this ability, in Clarence's case, to reverse the generations further serves his moral quest in two important ways: (1) in his mind, Clarence wins the competition with his father—who is the first major obstacle of authority in the child's life—by identifying with his grandfather, which in turn reduces his father to the level of a sibling; and (2) Clarence adds the capacity to envision a "spiritual father" based on this veneration of his grandfather.[19]

Learning the Ways of the Older Generation:
  Clarence, George, and the Old Haynes Automobile

Despite the often severe nature of his growing personality, Clarence was often morally adventurous and still a child given to childlike ways. When Clarence was about seven or eight, he took his brother George out to examine the old Haynes automobile that had been given to the family by his father's brother in Macon. The Haynes automobile was a large car built by Elwood Haynes, an automobile pioneer. His factory was in Kokomo, Indiana, where he created the earliest American design that could be used for mass production. The old Haynes model that had been given to Jim Jordan was a seven-seater and, as George Jordan remembered, about six feet longer than an average car of the day. Jim Jordan had to build an extension to the garage just to park the car. One day, Clarence got behind the wheel with George sitting in the front passenger seat. Both of the boys were barefooted and neither could see out of the car very well. Clarence, though older than George, could not see above the steering wheel. Clarence successfully started the car, however. In order to get a "feel" for the vehicle, Clarence began backing the car up a few feet and then going forward a few feet. He did this about six or seven times. Then his bare foot slipped off the brake pedal, and the car lunged forward into the back of the garage and knocked the entire back wall down.[20]

George suddenly had an attack of conscience and quickly remembered that he had a "settin'" hen who had abandoned her eggs, and that he had been told repeatedly to bury the old eggs. He told Clarence that he thought now would be a good time to bury those eggs. So he jumped out of the old Haynes car, grabbed the eggs, and ran back toward the county jail to bury them. From the distance of 100 yards, he saw his father—who had been summoned by Maude Jossey—come down and grab Clarence with one hand and, with a switch in the other, "tear" him up for that misadventure. The car, which had proven to be too big for Jim Jordan in any case, was given away.[21]

Learning the Stories of a People and the Ways of God

At an early age, Clarence began to learn other stories of his culture. One of the most important of those stories for Clarence would be the narrative of the Bible, which he learned while sitting on his mother's knee. These stories became doubly special—the words of the divine read to him in his mother's voice. Like other young school-age children, Clarence was intensely interested in stories, especially the stories of the book with all the pictures. He found that, about the age of seven or eight, those stories in the book with pictures contained the narratives that symbolize belonging to the church community. And he took in those stories and beliefs and appropriated them at this age with a certain literal sense, as he did with moral rules and attitudes.[22] His first image of God beyond the maternal matrix tended to be that of a "giant benevolent cop in the sky" who would enforce all the rules and bring about a larger sense of justice and peace.[23] It is likely that his mother's stories about his grandfather, Frank Jossey—a U.S. Treasury agent—merged in his mind with the stories about God, so that his understanding of the divine world was doubly ordered and secure.

It was through the exploration of biblical stories that Clarence was oriented to the mysteries of time and existence, and integrated into a larger family of faith with its stories about God, humankind, and society. Clarence would have learned the early stories perhaps by associating many of them with the pictures—idyllic nature scenes from the Garden of Eden, historic episodes from the legacy of ancient Israel, and portrayals of the infant Jesus—and the later public ministry. The narratives were understood in literal and concrete terms. Consequently, the righteous were on one side and the wicked on the other. But a striking thing also happened in Clarence's early reading of the Bible—Jesus looked like a woman, as he later proclaimed![24] Is this an adult testimony to an early childhood reality, that his first Christ-like teacher was indeed his mother, Maude Jossey?

So Clarence drank in the tradition of the church almost with his mother's milk. The reading of the book with pictures became for him the "great code" of life: the stories of creation, covenant, the stories of the great prophets, the narratives about Jesus, the early church, and the great apostle Paul. Growing up in the church, Clarence became immersed in the rich traditions of his Baptist past. He absorbed the Bible and its stories. In time, the scriptures provided Clarence with a compelling language world in which the mysteries of life were mapped out. The ancient rehearsals found in the Bible, and as practiced by the community through the centuries, imposed archetypes and paradigms on the chaos felt near by all. For a young boy like Clarence, the "overarching plot" of the Bible created a "graph of destiny." Talbotton became, for him, a "well-lighted" place providing orientation and coherence as he searched to know the ways of God and Christian people. And, as Clarence learned to read the scriptures, he was immersed in a "world story" that secured human life against death—meaning, against the irrational. The overarching story itself gave testimony to these realities. The stories of creation and covenant guaranteed the stability of the cosmos. Life was secured against death—meaning, against chaos—by the very power of word and story. Justice and salvation were promised to the faithful. The image of God as the great officer in the sky ordered the world in a secure way and promised that justice and equity would be the reward of all deserving lives, regardless of race or color.[25]

In his early schoolyears, Clarence also learned another powerful story: the American foundation myth articulated in the American Dream. Jim Jordan, the small-town tycoon and Mayor of Talbotton, epitomized this cultural story. From the beginning, Americans understood their history in religious terms. Early citizens envisioned America as a new Israel, the very_chosen of God. The old, established countries of Europe represented the "Egypt" of oppression, while America, with its openness and newness, stood for the "Promised Land." The hazardous journey over the Atlantic corresponded to the life-threatening crossing of the Red Sea. The small community of saints in New England felt called to be a "city on a hill," and on "an errand in the wilderness." But the Canaanites of the original Promised Land story were also represented in the mythic scheme. This negative image was projected on the Native American Indians. So the founding of the noble experiment was built on a primal crime—the Indians were often deprived of life and liberty and human rights by the new settlers. The beginning of this new society was witness to another major crime—slavery. Countless numbers of Africans with their own native culture and symbol system were forced to take up a role in the European dream—a dream that, for the Africans, became worse than a nightmare.

Clarence was morally precocious. He began to see rather early the conflict between the religious tradition that he was learning and the cultural tradition as it was practiced by the common folk. Eventually, Clarence learned that the dark side of the American myth merged with the plantation system, which reigned in the land of cotton, and that these cultural myths seemed to be undergirded by a human propensity toward "pseudo-speciation"—the "deep-seated conviction that some providence has made [one's] tribe, race or caste, and…religion 'naturally' superior to others."[26] In time, Clarence would come to see that the Southern church was propped up and controlled by deep-seated cultural myths that were most visible as a "plantation mentality"—which acted as a "god above God"—a powerful set of cultural mores and values that mitigated against a true spiritual life. But, for now, he was just learning the ways of the people—the idealized portrayal of that first Christian community, and the mores of culture and contemporary church. He recognized the conflicts, as when his father rebuked a black man for coming to the front door of their well-to-do home. And, already at nine or ten, he found the insight and the courage to contend for a more just and humane way.

Clarence Confronting His Father:
Homo Religiosus *and the Covenant Sealed with God*

This story just mentioned above about Clarence as a young grade-school child is very telling of his special nature as a religious person. It is a story that shows him with the "Grump" personality, contending with the discontinuity between the model of Jesus that he saw revealed in his mother and preached in the church over against the reality of everyday life among the folk. His mother read the Bible stories to him about Jesus and acted out the command of Jesus to love all people—red, yellow, black, and white. Maude Jossey was kind and generous to all. But Clarence's father, though an avid churchgoer, would sometimes talk down to and belittle black people. So, one day, when Clarence was nine or ten, a black delivery man comes to the front door of the Jordan home and is met by Jim Jordan, who promptly tells him that his "place" is at the back door (implying that his color makes him a second-class citizen unworthy of entrance to the home through the front door). Clarence "rebukes," "scolds," or "lectures" his father over the matter.

This is an extraordinary story for the year 1921. Jim Jordan was physically larger—and he was the father who often grabbed children and spanked them harshly for disrupting family life! How does a young boy in the fourth or fifth grade find the audacity to do such a thing? The story tells us much about the nature and dimension of the early religious life or spiritual pilgrimage of Clarence Jordan. The story essentially describes Clarence as a budding "religious innovator," whom Erik Erikson describes as *homo religious*. The extent to which Clarence pursues the ways of God without regard for his own wellbeing indicates his religious personality is that of *homo religiosus*. How does a nine-year-old like Clarence stand over against his father in this manner? He does so only by becoming his father's father—that is, by reversing the generations.

In Clarence's case, it seems that his identification with the images and stories of his grandfather, as portrayed by his mother, takes him beyond that first conflict with the father's authority and allows him to imagine God in terms of a strong, resolute, and just spiritual Father. In so doing, Clarence makes a covenant with God. Though Clarence is surely only a young schoolboy in this story, his personal narrative reflects an emerging sense of religious selfhood—a "budding 'I,'" as Erikson describes it, which believes that he "harbors a truthfulness superior to that of all authorities because this truth is the covenant of the 'I' with God." This "overweening conscience can find peace only..." through such totalistic belief and action, and by assuming that the covenant with God is "...more central and more pervasive than all parent images or moralities." This, Erikson writes, is the "core of a *homo religiosus*." It is on this basis that Clarence stands up to his father and rebukes or lectures him. The motto for a special young man like Clarence at this age is a kind of totalism reflected in "allness or nothingness." The covenant sealed with God allows one the ability to face danger and, eventually, death itself. It is this sense of an "I" sealed in covenant with God that allows Clarence to stand unprotected against his father, who could have grabbed him in a moment of rage and beaten him, as he sometimes did the other children. This is the core of Clarence Jordan's personality—the person behind the legend and legacy, here only in embryonic form. Yet it is this core reality that later will go on the long pilgrimage and seek to overturn an entire society, and eventually be joined with an entire generation. In due course, we will have to ask how Clarence's own individual conflicts match those of his generation.[27]

Mythos and Childhood Faith: Story and Ultimate Environment

Clarence's schoolyears found him expanding his spiritual landscape. His propensity for faith grew as he began to envision a spiritual father and as he took up the religious quest. Clarence's identification with the images of his grandfather, as portrayed by his mother, helped him win the competition with his own father at an extremely early age, but left him with a precocious conscience and an abiding sense of guilt. This overactive conscience and continuing sense of guilt marked Clarence's early years, as did his identity as "Grump."

Clarence's childhood years indicate that he likely grew to maturity in an environment where he was "called," like Jeremiah, at an early age. That is, he lived with a sense of obligation—grounded in a severe and profound sense of guilt—to succeed, to create, and to redeem. It is this call that is the foundation for his later legendary status. It is this dynamic of obligation—as seen in his relationship with his mother—grounded in guilt that, for Clarence, is the "guilt of overabundance," which later pushes him as a budding innovator to envision an entire people as the object of his rescue. It appears that Clarence did indeed shoulder the burden of greatness at a very young age. This view is borne out by the extreme nature of his childhood faith—a faith that, if only in the immature dreams of a teenager, sought to redeem his region.

Yet Clarence as a child, and later as an adult, would be sustained and nurtured by the stories he learned on his mother's knee. For a time, Clarence's spiritual geography was linked directly to the narratives he first heard from his mother, which helped him to define a larger world. As a child, these stories helped Clarence understand who he was and what he was commanded to do. They illuminated his world, gave him models to live by, and became a guide for the pathways that unfolded before him. Clarence seems also to have been deeply influenced by the lived faith of both his parents. He "read" their stories, emulated some

aspects and reacted to others. He seems to have been especially influenced by his mother's use of humor. In time, the stories he learned on his
mother's knee would be rewritten as the "Cotton Patch" gospel in a quest
to give new meaning for an entire generation. The stories and the story-
tellers were a foundational aspect in Clarence's growing and developing
faith. Both would live on in Clarence's spiritual geography and provide a
wellspring for later nurture and inspiration. Originally encountered in
the realm of the first naiveté and read with a literal sense, these stories
would come to live again in Clarence's re-appropriation, characterized by
the world of a second naiveté with an expanded sense of meaning and
reference.[28] But, for now, the clash between the stories he learned first on
his mother's knee and the larger culture itself will mark the end to one
era of faith and the beginning of a new one.

Chapter 4

The Curse

I am going into this project in order to pay a debt....I owe them a debt, which by the grace of God, I want to pay.
—Clarence Jordan

Fortified by the stories his mother read to him and the images of God as just and benevolent, all appropriated in a literal manner, Clarence Jordan spent his grade-school years "contending" for his emerging faith and a just and humane view of his world. With this faith and worldview, he challenged his siblings, who rewarded him with the nickname "Grump." And, with this egalitarian perspective and unusual courage, he responded to his father when he thought justice had been breached. But this era came to an end in August 1924 when he was twelve years old—when he got mad with God. This story of his anger with God serves to bring his childhood faith to an abrupt conclusion and open a new era of his teenage years.

The story itself is well known. Jordan, as an adult, tended to tell it to explain how his racial attitudes were shaped. It is the one story that is used most often by Jordan, and by those who read and try to understand his work, to summarize his response to the injustice he saw in his society. There are a couple of versions of the story, indicating that Clarence's memory on the issue was not precise.[1] Though this one story gives a specific time and locale to Clarence's rebellion against injustice, the totality of the experience was more than likely gradual. Yet this episode came to represent something of a marker event of his final rejection of the abuses in culture that he saw and experienced over time.

The Talbot County Jail was a few hundred yards behind Clarence's house, and he passed by there on his way to school. In those days, the area around the jail was also used as a camp for the chain gang and included five or six portable prison wagons, which were used to take the prisoners to temporary worksites. Each wagon was entirely metal and could hold up to ten to fifteen prisoners.[2] Walking past that camp on the way to school became an education that could not be taught or read in a book. As a precocious and sensitive young man, Clarence was also very impressionable. He would hear the wake-up gong every morning at 4 A.M. He also remembered the scenes at the camp for a lifetime. No doubt, his effort to befriend the prisoners and get to know them was something of a sensitive child's way to bring some sense of humanity to an inhumane situation. Clarence later recalled, "I stopped and made friends with them. They were almost all of them black men, but they seemed more alive, more genuinely human, than the people I met at church."[3]

Since this camp was just behind the Jordan home, it is likely that the Jordan boys often went there together and got to know some of the men. Dallas Lee writes that "Clarence was fascinated by the rowdy, profane humanity of the men who lived out a portion of their lives there...."[4] Clarence's sister Cornelia said that Mr. MacDonald, the warden, would come walking by the Jordan house, down the driveway to the jail, carrying food for the men, and the boys would run out of the house and follow him back to the prison.[5] Clarence, especially, seemed to like to go there. And he made friends with several of the men, and the cook who routinely gave him cornbread and fatback. For a young boy to be near a jail and a chain gang while growing up in a small town would have been an exhilarating and daring experience. Yet, for Clarence, what he saw and learned was revolutionary. To get to know the men and to find them to be "more alive, more genuinely human, than the people...at church" brought on a sense of contradiction in his literalist world. He saw brutality beyond what a young child could bear—harsh realities that called his world of immanent justice into question. He saw men with short chains on their feet and heard the "clank of the chained feet" as they tried to walk. He heard the "muttered curses of the wretched" whose lives were being swallowed up by a system with no justice or hope.[6] He saw men locked into the shame of primitive pillories. He saw strong men beaten by whips and vulnerable souls put through the agony of the "stretcher." And he saw that almost all of them were black.[7]

Clarence's moral education from the edge of his culture came to a climax one hot week in August in Talbotton. It was 1924. Clarence was 12 years old. During the revival meeting—typically held at this time in Baptist churches across the South—Clarence had just made a "profession of faith" and joined the Talbotton Baptist Church. This was a very serious and public identification with the "body of Christ" gathered in his hometown. He knew all the people and had known them for years. He knew Mr. MacDonald, who was the warden at the prison and also sang bass in the choir. A couple of nights after Clarence made his public profession of faith identifying with the other Baptists of the town, Mr. Mac, as he was called, was singing in the choir and really got "carried away" singing "Love Lifted Me." Then, on the very next night, Clarence, sleeping in a house with the windows open, was jolted awake by the "agonizing groans" that came from the chain-gang camp. Almost immediately, Clarence knew what was happening and who was doing it. Ed Russell, one of his acquaintances from the camp, had been put in the stretcher by the warden, Mr. Mac. The same man who had been carried away singing "Love Lifted Me" just a few hours before was now pulling the rope and putting a prisoner in excruciating pain. At this point in his interview, Clarence says a striking thing: "That nearly tore me to pieces. I identified totally with that man in the stretcher. His agony was my agony."[8] This confrontation between the brutality of the chain-gang experience and the faith he had just affirmed "caused a fermentation to take place inside...," Clarence said. He went on to indicate, "...and it hasn't stopped yet."[9]

For an idealistic and sensitive young man aspiring to be a follower of Christ and attempting to construct a world of justice and faithfulness, this was a devastating experience. The pain of what he saw, heard, and internalized stayed with him for a lifetime. His ability to identify with the man in the stretcher—and to be able to say, "His agony was my agony"—indicated a profound and precocious sense of guilt. Clarence took this experience with him for a lifetime and attempted in some manner to compensate for it—to repay the debt. After Clarence had decided to return to Georgia to establish Koinonia Farm, he wrote to a black pastor in Cleveland and said, "I am going into this project in order to pay a debt....I owe them [the black people of the region] a debt, which by the grace of God, I want to pay."[10]

The Curse: Clarence Jordan's Existential Debt

The brutal and inhumane treatment of the men Clarence had be-friended and gotten to know, combined with his own inability to alter the situation in any way, stayed with him as a type of existential curse.[11] That is, the suffering of these black men, along with the unjust treat-ment, was etched so indelibly into his childhood consciousness that it continued to haunt him for a lifetime. What does the "curse" mean in the life of an individual like Clarence Jordan? It means that Clarence carries some form of "existential debt" throughout his life. But the suffering of Ed Russell is not likely the cause of the debt. This particular episode is more likely the "cover memory," or the projection of an earlier childhood conflict onto this dramatic scene.[12] In essence, one could say that this memory is in some way tied to that earlier struggle, the Oedipus conflict. But this crisis may also be better understood as the "generational com-plex," or rather, that human beings experience the ultimate conflicts of life as the issues of life and death, past and future, the change of the gen-erations. Thus, it may be that a young man like Clarence experiences such remorse and guilt because early in life he has already begun to sense some aspect of "originality," which in childhood seems to him to point beyond competition with the father. In this sense, Clarence's precocious conscience and single-mindedness help him to appear older even while young. When his parents look to him with such expectation, as Clar-ence's did, then he can grow with something of an obligation to fulfill parental hopes and dreams—the dream of his mother, that he would be a great man in the church! Clarence's precocious conscience belies his al-ready long-term struggle to deal with his own felt guilt of—early in life—having gone beyond his father in some way. Consequently, this dramatic scene becomes the repository for the burden of memories and expectation, which in actuality go to earlier childhood days. These mem-ories and previous burdens only make the contemporary scene more traumatic and filled with guilt. His only solution, therefore, is to find a way to fulfill the original expectation. In order to do so, a young near-adolescent like Clarence often has a prolonged identity crisis while he searches for the moment that "he (and he alone!) can reenact the past and create a new future in the right medium at the right moment on a sufficiently large scale." But there are other factors in Clarence's moral and spiritual journey. What are they, and what do they have to do with Jordan, the man?[13]

Unmaking a World: The End of an Era
    and the Loss of Childhood Faith

A part of the pain that one hears in Clarence's often-told story about Ed Russell, Mr. MacDonald, and the chain-gang camp is his own childhood sense of devastation at the loss of a way of making meaning, and the image of God that went with it. After saying that Ed Russell's agony became his, Clarence adds, "I got really mad with God."[14] In another context, Clarence says, "I was 12 at the time and for a long time I was mad at God."[15] Though Clarence continued to reflect on how he could help lift the burden from the backs of the poor, there was "little of God in my motives," he said.[16] His strong image of a God as the divine officer in the sky who provided reciprocal justice for all had, in fact, died. That image could not withstand the sense of contradiction Clarence began to see when his childhood faith saw the collision between the injustice and brutality of the chain-gang world and his ideals understood literally.

Martin Luther King, Jr., had a similar experience as a 12-year-old. Young Martin had "slipped away to watch a parade when he was supposed to be studying." While he was out, his beloved grandmother, Jennie Williams, "had gone home to glory." Martin's response was to think that God was now punishing his grandmother and his family for his "sin"—going to the parade without telling anyone. Young Martin "cried off and on for several days…and was unable to sleep at night." Having appropriated the religious beliefs of his black Baptist church with literal interpretations, his worldview at the time, was like that of Clarence wrestling with the injustice of the chain gangs: reciprocal fairness and immanent justice. Young Martin must have thought that the God of justice and judgment must have visited the punishment for the guilt of his iniquity upon the family through the death of Grandmother Williams. Martin could not understand how a just God could so punish his grandmother, who was "saintly." The principle of reciprocity that had undergirded his childhood faith was now breaking down, and with it went the demise of the faith perspective of a troubled 12-year-old.[17]

*Becoming a Baptist: Clarence and the
     Emergence of Conventional Faith*

The story just rehearsed above about Clarence, Ed Russell, Mr. MacDonald, and the old-fashioned Georgia chain gang was also a narrative about a young man publicly affiliating with his religious group. This event had occurred just a couple of days after Clarence had become a member of the Talbotton Baptist Church. The story serves to seal one era of faith and to introduce another. That is, this story also announces the beginning of Clarence's conventional years. Though, in later telling, this event seems to loom large as a major marker event in Clarence's young life, in truth, at the time he was very quiet about it. The story itself is very much a reflective narrative that looks back in time and attempts to make sense of life as it has unfolded over the years. Though Clarence will in time become one of a few well-known "dissident" Baptists, as a young teenager, he was beginning to experience a sense of "moratorium"—a quiet, inward-looking time when he would continue to struggle to make sense of the things he had seen and heard. But those subterranean forces and struggles would be, for the most part, hidden from the view of the world. And, like other teenagers, his adolescent faith would be unreflective, naive, and based upon group opinion.[18]

Like most young boys, early in his teenage years, Clarence began to explore a larger world. His father had farmland and he liked the outdoor life. He and his brothers would go to the farm where Jim Jordan was growing corn, peas, sweet potatoes, and later, peaches. They also saw the world of sharecroppers because, as head of the local bank, Jim Jordan would be in charge of bank-owned lands, which meant overseeing tenant farming. On the farm, there were two mules, Jib and Jody, which they would occasionally plow. With his brothers, he would often go down to the creeks and ponds and explore the woods. He learned to ride a motorcycle. His brothers would ride with him on occasion. His brother Robert remembered riding on the back of the motorcycle and hanging onto Clarence for dear life as they went out to Juniper Lake, where they would go swimming. Robert said Clarence was a "daredevil" in his teenage years. "He didn't have any fear for anything, in later life or when he was young. He was fearless."[19]

When Clarence went out to the farm with his brothers, there were experiences that would lead him to further reflection. He would often play with the children of the workers. He tried to understand why these young black children looked so tattered, and why they wore dirty clothes. He understood that he, too, got dirty, but he was able to go home and clean up. He came to realize by his visits to the farm that the black children did not have running water, and that it was not easy for them to "spiff up" like he did. Clarence came to the conclusion early that black people are different from white people, but "it's not because of the color of…skin[,]…it's the opportunities that they have…." Clarence was also learning that young blacks did not have the opportunity to go to school that he had. The black children had to stay out of school to pick cotton and "shake" peanuts, and were allowed to go to school only a few months during the year. The days that they were allowed to go to school, they had to walk three to five miles to a one-room schoolhouse that would house grades 1–7, with a teacher who had minimal education herself. He also began to wonder why the black children could not go to the big school for whites in Talbotton. Several times he thought of trying to teach the black children something he had just learned, but he realized that many of his friends on the farm were illiterate. And Clarence did not know how to begin.[20]

As teenagers, the Jordan boys also worked in the hardware store. Jim Jordan did not like for his employees to sit down while they were working. One day, he came in and found Clarence and the other boys sitting down while no one was in the store. Jim Jordan scolded the boys and told them that they were supposed to be working. Clarence fired back, "Dad, put hobnails on your boots and you won't catch us sitting down."[21] Clarence always had a comeback, always sought to win the argument. Perhaps his father saw that Clarence's lighthearted jab did not carry a sense of disrespect because, when this happened, his father did not come back with more banter.[22]

Robert Jordan remembered that there were other episodes from Clarence's teenage years that illustrated his daredevil ways. One such occasion occurred in high school. Hugh Carter, the son of the local physician, had a car—a Model-T. The group had just come home from school. Clarence was riding on the running board, standing up and holding onto the car. He had his trumpet in his hand. Hugh Carter slowed the car down so Clarence could jump off. Just as Clarence jumped, a motorcycle came by and hit him. His trumpet went flying into the air, and his body did also. His brother Robert was watching. It "scared me to death," Robert said. When Clarence came down, he landed hard and his head hit the dirt pavement. Robert thought Clarence was dead. After a few minutes, however, Clarence got up and walked away. His brother began to see that "nothing could get him down, not even a motorcycle."[23]

In summer 1926, when Clarence was 14 years old, the home burned. Lille Lee Ford, their cook for fifty years, discovered smoke coming from the kitchen and sounded the alarm. But the fire department, with the limited firefighting equipment of that day, was unable to save the home.[24] Beginning in 1927, Jim Jordan built another home across the street. It appeared to be a stronger, more fire-resistant home. Jordan bought 180,000 bricks for the project, and the walls were built fourteen inches thick.[25] Maude Jossey wrote to Clarence on August 10, 1927, of the exciting news that their lot was being cleaned in preparation for the start of the building process. Clarence had gone away on a trip. His mother ends the letter by saying, "Take good care of yourself and don't take any *risks*, especially in the swimming pool."[26] When the family moved into their new home, Clarence was given a room by himself.[27]

In high school, Clarence studied literature and left notes on Shakespeare. In his courses on English grammar, he left notes on paragraph development, one of which was a brief essay on "A Famous Man I Should Like to Have Met." For Clarence, that man was Robert E. Lee. This is somewhat surprising, given his later stance on war and the military. But, during his adolescence, Clarence was exploring the ways of his culture and his past. Later, in college, Clarence explored the Reserve Officers Training Corps, and that story sealed and closed his adolescent era of faith. According to Clarence, he would have liked to have known Lee because of "some of his fine qualities." Those qualities included: the control of his temper and the fact that he did not swear oaths or use intoxicating liquors. Lee, like some of Clarence's ancestors, was born in Virginia. Robert E. Lee was, of course, commander of the Confederate army, and was the "hero of a lost cause."[28]

When Clarence was 16, he gave his mother a Mother's Day card with the inscription, "To the sweetest mother a boy ever had." And then the note: "A Token of Love to Mother." On the inside of the card, Clarence wrote, "Because I know you care for me, Because your love endures, Because of faith you bear for me, My heart's best love is yours."[29] About the same time, he received a letter from his sister, who was away at college. She counseled him: "Now, just don't let all that popularity with the fair sex get in your way. That's alright in its place, but don't let them have much of your time."[30]

Clarence's older brother, who was at the University of Georgia, also wrote to him on several occasions. In Clarence's junior year, Buddie wrote to say, "I think you are 'quite' the stuff." Then he challenges Clarence to "determine to make a success and nothing in the world can stop you."[31] In a later letter, Buddie encourages Clarence in his music lessons and pronounces his blessings upon Clarence's "debut" in the social world, which probably refers to Clarence beginning to date—likely Mary Adelaide Seigler, who was Clarence's high-school "sweetheart." Mary was very attractive, tall, slender, and a "nice dresser." She was his closest friend in high school. Buddie went on to tell Clarence that he had "a lot of things to talk…about that will help you." He goes on to tell Clarence to remember to "have a strong willpower and determination to do right." At the end of the letter, Buddie warns Clarence that "you certainly have to watch your step or it is mighty easy to go wrong. Remember that I am with you in anything that you undertake."[32]

About this same time, Clarence got a warm letter from his sister, Cornelia, she was addresses him as "Grump ole dear."[33] She describes his "last epistle" as a "go-*fetcher*."[34] Then she writes: "Come on you, I'm bettin' on you," and she asks if he has learned to play "Turkey in the Straw" or "Bake Dat Chicken Pie"? Clarence was taking lessons on the trumpet. Cornelia ends her letter telling Clarence that she has heard how powerful he is in "expression," apparently a reference to his debate and literary skills. And then she asks about the "societies." With Martin McGehee, Clarence started an honorary fraternity and, in his senior year, was president of the literary society.

During his early years and on into high school, Clarence later recalled that "being a follower of Jesus was perhaps the predominant thing" in his life.[35] During this time, he considered being a lawyer with the hope that he might see justice done. Clarence wanted to do something for the people he knew who were in jail and on the chain gang. He knew that many of them were "treated brutally."[36] But, as his experience broadened beyond his immediate neighborhood, his ideas began to change. The more he traveled around the farms and rural areas of Talbot County, the more he realized that "most of the blacks did not end up on the chain gang."[37] Instead, Clarence learned that most blacks were living in poverty trying to eke out a living—struggling with hunger and economic oppression. They, in fact, needed justice for every area of living. This realization led Clarence to the idea that perhaps the study of agriculture might be a way "to help the poor lift the awful burden off their backs."[38] So, gradually, Clarence came to the understanding that, though there were clearly injustices in the prisons and chain gangs, there was also a pervasive sense of injustice on the farms, which involved the totality of life experience for black Americans. When Clarence was able to put together his own inclination toward the outdoor life and farming with his innate sense of "social and religious consciousness," then he could see himself studying agriculture at the University of Georgia.[39]

Clarence's father was, however, less inclined to see his son make such a decision. Perhaps Jim Jordan was disappointed that Clarence did not decide on law. A lawyer could have fit well with the booming business that was located in "Jordan city." So he said to Clarence, "If you want to be a farmer, why go to school? I'll buy you a mule and you can start right now." Despite this initial pessimism, Jim Jordan would support his son as well as he could in the days leading up to the "Great Depression."[40] As Jim Jordan reflected on Clarence's desire to study agriculture, he may have had second thoughts. Perhaps he could see Clarence taking over the supervision of the 2,000-acre farming operation within his larger business enterprise. Maybe Jim Jordan thought Clarence would supervise the large farm on horseback and relieve some of his workload. Martin England remembered it that way: "Clarence, until near the end of his undergraduate days in the University of Georgia, had been marked to go back to take over the operations of the farm. That was to be his farm...."[41] While Clarence came to see agriculture as part of the solution to his quest, he wrestled with larger issues that were not settled with finality until his Louisville days.

Clarence graduated from the Talbotton Public School with the Class of 1929. The event was held in the school auditorium on June 3 at 8:30 P.M. Edward Martin MeGehee was the valedictorian, though Clarence's brothers always wondered if there were political considerations made for Edward, whose father was a prominent attorney in Talbotton. His brothers thought Clarence was brighter than Edward, who was Clarence's main competition in literary and speaking events in high school. Though Clarence had a splendid academic record, it did not appear to be something he wanted to talk about, except with his mother in his letters.[42] It is very likely that the letter his mother wrote to him a few days before graduation meant more to Clarence than did the actual graduation service.

Maude Jossey had gone on a short trip and was unable to be present at Clarence's graduation. So she sends a note to help Clarence celebrate the occasion and mark the significance of the event. She begins by saying that she wished she could be the first one to greet and congratulate him after the service. But, since she could not be there, she wanted Clarence to know that she was with him "in mind and heart." She told Clarence that she was the "proudest and happiest mother in all the world" because of the work that he had done. Maude Jossey goes on to say that the "greatest reward" you will have will be the "love and devotion of your...proud parents." Then Maude Jossey proceeds to summarize his young life, ask for God's blessings on Clarence, and reinforce the importance of spirituality over wealth and fame.[43]

His mother writes that "since babyhood you have been all that a mother could ask of a child." She praises him for his patience while sick, for being "sweet and gentle" with his siblings, and for being "so thoughtful and considerate of my every wish."[44] His hard work and "splendid record" cause her heart to swell with pride. The life he is living causes her to love Clarence more. Maude Jossey says, "I'd rather have my fine, splendid sons and daughters [sic] than all the wealth, honor, or fame that the world can give." She encloses a gift and a benediction: "May God bless you, my dear son, and may He keep you and guide your footsteps aright. May the coming years be filled with happiness and joy, and may every day be as bright as this, your graduation day."[45] On July 12, Clarence received a letter from the "Committee on Entrance" at the University of Georgia. The committee had received a certificate of the work he had done in high school, and Clarence had met the requirements for entry to the university. Within a couple of months, Clarence would enter a new world, and his mother would have cause for concern and bitter disappointment.

The World of "They": Clarence Jordan and Conventional Faith

Clarence ended his childhood years deeply troubled by the conflict that he saw between the ways of his religion literally understood, and the realities of his culture, especially the discrimination and brutality he was learning about. The stories of the chain gang and conflict with the church seal one era and open another. During his teenage years, Clarence entered into something of a moratorium—a quiet, reflective time when he began to explore a larger world of group opinion, and activities of friends and schoolmates. The stories told about Clarence from this period indicate that he was something of a risk-taker—a daredevil. He was learning that he was fated to survive, and perhaps he had the added responsibility to make something of his life. He was looking for a time and a way to rework those events that were rooted in his soul. How would he relive those core events in his young life—which was remembered as a curse—so as to release himself from the "curse" of existential debt (which came to him as a memory of things deeply embedded in his very being)? Could he be a lawyer and change the brutality done to blacks? Was the situation more complex than that? Could he be a military officer like Robert E. Lee, whom he had learned to admire? Could he be a new kind of farmer who shared his understanding with others and, thereby, help promote the common good, especially for the tenant farmers he had gotten to know? How would he use his skills in music and debate that he was beginning to cultivate in high school? How would he be a faithful and honest Christian in the world that he was coming to know? As for now, Clarence was going to the University of Georgia with the idea that he would be a scientific farmer. But the issues were far from settled. He would continue to explore possibilities, and be very tempted by one vocation that would break his mother's heart.

Chapter 5

Athens I: Dancing to Every Tune

[Clarence Jordan] was a party guy, a good storyteller, and...a live-wire personality in a quiet sort of way.

—Dallas Lee

In September 1929, Clarence Jordan left Talbotton for the University of Georgia in Athens. His father gave him a checkbook and told him he did not have to worry about money. What Clarence did worry about was how to make sense out of the ideas that were swimming in his head. No one else seemed to talk about the things that were so important and central for him, especially his concern for the poor and a way to respond that would make a difference. His four years in Athens would bring about a major turning point in his life and set the stage for his radical journey.

In late October that year, another momentous event took place: the stock market crash, which devastated the American economy and brought on the Great Depression, which profoundly affected the Western industrialized world for the next ten years. Clarence Jordan's life would also be impacted by going to school and working during this economically turbulent time. Both his father's bank and the store would fail in spring 1933. The times would require his best, both economically and spiritually.

Yet Clarence, like his father, had a certain intensity that allowed him "to get down with it," his brothers remembered. He was resourceful and able to manage. Like his mother, however, there was an innate sensitivity that meant he would respond to the larger environment. And Clarence took with him to Athens the "guilt of abundance" from his earliest years along with his desire to understand how to be an "honest" Christian, and his quest to find a way of service that would change the world that he knew.[1]

When Clarence went off to Athens, his mother continued to write to him, as was her practice whenever he was away from her. Clarence received several letters the first week. And, on Sunday of his first week away, Clarence began a tradition that he kept up until Maude Jossey's death. He would faithfully write to his mother. In his first letter from college, Clarence begins, "Dearest Mama...." Then he tells her that he has done as he promised, except the communication was a letter and not a card. He tells his mother that he is glad to get her letters. "They are an inspiration to me to make good." This is true, Clarence says, "because with such fine parents as you and Dad, I would be ashamed of myself if I didn't do good. Since God has blest me with such wonderful parents, certainly I can honor him and keep his word." Then he tells his mother that he had been to church that morning, and there were ninety-nine people in his Sunday-school class and 125 in the BYPU (Baptist Young People's Union). So church is a little different in Athens. Finally, he tells his mother about his schedule. He is in class every day Monday through Saturday from 7:40 A.M. until 2:30 P.M.[2]

The letters from his mother came as "an inspiration...to make good." They also came with a good bit of pressure. What if he did not "make good"? At the university, Clarence would be driven toward accomplishment, perhaps trying all the while to meet family expectations. He joined everything that he could, and eventually became a leader in most of those activities. His letters home would carry a theme of "shame," perhaps connected to his own guilt of abundance, and the growing realization that his own personal circumstance of wealth came at the expense and deprivation of others, which continues a historic and national shame.[3] On the one hand, Clarence feels driven to succeed, in part because of pressure from the family matrix—especially his mother's expectations and presence through her writing. But, on the other, Clarence feels increasingly compelled to rely on the presence of God and the shared life of divine expectations, which includes an unconditional grace overcoming shame and guilt. At the end of his first year, Clarence writes a letter to his mother in which he describes something of his early struggle. First, he tells his mother that he (his team) won the last debate, and that he is now wearing the "gold key" as a winner. He also tells his mother that he is rather proud of the medal because "it is considered something of an honor to win in the Freshman Debate." Then Clarence explains that it is exam time, which is not a problem except for chemistry. "I don't know whether it's the professor or me. I guess it's both but the average of the *whole* class is less than *60*." Then Clarence admits, "I think mine is less than that." Immediately following this admission, Clarence describes his first sensation of being homesick. While listening to a radio program with someone reading from a scrapbook, he tells his mother that he could see her and the whole family gathered and listening, too. Though surrounded by a crowd at the fraternity house, Clarence feels lonely and isolated and in need of the presence of his mother and his family. "Well, that was a little too much," he wrote.[4]

Trying to Be an Honest Christian and
a True Follower of Jesus

When Clarence went off to the University of Georgia, he was serious about being a follower of Jesus and finding a way to be an "honest Christian." From his first experiences with the church and the chain gangs, Clarence learned that there were "dishonest" Christians, people who were essentially hypocrites. These folks, Clarence thought, were not happy or fulfilled. They were simply playing roles, wearing masks, and hiding their true identity. Clarence was troubled by this kind of response, and early on he began to look for a more authentic way to respond to the serious issues of the day as he perceived them. But, in those days, he himself did not talk to anyone about his own inner feelings or thoughts. He wanted to continue to be popular with the crowd.[5] This shows that his faith at this point is essentially conventional in nature. His way of thinking and relating is, for now, based in large measure on acceptance by the group. What will happen to Clarence to give him the strength to stand over against the group and the accepted mores of his culture to the point that he will be willing to risk his own life and the lives of others for his own hard-won truths?

Because of his quest to be a true follower of Jesus, Clarence began to search out the groups on campus that he thought were doing authentic discipleship. He joined the college YMCA and the local Baptist groups.

He also joined the staff of *The Georgia Agriculturist*, a student-managed quarterly sponsored by the Agriculture Club. By summer of his junior year, Clarence had become something of a "man for all seasons." His brother George wrote to his mother and said, "You don't know how popular Grump is until you follow him around a while."[6]

About the same time, Clarence wrote to his mother and listed all of his accomplishments during his first three years at the university. By that time, he had been chosen as president of the agriculture honorary society, elected editor of *The Georgia Agriculturist*, made chair of the debate council, gained membership in the drama club and the Pelican Club, elected state president of the Baptist Student Union, elected to the Gridiron Club, and elected as delegate to several national conferences, and much more! Clarence at the University of Georgia was a young man on a mission, but what was the mission? His first three years at the university were extremely busy. Outwardly, he seemed to thrive and he joined everything he could join. He was a good dancer, and something of a party guy. That is, Clarence knew how to have fun and how to mix and talk to people. He was quickly elected to leadership positions in the organizations he joined. By summer 1932, however, when he wrote to his mother, he said, "I'm about ready to quit."[7] Quit what? Perhaps all of the dizzying activity to concentrate on the emerging awareness of what his life should be about. By summer 1932, Clarence's life would begin to show signs of change. While Clarence's first three years at the university were extremely busy, by the end of his fourth year, his faith would take a radical and mature turn.

For God and Country: Clarence Jordan
As an ROTC Cadet

All male students at the University of Georgia in 1929 were required to be part of the ROTC. While the first two years were compulsory, Clarence Jordan was a cadet throughout his educational career. He volunteered for advanced training and, at the end of his four-year career in Athens, he was very near to receiving a commission in the U.S. Army. Clarence was apparently investigating the possibility of service as an officer in the military. Like his father, Clarence had a drive toward success and excellence. Anything he did, he did well. "Whatever he was in, he was the top one," Frank said.[8] When Clarence Jordan first went to the university, he was "gung-ho" for the military. When he came home to Talbotton from the university the first time, he brought his Calvary uniform, including the boots and spurs. He told his family, "I am a military man." He went on to say, "If war comes, I am ready to go to war." Maude Jossey Jordan, who was "tenderhearted," did not want to hurt anyone. Though Clarence later said about his mother that she was a member of the United Daughters of the Confederacy, and quite proud of the South with its traditions and heritage, his mother could not bear to see him with military regalia in hand. Clarence was Maude Jossey's favorite son. For her to see Clarence walk through the door of her Talbotton home wearing an army uniform complete with boots and spurs, and to hear him say that he was now a military man ready to go to war disappointed her to no end.[9]

Dancing to the Tyranny of "They": Clarence and the Expectation of Others

How does one explain such a situation—Clarence Jordan wearing a U.S. Calvary uniform, and with a "gung-ho" military spirit? His brothers wondered if he had been indoctrinated by the officers of the ROTC program at the University of Georgia. If so, in three short years, Clarence would begin to change his mind and move in an opposite direction. What role would his beloved mother play in this reversal?[10] What would a disappointed Maude Jossey have said to Clarence? What we know is that, by the end of his university career, he would renounce militarism and spend a lifetime in opposition to it. But, at this point in his life, his faith was a reflection of the environment around him and was conformist in nature. That is, what seems true and real was mediated to him through the authority of his friends, teachers, and cultural stories. Clarence does not yet have the ability to think through issues and reflect on them critically. In part, the "tyranny" that controlled him during this period was the shared naiveté of conventional answers and the pressures he felt from various groups and significant others.

In high school, he had been impressed with the life and career of Robert E. Lee. Perhaps, at this age, Clarence was also impressed with the uniform and the *esprit de corps* of his ROTC unit. Clarence wanted to serve. The question was where and how.[11] One might say that, at this juncture, Clarence was "trying on" ideologies and worldviews like the uniform that seemed to impress him so. But, at this point, he had not experienced the liberation that comes with the free exchange of ideas, nor did he yet have the strength of person required to choose his own beliefs apart from the crowd. That individual and reflective faith would come within a few years, and Clarence would begin in earnest the move toward a radical faith. What were the factors that pushed, pulled, and lured Clarence toward that level of a more independent and mature faith? It seems to have been the convergence of several factors: an economy that took away his father's checkbook;[12] travel across the nation that tended to broaden his horizons and awareness; the academic experience at the University of Georgia, which included a department whose motto was service, and extracurricular activities that involved creative writing and debate; and his own innate sensitivity and spirituality, which included a lifelong conversation with his "saintly" mother, and a Baptist heritage that emphasized independence and the reading of the Bible.

Ascent of the Mountain:
Jordan's Travel Beyond Home

Many of the key transformative experiences that Jordan had in his university days actually took place beyond Athens, particularly in the mountains of Western North Carolina. The maturation necessary for Jordan's growth in faith meant that he had to go beyond the sources of authority that had been his home in his teenage years. It seems that, in the new physical surrounding of the Blue Ridge Mountains—far from Talbotton—Jordan gained a new freedom and was able to critically reflect on his culture and religion in new ways.[13] There he found not only physical but critical distance in the liberating words of challenging speakers and teachers, and the freedom to talk about relevant ideas. It was not until summer 1930—the summer after his freshman year—that Clarence heard anyone address the race issue openly. It was at a YMCA conference at Blue Ridge, North Carolina, when Clarence first heard the issues addressed publicly. "It was an exhilarating experience," he said, "to be at a place where people talked openly with a Christian attitude...." This was, in part, a liberating moment for Clarence personally because, as he said, this "was the first feeling of assurance that I wasn't just a crack-pot." Up to that point, Clarence had kept his own musings to himself, and his own thoughts were not revealed to anyone. The speaker for this event was a well-known Baptist minister of the day, Edwin McNeil Poteat, who was at that time pastor of the Pullen Memorial Baptist Church in Raleigh, North Carolina.[14] This experience in the Blue Ridge Mountains in the summer after his freshman year was clearly an important event for Clarence. In late December 1931, Clarence went with other members of the university delegation to the 11th Quadrennial Convention of the Student Volunteer Movement in Buffalo, New York. He marveled at the grandeur of Niagara Falls, which he thought was near indescribable. He wrote to his mother, "If a man can stand there and watch the water plunging down over 180 feet, and listen to the mighty roar, and look at the rushing, dashing rapids, and still say: 'there is no God,' then that man has no soul…."[15] His return brought him back through New York City, Philadelphia, and Washington, D.C. The next summer, he went back to the mountains of North Carolina. Before returning to the university in fall 1932, he wrote to some friends and said that, when thinking of the Blue Ridge Mountains, he could still see the "lofty mountains" and "remember the soul-stirring messages." Then Clarence wrote, "I find myself resolving to live a better life for having been there."[16]

In a letter to his mother in summer of his junior year, he wrote, "I wish I could describe my stay at Ridgecrest. I don't need to, though, because you've seen and been in the mountains yourself and know how beautiful the scenery is, how cold the water, how exhilirating [sic] and cool the air, and how close to God it makes you feel." But, even greater, Clarence wrote, were the speeches by men like Kyle Yates, Frank Leavell, and Roy Angell. For Clarence, the most impressive services were the ones around a campfire at the close of the day. The service concluded with prayer and the soft tones of a violin and a bugle that came from across the lake.[17]

Clarence Jordan was a very sensitive human being. He appears to have had a unique ability to respond to his environment. His travels to the mountains of Western North Carolina seem to have an impact upon him—as he put it, this environment makes you feel "close to God." For Clarence, the mountains of Western North Carolina seemed to function in his life as a special, sacred space. There he not only encountered a beautiful vision of the handiwork of God, but also a special place where he could encounter teachers willing to speak freely and openly about the religious ideas of the day. In this way, the Blue Ridge Mountains and the religious assemblies of the area brought Clarence into a context of undeniable transcendence. It was a time and space where Clarence approached a vision of the grandeur and greatness of God, and was drawn, as in Rudolf Otto's "Idea of the Holy," to the *mysterium tremendum.*[18] Physically, the setting of the Blue Ridge Mountains accompanied by the messages of the special speakers seemed to work for Clarence, much like visual art often does in the lives of others—it has the capacity to inform and transform. It informs one of how life is and yet somehow transforms one into another state of consciousness, where the individual now understands more clearly how life should be. From the standpoint of this new state of consciousness, brought on by the mountains as a reflection of God's handiwork (or art) and the messages of the speakers, seen as special by Clarence, Clarence came to a place where he wanted to be a stronger person. Mountains have long held a key place in the sacred space of many religions.[19] The Blue Ridge Mountains seemed to have that role in the early life of Clarence Jordan.

At Home in the Baptist Student Union:
Clarence and the Beginning of a Baptist Ministry

Clarence grew up in the Baptist church. When he went away to the university, it was natural for him to continue to pursue his allegiance to the Baptist tradition, which tended to mirror the culture of the region. Clarence found a home in the Baptist Student Union in Athens, and eventually was elected as president. Like many others, Clarence encountered more liberal ideas for the first time in his own denomination. His activity in the Baptist Student Union continued throughout his years at Athens and beyond. Clarence became friends with D.B. Nicholson, who was both the local and statewide Baptist Student Union director. He and Nicholson discussed many things, including racism and its implications for spirituality. Nicholson acted as something of a mentor for Clarence. While at Athens, Clarence made connections with leaders within the Southern Baptist Convention primarily through his work in the Baptist

Student Union. As a student at the University of Georgia, Clarence was elected as the President of the Georgia Baptist Student Union. He— along with other state Baptist Student Union presidents, like Frank Stagg from Louisiana—was invited to Nashville by Frank Leavell, who was the convention-wide director of Baptist Student Union work. Clarence became one of Frank Leavell's "fair-haired boys," as Martin England put it.[20]

Many years later, Frank Stagg remembered his first meeting with Clarence Jordan in Nashville. Clarence was an "entertainer," Stagg recalled. During the fellowship hour of their presidents meeting, Clarence entertained the group with a presentation of "The Midnight Ride of Paul Revere." He made Paul Revere and his famous ride come to life again. Clarence as Revere was riding his horse and making the sounds of the experience. "By slapping his hands on his thighs, he could get the clap of the horse's hooves." Then he took the group with him from town to town as he began crying out, "The British are coming!"[21]

Clarence also began to travel to churches in Georgia while he was in Athens. Frank Leavell's brother, Roland Q. Leavell, was pastor of the First Baptist church in Gainesville, Georgia, which was not far from Athens. Roland Q. Leavell was very interested in working with his brother Frank. So he often went to Athens to speak to the Baptist Student Union and at Vesper services. During Clarence Jordan's time in Athens, his name became a household word in the home of Roland Q. Leavell because he thought so much of Clarence. Consequently, Leavell invited Clarence and other young men to his church in Gainesville to help in youth revivals. There Leavell came to admire Jordan's "brilliant mind" and his ability to converse "on a level that was way beyond his years and experience." At that time, in the company of a larger group, he was a quiet person, not flashy or flamboyant. His eyes were warm— nothing fierce about them—and his voice was soft.[22] Yet there was a serious look on his face. There was a look of firmness in his chin. His face had a searching demeanor, but with a hint of a smile and an intelligent air. He had the look of being well-bred as he gazed straight at the world.

What did Clarence Jordan learn about Baptist life when he went to Gainesville? As pastor of the First Baptist Church of Gainesville, Leavell lived in an old Georgia home with big, white columns in the richest part of town. There was a large dining room with a long table and high-backed chairs, surrounded by Queen Anne furniture. The table was set with silver, fine china, and white linens on a linen tablecloth. Two maids kept the house going. One of the maids served Clarence and the other young men from the university Baptist Student Union. Roland Q. Leavell's daughter later wondered what Clarence Jordan would have thought of such a setting—being served by a black maid in the context of such materialism in a pastor's home.[23] For the time being, Clarence was content to take things in and learn the landscape. His serious conflict and decisions for the future would come later.

Dancing to Every Tune and Climbing the Mountain: Jordan's Early Collegiate Ultimate Environment

For a time, Clarence was content to lead a frenetic life trying to dance to every tune. He felt tremendous pressure from his family, especially his mother. He tried very hard to live up to the expectations that were placed on him. In his first three years at Athens, he was the man for all seasons, maintaining popularity with the crowd while running for office and playing the entertainer at every opportunity. His faith was a reflection of the environment around him and was conformist in nature. That is, what seemed true and real was mediated to him through the authority of his friends, teachers, and cultural stories. Clarence was, in his early college years, controlled by a certain tyranny; he did not yet have the ability to think through issues and reflect on them critically. In part, the "tyranny" that controlled him during this period was the shared naiveté of conventional answers and the pressures that he felt from various groups and significant others. But Clarence was growing toward maturity and beginning to make his ascent of the mountain. He was also going deeper into himself, and would soon find mature reflections of deeper selfhood and faith.

Chapter 6

Athens II: Climbing the Mountain

I am a military man. If war comes, I am ready to go to war.
—Clarence Jordan

The frenetic nature of Clarence Jordan's college career continued until his senior year in 1932–1933. There are signs of emerging maturity toward the end of his stay in Athens. His letters to his mother throughout this era seem to suggest that he is trying hard to meet the expectations she has of him. Yet Clarence grows in many ways while at Athens. He deepens his understanding of faith and recommits himself to religious resolve, and eventually makes a public decision that he will enter the ministry.

Letters from a Saintly Mother: The Foundation for Jordan's Radical Pilgrimage

More than artifacts from a long-ago era and examples of an earlier day when people practiced communication through written letters, the corpus of correspondence between Clarence Jordan and his mother allows one to trace the growth and development of a young man's life and the major impact of his "saintly" mother upon that life. Taken as a body of literary correspondence, this corpus demonstrates certain qualities. They are an extraordinary and singularly impressive collection of valuable information that has been heretofore unmined for the treasure of information revealed about Clarence and his mother. One of the most obvious qualities that the letters reveal is the extraordinary devotion they shared. The relationship was clearly a mutual-admiration society. The letters date from 1927, when Clarence was 15 years old, to 1935, when his mother died.[1]

Clarence dedicated his doctoral dissertation to his father and mother and, in so doing, described his mother as "saintly." His letters to Maude Jossey clearly demonstrate a warm, close relationship that lasted until she died. Clarence was singularly devoted to his mother, and she to him. His mother's devotion to Clarence as the one she loved the most seemed to cost Clarence quite a bit, and indeed put pressure upon him. One of the recurring themes in the correspondence is that of Clarence sending a list of his accomplishments to his mother. Sigmund Freud, who was also the focus of his own mother's grandest hopes, said, "I have found that people who know that they are preferred or favored by their mothers give evidence in their lives of a peculiar self-reliance and an unshakeable optimism which often bring actual success to their possessors."[2] Is it possible that the foundation for Clarence Jordan's radical journey is to be found in his lifelong relationship with Maude Jossey Jordan?

Maude Jossey told Clarence that she loved him more than the other children. She wrote him long and devoted letters demonstrating her care continually. Clarence not only describes his mother as "saintly," but says that, for him, the words "God" and "Mother" are, in fact, "closely allied." "One is not complete without the other," Clarence wrote. "I believe that Mother is only God come to earth and that in Heaven God will be Mother gone to Heaven."[3] Clarence also says that, as a senior at the university, "I'm just beginning to know my dad."[4]

In his important study, *Young Radicals: Notes on Committed Youth*, Kenneth Keniston studies a group of young people whose lives take radical trajectories. These young radicals, as Keniston called them, became committed to the antiwar movement in the late 1960s and were involved in "Vietnam Summer." Keniston discovered that his young radicals were intellectually talented youth who came from families that were highly principled and that gave their child the feeling that he or she was special, a feeling that was rooted in experiences from very early in life. These young people grew up with unusual verbal skills, but also had the capacity for self-control in the midst of intense feelings. For the young men who became radicals, there was typically an "unusually strong tie" with the mother from the earliest years of life. While this is not unusual in American families, this relationship seems to have been "particularly in-

81

tense" for the young men who grew up to be radicals. This maternal bond, likewise, seemed to evolve in the life of the child to the point that the young man took on an "unusual responsiveness" to the wishes of the mother. This seemed to be especially true in terms of academic accomplishment. The pressure from the mother seemed to "will" the success of the child in school, so that the young men exhibited signs of being not only gifted, but precocious, from a very early age. Interestingly, almost all of the young men interviewed by Keniston had a very ambivalent relationship with their fathers. On the one hand, the father was portrayed as principled, ethical, involved, and idealistic, while at the same time there were contexts where the father was seen as weak and inadequate. This "split" in the image of the father seemed to be a universal in Keniston's interviews with the young radicals.[5]

Clarence's relationship with his mother clearly qualifies for Keniston's requirement as "intense." Likewise, his relationship with Maude Jossey began in his earliest years. All of his brothers and his sister remembered that Clarence would stay behind with his mother when the other children went out to play. His listening to his mother's stories—when all the other children grew tired—demonstrated an unusual responsiveness to Maude Jossey. Clarence likewise knew that he was special early in life, as his mother continually told him she loved him more than the others. Furthermore, he lived through a near-death experience when others did not. Clarence displayed qualities of the gifted and precocious figure in both grade-school and in his university years. In the school at Talbotton, Clarence had an unusual ability to talk and to reason with his classmates. That ability continued in Athens in debate and creative writing. Clarence continued his close relationship with his mother even when he left for Athens through his weekly correspondence. In those letters, Clarence often reported on his academic success as if it were important for him to do so. And, again and again, he affirms his special relationship with his mother. He never seems to tire in thanking her for all that she does for him. In one of those letters, Clarence wrote to his mother and said, "Without your sweet and frequent letters, I wonder how I could ever get along, how I could *live*. They are indeed a great source of comfort and cheer to me, and each one…serves to lift me a little higher, a little nearer to God and man."[6]

Writing Toward Religious Selfhood:
Clarence Jordan Rewriting Himself

When Clarence Jordan went to the University of Georgia at Athens, he did not go there just to have a good time, though apparently Clarence had something of a love for life. Behind the ready smile and quick ability to talk to anyone was a serious desire "to get down with it," as his brothers described his skills. Clarence was wrestling with vocation, and the thought that he could be a minister. When he came to the university, Clarence was not sure how his life would unfold. Like many young people, he found his way through his coursework and through the opportunities that came his way. Clarence continued to be influenced by the dialogue with his mother. He had important transformative experiences in the Blue Ridge Mountains. But another barely-noticed opportunity for growth came during his role as editor of *The Georgia Agriculturist*. One can trace an important development in his writings from that period.

Why are Jordan's college writing assignments important? They show the issues of concern to him at the time. Perhaps, as Roland Barthes suggests, the very basis of narrative (writing) is, in this case, the son's search for the father, that narrative is "always a way of searching for one's origin…." Put differently, for Jordan, "every narrative…is a staging of the…father."[7] Was Jordan's writing a response to the summons of the father? His father had wanted his son to come back and manage the family farm. Could Clarence return to the family farm? Late in his college career, Clarence wrote to his mother and told her that he was just now getting to know his father. But writing is not always simply a matter of searching for origins. Writing can also be the process of interrogating the self about one's name and identity. Writing for Raczymow, a post-Holocaust Jew living in France, became "the desire for a place, for an identity. It is the search for a connection with the past through the processes of the imagination." "Writing," Raczymow says, "turns into an archaeological and an analytical enterprise during which I reconstruct my past by imagining it. I dig out something with which to build my identity."[8] This sense of place was also "psychic space," which one used to build a new identity and a new role—a safe place one used to create a sense of destiny and individuality that offered more possibility than one could at the moment imagine. It may be that, in his early writing, Clarence wrote creative fiction and nonfiction to build a new identity, to create a world—an alternative life etched in his lively imagination.[9] In remaking the world through the creative process, Jordan was also in dialogue with the Heavenly Father, and the real Creator. Consequently, writing, for Clarence, became a spiritual exercise and can be used to trace the change in him that took place during his college years. How does writing bring on such a change in an individual? What happened to Clarence when he began to write? As Walter Ong puts it, "Writing restructures consciousness."[10]

Writing reshapes the void within the human through the power of language and imagination to create an "increasingly articulate introspectivity." That is, writing is able to create an introspective nature, because writing as a human project is an "artificial" creation that allows the knower to become separate from the known. As discourse, detached from the author, writing opens the psyche for possible investigation of the interior self. Put another way, writing brings some distancing from that aspect of the self, which in time allows for the evolution of consciousness.[11] Thus, when Clarence begins to write his creative essays, he starts the process of transformation that is the beginning of his spiritual pilgrimage toward a more reflective faith, for it is in the writing process that he finds the necessary space from which to envision alternative destinies, and from which he can begin to remake the world.

While in Athens, Clarence wrote six articles for *The Georgia Agriculturalist*. This was a quarterly student publication put out by the College of Agriculture and sponsored by the Agriculture Club. The first two articles deal with basic issues: "Should College Graduates Return to the Farm?" and "What Price Should We Pay for a College Education?" The last four are more creative in nature and tend to demonstrate Jordan's gifted nature as a writer even at a young age. The first two essays likely represent something of a student response to the culture of the College of Agriculture in the early 1930s at the University of Georgia. But even these essays seem to have some autobiographical dimensions. The first essay—"Should College Graduates Return to the Farm?"—raises the issue of national farm relief. But Jordan re-construes the nature of the question and suggests that the real issue, and real farm relief, is for college graduates to return to the farms and turn them into "real paying enterprises." The essay implies that, since the state—through its funding of public institutions like the University of Georgia—pays two-thirds of the cost of a student's education, the student should repay the debt incurred to the state through service on the farm. In apparent autobiographical reference, Jordan writes: "Would not both father and son profit by such a move? Would not such a change give the state more of which to be proud?"[12] Does this essay suggest that Clarence, at this point in his college career, is wrestling with what he should do? Should he return to the farm and do as his dad wanted? If so, the argument of the essay is as much for him as his other readers. The article also implies that the issue of "debt" is very much on his mind as a serious and sensitive student attempting to be responsive to his parents and larger society.

The second essay is, likewise, an apologetic for the dogma of the College of Agriculture: "What Price Should We Pay for a College Education?" Once again, Clarence re-construes the topic so that his theme becomes the "value" of a degree in scientific farming. The agriculture degree comes with a tremendous cost, he argues, so one should try to get the most for the money. "One man," Clarence writes, "highly trained along scientific lines, can do more for the advancement of society than hundreds of men without this same knowledge....He goes back to the farm and sets an example for his neighbors."[13] Then, eventually, the whole country benefits from the work of this one man and his influence. The service of the dedicated farmer makes the world a better place. Though the argument is, technically, an argument about scientific farming and its value to society, one also hears an autobiographical component written for the writer and his own quest for identity and wellbeing.

The last four essays tend to be more creative and illustrative of Jordan's deepening awareness of the nature and rhythm of narrative. They are also more fictive in nature. There are two essays celebrating nature itself: one about a dog's devotion to his master and one about a young boy who saved money for college. The essay titled "When Night Meets Day" is noted as a "prize-winning essay." It is a narrative about a hike up to "High Point Peak," one of the highest points in the mountains of North Carolina. The group had agreed to climb the mountain in order to see the sunrise. Jordan narrates the climb up the mountain and describes the arrival of dawn: "Then the Eastern skies began to rain their splendors....Was not some Supreme Artist carefully painting this masterpiece?"[14] The essay titled "A Stroll with Mother Nature" is a reflective response to the beauty of nature and its contrast with the human. A college student takes a walk in the woods after a busy day in the academic realm. Jordan shows his sensitive awareness of the natural world around him. He describes the wind blowing through the trees, the falling leaves, the industrious activity of a squirrel storing food for winter, the discovery of mother partridge by her nest, the vision of an old woman reading her Bible in front of her homestead. "As I made my way homeward," Jordan writes, "the sun slowly began sinking in a golden fire. Never before had I beheld such a preponderance of color."[15]

The story of "Dan's Death" is perhaps Jordan's most ambitious and creative of his published college essays. It is the narrative of a pointer bird dog that was completely devoted to his master, Grady Nicholson, who had spent much time training him as a pup. Grady was taken ill one day and Dan lay at his bedside. "But, in spite of Dan's vigilance, a grim imposter slipped by him one night, and Death made his capture." Dan mourned so much that he, too, grew weak. He found a life-size portrait of Grady and lay down in front of it. "It was while he was thus at the feet of his master's portrait that a fit came over him, and a noble heart beat no more."[16]

Jordan's creative essays written for *The Georgia Agriculturalist* show the maturation of his writing skills and the development of his consciousness. His writing moves from the elemental and apologetic to a more complex and mysterious realm, and shows Clarence moving toward a more mature, reflective, and individual vision of faith. These essays also show Jordan concerned with the issue of his debt, his sense of obligation, and the concept of service and stewardship. But the later essays also show an appreciation for the transcendent aspects of nature, and his understanding of God as the Designer and Great Artist. But, like Gandhi's holistic view of *ahimsa* and nonviolence toward all things, Jordan demonstrates an early awareness of the interconnectedness of the species, and the devotion that is possible between the human and animal realm. Jordan's view of a nonviolent, interconnected universe is not dependent upon Hinduism except for similarities. Jordan's vision sprang from his own native religious tradition, no doubt influenced by the sensitive and caring spirit he found first in his own saintly mother.

Toward Adult Faith: Clarence, the Call, and Refusing the Commission

In 1932, the summer just before his senior year, life began to change for Clarence. In a letter to his mother, after summarizing all of the awards he had won, he announced to her, "I am about ready to quit." After three years of frenetic activity and dancing to every tune, Clarence was apparently tired and ready for a change. The devastating Depression was catching up with his family. Clarence was facing other pressures. He was wrestling with a variety of models for his sense of vocation. He wanted to "serve," but what was the best way to do it? The frenetic activity of his early years in Athens masked a good bit of inner turmoil and searching. By that final summer before his senior year, he had lost interest in the social scene. He thought little, now, of Alpha Tao Omega, a leadership fraternity. He moved out of the frat house where he had spent his junior year. When he went to Ridgecrest in the Blue Ridge Mountains of Western North Carolina that summer, he had a religious experience during which he felt drawn closer to God. Perhaps this was the experience where he initially felt called to serve God in some form of ministry.[17] If so, his announcement of that call does not come until spring 1933. Meanwhile, in fall 1932, Clarence moved into Ag Hall, a large dorm with common rooms where everyone had a bunk and a shelf. He also took a job with his brother George. They would collect clothes to be dry-cleaned, for which they made approximately eight to ten dollars a month.[18]

Clarence had spent three years studying agriculture. Would he return to the farm, his father's farm, about which he indeed had already written? Would he use his education in that manner? Would he follow his father's influence, ride around the fields and supervise the farming operation in the way that his father wanted? Would he take a commission in the U.S. Army? This option was a real possibility. When he completed the final course, he would get a commission as part of his graduation ceremony. During this last year, Clarence seemed to struggle with many ideas. What about the ideas his mother promoted?[19] She had apparently dreamed that one day Clarence would be a minister. If that had been the case, to this point, Clarence had not taken her ideas about ministry very seriously. Yet the more he thought about the idea of ministry, the more real the option became.[20] Clarence talked with his mentor, D.B. Nicholson, several times, and often with his friend Claude Broach.

Clarence had thus far been driven by the idea that he would help the poor by teaching them to grow better cotton. But it dawned on him during his senior year that many well-to-do white farmers already had better cotton, and "they were for the most part living in hell." So what guarantee did he have that teaching the poor to grow better cotton was the answer? Clarence was therefore driven toward spiritual resources and the eventual question: "Lord, what do you want me to do?"[21]

On March 4, 1933, and with a spirit of relief, Clarence wrote to his mother with the news: "No mortal has ever known the joy that floods my soul now. It seems that God has smiled his sweetest on me, because he has given me the privilege of serving in His vineyard by entering the ministry." Clarence assured his mother that he understood the nature of the task he was about to undertake, and that several more years of school would be involved. However, he told her he would not accept any more financial aid from his father. What he did want, though, were the prayers of his mother. "I know that you have always prayed for each one of us," Clarence wrote, "but I want to ask that you do so especially for me, because I'll need them in this undertaking."[22] A few months later, Clarence writes a statement on his call to the ministry, perhaps in connection to his application for the Southern Baptist Seminary. In this statement, Clarence writes that there was no protracted struggle, just a personal response to an audible voice: "My child, I want you to preach for me." His response was simply. "Yes, Lord, whatever you say, just promise me that you'll go with me."[23]

Ten days after his letter announcing his call, Clarence wrote back to his mother thanking her for all the "sweet and frequent letters." The letters bring not only "comfort and cheer," but also serve to bring him "a little nearer to God and man." He tells his mother that he has just preached his first sermon, really "just a talk." He shared the opportunity with Claude Broach and J.C. Adams. Clarence thanked his mother for her letter to Frances, who has also been an "inspiration" in "many, many ways." Last of all, he thanked his mother for "the money." Then he closed by saying, "You have no idea how good...[the money] comes in."[24]

Apparently, Clarence came into the spring semester of his senior year not knowing exactly how his vocation would unfold. He had spent four years in Athens getting an agricultural degree, but also growing spiritually. Yet, even in the last semester at the university, Clarence was still running for office and seeking approval from his peers.[25] He was elected to the presidency of the university YMCA. Clarence was still able to compartmentalize his experiences.[26] He had just made public his decision to enter the ministry and preached his first sermon, but he had not yet been able to integrate his vision of ministry with the military to the degree that he would soon need to do when he would go to ROTC camp at Gainesville after graduation.[27]

The decision to enter the ministry came as a convergence of several factors and forced Clarence to search for spiritual resources. His father's business had been greatly undermined by the Depression. In his last year in Athens, Clarence was forced to take responsibility for his life and finances in new ways. His experiences at Ridgecrest had brought him closer to God. He continued to be in dialogue with his mother, who invariably embraced a religious vision in the context of problems. Clarence came to a new understanding of his sense of mission with agriculture. And, as he put it, he was "just beginning to really know" his dad.[28] About the time Clarence publicly affirmed his relationship with his Heavenly Father, he was able to affirm his earthly father in a new way. At the end of March, Clarence met his father in Atlanta and the two of them went to hear Dr. Stanley Jones, the Methodist missionary and theologian who spent much of his life in India speaking to educated Indians on interreligious dialogue. Clarence was thrilled to hear Jones, who spoke for three hours with no one hardly moving. He described Jones as "a powerful man, due to the fact, I believe, that he has completely surrendered himself to God." Jordan went on to say that "you can see it written on his face." God is able to use all people in a "great way," Clarence said, "if we will only surrender ourselves and *let* him." He asked Jones to autograph one of his books, *The Christ of Every Road,* which is a study of Pentecost.[29]

On June 8, 1933, Clarence left Athens for the forty-mile trip to Gainesville and his last ROTC camp.[30] During the past months, his quest for spiritual resources had brought him back to his Baptist tradition, especially *sola scriptura* and *sola fide*—the Reformation ideals emphasizing scripture and faith. His Baptist tradition had also emphasized the concept of the priesthood of the believer. These concepts helped Clarence move in the direction of an individual quest. All of this meant that, when Clarence left for Gainesville, he had for some months been steeping himself in scripture and the basic ideas of the faith, which pushed him in the direction of an individual faith. Up to this point in his life, he had not seen that there was a basic contradiction between what he was reading in the New Testament and what he was learning to do in ROTC. Now, however, he was reading the text with a new intensity and beginning to make plans for a life of service. But his previous compartmentalizing of everyday life and faith would come into open conflict.

While searching for spiritual resources, Clarence began to study and memorize portions of the New Testament. He had memorized the Sermon on the Mount before coming to his last ROTC camp. The last text that he had memorized was the one in Matthew that reads, "You have heard it said, 'You shall love your neighbor and hate your enemy'; but I say love your enemies, pray for those who persecute you, bless those that hate you." That day, the class exercise was a mounted drill on the edge of the woods. The goal of the class that day was for the student to ride through the woods with pistol and saber in hand. With the pistol, the student was to shoot the cardboard figures and use the saber to run through the straw dummies. So, as ROTC cadet Clarence Jordan mounted his steed and charged into the woods to complete the exercise by shooting at the cardboard figures, the words of Jesus came to his mind: "Love your enemies." At that moment, his previous ability to compartmentalize was broken down, and he saw with clarity the conflict between the spirit of Jesus and the mindset of the military given through the commanding officer. When he reached the other side of the field, Clarence told the officer that "something had happened and that I just couldn't go on with it." Specifically, Clarence told the officer, "You and Jesus are teaching me opposite things. I have to relinquish either one or the other."[31]

The next day, Cadet Jordan had to speak to the commander, Colonel Colley, who was regular Army. Colonel Colley was a veteran of World War I. He listened patiently to Clarence's story. Then he told Clarence that he had only a few more weeks until his commission as a second lieutenant. Then he told Clarence that he would not have to do any more drills and he could still get his commission—that it would be worth a great deal to him. When Clarence rejected the initial offer, the colonel then presented other options. He questioned Clarence thoroughly about whether he had thought the matter through. Then, when the process was finished, the colonel sat silently for about five minutes. Then he got up, put his hand on Jordan's shoulder, and said, "God bless you, boy. I hope someday you can make my job impossible."[32]

Clarence and the Conventional Landscape of Faith

Two poignant episodes mark the beginning and the end of Clarence's conventional faith. The story of Clarence's precocious discovery of the Georgia chain gang and its abuses of justice, which left him with bitterness and resentment toward God, closes his grade-school years and opens the adolescent/young adult quest for a vocation. And the story of Clarence's dismounting his steed to refuse his commission in the Calvary marks the end of his conventional faith, with its ability to compartmentalize truth. During his early adolescence, Clarence seemed to be in a kind of moratorium—his quest had little to do with God, at least on the surface. When Clarence went off to Athens, his religious life began to take on an emerging vitality but without the ability for critical reflection. Consequently, he marched and danced to many tunes. He seemed to wear himself down in his quest to be popular—and, perhaps, to please the demands of his parents, especially his mother. Several factors continued to push Clarence toward a more reflective and individualized faith in his early college years. These were his ongoing dialogue and relationship with his mother; his coursework and extracurricular activity in the college of agriculture, which emphasized service; his creative writing for the college quarterly; the Baptist Student Union and YMCA in Athens; his travels; and student meetings in North Carolina. The end result of his years in Athens was that Clarence began to metaphorically (and literally) climb the mountain—where a new consciousness awaited, where he forsook the tyranny of group expectations and found faith to be an emerging path toward depth in spirituality, which led to a commitment for a lifetime of ministry—and, eventually, found the sensitivity and courage to reject militarism as a way of life. His ascent up the mountain did not end here, and it did take a more dangerous and radical turn later.

Chapter 7

Louisville

The year 1933 was a turning point in world affairs. In January that year, Adolf Hitler was appointed chancellor of a coalition government in Germany. His rise to power was almost complete. In a short span of six years, Germany would invade Poland and the world would soon be at war—the most widespread conflict in history. This year was also a major transition for Clarence Jordan. His father's businesses would close under the pressure of the Great Depression. Clarence would make a public decision to enter the ministry. He would also come to a dramatic decision about the Christian's involvement in warfare. And he would decide to go to the Southern Baptist Theological Seminary in Louisville, Kentucky.

Founded in 1859, this was the oldest of the Baptist seminaries. While Jordan was in Louisville, the seminary would be among the first group of seminaries accredited by the Association of Theological Schools in the United States. It was a natural decision for Clarence to apply to "Southern," as the school was called. Some of the speakers who had so impressed him while attending conferences at Ridgecrest, such as Ewin McNeill Poteat and Kyle Yates, were from the seminary. A.T. Robertson, a well-known author on the Greek New Testament, was also teaching in Louisville when Clarence went to the seminary in fall 1933.

Toward an Adult Faith:
    The Journey Beyond Home

Clarence seemed different in September 1933 when he went off to Louisville. He was tall and thin, and still maintained a boyish face. And, even though he had traveled a good bit for a young person of his day, he was still a good bit inexperienced in his early days in Louisville. He would often mistake the older-looking students for the professors. They all looked sophisticated to Clarence when he first arrived in Louisville.

Though he was older and more mature than most, and had decided on a new direction for his life, he was also very far from home. He would not be able to travel back and forth to Talbotton the way he did when he was at the university in Athens. He would not have a brother or sister nearby. In some sense, Clarence was on his own for the first time in his life.[1] He would now begin to establish the parameters of adulthood for himself in a way that he had not done before. Clarence had made an important beginning in his journey toward an adult faith while in Georgia. He had publicly declared a new focus toward vocation—his life would be lived as ministry, a life of service. And he had made a mature decision about the role of violence and the military.[2] But, in Louisville, his journey would take him deeper into himself, and again he would make important decisions about the nature and direction of ministry. He would establish himself as an excellent student in the area of his larger vocation; he would choose a life partner; and he would have a spiritual "awakening," which would set the stage for the rest of his life's work.[3]

The transition in Clarence's life is noted in the communication with his mother. Maude Jossey seems to sense that her son is moving away from her not only physically, but perhaps emotionally as well. In her first letter to Clarence in Louisville, she reaches out to him and reminds him of her great love for him, which "can never be filled by anyone else in my heart and in our home." She says that "only three days have gone by since you left, but they seem as if three months."[4] Clarence responds to his mother and tells her that she had written "some mighty sweet things." And, in a characteristically humble way for Clarence, he says, "I'm afraid that I do not deserve them." But he goes on to say that he will keep the letter "always," because it is the first letter from her that he received in Louisville and because of what she wrote in the letter.[5]

The campus where Clarence came to prepare himself for this new era had, ironically, just been moved in 1926 from downtown Louisville to the suburbs on the eastern side of town. So, when Clarence arrived in September 1933, the buildings were barely seven years old. The campus was built in Georgian architectural style and was very impressive to a 21-year-old young man from Talbot County, Georgia. He was living in Mullins Hall, which was the main housing complex on campus and was named for the recent seminary president and Baptist icon, E.Y. Mullins.

The building was steam-heated and had hot and cold water in each room. Mullins Hall was quite an upgrade from the Ag dorm at the University of Georgia. Now Clarence had a private room furnished with a mahogany desk and bookstand, two closets, and two chairs. He told his mother that "nothing could be nicer." All of this, Clarence told his mother, came as "the result of *free will gifts*, coming from the hearts of Southern Baptists!"[6]

Searching for a Dream, a Partner, and a Band of Brothers and Sisters: Clarence in Louisville in the Early Years

As a young man of 21, Clarence was trying to refine his dream, and to find a life partner with whom he could live it out. He found a young, attractive lady who worked in the library that caught his eye. Her name was Florence Kroeger. Three years later, Clarence would ask her to marry him. As his dream began to materialize, he found that he was also searching for a band of brothers and sisters with whom to live in a "koinonia" as a demonstration plot for the true kingdom. Clarence would, in due course, find all of these components for his life—a dream, a partner, and an ever-growing community of friends and colleagues in ministry. He would also develop another passion—one that would stay with him for a lifetime: the study of the Greek New Testament.

In the early 1930s, Southern Seminary, like a number of other schools in the country, placed heavy emphasis on the study of the original languages, both Hebrew and Greek. Clarence came to Louisville at a time when both were required for the master's degree. The majority of students would take three years of Greek and two years of Hebrew. In fall 1933, when Clarence arrived, A.T. Robertson, widely regarded as one of the leading biblical scholars in the country at that time, was teaching Greek at Southern.[7] W. Hersey Davis was also there and he, too, was highly regarded as a master teacher and exegete. It was in this context that Clarence would go on to develop a lifelong passion for the study of the Greek New Testament. After he finished his master's-level coursework, Clarence entered graduate studies. So his intellectual pilgrimage in Louisville was "ever-deepening" and found focus in the Greek New Testament. There "he began to discover firm theological foundations for the human impulse that was already alive in him."[8]

Though there was little in his early years in Louisville to predict how much of a dissident Clarence would become, or that someday he would be *persona non grata* at his own alma mater, the nature of Baptist life in the 1930s across the South and in Louisville would inevitably mean that he was bound to go against the spirit of the times. John R. Sampey was the fifth president of the seminary. He had taken the position after the death of E.Y. Mullins in 1928. He was already an icon of Baptist piety when Jordan arrived in 1933. In earlier days, Clarence would have had more in common with Sampey, who often reflected the cultural values of his country. Sampey's hero was Robert E. Lee, who was, in his mind, "the greatest Christian since Paul." Accordingly, Sampey would often say in his chapel talks to the students at the seminary, "Some of you low-down rascals ought to get up and go into the chaplaincy." Sampey also reflected the views of his denomination and nation on race as well.

His fellow students in Louisville remembered Clarence in his early years as quiet and reflective. He tended to be studious, but he had another side. There was a playful dimension in his personality. So, after times of serious study, Clarence turned to games of football on the Louisville campus, or basketball in gym. In spring, he would fly kites with the other students in the winds of March and April. But he also loved to tell jokes, and to be the entertainer for the group. In those times, it was as if Clarence were the actor taking center stage in a one-act comedy. He was also a musician and would sometimes sing with a choir or play his trumpet. But, beyond the playful self, in the mind and heart of Clarence Jordan, there was emerging a sensitive and courageous response to the culture of his day. He was looking for a way and the proper time to replay the drama that was deep within his soul.

During his first year in Louisville, Clarence continued to demonstrate his skill as a student. According to his own testimony, he grew spiritually and began to develop a social conscience through his connection to the various forms of practical ministry available to him. In the spring semester, while taking a course with Kyle Yates, Clarence wrote a creative piece on Job that foreshadowed his work in the Cotton Patch Gospels years later. The booklet became so popular that ten or so of the larger churches in Louisville requested that Clarence and some other students do a dramatic presentation. A local radio station also requested a broadcast. By the end of March, 900 copies of the booklet on Job had been produced. Clarence joked with his mother that he could perhaps play the part of Job if a few more bad things happened to him. In the spring semester, he had a bout with the flu and a badly sprained ankle from basketball.[9]

A constant in his first year in Louisville was a carry-over from Athens—his continuing relationship with his mother. He would later call her "saintly." But, in March 1934, Clarence told his mother that there are "a few outstanding high spots of my life." The first, Clarence wrote, was the letter she had written to him after his call to the ministry. The second was the letter that Maude Jossey wrote to him in mid-March 1934, Clarence's first year. Clarence described this letter as the "most precious thing that has ever come my way." Maude Jossey continued to be a sustaining force for her beloved Clarence.[10]

After a year of study, Clarence summarized this part of his life in Louisville by saying, "It has been a great year for me, so much so that I wonder if it wasn't just a dream after all." Then he went on to say, "I don't guess I've learned very much, but one thing I know: I'm a bit nearer, and have a deeper conviction of the reality of, the God to whom I want to be ever true. For me, the year has been one continuous revelation." He was exempt from all of his exams in the second semester, and before he headed back to Talbotton, he attempted to do a series of additional readings, including some in Hebrew.[11]

By summer 1934, Clarence appeared to be trying to find the personal space for a sense of autonomy. He returned to Talbotton for only a very brief period, and then went back to Louisville. Clarence had become a popular "supply preacher" in much demand.[12] But he had also established a social network in Louisville. Clarence wrote to his mother about his July 4 trip and how "several couples of us" drove to an Indiana state park sixty miles from Louisville. The girls brought the lunches, and they all enjoyed climbing mountains and looking at the waterfalls. "The scenery was…such…that I couldn't help wishing that you could be along, for I knew you would enjoy it so much."[13] Though Clarence was looking for someone with whom he could share his emerging dream, he would not marry until after the death of his mother, which would come the next year.

Clarence Jordan As a Young Pastor

One of the hallmarks of Jordan's life was his commitment to hold scholarship and faith in practical tension. From the early years of his ministry, he sought to find ways to live out his faith. Dale Moody later remembered Clarence for his "marvelous combination of the best piety in Baptist history and the finest scholarship in the…[s]eminary."[14] Indeed, Clarence's homiletical skills displayed during his early days as a "supply" preacher soon brought him an opportunity to be a pastor in a series of small, rural Kentucky Baptist churches. They would be the only churches of which Jordan would be pastor. All in the rural area just south of Louisville, the churches were among some of the poorest people in the region. But Jordan, from his earliest days in ministry, was able to embrace people from all circumstances, and he seemed to have a special desire to seek out the disadvantaged. The first of the churches to "call" him as pastor, as the Baptists put it, was the Knob Creek Church in Bullit County. Then he was also called to the Mt. Carmel Church on Wilson Creek, which was near Lebanon Junction, and finally, the Vine Hill Church. After a time, he also served concurrently as pastor at the Clermont Baptist Church.[15] Jordan's work in these early churches demonstrated characteristics that would follow him through life: he was a popular and engaging speaker, he worked among the poor, and he seemed to enjoy using his knowledge of scientific farming to the benefit of the local population. A fellow student at the Louisville seminary remembered following Jordan as a "supply" preacher in churches: "More than once I followed him in a church. They had great joy in telling how a good Bible preacher could improve the number of good laying hens on the farm!"[16]

While serving as a pastor in Clermont, Clarence found himself in a city on the Kentucky Bourbon Trail, near a major whiskey distillery where Jim Beam products were produced. As pastor, he was often paid in kind—live chickens or garden vegetables from church families, many of whom were impoverished. Jordan spent much of his time counseling church members who also worked at the distillery, but were struggling with alcoholism. He apparently did such a good job as counselor in the small church that his reputation became known at the distillery. Clarence was surprised to learn that he had a job offer from the distillery to become a chaplain for Jim Beam and to do counseling for the other workers in the distillery. To a young seminarian, such an offer seemed attractive at first thought—a way to overcome his own economic woes. But he finally concluded that he had to turn it down. Clarence knew that he could not "sell his soul" to the very company that was destroying the lives of many of the people whom he served as pastor in the Clermont Baptist Church.

For his part, Clarence also seemed to draw emotional and spiritual strength from his interaction with the church members. He began his work in the churches by going out to the churches on Sunday and returning the same day. But he found that this practice provided so little time with the people themselves. So he began the practice of staying over an extra day, which gave him more time to visit the sick and elderly. Clarence wrote during that time, "It brought me immeasurable happiness because I could bring just a little happiness and comfort to them....I saw and felt the softening, soothing powers of the Gospel as I read to them."[17]

Clarence As Benediction and Legacy:
The Last Letter of Maude Jossey Jordan

Perhaps out of her own sensitivity to the growth of her son, Maude Jossey wrote one of her most extraordinary letters to Clarence for his twenty-second birthday—July 29, 1934. The nature and timing of the correspondence gave his mother's writing something of the quality of a last letter. In less than six months, she would be dead and this letter would be one of her last major contributions to the life of her favored son. Clarence would keep the letter, as he did so many others until his own death. His mother began, "My darling Son...." She congratulated Clarence on his birthday and then began quickly to narrate the religious dimensions of his life. Clarence was, in his mother's estimate, a gift from God who grew up to be her "pride and joy," whose "wonderful life throughout the years" can now be summed up as a "benediction." Clarence was described as "our Life, our crowning joy, our All." Maude Jossey Jordan went on to say, "I am quite sure that God placed his seal upon you and set you apart to do his bidding, even before you came into the world, for at a tender age you loved to read the Bible and found for yourself a Savior's redeeming love." One of the last things Maude Jossey Jordan did for Clarence was to tell him that his life had been "set apart," like Jeremiah and Jesus before him. She told Clarence that the beauty of his life had drawn him closer to her than any of the other children, and that it was natural for her to love him more than the others. In reading this stunning letter, one gets the sense that Maude Jossey Jordan could be using the word "benediction" in more than one way. Perhaps Clarence was not simply a blessing to her, but perhaps an invocation for God to bless and reshape the world, or maybe for others to see that Clarence was also her lasting legacy.[18] If this is a proper way to read Maude Jossey Jordan's "benediction" letter, there is more. If Clarence is a benediction to her, she takes up the mantle and pronounces a benediction on Clarence: "May God continue to bestow…his richest blessings, and may He always keep you 'neath the shadow of His wings, and may many long years be added to your life so you can finish the work your Master has given you to do." Then Maude Jossey Jordan enclosed 300 pennies in Clarence's birthday package—100 each from his father, his brother George, and his "dear mother"—so that he could go to the bakery and buy a cake for his birthday.[19]

The End of an Era and a Continuing Curse:
The Death of Maude Jossey Jordan

Clarence's mother had been "sickly" all of her life. She had given birth to ten children. By fall 1934, she was very sick and could no longer keep up her weekly correspondence with Clarence. In early October, James Jordan wrote to Clarence, saying, "I am sorry to write you that for the past week she [Maude Jossey Jordan] has not been doing so well and has grown much weaker. Dr. Carter does not encourage us…." In the same correspondence, James Jordan wrote, "Robert came up and spent the weekend with us and he was lots of help in nursing mama.…He is close by and can come up almost any time."[20]

Clarence did not go home immediately. There are letters describing his work through the holidays. He wrote, telling his mother, "I love you and thank God for a mother like you." In another letter, Clarence thanked her for all her kindness. He also told her about his loneliness during the holidays, but he assured his mother that "you couldn't have done more to make my Christmas away from home happier and more real." At the end of the letter, Clarence described his preparation for final exams. "Exams start again next week, so I plan to spend today bringing my work up to date. I hadn't realized how much I had to do until I started making a list of it." Then, next to the signature block, Clarence wrote, "You should see the five-inch blanket of snow that covered everything last night."[21]

On January 19, 1935, Clarence got a telegram in Mullins Hall. It read simply, "Mama worse. Come as soon as possible. All Think [*sic*] Best._Dad."[22] Apparently, Clarence left immediately and arrived in time to spend several days with his mother before she died—one day before she became unconscious. One of Clarence's aunts wrote to him and said, "I never saw such will power as she exerted the day you came. She knew the end was near and seemed determined to wait for you."[23] In his adolescent theology, Clarence had described his mother as an angel of God. And then, with the wisdom of qualification, 19-year-old Clarence said, "Whether this be so or not, God has certainly created a lot of himself in our mothers."[24]

Ann Louise Coble was likely correct when she wrote that Clarence was "quite traumatized" by his mother's illness and death.[25] Clarence's roommate's mother wrote him a sympathy card, which informs the reader's understanding of how Clarence began to deal with his mother's death. Mrs. Broach implied that Maude Jossey Jordan could still relate to Clarence beyond her death. Mrs. Broach wrote, "May you feel even closer to her now than ever before. She can and will guide, bless, and love you—even more fully than ever she could when burdened in her earthly temple." This is true, Mrs. Broach wrote, because "the great things of the Spirit are *never* lost to us, but bloom and bloom into fadeless flowers, beautiful and fragrant with heavenly incense."[26]

How could Clarence re-envision the loss of his mother? She could serve as a model interpreter of the human situation. Put another way, his earliest relationship and dialogue with his mother shaped and formed his religious vision and set the stage for his later understanding of Jesus, the rebel who "identified with the poor of all races" and, therefore, had to be understood as the "leader of a revolutionary movement." In a sermon titled "The Mother of Jesus," which Jordan preached at the Mt. Carmel Baptist Church two years after his mother's death, he said that "the mother receives a child like an unstamped coin and stamps her own image on it."[27] This autobiographical statement is something of a key to understanding how Clarence dealt with his own grief over his mother's death. He came to realize that his mother was still with him as a factor in his daily living. In another later sermon on "Jesus the Rebel," Jordan reflects on his early life and the Bible that his mother had given him.[28] In that Bible was a picture of Jesus, and Jordan remembered that he "almost thought he was a woman." Though the adult Jordan likely could not admit it, it seems clear that, for him, Jesus has a feminine face, and that face looks a great deal like Maude Jossey Jordan. It is also possible that, as Clarence read and spoke to his congregations, he was in touch at some deep personal level with the one who first taught him to read and understand the metanarrative about Jesus the Rebel. That is, as he read and spoke to others about his own understanding of the Gospel, he was in some way reliving and re-creating that first matrix that became foundational and formative for his view of the world.[29] On some level, it is this re-creation that helped give Clarence the power and authenticity that became hallmarks of his life's work. A part of the driving force that was Clarence Jordan was the desire to share the first "koinonia" that he had known with others, and thereby help to resituate the human family. In so doing, Clarence could begin to pay what he saw as his own "debt" and begin to overcome his sense of shame and guilt.

Florence Kroeger, Clarence, and the Envy of Every Single Man

She was tall and very attractive, with deep blue eyes. With her head held a bit higher than the other girls, she seemed to carry herself a bit differently. Her name was Florence Kroeger and she was born in Louisville to a family that had come over from Germany. She had a "continental" upbringing—she was never discouraged from doing things. Rather, there was in Florence a sense of willingness to risk—a sense of challenge for adventure balanced by commitment to ideals. She seemed to have more substance than the other girls. She wanted to go to Columbia University and study Latin and Art. But the days of the Depression came about the time when she would have gone to New York. Her father was a builder and, though wealthy for a time, lost virtually everything in the Depression era. Florence wound up working in the seminary library as an assistant to the librarian.[30]

Florence took her job in the library in summer 1933. Clarence came to Louisville in the fall semester of that year. The seminary was a fairly small institution of about 400 students in those days. When Clarence first came to the library and saw Florence, he said to himself, "That's for me." But there were a couple of problems. Clarence's reaction was shared by virtually all of the young men there. And Clarence was not that impressive of a figure in fall 1933. Florence remembered Clarence as a tall, boyish figure from a small country town. Yes, he was highly educated, but he was a country boy. She was a city girl with a Germanic background. Florence later remembered that when "Clarence came up from Georgia...I didn't pay a lot of attention to him at first, I'll have to admit that." She was going out with others. Clarence was very busy with his studies and as pastor. Sometimes a group would do things together, and Florence and Clarence would be together in that way. But they did not begin to date quickly.[31]

In those days, Clarence Jordan weighed only 135 pounds. And, at 6'2", that made him look very slender. Florence came to see him as a "nice-looking guy." But "he was not what you would call handsome in the sense of being picture-book handsome." She remembered that, from those early days, he had a "good face and beautiful eyes." And, in his jovial way, Clarence convinced Florence that she had asked him for the first date. They were both members of the Clifton Baptist Church. And, on one snowy night after church, Florence saw Clarence and told him to tell J.R., a married student from the seminary, that he should wait for her so she could ride back with him. After Florence finished talking with a friend, she went to look for J.R., with whom she had ridden to church. J.R. was not there, but Clarence was waiting for her. He took her home to Galt Avenue off of Frankfort. They began dating after that.[32]

Once Florence and Clarence began to date, they soon came to the conclusion that "there was something there." Even though Florence continued to date others for a time, she began to think that she "had found the right one." In the back of her mind, she began to feel like "this was it." Clarence received his first seminary degree in May 1936. When the couple began to talk seriously about marriage, Clarence told Florence, "If you want to be the wife of a pastor of the First Baptist church someplace, you don't want to marry me, because I'll never be pastor of a First Baptist church, or any church maybe." Then Clarence told Florence about his dream to go back to the South to "help the poor." Florence was not scared easily. Florence and Clarence married at 4:30 P.M. on July 21, 1936, at Florence's home on Galt Avenue. Claude Broach, Clarence's friend and former roommate, was best man. The seminary librarian, Thomas Johnson, performed the ceremony. So began what was to be a strong relationship and marriage. James Wm. McClendon wrote that Florence "was independent enough of mind, and free enough from the Kentucky culture, to encourage Clarence's own independence of thought and action."[33] Clarence's father wrote to his son and told him that "a good woman is one of God's greatest gifts to man."[34] In Clarence's case, Jim Jordan was exactly right—Florence was a partner in every sense of the word, and a continuing gift to Clarence even after his death.

The First Years in Louisville: Clarence and the
  Early Adult Ultimate Environment

As a young adult making his way into the world on his own, Clarence Jordan began to demonstrate some important characteristics. His life was already very disciplined and committed. He worked and studied hard in the midst of tough economic times. Clarence's world as a young seminarian was serious and praxis-oriented. He held together theory and practice as he looked for ways to live out his faith and demonstrate his abilities in the classroom. But his head and heart were attuned to the world around him, and he was alive with dreams and imagination of a world changed, and moving closer to his growing understanding of Jesus the Rebel. His dream was just beginning to form, yet, Clarence lived, like many other seminarians, with a sense of guilt, and his early life seems to have been driven by a search for redemption for himself and the human family. Perhaps he did not know it, but on some level and in some manner, in his reading and teaching of the Bible, he was in touch with his first matrix of learning— his first sense of koinonia. His life began to take on new dimensions of authenticity and authority. What he did not yet know was how his dream would unfold, or how he would have the courage and insight to make it happen. There was a spiritual awakening for Clarence still ahead. How would it unfold, and what would it mean for those dreams buried deep in his heart?

Chapter 8

The Haymarket Years

For four years I worked in...the heart of the ghetto. It was a spiritual awakening for me.

—Clarence Jordan

Several themes began to emerge in the life of Clarence Jordan in his early years in Louisville: commitment to scholarship and pastoral ministry, increasing sensitivity to the poor and downtrodden, and an ongoing search for clarity of his dream and someone with whom to share it. As he committed himself to the task of study—often eight to ten hours a day—he found himself going deeper intellectually and spiritually. The most important influence on Jordan was Edward A. McDowell, who taught him not only to search the deeper recesses of the Greek New Testament for the true meaning of the Word, but also to know "that the Word must come alive in currents of history and social change." Jordan later wrote to McDowell—who had also taken him to an important conference on race—that this was a "turning point in my life." This way of reading the Bible in dialogue with the culture "seemed to bring into the open the deep feelings which had lain, like molten lava, within the inner recesses of my heart."[1] What Jordan was learning about the Bible was increasingly radical because he sought for the root meaning of Christianity. Applying the insights he learned in his quest would take Jordan in a radical direction, because it meant that he would have to go against the accepted traditions of Southern society.[2]

The second most important influence on Jordan during his Louisville years was his work in the inner city. Jordan later described his four years of work there as a "spiritual awakening." There he found many refugees from the farmlands of Georgia and Alabama. The ghetto, Jordan said, "was grinding them up." So Jordan saw this as the clarification of his call: "It drove me to get back to the area that was vomiting these people up and see if we couldn't reverse the trend from the farms to the city."[3]

The Haymarket and the Drama of
Clarence Jordan's Spiritual Awakening

The Haymarket of downtown Louisville was an outdoor farmer's market that occupied the large block located between the four streets: Jefferson, Liberty, Floyd, and Brook Street. The market began in the 1880s when local farmers started bringing their produce to town to sell directly to the consumers. By the 1890s, farmers had formed a company to buy space. Many of the customers were local merchants who bought produce to sell in their own stores. The market began to decline in the 1940s with the rise of chain stores. But, even before then, the area had taken on more than ethnic charm. In the late 1930s and early 1940s, the canopied sidewalks and hucksters hawking their wares were still there.[4]

In the surrounding neighborhood, there were, by one account, "*ninety* whiskey stores, bars, 'honkytonks,' nightclubs, gambling dens, porno shops, and houses of prostitution, all within a radius of three blocks."[5] Florence Jordan remembered it as the roughest part of downtown Louisville. There was a certain danger in just being in the area. One could be robbed, mugged, or shot. Strangely, Clarence Jordan did not seem to be afraid in this troubled environment. Ironically, he appeared to thrive here. He would later say that this was the place of his spiritual awakening.[6]

Indeed, there had been a Christian witness in this neighborhood since 1881, when Steve Holcombe, a former riverboat gambler who was reputed to have killed two people, came to town and was converted, after which he established the Holcombe Mission, which, in time, became the Union Gospel Mission. Jordan's involvement in Louisville's inner city can be traced from his first month at the seminary. In his first four weeks in Louisville, Clarence ventured into the inner city on two occasions with other students to conduct services on the streets. After having done so, he wrote, "I have seen life in all its stages and conditions—the poor, the wealthy, the sick, the healthy, the blind…the crippled, the starving (you should see the length of the bread lines), the homeless, the motherless—

yes, I've seen it all, and it makes me realize how fortunate I am and how richly God has blessed me." He also added, "It makes me rejoice that I have a place in the service of suffering humanity."[7]

Clarence Jordan and the Guilt of Abundance:
A Seminarian with an Overweening Conscience

About ten months later, Clarence once again writes about his experiences in the inner city. He had been to a "little mission" in the "slums." The service was composed of a "handful of ragged, dirty, hungry, yes starving humanity." A young mother and child caught his eye. She was, Clarence wrote, not more than 16 but she held a 5-month-old child who weighed no more than eight to ten pounds. When he inquired about her, Clarence learned that the mother and child lived in squalor. Their ratty home provided virtually no shelter. The makeshift shelter was filthy, disease-ridden, and lacking in food. Both mother and child had rags for clothes. What Clarence also knew was that this home in the ghetto existed "alongside the mansions and palaces and luxury of another part of the city." This realization led Clarence to affirm, "No, America isn't Christian yet." Then he made his analysis personal: "Every time I see something like that, it makes me sorta hate to sit down to a full table. The food sorta chokes, as if I were eating and taking bread from a starving man....Isn't that what I'm doing when I have plenty and to spare and others haven't even enough to begin to ease the pangs of hunger?"[8]

About the same time period—the first year in Louisville—Clarence wrote about another episode. His mother had sent a package containing Georgia pecans. Clarence wrote back to thank his mother and said, "I am very appreciative, and knowing that you picked them out with your own fingers makes me appreciate them all the more. You shouldn't have done it tho [sic], Mama, for I am sure that you need them for other things at home."[9] Both of these episodes imply that Clarence enters into this period of spiritual awakening with a great deal of sensitivity, arising, in some sense, from a feeling of guilt.

It is not unusual to find young seminarians plagued with some form of guilt. Since the time of St. Augustine, the Western understanding of religion in the Catholic and later Protestant traditions has been dominated by the concept of original sin and its paradigm of guilt and redemption. The seminaries and divinity schools have been historically populated by sensitive young people attempting to participate in the larger drama they see in terms of anticipated redemption. So one should not be surprised to find Clarence Jordan working with a sense of guilt. But it appears that, for Clarence, this drama and his place in it were more deeply felt than usual. His sensitive spirit caused him to compare his life with the "plight of…[the] poor wretched souls" he had seen in the inner city. His sensitivity to the situation seemed to make his food choke, and made a small, inexpensive gift of pecans from his mother problematic. Clarence Jordan, as he moved in the direction of a spiritual awakening in the inner city of Louisville in the 1930s, had an ongoing severe and sensitive conscience—an overly sensitive conscience. This overly severe sense of conscience is what Erik Erikson described as "overweening," and the core of the religious genius, or *homo religiosus.* We will need to ask later how this unique personality orientation relates to his earlier days and how it compels him toward the future. For now, it will be enough to note the striking element of Clarence's compassion that he had for the poor and his ongoing sensitivity to the plight of "starving humanity," and that it will be his unique response, through a continuing sense of shame and guilt that will provoke him in the coming years, to fashion a dream for a land where people can live in decent housing and have food enough to eat. But, for now, Clarence can only write to his mother and tell her that he is having trouble eating because he remembers what he has just seen in the ghetto of Louisville. Then, out of his own "guilt of abundance," he thanks his mother for the stamps she has sent him, but goes on to gently rebuke her: "Don't you do it anymore because I know how things are and how scarce money is. You might sacrifice too much for me."[10]

Confronting the Challenge: Clarence Jordan's Dangerous Quest and the Religious Self

Florence Jordan knew the Haymarket area was the most dangerous part of Louisville. But Clarence seemed undaunted. He seemed compelled to make a difference somehow. In fall 1936, as a part of his growing sense of vocation, he accepted a teaching assignment at Simmons University, a school for bi-vocational black ministers. This meant that Clarence was taking classes at the seminary, teaching at Simmons, and serving as a pastor on the weekends. In the final year of his doctoral studies, he resigned from the church at Clermont to concentrate more on his studies and to spend more time at home. His first child, Eleanor, had just been born. About the same time, however, he was invited to become director of the Sunshine Center mission. He accepted this position in January 1939. When Clarence graduated from the seminary with his Ph.D. a few months later, he was invited to become the director of missions for the Long Run Baptist Association. This position would also oversee the Union Gospel Mission in the Haymarket.

Both the Sunshine Center and the Union Gospel Mission were unique buildings. The Union Gospel Mission had been founded by a riverboat gambler and murderer. Yet the Sunshine Center, which became the Fellowship Center, was the most ornate and had an even more dubious past. It was the original setting of the first "koinonia," yet, ironically, it was at one time a house of prostitution—one of the most famous in Louisville. One entered on marble steps. There was a large room that had a fountain in the center. Apparently, as the customers came in, the women would dance around the fountain in the nude. Each of the women was assigned a room, which later became space for Sunday-school classes. On the banister for the steps leading to the rooms, a devil's head had been carved, and on the wooden wall of the hallway, someone had carved "house of sin." Such was the physical setting for Jordan's first mission.[11]

On one occasion, Clarence Jordan was down in the Haymarket area with Henlee Barnette. They were standing across from Stony's Honky Tonk. There had been fifty-two crimes reported in the newspaper for that area in the previous two years. Jordan was making a film to be used in presentations to local churches. When the owner of Stony's saw Clarence across the street taking pictures, he came running out, ready to attack him. He was enraged, cursing, and threatening to beat the hell out of Jordan. It appeared as if the owner intended to do just that, but Clarence stood there calmly and said, with his South Georgia accent, "My friend, it *is* a free country, is it not?" That soft answer turned the man away. And, as he returned to Stony's, he said simply, "Aw, to hell with you."[12]

The Haymarket As Parabolic Event:
The Secret of Clarence Jordan

Another dangerous episode developed in the Sunshine Center. A crowd of angry blacks had gathered in the center. A crime had occurred—a white man had raped a young black woman. The black men were justifiably enraged. A large black man stood up with an iron pipe in his hand and said, "Just like the whites kill a Negro for this, I am going to kill a white man." When the fellow said this, Clarence came to the front of the room, put his head down on the table, and said, "If a white man must die for this rape, let it be me. Do it now." The man dropped the pipe and the crowd began to murmur. After a time of shared astonishment, the group began to talk about what could be done without violence.[13]

How does one begin to understand such a story? Seventy-five years later, it can be traced to four different narrations. The story was told by Bob Herndon, who worked with Jordan in the Haymarket. It was heard and told again by Victor Glass, a fellow student in Louisville. Somehow the story was told to D.B. Nicholson, the state Baptist Student Union director in Athens, who published an account in *The Christian Index*. And, finally, Clarence himself told the story in 1946 at the Woman's College in Greensboro, North Carolina, where it was heard by Sara Owen, who later recounted the telling.[14]

Clarence participated in the process of telling, which indicates that autobiographical narrative is at the base of this legend. Clarence, either in public speaking or in response to questions, often narrated his own story. The autobiographical element helps to place this unusual story in larger perspective. That is, in some way not always known to the autobiographer (or to the reader/hearer), this telling of one's story illumines the unknown mystery of the self through metaphor. Further, some of the events in autobiographical telling can be understood as "parabolic events." The self of autobiography is incarnated through concrete events, and these aspects of one's life become parabolic when, as complex images, they embody a part of the secret of the individual's life.[15] Such appears to be the case with this gripping story. Something in this narration chronicles the life secret of Clarence Jordan and bids the narrative to be told again and again.

The contemporary setting of this story is that of a young, devoted seminarian learning to read the Bible in dialogue with the surrounding culture. When he began this practice, he rediscovered his earlier quest to answer questions on race, poverty, and violence. This reading also pushed him to find the earliest and most authentic form of Christianity. In the Book of Acts, Jordan found the first Koinonia, where followers of Christ pooled their resources and shared according to need. Reading for the doctoral degree, Clarence was involved in an intensive study of the Greek New Testament—immersing himself in the text. What Clarence discovered while reading was "more than forms and syntax; he found the example and teaching of Jesus."[16] And Clarence heard the voice of Jesus say that losing the life was the way to find true life—the greatest love and commitment was to lay down one's life for others. Clarence took the words of Jesus very seriously, and he was formed by those words in such a manner that stories were remembered about his lived interpretation. He sought to live out the teachings of the New Testament as much as humanly possible.

The Haymarket/Sunshine Center incident can be read in this light: Jordan was attempting to follow what he understood as radical discipleship—the greatest love and commitment was a willingness to lay down one's life for another. Fellow students who knew Jordan during Louisville spoke, almost universally, with an extremely high regard. One of those students from that day was H. Cornell Goerner, who said of Jordan that he "was the most completely dedicated Christian I have ever known." Goerner went on to say, "With childlike simplicity, he took the Sermon on the Mount seriously and tried to follow the teachings of Jesus literally and absolutely."[17]

This story shows Clarence Jordan moving in a specific religious direction—an increasing identity with the one he will later refer to as "Jesus the Rebel." In his sermon titled "Jesus the Rebel," Jordan radicalizes the concept of love as the antithesis of violence. Jordan said that "Jesus the Rebel did not seek to escape the guilt of a society that could produce a Ku Klux Klan." The Haymarket incident portrays Jordan as one willing to take upon himself the guilt of society in order to create a new sense of community. This story—however one is to read it—gives the reader the impression that here is a young man with a radical sense of identification with the life and teachings of Jesus. Because of that sense of identification, he was free to lay his head down on the table in the presence of the racial animosity and invite the group to take revenge upon him. According to this element in the narrative, the life of Clarence Jordan is beginning to take a cruciform shape—the shape of a cross.

As a parabolic event, the Haymarket incident seems to indicate that Clarence Jordan knows the building of "koinonia"—reconciled human community—requires vicarious suffering and the willingness of the disciple to lay down his life for others. At the same time, the narrative as parabolic event also seems to imply that Jordan knew, on some level of his being, that he was fated to survive. This reading of the Haymarket incident also suggests a connection with the earlier drama in the life of Clarence Jordan. That is, the central drama of his life was a sense of solidarity and community over against a prevailing condition of neglect and abandonment—a theme of fractured community. As a parabolic event, the Haymarket incident is related to Jordan's first view of the world and an intense effort to rebuild the fractured human community.

The Covenant Sealed with God:
The Core of Jordan's Religious Personality

This incident, on another level, also helps to establish Jordan as *homo religiosus*. The narrative clearly portrays Clarence as a young, sensitive, and impressionable religious personality. Yet the extent to which Clarence pursues the challenges of ministry without fear, and with something of a disregard for his own wellbeing, indicates something remarkable about him. The story shows a young man reaching a state of total involvement in what turns out to be a dangerous religious mission in the toughest part of the city. Clarence himself gives us a clue to how this development comes about, in a letter written to his mother when he was in his twenty-first year, when he writes, "I am just beginning to know my dad." Twenty-one years of age and just beginning to know his father? This implies some lack of relationship, or some disregard for twenty-one years of life. Perhaps, in some fashion and on some level, at a very young age, Clarence, freed from both conflict and relationship with his father, constructs an image of God as Father. If so, Clarence would have made an early covenant with God. These stories from his Louisville days, thus, can be seen as an effort to reimage that original covenant. As he had written to Edward A. McDowell, his work in relating scripture to culture already "seemed to bring into the open the deep feelings which had lain, like molten lava, within the inner recesses of my heart."[18] Perhaps one of those things now being brought into the open was his long-ago covenant made with God, which harbored a truthfulness superior to all other authorities and, thereby, freed him to live with "totalistic belief and action." If so, this is what gives Clarence Jordan the freedom to so live in Louisville. It is the covenant sealed with God many years ago now remembered and activated. If this is possible, then it may be this sense of an "I" sealed in covenant with God that allows Clarence to stand unprotected in that moment of violence and threatened terror from the mob in the ghetto, and will sustain him in campaigns of later violence from the Klan in Georgia.[19] Perhaps this is the core of Clarence Jordan's personality— his religious self—the person behind all the stories, that is beginning to emerge. Could this be the core reality of the man who left Louisville in winter 1942 to go south and confront head-on the assumptions and values of a whole region—a dangerous and radical pilgrimage of faith lived out just a few miles south of Americus?

Koinonia in Louisville:
  The Development of a Radical Ideology

As Clarence read the pages of his Greek New Testament, he discovered that the first Christians shared all things in common. He sought to go back to that ideal. Though Jordan's Baptist heritage envisioned the congregation as a community, his study of the New Testament took him further. He discovered in the early Christian story that "all that believed were together, and had all things in common; and sold their possessions and goods, and parted them to all men, as every man had need."[20] Based on this reading, Jordan came to think Christians should live in community and share their worldly goods. In this way, Christians act as the body of Christ and not as individuals.

In reading the New Testament, Jordan discovered that the message of the kingdom of God was the central Christian theme. But the announcement of this kingdom was not for an otherworldly reign but, rather, for the here and now. In other words, the kingdom of God is the life of the family of God here on earth. For Jordan, being a follower of Christ meant membership in a spiritual family in which God is the Heavenly Father and fellow believers are, essentially, brothers and sisters in a new relationship. The new family was beyond race and class. For Jordan, this meant that, as the family of God, Christians must cooperate and relate in a new interracial and egalitarian way, which stunned many who observed this belief in action. It would prove to be a truly radical ideology for a young disciple from Talbot County, Georgia.

On stationery from the Baptist Fellowship Center on Madison Street, Jordan wrote down six definitions of the Greek word "koinonia," and then went on to translate the texts where the word was used.[21] But Clarence was not just idealistic; he was also very praxis-oriented, forever trying to hold thought and action together. He was driven to live out the faith in very practical ways. Clarence had, for some time, wanted to set up a "koinonia," which would seek to replicate the first Christian community. Apparently, in Louisville, there were two such efforts—one on the seminary campus and another at the Fellowship Center.

Discovering Jesus the Rebel and
the Vocation of a Lifetime

As Clarence read his New Testament, his understanding of Jesus took on a particular slant. Jesus was a rebel, the leader of a revolutionary movement who brought in a new era of human relationships. Edward McDowell was teaching Clarence that the New Testament must be read in dialogue with culture so that the true Word comes alive in the crosscurrents of human history, where social change could help bring in the new era. When Jordan began to do that, he saw the ghetto in a new light. He began to see the poor and lowly living on the streets of downtown Louisville as members of this new egalitarian kingdom. And he began to wrestle with a concept of ministry and vocation that could bring human wholeness to them. He eventually concluded that his vocation should be to go back to his own native region—the Deep South—and there attempt to reverse the circumstances that pushed these folks off their land and made them flee to the inner cities of northern areas, where they continued to be abused by a system out of control.

Clarence expressed his dreams to members of the Louisville "koinonia." He talked about pacifism, equality among the races, and the concept of stewardship that involved complete sharing. And, in time, Clarence described his emerging dream of a farm that could sustain a "koinonia," or fellowship of believers who had committed themselves to peace, equality, and a common life, and could at the same time become a transforming resource for the South's rural poor. In his quest for larger vocation, Clarence became a member of the Fellowship of Reconciliation, and he began to read the newsletter of Walt Johnson, a pioneer in stewardship who also promoted economic justice and equality among the races. In July 1941, Johnson published a letter by Martin England, a missionary to Burma now on furlough because of the war. England wrote to Johnson proposing the idea of an interracial community. Jordan read England's letter and met with him some months later in Louisville in spring 1942 at a chapter meeting of the Fellowship of Reconciliation. What England proposed was exactly what Jordan had dreamed of doing. After a series of meetings, which often involved their wives, they agreed to search for a place for the farm and to solicit funding.[22]

During that period, Jordan's reputation continued to grow, and he was given many opportunities to speak to student groups and to write articles for church groups. But his outspoken approach to the issues brought both supporters and detractors in Louisville and the larger Baptist world. His detractors foreshadowed, in some sense, Jordan's growing alienation from Southern culture just as his work won for him many admirers and supporters. Just as many church groups around Louisville asked him to speak on race, and his reputation for being a good speaker grew, so also did the critique whereby many leaders tried to rein him in and tell him he was trying to do things too quickly in the area of race relations.[23] Convention leaders attempted to edit and tone down his articles, especially the ones in *The Baptist Student*.

In a very revealing letter from the assistant editor, Marjorie Moore, Clarence was told that editor Frank Leavell "greatly enjoyed your article." But then Ms. Moore wrote that, before final approval was given, Leavell asked that she take the article to Dr. Holcomb. This was done, she wrote, because "we want always to be careful that what we publish…for student 'consumption' is in line with the Board's policy." Holcomb was "pretty much riled over it." It was "that part about the white man's treatment of the Negro and Hitler's treatment of the Jews being two sprouts from the same bush [that] made him indignant." Holcomb was of the opinion that, for Negroes to advance in society, they needed opportunities for leadership on their own and, therefore, did not need to worship with whites. If those two items could be deleted—the statement on Hitler and integrated worship—then the article could be accepted. Of course, Ms. Moore wrote, Holcomb also wants to omit the last line: "To plunge into danger-laden jungles requires less courage than to cross racial boundaries in one's own homeland…." Then Ms. Moore, who was a personal friend, wrote to Clarence, "I hope Dr. Holcombe will get acquainted with you at Ridgecrest. His first impression is not wholly favorable…." But Ms. Moore assured Clarence that he wasn't "the first sane person in the past two thousand years who has had 'crazy notions,' as he calls them." She closes by telling Clarence that Holcomb thinks Clarence must be some "Yankee boy!" As if to say not to worry, she adds, "He'll like you immensely when you meet."[24]

Though Frank Leavell reportedly liked the article, he was less affirming about Jordan's idea that an African American be invited to participate in his upcoming seminar on race relations scheduled for Ridgecrest. In planning for Ridgecrest, Clarence wrote to Leavell and said, "It just occurred to me the other day that a great contribution could be made to my seminar on race relations if an outstanding Negro student were there to present the Negro's viewpoint." Leavell wrote back, "I read your letter carefully and have conferred with my associates. I am obliged to answer according to my judgment rather than my wishes. In my opinion, it would be better not to create a problem by bringing the Negro student to Ridgecrest."[25] Clarence responded in a polite but somewhat patronizing tone: "Mr. Frank, don't you think the time has about come when the 'powers that be' should at least begin to weigh the evidence for and against having Negroes at Ridgecrest, not only for the student Retreat but for some of the other meetings? …I believe if ever the time was ripe for Christian forces to take the lead, it is now." Clarence went on to write, "In this hour of crisis, it would be tragic for the leadership to lag behind the laity."[26]

Clarence was also very busy speaking at Baptist colleges and universities at this point in his life. He got far more affirmation at the Baptist schools than from the "powers that be" within the denomination. Throughout 1941–1942, Clarence spoke at several different Baptist colleges, including Ouachita, Furman, Mercer, and Baylor. In virtually every case, the response was overwhelmingly warm and affirming. Wayne Ward wrote from Ouachita to thank Clarence for "the great inspiration" he was for Ward personally. Ward found that Jordan embodied a "Christ-like humility" that pervaded "every word and act." In speaking of Jordan's effort on the campus, Ward wrote, "We have found that this week touched more phases of campus life and reached more individual lives than any type of religious effort on our campus has ever done."[27] The President of Ouachita, Thomas Jones, wrote to Clarence, "There was one thing above all else that stood out in the minds of the entire student body concerning Focus Week and that was the Christ-like character of Dr. Clarence Jordan."[28] Concerning his time at Mercer, one student said that "he is the spirit of Christ."[29] A student from Arkansas who came to his seminar at Ridgecrest wrote to Clarence, "I felt the Lord so near…God gave me new hope and faith from that hour. Your meek, humble, Christ-like disposition touched all of our hearts."[30]

As a young 30-year-old man, Clarence Jordan was a rising star in Baptist student work, and in the denomination generally. Job offers began to come his way, but he felt pulled in another direction—toward another vocation. In June 1942, W.A. Colvin contacted Jordan about whether he would consider becoming pastor of the Eighteenth Street Baptist Church in Louisville.[31] Jordan wrote back with a polite but revealing response. "It seems," Jordan wrote, "that the Lord has laid His hand upon me to work among the poor, the outcasts, the friendless, the downtrodden. I have offered myself to Him to go where others hesitate to go. It's a road that sometimes breaks a fellow's heart, but when God's voice…speaks, His servant has no alternative but to obey."[32]

Called to a New Frontier: Jordan, a Pioneer in the New South

In October 1942, when Jordan was leaving Louisville for his new work, an appreciation dinner was planned to which Edward McDowell was invited. Unable to attend the meeting, McDowell sent a letter expressing his appreciation for Clarence, along with an assessment of his work: "Dr. Jordan pioneered in such a way as to break down barriers between the races and build a permanent foundation for better cooperation and more wholesome relations in the coming years." McDowell went on to say that Jordan "will leave behind an example of Christlikeness and practical Christian idealism that will never be forgotten in Louisville. Clarence Jordan is one of the greatest Christians I know."[33]

When Jordan began to describe his new work, he also picked up the image of the pioneer. He wrote to Howard Johnson and said, "The time has come when Christians must once again be the pioneers and lead the way to a new world o[f] righteousness, justice, and peace." The South, Jordan wrote, offers "one of the most challenging frontiers...." Koinonia Farm would be an experiment on that frontier to live out basics principles "emphatically enunciated" by Jesus. Jordan's strategy was first to identify with the farming community—attempt to win the hearts and minds of the people by being good neighbors. Then, after having won the confidence of the people, there would be an effort to bring forth the principles that are foundational. The dream was eventually to bring in other people, like a doctor or a mechanic. "We will hold all things in common, distribution will be made to each *according to his need*, and every worker will be given equal voice in its government."[34]

Initially, Jordan and England had hoped to settle in Alabama, but the two farms identified there did not work. But then Jordan's brother Frank, who was a farm appraiser for the Federal Land Bank, told him of a 400-acre farm about nine miles southwest of Americus, Georgia—a city of approximately 10,000 people. The land was about average for the region. Two hundred acres had been used as pastureland, 100 acres had been cultivated for crops, and 100 acres had been in timber. After investigating this site, Jordan said that "it looked so much like what we had been looking for, that we decided to buy it."[35] The farm seemed to "afford every opportunity for the development of the project." Jordan and England arrived in the middle of November 1942.

The Haymarket As an Ultimate Environment:
A Spiritual Awakening and the Call to Be a Pioneer

Clarence Jordan's Louisville years were formative for his adult life. It was here that he found a life partner, learned to read the Bible in dialogue with culture, and experienced a spiritual awakening. These years embody a "turning point" during which he is able to go deeper into himself and rediscover "the deep feelings which had lain, like molten lava, within the inner recesses of…[his] heart." Once he does this, his life unfolds as that of a pioneer on the frontier of a new South. These years also demonstrate much about Jordan's faith. His experiences in the Haymarket region of Louisville touch him deeply and show his remarkable sensitivity and, indeed, "overweening" sense of guilt.

These stories point backward and forward in time. His overactive conscience leads the reader to reread the stories of his youth and remember earlier experiences, especially how he went beyond his culture and culture heroes, such as his father, allowing for an image of God the Father. These stories from the ghetto also help to document the interpretation of Jordan's life as that of a *homo religiosus*—a religious genius who, as a cultural worker, shows the way forward for his generation. Louisville, for Jordan, points backward in the sense that these stories pull from him the lessons that have been uncultivated in his own heart for all the years now, only to be brought to life again by the heartbreaking experience of reading the Bible in light of the ghetto.

Jordan learns that the Haymarket is a microcosm of the South and, eventually, the world, so that it can become a metaphor for his growing and developing faith, so that it can be the repository for his radical ideology of communal life, pacifism, and egalitarian race relations. Religiously, Clarence's experiences in the ghetto show how his own deeply reflective spirituality is being formed by his image of the rebel Jesus. His own life and exegetical spirit at this time are not only reflective but demythologizing—tearing down the icons built by Southern culture. His image of Jesus is the leader of a revolutionary movement, and Clarence is now ready not only to join that movement but to be a leader on a new front, on a new frontier. As an image of the faith of Clarence Jordan, the Haymarket looks forward as well and anticipates the hayfields of South Georgia as he prepares for a lifetime's work on a frontier that will demand the best efforts of this young and optimistic religious genius.

Chapter 9

Koinonia I: Man and Event

The theme of Clarence Jordan's life was "koinonia." He wanted a Christian community in which people of all races could come together and share the common life.

—Henlee Barnette

In fall 1942, when Clarence Jordan was preparing to head back south to establish Koinonia Farm, Martin Luther King, Jr., was getting ready for his sophomore year at Booker T. Washington High School in Atlanta, where he would struggle with the "tyranny" imposed by his teenage peer group. Mohandus K. Gandhi was in prison because of his famous "Quit India" speech, in which he demanded that the British leave the historic land and grant immediate independence. Dietrich Bonhoeffer was involved in an effort to help German Jews escape to Switzerland and in a resistance movement to stop Hitler. Within a few months, he would be arrested by the Gestapo. For his part, Clarence Jordan spent spring and summer 1942 planning another type of resistance effort—the establishment of Koinonia Farm as an interracial farm in the heart of what Dubois had called the "Egypt of the Confederacy," the heart of the famous Black Belt.

As a gifted young scholar/preacher, Clarence had recently finished a doctoral program in New Testament at the oldest of the Baptist seminaries. He was also one of the "up-and-coming" stars of the Baptist Student program, which coordinated programs at Ridgecrest in North Carolina and special events on Baptist University campuses. In this capacity, Clarence had the "ear" of many of the prominent leaders of the Southern Baptist Convention. In July 1942, Clarence wrote to his brother Buddie and told him that he had spent "almost all of June" at Ridgecrest speaking to some 2,200 students. While he was there in Western North Carolina, Clarence wrote to his brother, "I had opportunity to talk with all the

Southern Baptist 'big-wigs' about a project that I've been thinking about for years and to which I have finally definitely committed myself." Clarence described the response as "very enthusiastic...the most forward-looking venture that they had ever seen among Baptist ranks." Clarence thought the project would be a combination of a practical school for Negro preachers and a "springboard" for mission work in the rural areas. This fits a need, he wrote to Buddie, because the Home Mission Board has no plan for such mission work. This venture will be completely on faith, he wrote. "So, Bud, if at any time you'd like to make an investment in this project, which we believe to be the Lord's work if there ever was any, it would sure make me feel mighty good."[1]

Through spring and summer, Clarence also continued to write friends and acquaintances about his new effort. He wrote to Liston Pope at Yale Divinity School. "Like you," Clarence wrote, "I am a native Southerner [and] for many years have been...interested in the rural situation and the Negro." Then he described his project to Pope. It will be "interracial," "communal," and "missionary or religious." "We're just trying to take some of the social theories our seminaries have taught us and put them into practice," Jordan said. Clarence also wrote to Mack Goss that both he and Martin England had agreed it would be far better to get a large number of people to support them with small donations as opposed to one donor with a large check. And he closed his letter to Mack by saying, "Every chance you get, help us to spread the word around."[2]

The most basic need was the money to buy the farm. The first contribution was from Elizabeth Hartsfield in New Albany, Indiana. She sent a check for fifty dollars. When Clarence wrote her back, he thanked her and congratulated her for being the "first contributor to Koinonia Farm." "Your belief in us is a challenge, and this first gift is a great encouragement." The land cost approximately twenty-five dollars an acre. So the first check paid for two acres. There were, of course, other needs. Sara Owen was a senior at Mercer University in 1942. The Mercer Baptist Student Union joined other student groups across Georgia in collecting funds to "buy a mule for Clarence Jordan's farm." The students felt "a real sense of participation."[3] In September, Clarence wrote in a form letter to his friends that there were other needs such as "implements, livestock, feed, fertilizer, seed, etc....." But he said, "[T]he Lord is laying it upon the hearts of friends to respond graciously, and we are confident that...the Lord will provide."[4]

In November, when the Jordans and Englands made preparations to go to Georgia, they decided that the buildings were in such disarray that repair work was needed before the women and children should come. So Florence and her two children, and Mabel and her three children, stayed in Kentucky until December. When Clarence Jordan left Wakefield, Kentucky, in mid-November 1942, dreams danced in his head. He was on his way back to Georgia to live out the vision that had lain fallow in his mind and heart since childhood. Now his dream would be turned into a deed—the man and the event of a lifetime would come together. But it was no small deed he had envisioned—it was daring and dangerous. Clarence Jordan wanted to do nothing less than restructure Southern society and, thereby, create a new place where people of all races could live in harmony overcoming the barriers that had divided people.[5] He was leaving Kentucky with the zeal of a missionary. "We felt like Abraham: 'Get thee out of this country into a land that I will show thee.'"[6] He was passionate and optimistic. But Clarence knew the challenge would not be easy. "It scared the devil out of us to think of going against Southern traditions," he said. Clarence knew that, in the South, a white man could disappear just as easily as a black man. Yet the challenge, as he put it, was not success but obedience. "Surely," he thought, "no one could argue over the revelation of the New Testament that God is no respecter of persons."[7]

Clarence was also afraid of what was happening in the churches. The song of the Southern church was "war, hate, and destroy your enemy." He knew he would have to stand against that. Jordan was not going in order to pick a fight, but to demonstrate a different way of living. In that sense, he would fight with different weapons—not just nonviolence, but active goodwill to those who would oppose him. As an alternative to the war, Clarence saw himself fighting Hitler and fascism in South Georgia as opposed to Germany.[8] A few months before, he had written to Mack Goss and described his new project. "It will be cooperative and communal; interracial; based on the investment of time and energy, instead of capital; operated by distribution based on need; motivated by Christian love."[9]

Koinonia: Man and Event

Founded thirteen years before the beginning of the Montgomery Bus Boycott and the Civil Rights Movement, Koinonia was nonetheless something of a period piece—a creation out of the spirit of the times. Koinonia was, in some sense, a creation in response to the economic cataclysm that was the Depression. It came out of Jordan's desire to work on the "economic emancipation" of the Negro and to respond to what he had seen in the ghetto in downtown Louisville. As an attempt at reconciliation of the human family, it was also a response to the violence of World War II.[10] Yet it was far more than either of these more immediately apparent efforts. For Clarence, it was the event of a lifetime and embodied the theme of his life, the fulfillment of his youthful quest to make a difference and reorder the society that he knew to be tragically unjust.

Clarence Jordan was one of the special ones of his day, willing to risk his life and the lives of others to right the wrongs of society—to genuinely make a difference in the human family. How did Clarence get to this point of extraordinary moral commitment and courage? His story and that of the community he founded has yet to be told. When asked what he saw in the radical trajectory of Jordan's life, Joe Hendrix, who was an early follower and observer, admitted that he could not figure out how Clarence "came to be awakened" because he saw "no line that leads from Talbot County to Koinonia."[11] What was it that motivated Clarence Jordan to adopt such a cause and accept a whole race of people as the object of concern and deliverance? What were the elements of his spiritual formation that led to the awakening of this religious genius provoking him to accept this radical and dangerous mission?

The Child As Father of the Man:
Clarence As Homo Religiosus

The current consensus is that the foundational religious experiences of someone like Clarence Jordan take place in early childhood. That is, in the language of the poet Wadsworth, "The child is father of the man." Following this consensus and poetic dictum takes the reader back to Jordan's childhood, where one is asked for experiences that have the potential to shape his adult perspective, and, especially, why he would accept such a challenge as Koinonia. The argument of this book is that Clarence Jordan demonstrates the characteristics of a *homo religiosus*—a religious genius. This thesis and the evidence for it help one to understand the radical pilgrimage that was the life of Clarence Jordan. As a religious genius and spiritual innovator, a conflicted individual like Clarence Jordan looks for a way to join his own personal and existential struggle for meaning and identity with the quest of the group. His struggle is totalistic. It is "something like Jacob's struggle with the angel, a wrestling for a benediction…" and the right to a new name.[12] Therefore, in trying to resolve his own struggle, this figure projects his own solution onto the group and attempts a new sense of identity, not only for his fragmented life but for the entire generation as well. This leader attempts also to restate in positive terms what has been experienced as a negative overstatement.

Such a reading is contrary to the popular view. Yet the spiritual innovator, like Jordan, lives a life of extraordinary conflict that begins in childhood or youth and becomes an existential debt that remains unsettled for a lifetime. As a part of his effort to find a cure for his own dilemma, he is likely to attempt a new ideological synthesis that brings together old and new patterns from religion, politics, or economics. As a cultural worker, this protagonist in the drama of his day creates a new identity for the young people of his age by his own answer to the central and basic conflicts of the age. Put another way, the religious genius is that individual whose personal-identity conflicts merge with the group, and who eventually seeks to establish a new and more humane sense of personhood for himself and for his generation.[13] This is the story of Clarence Jordan's search for a "koinonia." The founding of this community was the outcome of a lifelong struggle. But what was his struggle, and what pushed him in the direction of "Koinonia"?

Like Will Campbell, Clarence Jordan grew up in a family that considered him to be special, based in large measure on the interpretation and explanation of the mother. Both mothers, in fact, tell their sons that they have been "set apart." Furthermore, both Will and Clarence live through a life-threatening illness. And, having done so, each must have sensed some new form of courage and purpose—if only in embryo, to be later discovered in some fullness. Clarence's mother tells him he has been called and set apart like the great biblical figures—consecrated before birth, like Jeremiah and Jesus, whose earthly lives were somehow prefigured by the work of God. And, if only gradually, Clarence, like Will, must have come to understand his life as having a "cruciform" nature to it so that, somehow, some way, he grew up learning to live vicariously. As Will's mother put it, if the family is quarreling, you will be the one to bring them back together and, because of that, you might die early. Likewise, Clarence would grow up with a deep desire to mend the broken nature of the human family, perhaps stemming from his own early experience of alienation and separation from his brothers and sisters during his near-death experience. Both Will and Clarence seemingly were born special, and called somehow even before birth, Clarence's mother said.

Clarence's mother was a gentle, caring woman whom he later called "saintly." And he was greatly influenced by her. He felt the love that came from his mother was so deep and pervasive, it appeared to him to be coming from God through his mother as an earthly angel. The larger framework of Clarence's early life, which helps to make sense of his later radical trajectory, is a sense of perceived abandonment over against a sense of community. That is, his lifelong quest for community—or, as he would later discover, Koinonia—was the adult focus of an experience that was so traumatic in childhood that it sent him on a long journey to discover an antidote. The story of the establishment and founding of Koinonia is, then, a young-adult response to this first crisis in life.

What was that first crisis? For Clarence and his biographers, the first crisis noted is the well-known story of conflict when he was 12 years of age and awakened by the agonizing groans of a prisoner in the jail behind his house. But this story, which Clarence used to explain his adult views, is likely a screen memory concealing an earlier and more painful experience.[14] For all young children, the first major crisis is the challenge of learning trust over against a measure of mistrust. The quality of the child's exchange with the mother is one of "trust versus mistrust." It is clear from Clarence's lifetime of love and adoration for his mother that the quality of trust he carried from his earliest years was both high and profound. What could have brought on the mistrust was the absence of his mother in those formidable years. His mother was often sickly, and Clarence grew up thinking, at times, that there was no one to care for him. His near-death experience may have exaggerated this fear when he was quarantined—and his brothers and sisters were sent away. As his family life was disrupted, he felt abandoned. Yet living through the near-death experience must have given Clarence a measure of courage on some level of his being, as it also gave an added sense that his life must have been saved for some purpose. And the illness likely drew him even closer to his mother, who was his first teacher of things spiritual.

Despite the abundance of his mother's love, the absence of his parents and the loss of his brothers and sisters in the context of his illness must have pushed Clarence in the direction of a "melancholic 'I.'" That is, on some level of being, he moved toward despair and melancholia—hence, his declaration to his Aunt Corrine when he was 5 years old that there was no one to look out for him. The "Grump" personality emerges in connection to his perceived sense of loss of the presence of his parents and siblings, and to his sense that there are those who now see him at his most vulnerable point. This aspect of his personality will grow into an ability to critique, analyze, and challenge the culture, beginning with the foundational aspect of culture, the family. "Grump" became a nickname that stayed with Clarence well into his college years.

At this point, Clarence's spiritual formation is beginning to become clearer. His life trajectory bears the influence of his saintly mother. His faith followed the deep contours of her caring life. Clarence's relationship with his saintly mother established a strong foundation for trust and faith, but her absence due to illness became the basis for a sense of mistrust, which grew more profound with his own illness and near-death experience when he began to experience the fractured nature of life through the imposed quarantine. This sense of the brokenness of life became central to his first composition of the world, and brought on the childhood "melancholic 'I'" that resulted in his nickname of "Grump." The influence of his mother's saintly personality and the fact that he lived through the near-death experience gave him a childhood sense of courage and the idea that his life should have purpose and a religious understanding—and, perhaps, a cruciform shape. But what was it that pushed him toward "Koinonia" and the willingness to take on the welfare of an entire group as his own responsibility?

Clarence's "Grump" personality took the shape of contention in family life—he challenged, argued, and contended. Clarence became frugal in contrast to the family's abundance. He began to resent the family "bounty"—food or anything. He challenged his father when he was condescending to black people. Clarence seemingly responds to the childhood matrix of an absent father and sickly mother with an effort to identify with the strong image of his maternal grandfather, who stands, in his mind, for justice. This transaction comes at a great price—a precocious conscience. Clarence absolves himself of this internalized guilt by assuming responsibility for the pain of the powerless ones around him. He wants justice for the larger family. Clarence seemingly understands intuitively at an early age that this means his family should make do with less. This identification with the maternal grandfather, a figure of justice in his mind, also helps us understand his childhood rebuke of his own strong father. But, most of all, the dimensions of Clarence's childhood drama helps one understand how he begins to formulate the need for a "Koinonia" and why, at age 30, the establishment of the Sumter County "Koinonia" is the dream of a lifetime now come to reality.

The Faith of the Fathers and Grandfathers: Koinonia and the Composition of Radical Faith

The establishment of Koinonia Farm in fall 1942, thirteen years before the beginning of the Montgomery Bus Boycott and the Civil Rights Movement, in the heart of what Dubois called the "Egypt of the Confederacy," was an extraordinarily courageous and idealistic event. The fact that Clarence Jordan stayed on the farm and continued this ministry for twenty-seven years until his death only underscores the extraordinary nature of this undertaking, as well as the lifelong and enduring commitment to the cause. The stunning thing about the establishment of Koinonia Farm and the decision by Clarence Jordan, Martin England, and their families is that this was done in spite of the faith of the fathers—individually and collectively. Clarence Jordan became the "black sheep" of his family. He was an embarrassment to his family, and they did not know how to handle what he was beginning to do. Likewise, the dominant Southern white culture of the region, frankly, did not understand either, and accused Clarence of being a communist.

If Clarence did not go to Sumter County, Georgia, with the support of his father and the surrounding culture, how did a young man of 30 years of age find the courage to withstand the backlash? Clarence knew that there was a cultural tradition and a church they would have to oppose. In fact, he said that going against Southern tradition "scared the devil" out of him, and that he was greatly bothered by the stance of the Southern church on issues of race, war, and materialism. To take a stance that was in opposition to this faith of the fathers was no small matter, and it put fear into their hearts.[15]

If Clarence Jordan and Martin England did not have the support of the faith of the fathers in their endeavors, they did, ironically, share a major influence in their individual faith compositions by their grandfathers. Both Martin England and Clarence Jordan developed attitudes toward race that were unusual for their time and locales. England grew up in South Carolina and Jordan in Georgia. The social climate of each state was segregationist. Both men had grandfathers with strong stories that influenced the grandsons. England traced his desire to be a missionary to Africa back to a story he was told about his maternal grandfather, Jasper Wilson, by his wife.

Jasper Wilson was drafted by the Confederacy and saw duty at Fort Sumter in the early days of the war. He was so badly wounded that he and some of his fellow soldiers thought he was going to die. Jasper Wilson wanted to die at home, so some of the Confederate soldiers put him on a train bound for Western North Carolina. When he came to Walhalla in Oconee County, the train crew lifted him off the train and onto the station platform. He was still forty miles from home. Jasper Wilson lay on the platform for two days begging people to take him home, and to send word to his family. After the second day, a black man who had a horse and wagon came by and picked him up and carried him home. When the two arrived at Wilson's mountain home, they crossed a small creek. The black man lifted Wilson from the wagon and took him down to the creek, bathed his wounds, and then carried him up to his house where Wilson's wife was waiting. Martin England heard the story from his grandmother, who added her own admonition: based on what she had experienced through the kindness shown to her husband, no one should ever speak ill of black people or treat them in an unkind manner. This family narrative presages Clarence Jordan's retelling of the parable of the Good Samaritan. In this case, a black man plays the part of the Good Samaritan—and, for Martin's grandmother and, later, for Martin, this fact becomes "world reversing."[16] For his part, Martin England heard his grandmother's admonition, took it to heart, and went beyond it. It became the basis for his desire to be a missionary to Africa.[17]

Clarence Jordan was also the recipient of a rich oral tradition when he was also young and impressionable. His mother was his first and most influential teacher. She taught Clarence not only about the Bible, but also about her own younger days and about her family, especially her father and Clarence's grandfather, Frank Jossey. In the mind of Maude Jossey Jordan, her father was a very special person. She was so devoted to her father that she had promised herself she would not marry as long as he was alive. And she did not!

Frank Jossey was a U.S. Treasury agent who received a presidential appointment to work in the western and southwestern parts of the United States. He took his family on an exciting life beyond Talbot County, Georgia, the narrative of which Maude Jossey Jordan wanted to pass on to her children. In those stories, her father was portrayed as a person of strength, dedication, and integrity. He tried to make a difference in the world. His life was not only the embodiment of competence and courage, but also justice in a larger world. Because of Maude Jossey Jordan's enthusiasm to portray her father in a good light, and because Clarence often found his own father "absent," it is likely that Frank Jossey came to embody, for Clarence, a "provider of identity" and what Erikson once called "one of the last representatives of a more homogeneous world."[18] What do the grandfathers' stories have to do with Koinonia?

An identification with the grandfathers and their worlds and values provides a way around the world of the fathers and the cultural fathers. This phenomenon provides for what Ernest Jones calls the "reversal of the generations," which allows for a way to win the confrontation with the values of the father and his generation and to begin the process of envisioning a spiritual father. In Clarence's case, his first image of God beyond the maternal world was, no doubt, that of a policeman in the sky who would enforce the rules and bring about a sense of justice. This image likely would have merged with the stories his mother loved to tell about her own childhood and the strong father who made a difference in the world.

Clarence's own hearing of his mother's stories, with her emphasis on a strong father/grandfather, became a fertile ground for Clarence to begin to imagine a spiritual father—a God who would make a difference and order the world with justice. The stories, as told by Clarence's mother and Martin England's grandmother, allowed these young men to conceptualize a time and place when justice might return to the land, and gave them the freedom to think they might be a part of that grand dream. Ironically, based in large measure on these stories of faith they heard about their grandfathers, Clarence and Martin were able to envision an alternative narrative to the way things were. In theological vision, they were "soul" mates. That is, as David Stricklin puts it, they "had the same vision for an interracial agricultural community."[19]

Koinonia As Ultimate Environment

Though the farm and its buildings were so run down when they first bought it that Florence Jordan had to wait in Louisville for repairs to be done, in time, Koinonia came to embody the idea of the dream Clarence and Martin shared. In fact, Martin Luther King, Jr., could well have evoked the vision and reality of Koinonia when he said in his famous speech, "I have a dream that one day on the red hills of Georgia, the sons of former slaves and the sons of former slave owners will be able to sit down together at the table of brotherhood." Indeed, that was exactly the vision Clarence Jordan had when he went to Sumter County, Georgia, in 1942. The rundown, 400-acre farm that he bought and named "Koinonia" came to mean far more than a red-dirt agricultural plot in Southwest Georgia. It came to stand for his dream at mid-life—for him, his thirtieth year. It was an ecological metaphor standing for reconciliation, for grace, for making the world whole, for repairing the fractures and brokenness of the human family.

As an ecological metaphor, Koinonia was first a dream—a life of thirty years in the making. It was a daring and dangerous, iconoclastic conception that was willing to risk all. It was a deeply sensitive dream that cared immensely. It was a dream—an imagined and lived reality—that required a life lived "in scorn of the consequences." At age 30, Clarence's conception of faith was reasoned and articulate. He had spent years working through the ideology in his mind. He had discovered the intellectual foundations for his ideology in Louisville, where he also learned to bring it to life in the ghetto. He had now come to Southwest Georgia to make the statement of his life. Koinonia was not, however, just an intellectual endeavor discovered in graduate school. It was the embodiment of a human struggle that extended backward in time to his early childhood. But it was also a personal struggle toward human wholeness that matched the struggle of an entire region—black and white. It was economic, it was social, and it was religious. Koinonia was the restatement of 100 years of history, and an effort to rework the religious, social, and economic identity of two groups of people who had lived at odds for over 200 years, depriving both groups of human wholeness.

Therefore, Koinonia as a metaphor for an ultimate environment, for Clarence Jordan at age 30, was a dangerous conception challenging a historic injustice and human *rapprochement*. As an alternative dream of ultimate reality, Koinonia, the mid-life conception of Jordan's faith, shattered the conception of normalcy as it had been conceived for 200 years. But, just as it demythologized that old vision of reality, it evoked a new dream of human possibility—of human relatedness beyond difference—for, in the dream of Koinonia as conceived by Jordan, God was no respecter of persons. Beyond shattering and evoking, however, Koinonia as ultimate vision gave energy to "enact," to live out, to demonstrate that new reality. This was the faith that Clarence Jordan and Martin England shared as they came to Sumter County, Georgia, in late fall 1942.

Chapter 10

Koinonia II: The Outpost of a New Order

We're gradually getting things underway here.... [But] the hardest thing about Koinonia Farm will not be making a crop but doing what Jesus said.

—Clarence Jordan

The Journey to the True Country:
Jordan's Narrative of the First Day

Despite the dreams and high seriousness, the narrative of Clarence Jordan's trip back to his native Georgia reads like the beginning of a Flannery O'Connor short story, with its emphasis on the grotesque. Clarence left Wakefield, Kentucky—the home of the Englands—at 5:30 in the evening in an old truck and trailer, both "loaded to the gills." The first six hours were fine. But, a little after midnight and about twenty-five miles outside of Nashville, Clarence ran out of gas. Thinking he could perhaps restart the engine, he allowed the truck to roll down the grade of the Tennessee hill, which led to an even greater problem. As he rolled down the hill, the trailer buckled and got "lengthwise" across the highway. Of course, there was nothing to do but unhook the overloaded trailer. When Clarence unhooked the trailer, the disproportionate weight on the back of the trailer caused it to "rear up," and it started rolling further down the grade. Then he wrote, "I swung onto it and, after bouncing up and down several times, I got it stopped." Then there was no other option but to take a can and walk to the nearest gas station. It was a cold November night in the Tennessee hills. The chill seemed to penetrate his bones. He began to look for ways to make the time pass quickly. So he started counting the fence posts. Cars passed but no one stopped until, finally, two young men in an old "flivver" had compassion. But, when Clarence got in and the driver began again, he noticed that the young man must have been drunk—he "zigzagged" back and forth across the road, all the way into the town.[1]

After Clarence bought a gallon of gas, the good-natured young men offered to drive him back to the truck. He wrote, "I was so cold and tired that I couldn't refuse, even though I was afraid to ride with them." Clarence got into the back seat, and as the car swayed from the drunken driving, some of his gasoline "sloshed out." Then one of the young men lit up a cigarette. Clarence held his breath, fearful that a spark might fall in the back seat. For a mile or more, Clarence watched as the car swerved from one side of the road to the other. Then, "the driver said he must have a flat tire because he couldn't hold it on the road." Clarence quickly agreed with him and told him he should let him out and go back to town quickly to get some air in his tires. So the young men let Clarence out of the car, and he walked the rest of the way back to the truck.[2]

Koinonia: An Average, Rundown Farm

Clarence arrived in Sumter County on November 13. The very next day, he wrote a card to Florence. The note began, "Dear Sweet, arrived here yesterday A.M. thoroughly worn out. Felt like I'll never recuperate. The truck made it all right, but gas was a problem...."[3] The next day, he wrote a two-page, single-spaced letter, which he began with "Dear Sweetheart...." He rehearsed the story from the diary described above about running out of gas outside of Louisville. Then Clarence described how he drove all night and through the next day, arriving in the Columbus, Georgia, area after the wartime curfew. So he was unable to get gas and had to spend the night in the truck because he could not find a place to stay. The next morning, on November 13, 1942, he pulled into the farm. He ended the letter by saying, "I surely miss you and my chillun. It just isn't going to be home until you come, 'cause I love you so much. Here are some hugs and kisses for you, Eleanor, and Freddie.—** **"[4]

Four days later, Clarence sent another long letter to Florence. "Dear Sweet," he began, "Already I'm a seasoned hand at chopping wood, but this plowing is something else." He and Martin had borrowed a team of mules to break up the ground for a winter garden, but when they stopped for dinner, the two mules had broken out of the barn and gone to the pasture and could not be caught. So Clarence and Martin took turns

135

pulling the plow. Clarence noted that he thought he would "make a better farmer than mule." But, in any case, the garden was planted with "onions, cabbage, carrots, turnips, beets, lettuce, rutabaga, mustard, spinach, and radish." "Your letter," Clarence wrote to Florence, "surely did cheer me up....Be sure to write as often as you can." Clarence ended by telling Florence that it was 78 degrees there—"just like summer." So he and Martin would go to the creek tomorrow for a bath.[5]

When both Clarence and Martin had finally arrived in Sumter County, they faced three immediate challenges: the dilapidated nature of the farm, the need to plant a winter garden, and the strange fact that there was a "gruff" white tenant farmer on the land left over from the previous owner. The tenant initially refused to leave. The agreement had been that he was to move after harvesting the crops. He promised Clarence and Martin he would move soon, but he had something of an attitude. "He acted as though imposed upon and moved with the slow air of authority, as if he owned the place and Clarence and Martin were unexpected and unwanted visitors"—as if they were the true "displaced persons."[6] But he did move on rather quickly, leaving two issues: the rundown farm and the winter garden.

Koinonia Farm, in its early days as a "rundown" tenant farm, was a "rather desolate-looking place." The land itself was ripped with gulleys and had few trees. There were a series of buildings on the property: "an old house, an old mule barn, an old cow barn, all of them about ready to fall down."[7] The barns were "sagging," the outbuildings and sheds were in disrepair, and there were also two rundown tenant houses.[8] The main farmhouse was a large, unpainted building with a wide hall down the middle and two rooms on each side. Clarence and Martin did what they could to the old farmhouse to fix it up a bit—enough so that Mabel England and the children moved in Christmas 1942. Mabel and the children needed to come in December so that Johnny, the oldest, could start school in January. But the old farmhouse still had serious problems. It was "crawling" with insects. Mabel England had to put mothball flakes under the bedsheets to keep the fleas out of the beds. The old house leaked like a "sieve," so when Clarence built a new, "state-of-the-art" chicken coop, Mabel begged to move into it. "It didn't leak, it was well heated, and would seat 2,000!"[9]

In early December, Clarence wrote to Florence and began in his typical fashion: "Dear Sweet...." Clarence then told Florence they had bought two milk cows and were getting more than three gallons of milk per day. They now had four pounds of butter in the refrigerator and had been able to give both sweet and buttermilk to Negro families in the area. Clarence thought this would be a valuable contact.[10]

For a time, in those first months before Florence came to share the burdens, Mabel later admitted that she "was a very frustrated mother and wife and hostess...." As she said, "I was it, you know, canning, gathering peaches, entertaining, whatever. I was it." In his spare time, Clarence attempted to help Mabel England adjust to farm life. Though she had lived and worked in Burma, there was much she did not know about rural living in the South. She had only been on a farm once before, when she was a child. So Clarence taught her how to make cottage cheese and butter. When Mabel's mother came to "inspect" her new living conditions, she simply walked in and began to shake her head. "Your grandmother," she said to Mabel, "started as a bride on a stove just like that one." Mabel took that to mean she had made no progress from her grandmother's earliest days.[11]

To make things worse, Clarence could not obtain the necessary permit to build a house for the Jordan family. During the war years, building materials were difficult to obtain, as were permits for buildings. So, when Florence moved to Georgia, she came to Talbotton to stay with Clarence's family until April that first year. By then, Clarence had obtained a permit to build a shop with an apartment upstairs. When it was completed, Florence and the children joined the group. Florence described the house as "at least campable." After she arrived, Florence helped to finish the painting and other things that needed to be done in order to move into the new building. But there were no modern amenities—no running water, no bathroom. The water had to be pumped by hand from the well, and the cooking was done on a small wood stove. Clothes were washed in an iron pot. The early years on the farm were "hard," Florence later said. "These kinds of things really sound awful now," she admitted. "But when you are young, everything is an adventure. You know you can do it! So we did."[12]

After the garden was planted, they set out to improve the farm in other ways. They also "set out" a series of trees: "apple, pecan, peach, walnut, pear, plum, fig, apricot, nectarine, Chinese chestnut, Japanese persimmon." Then they planted an assortment of other fruits and berries, including "grapes, scuppernongs, muscadines, strawberries, raspberries, improved blackberries, Youngberries, and Boysenberries."[13]

Clarence also purchased two milk cows and two hogs. One of the hogs later provided the excess meat shared with the neighbors. She appeared to be a "nice brood sow," but after she broke through the fence and took Clarence and his neighbors on a chase "over field and fence," the "death sentence" fell upon her.[14] She was a 350-pound brood sow, but when they got her back to the farm, they discovered that she was "pretty wild." Despite their best efforts, the sow broke through every effort to keep her in the pen. The last time the sow broke out, she was found a mile and a half down the road. On the way back to the farm, she began to charge at Clarence. Six men gathered to help Clarence, and all of them laughed at him for running from a hog. But then she chased one of the six men all over a pasture and, finally, escaped again to the woods. By the time she was found the next day, Clarence had decided to make pork chops and ham![15] "What once was a ferocious sow," Clarence wrote, "is now lard, bacon, sausage, pork chops, and ham." Even though this was the first butchering job, Clarence noted with some pride that "the two colored friends who helped us said we did it up like 'store-bought meat.'"[16]

Joining with the Baptists: Membership at Rehoboth

Clarence had grown up as a Baptist. Though, in time, Clarence would come to look at Koinonia as his church, when he first came to Sumter County, he did not think twice about church membership.[17] He joined the closest Baptist church. In the 1940s, no other religious group was closer to the people of the South. The Baptist church in December 1942 was virtually identical to the Southern vision of life and reality.[18] So Clarence announced to Florence in his Sunday letter on December 7, "I joined Rehobeth church today. The people all were exceptionally nice, I thought." When the services were over, the minister asked Clarence, "You are a farmer? You look sorta like a ministerial student." Jordan did not reply except to say, "Is that right?" Then, at the evening service, the preacher let Clarence know he had found out that Clarence was, indeed, a minister. He said, "Why didn't you tell me you were a preacher this morning?" Then Clarence went on to declare to Florence, "There's a grapevine somewhere." The later years, especially during the days of the FBI investigations, would show just how right Clarence was: the church was, indeed, connected to Southern reality.[19]

Trying to Pay a Debt: An Ongoing Letter-Writing Campaign

Perhaps late at night, when the other tasks were done for the day, Clarence tried to keep up his letter-writing campaign to raise funds for the farm. He wrote to Mrs. R.P. Halleck in Louisville asking for support. "I wonder," he wrote, "if I may be bold enough and humble enough to make a request of you—that, as Mr. England and I have invested our lives in this cause, you might help us, if you see fit, by investing some of your substance." Clarence went on to say to Mrs. Halleck that "we make not this request for ourselves, but for those whom we shall serve, Negroes and whites, the exploited, the poor, the friendless, who at this moment are living in the shabbiest of shanties, with hardly enough cotton which they helped pick to cover them and barely enough food they helped riase [*sic*] to feed them."[20] Clarence affirmed that he knew these people, for they are neighbors that can be helped if only the proper tools can be purchased. "We need a tractor or a team and equipment," he wrote. The cost will be approximately $650 to $1,000.[21] Although Clarence did not articulate the idea here, as in other places, the fundraising in the Koinonia project was part of the way he wanted to repay the debt that he felt he had already incurred—that he owed to the poor of the region.[22]

Clarence also wrote to Howard Johnson describing the "tremendous difficulties" they were facing. Though "we're gradually getting things underway," he wrote, there is so much to do and so many obstacles. We have virtually "no stock," or "implements," or "tools." There are "government restrictions" on almost all items. "We've really got a job on our hands." Clarence went on to confess, "I don't know that I have ever before realized so much my need of divine guidance, and the need to pray for deliverance from COMPROMISE." And, in a reflective moment, he wrote, "The hardest thing about Koinonia Farm will not be making a crop, but doing what Jesus said."[23]

The Challenge of Confrontation and Compromise:
  The Scorn of Neighbors and the First Visit from the Klan

When Clarence and Martin began to work the fields for spring planting, they hired a black worker who was a former sharecropper. The three men ate their noon meal together, which was a breach of the accepted Southern tradition. Clarence and Martin had hoped to make a witness of their faith from the beginning without alienating the community. But, as Clarence had written to Howard Johnson earlier, the pressure toward compromise was ever present. Yet Clarence and Martin knew they could not begin by eating apart from black people and then try to change that custom at a later date. So, from the beginning, the three men ate together. However, as people from the community came by to welcome the newcomers, they unexpectedly discovered that these men were in the regular practice of violating long-held tradition—they ate with black people.

After word had made its way through the community, a group of men came by to talk with Clarence. They told Clarence that they were from the Ku Klux Klan. This visit was an obvious effort to intimidate the two young ministers. There would be more serious confrontations later, but this visit gave the signal that the cultural "leaders" were aware of what was happening and that they meant to resist. "We are looking for Clarence Jordan," one of the men said. After Clarence identified himself, the man looked him square in the eye and said, "We understand that you been taking your meals with the nigger." Jordan replied slowly, "Well, now, at lunchtime we usually eat with a man we've hired." The spokesman from the Klan responded immediately, "We're here to tell you that we don't allow the sun to set on anybody who eats with niggers."[24]

Clarence knew Southern people and how to talk to them. In fact, he had been practicing his quick wit since childhood days. Looking at the leather-skinned faces of the men who had come to give the sternest kind of cultural warning and threat, Clarence reached out to the spokesman of the group and began shaking his hand with a big grin on his face, as if he were playing a joke on his schoolmates in the yard at Talbotton. He said quickly, "I'm a Baptist preacher and I just graduated from the Southern Baptist Seminary. I've heard about people who had power over the sun, but I never hoped to meet one." Clarence had done what he would go on to do time and time again—use humor at the most crucial moment to penetrate the illusions held by groups and put their defenses off guard. The Klansman, not knowing quite how to respond, gawked for a moment and then said, "I'm a son of a—I'm a son of a Baptist preacher myself...." Then they laughed and talked a bit as the sun went down in the west behind them.[25] For Jordan, laughter was often meant to create a pause for self-reflection for the listener and to create an opportunity for the hearer to open one's eyes. In this case, Jordan seemed to use humor for self-defense. There is no evidence to think that the Klan "opened their eyes." In fact, they would be back with more deadly force in the years ahead. But Clarence felt deeply that he could not back down or compromise.

Trying to Win the Day: Relating to the Neighbors

Clarence and his fellow Koinonians tried hard not to alienate people. They, in fact, had an intentional plan to try to win the community over, and to get the neighbors to see them as good people who were helpful to others. To that end, they tried many "outreach" programs. One of the most successful of the Koinonia outreach programs was Vacation Bible School—an old habit for Southerners. In fact, for a time, local whites helped in this and other Koinonia outreach programs. And, during the "laying-by" time of summer, they would drive across the country roads within a five or six-mile radius and bring as many as seventy children to the farm, where they would hold Bible classes, show films, and teach crafts to an interracial group.[26]

Clarence also shared his understanding of scientific farming with the neighboring farmers. He instituted a "cow library" by which poor families could check out a cow and keep her as long as she gave milk to sustain them. Clarence also shared ideas with other farmers about the poultry business, which thrived at Koinonia. He helped other farmers set up and establish their own poultry business, and he also created a marketing cooperative with other farmers for eggs. In addition, Jordan created a mobile peanut harvester, which helped farmers cut back on manpower during those war years when labor was scarce.[27]

A community project that turned out to be rather controversial was the transportation of young black children to school. The local school system did not provide for the transportation of black children to and from school. When Clarence was able to get some extra ration stamps, he used them to buy gas to transport the children. But this so infuriated some of the county residents that one of them wrote to Clarence's father in Talbotton with the charge that Clarence "was endangering his family by stirring up the Negroes and defying local custom." Clarence's father was ill and in failing health and had suffered a heart attack. When Clarence visited his father, without knowing of the letter, he was met with emotional concerns for his wellbeing and that of his family. Clarence was so upset that he got in his car and drove back to Sumter County to confront the man who had done this. There were also accusations against him sent to the county schoolboard.[28]

Mabel England also attempted to relate to the women of the community through membership in a local club for women. At one of the first meetings, one of the women announced that "next time you must wear your feedbag dress to show it off." Mabel did not know what the woman was talking about. She had never heard that there was a Southern custom of making dresses from the material in which the cattle feed was packaged. So the ladies had to explain the idea to her. Although Mabel attended the "feedbag-dress fashion show," she did not have a feedbag dress or a sewing machine on which to make one. Yet Mabel felt that, in the early years, the women were entirely accepting of her and the other Koinonians. She and the others at Koinonia were invited into the homes of the people. The group of women would often share ideas and information on how to "can" peaches or pickles or the like. The antagonism would come later. It was clear, however, from the earliest days that the members of the community did not understand the ideology behind Koinonia. It was obvious when they came to the farm and saw blacks and whites eating together that they did not understand the concept. According to Mabel, many of the Sumter County folks could not even pronounce "Koinonia" in the early days. They called it "cornucopia" instead.[29]

Suspect from the Start: An Early Visit from the FBI

On some level, the Koinonians were suspect from the start. In 1944, when John England was in the third grade, he took his stamp collection to school for "show-and-tell." It included both Burmese and Japanese stamps, and that made school officials even more suspicious—so much so, that the principal confiscated the stamp collection. The rumors began to spread—"the Koinonians are about to be investigated as spies!" Sure enough, as things go, a dark-blue car pulled into the farm one spring morning not long after. The car had an official emblem on the side and was driven by a young lieutenant in the Navy. The car arrived just as the postman came by. Mabel England came to the door and saw both. After later reflection, Mabel said, "That's all the postman wanted to see." The postman, Mabel thought, declared up and down the mail route: "They're really being investigated now."[30]

Mabel England had just washed her hair and it was in a turban. The lieutenant asked to speak to Martin. The young man was "polite but very cold." When Martin came in from the fields, the lieutenant said to him, "I understand that you had service in North Burma." England indicated that he had. Then the young officer said, "Well, I want—if you've got any pictures, I want to know the topography of that area, including the Burma Road." To this, England said, "You could get a fourth-grade geography book and learn as much...as I would be able to tell you." He went on to assert, "That's all I'm going to say." In other words, "I would not tell you one single word that might cause the harm—or worse, the death—of one single person, regardless of the race." Apparently, since the Japanese had taken over the area, little was now known about the area. So the lieutenant was given the assignment to talk to a list of people to gather information. Later on, England received a letter saying that, if he were interested in a job with "strategic importance," he could contact them. For her part, Mabel England thought this just added to the suspicion of them in the community. Mabel thought they will see us all as spies because the Englands have been in Burma, near Japan. Florence has a German background, and Clarence advocates strange ideas.[31]

In fall 1944, the Englands were called back to the mission field by the American Baptist Mission. In September, they left for a period of training at Cornell University. Their departure, however, was a signal of how the people of Sumter County thought about the Koinonians. At their last Sunday at Rehoboth Baptist Church, just four miles north of Koinonia, the pastor asked Martin and Mabel England to stand at the front of the church so that the congregation could say farewell. The people of the congregation came by to shake their hands and wish them well. Mabel England remembered that "there was hardly a dry eye in the place, and we'd only been there two years and most of them slipped money into our hands."[32]

The Signed Blank Check:
Endorsing Another Generation of Disciples

Clarence continued his speaking engagements even after he went to Sumter County. He used those occasions for the larger cause—to spread his own interpretation of the kingdom and to make friends for Koinonia. Because of his own powers of persuasion and the magnetic and authentic power of his personality, many were drawn to him. And, in due course, after the war, many were drawn to Koinonia Farm. One of the first students to come to Koinonia for an extended time was Foy Valentine. He came to Sumter County in summer 1945. Clarence had invited Valentine to come and spend the time in the summer before he went to seminary in Ft. Worth in fall 1945. The Englands were gone, and Clarence needed help.

Foy Valentine was a twenty-one-year-old young man. Koinonia was not quite three years old. Valentine later wrote that it was a "glorious summer"—"a wonderful, rip-roaring, rousing, delightful time." Clarence showed the young man how to do many things: work in peanut patches, cut wood, gather wild grapes, build a room. Koinonia was in its earliest stages, and Clarence's sense of idealism was contagious for a young college graduate from Baylor. Valentine's assessment of Jordan at the time was that he had an "awesome" amount of courage, scholarship that was "impeccable," and an impact for Christ that was "emphatically growing."[33]

Valentine and Jordan preached and played music all over "that part of the country." Clarence played the trumpet and Valentine the saxophone. Some of the church members were "startled" to hear renditions of

"When Shall I Read My Title Clear?" and "Mansions in the Sky." But it was "Laying By" time in South Georgia, and the farmers were free to rest for a time and to come to church. In addition to the church activities, Jordan took Valentine to visit the neighbors, work on improving race relations, and study the Greek New Testament. When Valentine, who would later become a voice of conscience for the Southern Baptist Convention as the Executive Director of the Christian Life Commission, got ready to leave for Fort Worth—and did so with, essentially, no money in his pocket—Jordan put a piece of paper in his hand. The piece of paper was "a blank check, good for every penny Koinonia Farm had in the bank, made out to [Foy Valentine] and signed, 'C.L. Jordan.'" Valentine never cashed the check, but he kept it for a lifetime as a "tangible reminder of Clarence Jordan's trust, of his fathomless faith, of his contagious Christian experience, and of his profound commitment to be a doer of the word."[34]

Another student Clarence met in the 1940s was Will Campbell. Having just returned from the war in the Pacific, Will had enrolled in Wake Forest College. He had not heard of Clarence Jordan or Koinonia Farm, but Clarence came to Wake Forest in spring 1946 for a religious emphasis week. Clarence talked about race relations, pacifism, and economic equality—all in relation to the gospels. Will had never heard anyone speak like that before. He was both "intrigued and threatened." After listening to Clarence that week, Will went by to talk with Clarence personally. Will was interested in hearing more about Koinonia and the possibility of coming to join Clarence there. Clarence encouraged Will to stay in school and finish his education—the struggle would not be won before he finished, Clarence said. Will became close friends with Clarence over the years that followed, but he never came to live at Koinonia.[35]

A Radicalized Faith Tested:
The Reinstitution of a Military Draft

At the end of World War II in August 1945, the American people had demanded the demobilization of the military. But, less than three years later, signs of world conflict loomed on the distant horizon and President Truman once again called for a military draft. On July 20, 1948, he called for some ten million men to register for the draft in the next two months. Memories were still vivid from the years of sacrifice from 1941 to 1945. Clarence Jordan's own ideas about war had only "radicalized." Despite the atrocities that took place in World War II, Clarence would not accept any rationalization for war. Clarence concluded that he would render unto Caesar what was Caesar's, but not what was God's. In other words, since it was immoral to kill, and God had ordered that one should love the enemy, Clarence could see no redemptive element in being a soldier. In his mind, for churches to condone the process of war creates a sort of spiritual schizophrenia, which troubled both returning soldiers and young men contemplating forthcoming wars.[36]

In summer 1948, Clarence Jordan was 36 years old and beyond the age for draft registration. But he remained very concerned about the issue of the draft. Consequently, Clarence joined with 300 other ministers in signing a petition calling on young men to refuse to register for the draft. There were two young men—Millard Hunt and Jack Singletary—at Mercer University who were eligible for the draft and were very troubled by it. They both refused to register for the draft because of their faith, and gave statements to their draft boards stating so. Both young men were arrested by the FBI in October and scheduled for trial the following April. Jack Singletary spent the intervening time at Koinonia, and Millard Hunt often came down from Macon. Although Clarence attempted to vouch for them as a character witness, both young men were found guilty by the judge and sentenced to a year and a day. Clarence was investigated by the FBI for any role he might have played in the decisions of these young men to violate the registration act, but, apparently, there was not enough evidence for the legal process against Clarence to go forward.[37]

There were two statements in the trial that likely reflected the prevailing cultural assessment of Clarence's involvement, however. One of the character witnesses for the young men was a minister who had been a former Army chaplain, and he told the court he had tried to persuade the young men to take a less radical stand. He went on to say that the "real culprits" were not in the courtroom, and that he felt "nothing but contempt" for the 300 ministers who had signed the petition advocating the violation of Truman's registration act. Likewise, the judge said, "I may be wrong, but I have a feeling that these young men may have been ill-advised. I am certain in my own mind that they did not and could not have taken this stand from their religious training and from the institutions that I know of...."[38]

Koinonia and Dangerous Faith: Clarence Jordan's Ultimate Environment in the 1940s

At the end of the 1940s, with the Englands gone back to Burma and Clarence and Florence struggling to hold a dream together, a number of young, committed Christians were being attracted to Koinonia in large measure, due to the authentic and contagious witness of Clarence Jordan. Koinonia as a metaphor for Jordan's own ultimate environment—the map of his own vision of ultimate reality—was increasingly courageous as it began to encounter cultural resistance. Clarence was himself, as he indicated early on in the decade, struggling not to compromise with the culture. The stories about Clarence from the 1940s show that his faith during this era can be described as deeply reflective and critical of any cultural *rapprochement*. One of the dangers of such reflective faith is "an excessive confidence in the conscious mind and in critical thought...in which the now clearly bounded, reflective self over-assimilates 'reality' and the perspectives of others into its own worldview."[39] One can create caricatures of the other. For example, Carlyle Marney was once reminded that he should never forget the "bent knees and the loyal spirits of those who will never understand."[40]

Jordan began Koinonia with an iconoclastic, unbending faith, and the social interaction of the earliest years actually presaged the conflict that was to come. The theme of Koinonia, from its earliest days, was "faith against faith"—Jordan's iconoclasm against the conventions of an entire people. Despite his biting critique, Clarence worked hard in his personal interactions with the people of the region to demonstrate that he was a caring and constructive member of the community. In his interaction with the Klan, Clarence attempted to relate to the men as human beings. But the conflict was inevitable.[41] Jordan's individualized perspective on religion and race ran counter to the cultural assumptions. He felt strongly that he could not compromise, and the cultural assumptions required that if one were to be accepted. Consequently, Jordan, by virtue of who he was and what he thought, was a direct threat to the culture. And the threat would eventually erupt in violence.

Throughout the 1940s, Clarence continued to go to the churches and speak and teach and attempt to win the people over to what he saw as a larger vision—a Christian witness on behalf of the poor and exploited. But it is also clear that there was resistance, from the earliest days, to his faith and vision. The early visit from the Klan, the rumors that were abundant in the community, the investigation by the FBI—all were harbingers of the dangers of cultural conflict that would erupt violently in the years ahead. What seemed to bring some semblance of balance to the early years were the courage, humor, and wisdom Jordan demonstrated throughout that decade, all while maintaining his zealously reflective faith at virtually every turn. Yet the narrative of Clarence Jordan's lived faith of the 1940s leaves the reader all but knowing that the 1950s and 1960s will demand an even more steadfast, deeper, and ever increasingly profound faith, if his commitment to his dream is to continue "in scorn of the consequences." But one also senses that the iconoclastic and uncompromising faith of Clarence Jordan will, eventually and inevitably, erupt in serious conflict with the conventional assumptions of the region.

Clarence Jordan's childhood home, built in 1907 and burned in 1926.

Clarence Jordan's teenage home, built in 1927.

Photo by Jonathan Downing, 2016

Talbotton Baptist Church
Founded in 1828, the present structure was built in 1924 with
Spanish Colonial Revival Architecture. This was Jordan's church
during his teenage years.

Photo by Jonathan Downing, 2016

Talbot County Jail

During Jordan's youth, the jail yard was the site of a chain gang, an extension of the convict lease system. A series of five or six metal wagons were moved from place to place to utilize the convict labor on public work projects. The wagons were likely built by Manly Steele of Dalton, Georgia, and resemble the wagon currently on display in Fitzgerald, Georgia.

Photos by Fred Downing, 1987

A chain gang of prisoners in North Carolina, ca. 1910–1920
In the foreground is J. Z. McLawhorn who was a county
superintendent of chain gangs.

Mullins Hall

Built in 1926, Mullins Hall at The Southern Baptist Theological Seminary in Louisville, Kentucky, was Jordan's home while living on campus.

Haymarket, 1932
The Haymarket at Jefferson and Market Streets in Louisville, Kentucky.

Union Gospel Mission, 1935
Union Gospel Mission at 114 E Jefferson Street, Louisville, Kentucky.

Haywagon at Koinonia Farm, ca. 1943
Riders in the wagon include Florence and Clarence Jordan, and Mabel and Martin England. The Jordans' dog is in the foreground.

Koinonia Archives

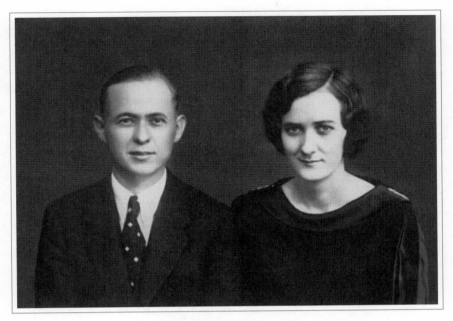

Mabel and Martin England in an early photograph.

Clarence Jordan at Ridgecrest, North Carolina.

Koinonia Archives

The Jordan Family, ca. 1946
Florence, Clarence, Eleanor and Jim.

Koinonia Archives

Planting Corn at Koinonia Farm, ca. 1950
Jim Jordan, Lora Brown, Bobby Engram, and Bo Johnson.

Photo by Howard Johnson, Koinonia Archives

First College Work Group at Koinonia Farm, ca. 1951
This photo shows the type of setting that Clarence Jordan
preferred for exploring the gospel.

Koinonia Archives

Foy Valentine, who became director of the Christian Life Commission of the SBC, spent several months at Koinonia in the summer of 1948. Pictured in the photo are Florence, Clarence with Jan Jordan, Mrs., R. F. Howard and son, Allene and Harry Atkinson, Foy and Mary Louise Valentine, and Maggie Moore.

Assembly at Vacation Bible School group, Koinonia Farm, Summer 1950.

Koinonia Archives

Clarence with Millard Fuller, Koinonia Farm, ca. 1968.

Koinonia Archives

Clarence's Writing Shack, Koinonia Farm.

Above photo by Wally Howard; below photo by Jonathan Downing, 2016

Clarence at Furman University, Greenville, South Carolina, ca. 1969.

Furman University Archive

PICNIC HILL

CLARENCE JORDAN 1912-1969

FLORENCE JORDAN 1912-1987

DAUGHTER, ELEANOR 1937-1991

GOD HAS MADE US OUT OF THIS OLD SOIL AND WE GO
BACK TO IT, AND WE NEVER LOSE ITS CLAIM ON US

Above, Picnic Hill, Koinonia Farm; below Picnic Hill Memorial

Photos by Jonathan Downing, 2016

Koinonia Farm, aerial view, ca. 1972.

Photo by Les Taylor, Koinonia Archives

Chapter 11

Rehoboth: The Struggle for the Southern Soul

Seldom in Christendom does one read of a more remarkable incident than that reported...[by] Clarence Jordan...that he and others
had been excluded from Rehoboth Baptist Church...because they
treated Negroes...as they believed Christ would approve.
—S.L. Morgan, Sr.

Clarence Jordan joined the nearly 100-year-old Rehoboth Baptist
Church on the first Sunday of December 1942, only weeks after his arrival in Sumter County. During his time there, he and Florence both took
a very active role in the church. Clarence often played his trumpet and
led the music, and sometimes preached in the services. Florence played
the piano, taught Sunday-school classes, and participated in the women's
organizations. But there was a grapevine. That grapevine carried any hint
of information about Clarence and Koinonia as a perceived threat to the
community's way of life.[1] Clarence would likely begin to understand that
"grapevine" more clearly once he began to talk with the FBI. But, in
truth, Clarence Jordan had come to Sumter County to be a "change
agent." As Florence later admitted, "The reason we came down here
[was] because we didn't think the church was teaching all of the things
that Jesus taught." For a time, "we were the fair-haired children," in the
same manner that a Baptist preacher and his wife often are in the South.
But then, about 1949, the church people began to see that "we really
meant what we were talking about."[2]

The Grapevine at Work: Intensified Suspicion for Jordan

From the beginning, Clarence and his fellow Koinonians were under the watchful eyes of the community, who were naturally wary of
strangers. But Clarence, hoping to maintain a sense of integrity to his
vision, sought not to compromise. The custom of eating with African-

American workers, adopted from the start, was seen by the local community as a "shot across the bow." The Klan was alerted from the very first awareness of this breach of tradition. Likewise, the effort to bus the black children to school was also seen as a dangerous and subversive attempt to destabilize the economy and the status quo. The school superintendent reported to a relative what he thought was the consensus of white people in the region: "Koinonia is a cancer that should be removed."[3] Furthermore, Jordan's pacifist approach was an affront to the cultural sense of patriotism. Yet, for a time, Clarence was able to work toward his dream unhindered, though the rumor mill was clearly at work.

Clarence was able to promote Koinonia both locally and across the nation for a time, and, toward the end of that decade, a number of students began to come to the farm to participate in the egalitarian ideal. However, during the last three years of that era, a series of events began to unfold that intensified local suspicion of Clarence and his fellow Koinonians. In truth, it was the growing suspicion of Clarence and Koinonia and the resulting tension that would presage the community's rejection of his dream. Clarence knew from the beginning that the issues were primarily religious and theological. As a Southern Baptist church, Rehoboth exemplified an accepted set of mores that were culturally affirmed. That is, the Baptist tradition in the South was a major component of the Southern soul and included an understanding of the "Southern way of life." Consequently, for Jordan to go up against the accepted values of Rehoboth Baptist Church was to challenge the Southern sense of custom and order—and, thereby, threaten the people at the deepest level. In that sense, when Clarence spoke of commitment to God and a lived faith, he was, in fact, describing a very different reality than what the members of Rehoboth knew deep in their souls. As Florence later indicated, the people of Rehoboth came to see how serious Clarence and his fellow Koinonians were late in the 1940s.

Pioneers on a Dangerous Frontier: Koinonia in Confrontation with the Culture

Although Clarence and others at Koinonia violated Southern tradition daily by eating with African Americans, by paying higher wages, and by being an example of how the two races could live together, the white

people of Sumter County did not seek to stop their activities. It was, rather, when the progressive attitudes began to spill over into the public
arena that the strong reactions began to come. It appears that the whites
of Sumter County and Rehoboth Baptist Church, as a traditional guardian of culture, almost instinctively began to impose limits on what Clarence and the Koinonians could do when they reached a certain point. At
issue, it seems, for the members of Rehoboth, was not just the willingness of Clarence and the members of Koinonia to violate the customs
and accepted mores of Southern life, but, rather, the nature of the violation and where it took place. Put another way, while Clarence and the
Koinonians saw real success in the first decade in cultivating and foster-
ing interracial relationships and advancing the cause of African Americans in Sumter County, at the end of that decade, they were confronted
by the church, which saw itself as the moral guardian of Southern society. Rehoboth began to establish real limits as to how far Clarence and
Koinonia would be able to go in living out shared ideals that ran counter
to accepted Southern tradition.[4] Clarence was right. The "grapevine" was
clearly in place.

One of the first incidents that put Koinonia in a confrontation with
Rehoboth involved Harry Atkinson, who had first heard Clarence at a
religious emphasis week at Stetson University in Deland, Florida. Clarence had been very helpful to Harry in helping him clarify his own thinking. Harry came to the farm in 1949 and soon became a member at Rehoboth. Being young, idealistic, and perhaps a bit naive about the power
and strength of Southern mores, he invited the black chauffeur of one of
the Rehoboth members to join his Sunday-school class. Church members at Rehoboth were so angered by the situation that they began to
pressure the Koinonians to leave the church. Atkinson did withdraw
from the church, but Clarence and the others resisted. Following this
incident, it became clear that relationships between the farm members
and Rehoboth were becoming very strained.[5]

A second incident involved Miss Willie Pugh, who was a recent
graduate of Blue Mountain College in Mississippi, where she was Baptist
Student Union president and had heard Clarence Jordan speak. For a
time, she taught in the public school system in Mississippi before coming
to Koinonia in 1949. At that time, she was the only woman at the farm

besides Florence. Willie Pugh and Norman Long organized the Vacation Bible School. She also helped to start a Friday-night fellowship for young people, and she would often go into the homes of local blacks for informal meetings.[6] At some point in 1949, Willie Pugh accompanied two young black girls to Americus to buy clothes. After shopping, she took them to get ice cream. A deacon from Rehoboth saw Willie Pugh walking back to the vehicle holding hands with the young girls. The deacon was irate because of the way Willie Pugh had violated the cultural tradition of separation between the races. The deacon went back to Rehoboth and told church members that the Koinonians should be dismissed from the church.[7]

Another potentially explosive event took place with Willie Pugh on the farm itself. As the story goes, the Koinonians were working around the clock to get the fields ready for spring planting. One night, Willie Pugh was assigned a nightshift for plowing. She drove to a distant field to take the shift after Bo Johnson, a young black man. Apparently, a neighboring farmer saw Miss Pugh go into the field where a young black man was in the dark of night. He promptly reported what he saw as an incident to the "authorities." When Miss Pugh came back in from the field the next morning, she discovered that the sheriff had already come by to "investigate." Another neighbor, who was a friend to the Koinonians, came by with his own questions in order to ensure that the "encounter" was truly just a shift change. Gossip along the "grapevine" was so intense that it was picked up by an out-of-town newspaper reporter, who also came by to ask questions. Bo Johnson had been put in a life-threatening situation and was sent to West Palm Beach, Florida, for two weeks until the tensions eased.[8]

Americus, Georgia, was like other small towns all across the South in the 1940s and 1950s. Segregation between blacks and whites was the rule of the day and was strictly enforced in the public arena of small-town life. Lunch counters, movie theaters, churches, public drinking fountains—all were protected by long-held customs and taboos. Consequently, when Norman Long, a graduate of Colgate Rochester Seminary who came to the farm in 1950, decided to take his black friend Alma Jackson, who had been coming to the Bible study, to the theater in town, Norman thought it best to go with Alma to the "Colored" section. Norman likely had no idea that, in doing so, he was also violating the Southern custom. It is very likely that he was greatly surprised when the authorities came and removed him from the theater.[9]

The Discovery of the Grapevine: Clarence, the FBI, and the Criminal Division

In 1949, Clarence came to understand that the Sumter County sheriff was not the only one wanting to investigate Koinonia and Jordan himself. On April 23, 1949, a case was opened against Clarence Jordan at the request of the Criminal Division, Department of Justice.[10] The suspicion was that Jordan had illegally counseled young men to refuse to participate in the draft. In reading the pages of Jordan's FBI report, one gets a vivid sense of how the FBI worked in this era and what the citizens of Sumter County, Georgia, thought of Clarence Jordan in those days. In short, the "grapevine" is clearly revealed. It involved a network of informants sending information to agents, who, in turn, sent the material to the bureau. But it also involved agents actively seeking information on Jordan and his motivations—and, finally, involved an interview with Jordan himself. There were three stages to the FBI's interest in Clarence Jordan. In the late 1940s, the FBI was told that Jordan had influenced Millard Hunt and Jack Singletary. This accusation could have resulted in criminal prosecution. Second, the bureau became interested again in Jordan and Koinonia after the Sumter County Grand Jury made accusations against Jordan and Koinonia that they were involved in subversive activity as a communist front organization. And, finally, the FBI began surveillance of Clarence Jordan again in the violent days after the death of Martin Luther King, Jr., especially when Jordan attempted to integrate the First Methodist Church of Americus.[11]

Jordan's FBI files reveal that there were two major issues of greatest concern to the local population: Jordan's association with blacks, especially eating with them in his home; and his attitude toward war, including his failure to participate in the war effort in any way, such as his refusal to buy war bonds. A related matter was his outspoken criticism of war itself. On August 1, 1948, the *Albany Sunday Herald* published an article on Clarence and Koinonia that tended to spark the criticism. The article was written by Sam Chambliss and was titled "A Matter of the

Mind: 10 Persons, Negroes and Whites, Live Together in Americus Plan." In addition to the portrayal of Koinonia as an interracial community, the article indicated that all members were conscientious objectors to military service, and that two young men eligible for the draft were refusing to register. The article "caused considerable comment and discussion in the Rehoboth Church circles...."[12]

A group of deacons from the church came to talk with Clarence after they read the Albany article. They told Clarence that associating with Negroes was "contrary to local custom." They also told Jordan that he was "becoming a disruptive influence" in the church, and they suggested that he should leave the church. Clarence began to justify his position by quoting scripture. Clarence told the group that all of the Koinonians agreed with him.[13] One year later, Clarence and all of the other Koinonia members would be forced out of Rehoboth.

Though the issue of associating with blacks was a serious breach of local custom, as the deacons informed Clarence, and would erupt a year later, it was the question of counseling Millard Hunt and Jack Singletary that actually brought the potential of criminal liability. Millard Hunt was interviewed by FBI agents on September 20, 1948. He was arrested on September 29, 1948, and indicted on January 19, 1949. He was later sentenced to a year and a day for evading the draft. His father, R.T. Hunt of Sanford, Florida, wrote to the FBI and stated that "he believed that his son's failure to register was the responsibility of [Clarence] Jordan." The elder Hunt wrote, "I have been trying very hard from every angle to find out why Millard took the stand that he did. I have traced it down to one angle. Millard has been closely associated with Dr. Clarence Jordan...and it is my belief that it is the influence of Dr. Jordan that has caused all this disturbance."[14]

After a lengthy investigation, Jordan himself was interviewed. Clarence denied the accusation that he had counseled individuals not to register for the draft. He said that, as a Baptist preacher, he did not try to coerce others into taking his position. He further stated that he thought the free discussion of ideas was neither illegal nor immoral, and that he always advised every individual that he or she must take responsibility for the interpretation of scripture and the formation of individual belief. Clarence indicated that he had registered for the draft under the Act of

1949, and that he had been a pacifist since 1932, when he resigned from the ROTC. The case was turned over to the U.S. Attorney in Macon, who declined to prosecute Jordan based on the lack of "positive and specific evidence that subject [Jordan] had actually counselled men within the draft age not to comply with the provisions of the Selective Service Act of 1948."[15]

The Struggle for the Southern Soul:
  Clarence Jordan Expelled from Rehoboth

By August 1950, local suspicion of Clarence and Koinonia had grown to the point that an open confrontation was possible. The event that moved the Rehoboth congregation to action again was another perceived violation of Southern custom. The members at Rehoboth were fearful that Clarence and the other Koinonians would bring blacks into their church, as, indeed, Harry Atkinson had attempted a few months before. So they were ever vigilant and overly suspicious of anyone who came with Clarence and the others. On the first Sunday of August 1950, the congregation thought their suspicions were well founded. A dark-skinned international student from India, R.C. Sharma, was studying at Florida State University. He had heard of Clarence's teaching on nonviolence and he came up to the farm to visit for a weekend. Perhaps, as a Hindu, like Gandhi, Sharma was interested in Christian interpretation of the Sermon on the Mount and its relationship to the Gita, which can be read as an internal dialogue involving one's deepest self—a struggle for self-mastery between the forces of light and darkness in every heart.[16] Yet Sharma had no way of knowing that he would, by his very presence in Americus, ignite such an observable human struggle that became a window into the soul of an entire culture—into the Southern soul.

Sharma had wanted to visit an American Protestant church while in the United States. So, while his skin was dark, apparently Clarence and the other church members at Koinonia did not conceive that it would be problematic in any way. Consequently, when Sharma asked to go to church, he was taken to Rehoboth with Clarence and the others on August 6, 1950. The members at Rehoboth, ever vigilant that Clarence might bring his radical ideas into the church, saw the dark-skinned Sharma and mistook him for one of the black farmworkers Clarence had employed. Florence later indicated, "We thought the people would be delighted to meet him." In reality, the people were outraged, thinking Jordan was trying to bring a black man into the church. The pastor, Ira Flaglier, came by the farm to tell Clarence that he and the others had brought "disunity" into the church.[17]

Apparently, after the pastor's visit, a group of men from the church also came by to see Clarence and asked that he and the other members from Koinonia agree not to come back to the church. Clarence did agree to apologize to the church if he had done anything wrong or had offended anyone. Then Clarence handed a Bible to one of the men and asked the group to show him where he and the others had done anything wrong. In response, the man slammed the Bible down and said, "Don't give me any of this Bible stuff!" Perhaps getting a bit exasperated himself, Clarence told the men that, if they could not accept the Bible as the inspired word of God, perhaps *they* should leave the church. At that point, the men left, apparently also very frustrated. Clarence and Howard Johnson, a young Auburn graduate who had recently come to the farm, began to visit each of the deacons individually. They met with three of them before Clarence received a letter saying that action would be taken the following Sunday, August 13, to expel them from the church. Clarence called the pastor and told him he would be out of town preaching at Dexter Avenue Baptist Church in Montgomery on that day, and asked if this action could be postponed. The pastor agreed that he would try to have the business session delayed. But, in fact, a resolution was read in church the following Sunday.[18]

The resolution listed the names of the members from Koinonia: Clarence and Florence, and their daughter, Eleanor; Howard Johnson and his wife; and Willie Pugh. The central argument of the resolution was that they "have brought people of other races into the services of the Rehoboth Baptist Church, and have done this with the knowledge that such practices were not in accord with the practices of other members of Rehoboth Church...." After a litany of similar charges, the resolution read, "Therefore, we recommend that the Rehoboth Baptist Church do on this 13th day of August, 1950, withdraw fellowship from any who are members of Koinonia Farm, and that their names be stricken from the church roll." Two-thirds of the congregation stood in favor of the motion. Then the people got quiet for a long time, Jordan recounted. Then someone began to sob, and soon others joined. For five minutes, the congregation cried quietly. Then they got up and, one by one, they began to go out the door.[19]

When Clarence returned from Montgomery and talked the matter through, he and the others decided to return to the church the next Sunday as if nothing had happened. But they were rebuffed the following Sunday and, later, told they were no longer welcome. Clarence agreed, so long as he could come back and read a statement to the church about why they no longer attended. So, on August 27, 1950, Clarence went to Rehoboth for the last time.[20]

In the church business session that day, a deacon stood and made a motion that anyone from Koinonia should be requested to refrain from attending services at Rehoboth. Apparently, this was meant to speak to the fact that Clarence and others had come back to the church services after they were expelled. During the discussion of this motion, Clarence stood and read a statement explaining why he and the others would not be back. He began by saying, "It is our desire…that it be clearly understood that our absence would be due, not to any malice or lack of forgiveness or willingness to attend on our part, but to the will and action of the church itself.…" He ended by saying, "May there be a ready willingness for a reconciliation which would involve no sacrifice of conscience or compromise of the Lord's truth."[21]

Were You There When They Crucified My Lord?:
The Spirituality of Deacon Bowen As a Divine Irritant

On the Wednesday following Jordan's last appearance at Rehoboth, the chairman of the board of deacons, Deacon Bowen, a sensitive and elderly man, came to Koinonia to see Clarence. Bowen said, "Brother Jordan, I need to talk with you." Then he told Jordan that there might be trouble in the days ahead. Bowen did not claim to know what would happen, but he wanted Jordan and his family to know that they could be in some danger. So Bowen asked Clarence not to travel in the manner that he usually did until the situation calmed down a bit.[22]

When Bowen got ready to leave, he still appeared to be very concerned. So Clarence asked if there were something else on his mind.

"Oh, nothing special," Bowen said. Clarence had a sense that the man had something important he needed to talk about. So Clarence said to him, "Well, if you don't have anything special, what you got 'unspecial' on your mind?" Then Bowen began to tell Clarence his burden: "Well, I'll tell you what it is....I haven't slept since Sunday." He added, "I have heard the clock strike every hour." Clarence asked, "What's your problem?" Bowen replied, "Every time I get ready to sleep, I hear singing, and it sounds like people are coming into the room." Then the old man started sobbing. Clarence asked, "Well, do you know what they are singing?" Bowen responded, "That's just it, I do know what they are singing." Clarence asked, "What is it?" And Bowen answered, "They are singing 'Were You There When They Crucified My Lord?'"[23]

Then Bowen painfully admitted to Clarence, "I was [there] and I helped....I have come to ask your forgiveness." Clarence immediately responded, "Well, you have it....You know that." Then Clarence went on to say, "I know the position you're in....Of course, you have my forgiveness." Then the old man asked Clarence if he would ask the Lord to forgive him, to which Clarence immediately replied, "No." The deacon did not understand—Clarence had just quickly forgiven him, so why would he not intervene on his behalf with the Almighty? Clarence explained that, when he wanted forgiveness from Clarence, he had come to Clarence, and that he would have to do the same with the Lord. Deacon Bowen asked Clarence if he would go with him in his prayers to God. There was a big tree out in the yard, and the two men knelt down under the tree while the old man prayed fervently. When he ended his prayer, he felt forgiven. But he did not know what to do next. He told Clarence, "I can't go into a church that won't have you in it." Clarence's response was, "What you do, you don't get out of the church; you live so that they kick you out." Bowen got the point and agreed, "I'll do it." So he started a new era of his life as a "divine irritant." Unfortunately, he did not live long after that, but as long as he lived, he kept his promise to Clarence.[24]

Who Is Their God? What Kind of People Worship Here?

In his famous protest statement, *The Letter from Birmingham Jail,* Martin Luther King, Jr., raised issues central to the Rehoboth episode. He states that he has traveled across the South—all the Southern states.

And, with impressive prose, he addresses an important question in Southern religion and culture. "On sweltering summer days and crisp autumn mornings," King writes, "I have looked at the South's beautiful churches with their lofty spires pointing heavenward." Yet, with his understanding of the region and its culture, King is motivated to ask, "What kind of people worship here? Who is their God?"[25]

Had King known about the Rehoboth episode, he could have addressed those two pointed questions directly to this church. Put differently, how can it be that a group of people, headed by Clarence Jordan, are put out of a church for acting in the manner that Christ most assuredly would have acted? What is the nature of such a church and a culture to which Clarence Jordan is attempting to address himself? In part, the answer is that Rehoboth Baptist Church was founded in 1845, fifteen years before the beginning of the Civil War, and that there is a burden of history this church has been called upon to bear.

When Rehoboth Baptist Church came into existence in the 1840s, other Baptist churches in the Deep South were in the process of institutionalizing a frontier heritage of revivalism and evangelistic fervor. The ministers continued a tradition of an uncomplicated gospel compressing the full sweep of the biblical revelation into one demand: get right with God before it is too late. The Civil War focused the issues for churches like Rehoboth. Feeling that they were responsible to hold Southern life together and to sanctify its ways, Southern ministers developed a proslavery argument before the Civil War, lest the demise of slavery doom Southern life and culture. After the war, Southern religion helped the people cope with anxiety, but churches like Rehoboth became more regional now than before. The religion of the South met the needs of its people by exalting an eternal spiritual victory placed in reach of all, and religion was often used to legitimate the cultural system. In other words, the primary task for the shared memory system after the war was how to make a way of life legitimate when it had been declared illegitimate. The primary role of Southern religion preached and shared at Rehoboth became that of conserving and reinforcing popular white Southern culture. The traditional values of Southern culture that Southern religion sought to uphold were: the inferior status of African Americans, the agrarian or semi-agrarian society as the moral arrangement for living, and Southern society as favored by God. Southern religion had been molded and shaped by the frontier and Civil War eras, and was basically status-quo or continuity-oriented. Such was the burden of Southern history and the gospel that came to be treasured at Rehoboth.[26]

But this is not just the story of one church in Sumter County, Georgia. It is the story of an entire region. And, in terms of religion, the region continued to be the "solid South" until the time of Clarence Jordan's death. That is, as a historically distinct region, the South continued as a coherent collection of values and assumptions. Consequently, the confrontation of Clarence Jordan and Rehoboth Baptist Church can be understood by the Southern legacy and distinctive role of religion in the region—to legitimize the culture and its people. The distinctive history of religion in the South gives Rehoboth Baptist Church a divided loyalty—in essence, the church is pulled in two directions, as illustrated by Deacon Bowen's dilemma. The love ethic of Christianity is modified by the traditions and values of Southern culture. Put differently, both religion and regionality are primary frameworks of meaning for the people of Rehoboth. In the practical, day-to-day ordering of society, regionality becomes predominant and the primary framework of meaning. The love of God takes a back seat to Southern custom. Consequently, as in the story of Clarence and Rehoboth, regionality—or "Southernness"—becomes a type of "god above God." There is so much pressure from peers and the shared assumptions of the culture that the Southernness as a cultural system demands something like a total loyalty. Southern mores take on a type of divine quality.[27] Hence, good people like Deacon Bowen are pulled into doing things they know, on some level, are wrong.

His Number Is Legion: The Spiritual
Schizophrenia of the Southern Church

The confrontation with such a severely divided religious personality would not be lost on Clarence Jordan, and would, in time, lead to his most scathing critique and become what Charles Marsh called "Jordan's biggest threat to the Southern Christian establishment...his relentless effort to demonstrate that Southern white evangelicalism was built on an ancient Christian heresy." Jordan, in his last years, would scandalize the Southern church by his proclamation that it was "docetic" to the core.

That is, the church never understood how to affirm the humanity of Jesus, which was, essentially, rejected for an otherworldly Christ.[28]

But, in 1950, the confrontation must have formed the foundation for his emerging critique and the springboard for later reflection and writing. In time, Jordan will focus on "Judas," whom he sees as the "true" beloved disciple, rather than John. It is clear that his reading of Judas is done with the Southern church in mind, in that he makes this disciple a Southerner from the stronghold of orthodoxy. Jesus, according to Jordan, knew about the "schizophrenia of orthodoxy." Judas, like the members of Rehoboth, "did not die of too little religion. He died of too *much* religion." Judas, like the Southern church, had two masters and he could not serve them both. Unfortunately, Judas and his spiritual schizophrenia were not limited in time or to his own unique circumstance. "His number is legion," Clarence later wrote. That is, those who feel the "pull of the professional religious establishment and the pull of this prophetic Gospel" are put in a great tension that can lead to a form of death. Jordan ends his sermon on Judas by saying, "One can but hope in the far reaches of eternity, Jesus and his broken, beloved disciple will meet again and Jesus will restore his soul to wholeness…and take him to the father saying rejoice with me."[29] In the same manner, Jordan spoke longingly about a reunion with Rehoboth, saying that someday they, too, would see him as a true son and brother. In May 1969, Jordan said to a group of American Baptists in Seattle, "I hope and pray before I pass on to glory that little church which expelled me from its fellowship will realize that I am really its son, that I do love it, and that it will gather with me at God's table."[30] Unfortunately, the reunion did not occur before his death.

Rehoboth and the End of an Era: Jordan's Ultimate Environment in Late 1950

Jordan's faith after Rehoboth would be different. He would never again have the youthful optimism demonstrated by the dream that drove him to come back to Sumter County. Clarence Jordan was a son of the church and had devoted his young life to understanding its deepest problems. He had fashioned his whole life, in a remarkable way, after his understanding of the life and teachings of Jesus, albeit "Jesus the Rebel." He worked hard to become a graduate of the denomination's oldest and most prestigious seminary. He was a "Doctor of the Church." He had been a "rising star" in the denominational machinery. He came to Koinonia with the backing of some of the most powerful and thoughtful people in the Southern Baptist Convention. Now, however, the confrontation at Rehoboth made him an ex-Baptist. He would never again attempt to join another church. In a sense, Rehoboth made Clarence Jordan a member of the church universal, beyond region and ideology.

Rehoboth as a landscape of faith, as a form of an ultimate environment, means the end of an era and the beginning of another for Clarence Jordan. It means the end of the youthful, reflective faith that had begun when he got down off his military steed in North Georgia and handed in his sword and spurs. The pain of the public rejection at Rehoboth brought to a close that period that began seventeen years earlier in summer 1933. Clarence had spent years challenging and demythologizing ideas and developing his own understanding of what it meant to be a person of faith in the world. He had rejected the cultural faith. With unusual sensitivity, he had identified issues of poverty, racism, and militarism. He had worked through these issues to his own individual understanding so that, now, students were drawn to him because of the authenticity, eloquence, and courage with which he articulated those ideas. He had come to be seen by many as an emerging leader on the forefront of change regarding the most important social issues of his day. He was a Christian pioneer.[31] But, now, his views—and he himself—were rejected by some of the very people he most wanted to help!

The pain inherent in the Rehoboth incident pushed Clarence deeper into himself, where he began to hear voices he had not heard before. In a sense, Rehoboth was a before-and-after event. It was not only the end of his youthful, individuative-reflective faith, but also an opening to a deeper, more communal faith. The pain of the events of 1950 helped Clarence hear beyond the principles of his experiment to a commitment to people in an increasingly larger "Koinonia."[32] The rejection at Rehoboth would force Clarence to ask not only what it meant for him to be a Christian, but also what it meant to be a Baptist and, now, an ex-Baptist. He would, in the coming years, also have to deal with the possibility that he would leave Sumter County. Would that mean an end to his dream of "Koinonia"? The year 1950 was a turning point for Clarence Jordan. He would never be so young again! Rehoboth, as a violent overreaction from the community, would, unfortunately, presage the most violent episode in Jordan's life, which is still yet to come.

Chapter 12

Too Many Enemies to Leave: The Boycott Years

We have too many enemies to leave.... The redemptive love of God
must somehow break through if it costs us our lives....
                                                    —Clarence Jordan

The Rehoboth incident not only brought a great deal of pain to Clarence, but also indicated how deep was the misunderstanding between Clarence and the people of the community—between a prophetic faith and the cultural faith. How could it have been otherwise? What the community in Sumter County saw was a "preacher in overalls" who had no congregation, but practiced "race-mixing." He was anti-military, lived at a subsistence level—like some called "white trash"—on an unpaved road that was barely passable in winter and thoroughly dusty in summer. Such was the context where Clarence began the dream of a "demonstration plot." The white community had no model by which they could understand this. It went against everything they had known. Consequently, they saw all of this as a serious threat to their way of life, as well as a violation of social taboo.[1]

Florence Jordan later said that Clarence was "very, very hurt at first because he thought, as we all did, these people knew us and loved us."[2] Both Clarence and Florence had spoken all over the county, not just at Rehoboth. But Clarence and the Koinonia fellowship did not make it clear who they were. They did not publicize the nature of their faith. Rather, they thought it was enough just to live it out.[3] But it was not, and the people did not understand. The majority-held cultural faith embraced a view of race and the military that was antithetical to the values held at Koinonia. Clarence and the Koinonia group underestimated the gap between themselves and the community. To that extent, they lived with a certain caricature of the social circumstance and the people involved.[4] Since the community did not understand Koinonia, they tended to listen more to the rumors—and to be highly threatened by their fears. Rehoboth was also an indicator of things to come, and in that regard, it presaged an unthinkable amount of violence that would be directed against Jordan and the members of Koinonia. However, after the Rehoboth incident, Clarence and his fellow Koinonians involved themselves in the life of the farm, with special attention given to issues of community. For a time, it seems, the Koinonians turned inward.[5]

In the 1951 newsletter, Clarence wrote that, while the "most far-reaching event" of the past year was the "breaking of fellowship" with Rehoboth, "we rejoice in the clarity that it brings to us regarding our witness....[which] is no longer divided."[6] Many visitors continued to come, including friends from Paraguay and South Dakota. "The presence of those friends with us was one fact leading us to a deeper-seeking self-searching....We gained a new feeling of belonging to a great fellowship stretching from one end of the Western hemisphere to the other, and as far as England and Yugoslavia—a fellowship whose purpose and principles we could share as with no one heretofore known."[7]

When Clarence and his fellow Koinonians were "turned out" of the church, as the pastor Ira Flaglier put it, it brought the first era of Koinonia to an end. The group began to talk naturally about the nature of "Koinonia" and what it should be like ideally. One of the highest ideals discussed was that, as a fellowship of believers, Koinonia should be seen as something of a continuation of the very humanity of God—an ongoing incarnation. Clarence came to see that "something has been set in motion here—something that is eternal....I'm beginning to see that I'm in this thing called Koinonia for life."[8] By that, Clarence did not mean the farm, but the fellowship of believers who were trying to live out the faith. Clarence admitted that one of his biggest problems had been to see things in terms of "principles." Now he was ready to give himself completely to people—"the people of Koinonia who are making the same struggle as I am."[9]

It seemed, at first, that the Rehoboth incident had brought the group closer together and closer to partners around the world. But, in truth, there were some serious internal struggles, some of which must have been very painful for Clarence. One of the most hurtful would have been the series of disputes he had with Jack Singletary, who eventually decided to leave the farm for one of his own nearby. Another major issue was the way both Florence and Clarence related to the rest of the group. The two of them were accused of not giving themselves completely to the larger group. Florence was an independent person by her very nature, and remained so all of the rest of her life (which was lived out at Koinonia). Clarence traveled a good deal and was, therefore, "absent" a good bit, perhaps one-fourth of the time. The group tended to resent his travels and his absence.[10] Though it must have been painful for Clarence to even think it, he finally offered to leave the farm if it would bring a sense of solidarity to the group.[11]

Eventually, the group renewed its allegiance to one another as people, and as members within a covenanted group, through a new statement of commitment. The document read, in part, "We desire to make known our total, unconditional commitment to seek, express, and expand the kingdom of God as revealed in Jesus.... The community of believers...is the continuing body of Christ on earth. I joyfully enter into a love union with the Koinonia." Ten members signed the statement. Another group could not and left soon thereafter.[12]

While Koinonia renewed itself internally, and rejoiced in new friendships and fellowship increasingly worldwide, the serious tension with regional cultural elements continued unabated. Few people in Sumter County were willing to say good things about Jordan and Koinonia. One informant declared to the FBI in 1952 that "the general feeling in the Americus community is that...[Clarence] Jordan is a subversive character."[13] The corollary was that Koinonia Farm was a front for a communist organization. Suspicion and rumor about Jordan and Koinonia ran rampant in Sumter County, Georgia, in the early 1950s. The *Albany Herald* article from August 1948 had made Jordan even more infamous. The logic for assuming that Jordan was a communist and a subversive contained the following elements: out-of-state cars seen coming and going from Koinonia; Jordan dismissed from Rehoboth because of racial views; Jordan aided in the defense of two Selective Service violators; Jordan refused to participate in the war effort; integrated living existed at Koinonia; Jordan came to Sumter County as a poor man, and he now had four farms; car radios often went dead near Koinonia, and there was a large, refrigerator-like object in the swamps of Koinonia, which was a short-wave radio Jordan used to contact Russia; and 600-pound foot-lockers, securely locked, came regularly to Koinonia by railway express. The sum total of this "evidence" must be that Jordan is a communist seeking to subvert American values.[14]

The Crucible of Race: The Emergence of Violence Against Koinonia

In their struggle with the issue of race, Rehoboth and Sumter County were not alone. Erik Erikson, writing in anthropological fashion, found that matters of race and tribe have been factors in the psychosocial evolution of the human species from the earliest days. Consequently, human history has recorded the development of the "deep-seated conviction that some providence has made [one's]...tribe or race or caste, and yes, even his religion, 'naturally' superior to others."[15] Churches have often joined this process, while the great religious leaders and visionaries have opposed it.[16]

After the Rehoboth incident, Koinonia turned its attention to farming and, for a time, lived a rather quiet, even if "uneasy but peaceful[,] co-existence" with the folks of Sumter County.[17] During this time, there were approximately sixty people living or working at Koinonia. However, while Koinonia was turning inward with a renewed focus on the communal life, the matter of race was becoming a national issue. After the end of World War II, President Truman had made civil rights an important agenda item. Indeed, it became a matter of foreign policy. If he were going to convince the nations of the world to align with Western democracies, then the United States must deal with racism. On July 26, 1948, Truman signed Executive Order 9981, which desegregated the U.S. military. For many, the revelations about the Nazi treatment of the Jews had delegitimized racism. However, resistance to Truman's agenda began to build slowly. After the Supreme Court decision on *Brown v. Board of Education of Topeka, Kansas,* conservatives had a new rallying cry. Race as a national issue also tended to galvanize white Southerners. Though a sense of black militancy began to intensify, so did the reaction across the South. One of the first targets of the reaction to the Supreme Court decision was Koinonia Farm.[18]

167

Before the Supreme Court decision handed down on May 17, 1954, there had been little public conversation about race relations in Sumter County. The status quo reigned and the age-old cultural *rapprochement*, which granted superior status to whites, was not questioned. But, after the Supreme Court decision, the citizens of Sumter County became increasingly agitated as the *Americus Times-Recorder* carried the headlines of the Montgomery Bus Boycott, which began on December 1, 1955, and the Georgia governor's race, which was dominated by the school issue. Marvin Griffin, who was elected governor, was a staunch segregationist and denounced the Supreme Court decision. In June 1955, the *Times-Recorder* described a rally of the "White Citizens Council," in which members came from three states and the group promised action against the leaders who had brought on the move toward integration. There would be "a social boycott of the 'scalawags and carpetbaggers of the modern era' who fail or refuse to join in the fight to preserve segregation."[19]

Igniting the Tinderbox: Clarence Jordan at the Georgia State College of Business

Perhaps unknowingly, Clarence Jordan lit the fuse that brought on the barrage of attacks from the community. The simmering resentment concerning Jordan and Koinonia, in the context of a growing national debate about race relations, created something of a "tinderbox" in Southwest Georgia. Clarence told P.D. East that "they feel they have to vent their anger on somebody and we are the natural ones for it."[20] The event that lit the tinderbox was an effort by Jordan to talk with officials at the Georgia State College of Business in Atlanta about the enrollment of two black students who wanted to take courses there.

In March 1956, four months after the beginning of the Montgomery Bus Boycott, suspicions of Jordan and Koinonia were high. A friend had asked Clarence to help Thelma Boone and Edward Clemons to register in the Georgia system, which had been an all-white unit up to that point in time. Since the 1954 Supreme Court decision had made it clear that the two young blacks could apply, Jordan was asked to help them meet the requirement for the application, to be signed by two alumni. When Jordan met with the two students, he found them to be sincerely interested in education and in need of the courses offered by the college of business. Clarence and the students first met with the president of the college, and then with the registrar. It was the registrar whose words essentially predicted the future: to do this "might set off a bomb."[21] After several different conferences with leaders of the college and the university system, Clarence was told that he could not sign the applications, because he had graduated from a different college within the system and was, therefore, ineligible.[22] So he headed home to Koinonia.

The response to this perceived attempt at altering the status quo was immediate. The word about what was happening spread like wildfire. Before Clarence had arrived back at Koinonia, the governor, Marvin Griffin, had called the Sumter County sheriff to "check out" this Jordan fellow. Con Browne was told that very afternoon by one of his egg customers that he would no longer buy from Koinonia. That very night, the threatening phone calls began. The next day, the *Americus Times-Recorder* printed an inflammatory account titled, "Negroes Fail in Attempt to Enroll at Ga. College; Endorsed by Americus Man."[23] It was clear that, in the minds of many, Clarence had violated a great taboo. He had attempted to desegregate the all-white university system, and, by educating blacks, thereby had begun to undermine the economy of the state. Those who were looking for a scapegoat found Clarence and Koinonia Farm to be perfect targets. "Jordan's attempt to help these students, combined with the agitation of the people of Sumter County over the race issue, suddenly transformed Koinonia from a community of Christians trying to live together into a threat against segregation."[24] The locals began quickly to attempt to remove Clarence and Koinonia as a threat to their way of life. The threatening phone calls came first. Then the egg business was shut down. When the local merchants stopped buying the eggs, Clarence had to liquidate the entire commercial flock. Then came the different episodes of violence, efforts at legal intimidation, and, finally, the boycott.[25]

One Tuesday evening in late spring 1956, the Koinonia children were playing under the peach trees in front of the farm buildings. Margaret Whitkamper was nursing her youngest baby when she heard a "splattering." She thought it sounded like rocks or nuts falling on the tin roof of the laundry room. But she could not figure out what in the world was happening—what that sound of splattering was. Then the kids came running into the house, and they were white as sheets. Margaret immediately asked what was happening, and they said in astonishment, "We were shot at!" Someone had come down the road in a car and had seen the children and fired over their heads, as if to intentionally scare or intimidate them and their parents—perhaps as a warning to both! The bullets fell on the tin roof of the laundry shed. Margaret Whitkamper said this was the first time she understood that prejudice and violence were so rampant.[26]

From that time forward, there were many forms of violence perpetuated against Koinonia—from small, random acts to potentially deadly acts. The violence began with drive-by shootings and anonymous, threatening calls. Sometimes the phone would ring every ten minutes, all night long. In the first couple of years, there were some twenty-three acts of violence with firearms, with fire, or with dynamite. With all of the violence, it was only short of the miraculous that no one at Koinonia was hurt physically. Yet there were some "close calls." John Eustace was on guard duty one night when his lantern was hit by a bullet, and the fragments of the lantern came up and hit him on the hand—without severe injury, however. Dorothy Day was visiting in spring 1956 and taking a shift on guard duty with Margaret Morgan. About 1:30 or 2:00 in the morning, a car came by, and someone from the car fired on the nightwatch car by which they were standing. It scared both of them terribly. The bullet came close, but neither of them was hurt. Ross Anderson was living in a house across the road from the farm, and one night, the house was hit with machinegun fire. One of the bullets ripped through his bedroom and passed about six inches above his head. Just a few days before, he had lowered his bed by sawing off the legs about six inches, because he liked a lower bed. There were other close calls, including bullets in Clarence's bedroom and several in the apartment of Con Browne.[27] One weekend, Eleanor Jordan came home from the University of Georgia and went into her room about 10:30 that night. When she turned on the light, a rifle bullet came through the wall and the mirror of her dresser, barely missing her by inches. Then the bullet went through the wall into the living room, where Clarence had been reading just minutes earlier. The bullet was stopped by the closet in the children's room.[28] There were also many random acts of vandalism. One day, while he was riding on a tractor, someone shot at Clarence in broad daylight. In addition to the roadside market that was blown up, signs were pulled down and destroyed. Beehives were burned; sugar was put in gasoline trucks, ruining the engines; orchards were chopped down; fences were cut; and fields were set on fire.[29]

After one round of violence, Will Campbell and some friends came to see Clarence. They found him, naturally, angry and afraid. In an effort to help, Will picked up a few of the thirty-caliber slugs and went to Albany to talk with agents from the FBI. The agents informed Will that their job was not enforcing the law, but investigating possible violations. Will, who had served in World War II, knew that the thirty-caliber slugs were fired from a machine gun, and that the only place one could get such a weapon was from the military. Perhaps these weapons and the ammunition came from the local National Guard Armory, clearly a violation of the law. Yet Will was not successful in getting the FBI to come to Sumter County.[30] When Will returned to Koinonia and told Clarence what had happened, he did not say much. But, after dinner, Clarence read from the Greek New Testament and ridiculed the work of theologians "who are forever talking and never doing." As Clarence continued, he translated: "It will be hell for you, theologians and preachers— phonies...[who] pass up the more important things in the Bible, such as justice, sharing, and integrity."[31]

Continuing Violence and Legal Maneuvers

In June 1956, the Sumter County commissioners filed for an injunction to block the opening of "Camp Koinonia." This was a successful, six-week summer camp that Koinonia had held for inner-city children. The charge was that Koinonia would operate this camp in a manner that would be "detrimental to morals" and that the facilities would be "non-segregated." Koinonia moved the camp to Tennessee. The case was dismissed when summer was over. Violence intensified in July, and the Sumter County boycott of the farm began to solidify in August. In September, the Sumter County solicitor general, Charles Burgamy, attended a States Rights Council meeting in a nearby county and was reported to say, "Maybe what we need now is for the right kind of Klan to start up again and use a buggy whip on some of these race mixers....I would rather see my little boy dead than sit beside a Negro in the public schools."[32]

In November, the roadside market was attacked again. Then the farm's butane supplier told the Koinonians that he would no longer be able to supply them with gas used for heating and cooking. In December, heavy-caliber bullets ripped holes in the farm's new gas pump. On January 1, 1957, the nightriders came again, ripping the sign in front of the farm with bullets and spraying the buildings. On January 14, the roadside market was bombed again, causing about $7,000 worth of damage.[33]

In late January 1957, in response to the terror, Clarence wrote a letter to President Eisenhower in which he said: "A community of nearly sixty men, women, and children is facing annihilation unless quick, decisive action is taken by someone in authority. I am therefore appealing to you as a last resort, with the hope and prayer that you might find some course of action before it is too late." Then Clarence summarized the violence that had taken place, noting that it was all public knowledge and had been printed in newspapers and magazines. He told the president these matters had been brought to law-enforcement officials and to the courts, to no avail. Nothing had been done, Clarence declared, to help. Instead, "groups of ten to twelve cars are forming and riding at night. We are told that the end is near." Then Clarence closed with a stunning statement to the president: "We shall not run, for this is America. It is a land where free men have the right—and the duty—to walk erect and without fear.... Should this freedom perish from our land, we would prefer to be dead." The last line reads, "We gladly offer our lives for its preservation."[34]

Uplifting Mankind and the Kingdom of Heaven: The Klan and Segregation As God's Law

Several weeks later, Clarence received a letter from the Attorney General stating that the violence against Koinonia appeared to be an issue for state law enforcement.[35] Since no federal laws had been broken, the matter would be referred to the State of Georgia. This letter must have been demoralizing for Clarence because, just days before, the Attorney General of the State of Georgia, Eugene Cook, had declared that, for more than a year, Koinonia had been under investigation for "subversive activities." This was an indicator of things to come for Clarence. The tactic now would be to openly "blame the victim." The Sumter County Grand Jury would investigate Koinonia that spring. Though there were no indictments, there were charges that would be spread far and wide: that Koinonia profited from the violence they had inflicted upon themselves; "that its practice of Christianity has no precedent in the religious annals of the United States"; that the farm profited from the destruction of the roadside market; and that the farm's egalitarian claim to equality among the races was false, because the African Americans who were there had "relegated themselves into a status of brainwashed peonage, while those few members of the white race…enrich themselves at the expense of the Negro's toil." Furthermore, the implication was that Clarence Jordan was a communist, and that his sense of integrity had been so compromised that his testimony was essentially unbelievable. The report, therefore, leveled charges of "perjury, fraud, disturbing the peace, and suspicion of conspiracy." Though this report was sent to Washington— as if to answer the query of the U.S. Attorney General—there were no formal indictments. The end result of the matter is that Clarence Jordan and Koinonia came under scrutiny by the FBI again.[36]

The focus of the FBI on this second occasion was twofold: the accusation of civil rights violations—that local authorities had not properly investigated the violence against Koinonia; and whether there were "sufficient subversive connections at Koinonia to warrant a security-type investigation." The bureau came to negative conclusions on both issues— that local authorities had not improperly investigated the violence surrounding Koinonia, and that "the inquiries fail to indicate sufficient derogatory data to warrant such an investigation." Yet, in closing, the memo read, "Recommend this case be administratively closed subject to reopening in the event additional data is received regarding personnel at Koinonia…."[37]

What was, perhaps, more immediately frightening and ominous for the Koinonians was the activity of the Klan. On Sunday, February 24, 1957, the Knights of the Ku Klux Klan held a rally in Americus at the fairgrounds. The group included 150 men and women and at least one robed child, all from across South Georgia. The group included the

"Great Titan of the Sixth Province" from Macon. The crowd, assembled in their robes and hoods, heard an opening prayer that proclaimed they were there to "uplift mankind and the kingdom of heaven." A spokesperson described the work of the Klan as a struggle "against the white men on the inside who are fighting the Negro's cause for money." One minister there declared that segregation was God's law, and called upon white people to uphold the teachings of the Bible.

After the rally was over, the Klan group got in their cars and drove in a motorcade—seventy strong—down to Koinonia Farm. They were greeted by Margaret Whitkamper, who thought the procession was a large funeral. So, when she was pushing her stroller across the road, she asked the man in the car, "Whose funeral is it?" The Klansman responded, "It might very well be yours." The Klansmen got out of their cars and spoke to Norman Long, who was asked if they were communists. He responded, "No, unless Jesus Christ was a communist." The purpose of the motorcade, the Klansmen said, was to protest the interracial lifestyle at Koinonia. The Klansmen also said they were there to represent a group of interested citizens who thought that Koinonia should move out of Southern Georgia. The Klansmen stayed less than ten minutes and they were gone.[38] Billy Whitkamper later said, "This was the first time that we could really see fear in the faces of the adults."[39]

Climactic Act of Terror on the Southern Frontier

After the Klan rally, the pressure on Koinonia began to increase. Though Clarence must have been encouraged by the letter from Herbert Birdsey in May 1957, declaring that his local feed store would no longer participate in the boycott, the bombing of that store with a dynamite blast on May 19 became the climactic moment of the reign of terror, as seven downtown establishments were affected. Once again, Koinonia was blamed by the local people, but the national media angered the people of Americus and the Georgia media. In the *Christian Century*, Harold Fey captured the spirits of the embittered whites by describing the Deep South as a "frontier," and Koinonia as a last "outpost" of a Christian testament. Dora Byron, in the *Nation*, gave a face to the community hypocrisy by quoting County Commissioner George Mathews, who said, "We got a good county, here, and God knows we treat the niggers right....We

aren't going to have a gang down here stirring up our Americus niggers."
Andre Fontaine's "The Conflict of a Southern Town," in *Redbook*, portrayed Clarence as a prophet who preached social equality, and characterized Blair, the editor of the town paper, as being fearful of "mongreliza-
tion." One of the local policemen told Fontaine that he would shoot a
"nigger" dead if he came into the police station and did not remove his
hat.[40]

Shortly after the Birdsey incident, a group of local businessmen
came to visit Clarence to discuss possible ways to end the violence. Essentially, they came to give their opinion, once again blaming Clarence
and Koinonia. The group told Clarence that his moral responsibility was
to move, in order to protect the welfare of the community. "We want to
appeal to your good judgment to pray over it and think over it and see if
you don't think you'll be serving the best interests of the community and
certainly the best interests of your Lord to move and leave us in peace."[41]

Why Don't You Sell Out and Move Away?:
Too Many Enemies to Leave

In January 1958, Con Browne had taken packages to Americus for
shipping. While unloading the packages, Browne was attacked and brutally beaten. Clarence was called and he, too, came into town. In the process, he was charged and arrested for driving a car with improper license
plates. On the way over to the jail, the officer also asked Clarence, "Mr.
Jordan, why don't you folks sell out and move away?" Clarence did not
take the time in the patrol car to answer the officer. But he did take the
time in a later speaking engagement in early 1958. The first answer,
Clarence said, is "plain sentiment." Fifteen years earlier, he had come to
this worn-out farm, ripped with gulleys, the land essentially crying out,
"Heal me." And, over time, Jordan said, we have seen the land come back
to life. It is no longer a simple matter to leave. One could just as soon
ask, "Why don't you sell your mother?"[42]

The second reason, Jordan said, is because of the people around us.
"All about us are people with personalities twisted and warped by hate
and prejudice," he said. In rhetorical fashion, Jordan raised the question,
"Shall we go off and leave these people? Is it the sick or the well that
needs healing?" And then, as if to answer his own question, Jordan says,

"We have too many enemies to leave them. The redemptive love of God must break through. If we must be hung on a cross to redeem our brothers and sisters in the flesh, so let it be." Jordan went on to affirm that such an act would be well worth the price it exacts, for to do anything other would be "to deny the redemptive processes of God." So, thirdly, Jordan said, "We cannot move away because the hand of God is upon us. We have heard the high calling of God in Christ Jesus."[43]

Restating an Overstatement: Clarence, Koinonia, and the Continuation of Slavery

When asked how to account for the violent outbreak of attacks on the farm, Jordan responded with a grim statement: "The South wanted to preserve the plantation system in this section, which was built on the exploitation of Negro labor. In order to keep that way of life, they wanted to root out anything that threatened it." Then he added that "the momentum of slavery is still carried on by men who are still trying to perpetuate the slave mentality, both in the master and the slave, even though they don't know why."[44] Jordan's dream of a "Koinonia" was a restatement of the issue—the African American as a slave or nonperson, property to be bought and sold, is negated by an egalitarian community in which race is not a factor in a person's worth or status. Ironically, the violence acted out against Clarence and Koinonia helps to sharpen one's understanding of who Clarence Jordan was in the context of his time—a spiritual innovator and religious actualist. As Erik Erikson puts it, in his work on Luther, "It is always good to find out what he was talking *against* at the time, or what previous overstatement he was trying to correct, for greatness is based on an excessive restatement of some previous overstatement...."[45]

The cultural story of the Southern establishment was told through the local newspapers, which portrayed Americus as a place of "peace-loving, church-going, cultured people," while the citizens of Koinonia were described as "menaces to democracy" who had bombed their own market in order "to obtain [the] sympathy of the general public."[46] Koinonia Farm became controversial because, in the minds of the editor and reporters of the *Americus Times Recorder*, the interracial practices of Clarence Jordan and the other Koinonians were seen as an extension of the

Supreme Court decision of 1954.[47] After the bombing of the roadside market, Clarence attempted "a calm and loving statement" regarding Koinonia's true identity. It did not work, however. Even though the Koinonians described the farm as a church run by ministers, and promised to respect the rights of those who disagreed, their efforts seemed to make little difference. The Christians who did not challenge the Southern mores could not hear the claims of those who did. One resident who claimed to speak for the masses came to the conclusion that Clarence should take the farm members "well above the Mason-Dixon Line."[48]

The Boycott and Scapegoating:
Jordan's Challenge of Integrity

Clarence and the other members of Koinonia were subjected to the challenge of their lives—how to maintain a sense of integrity in the context of this serious crisis. In truth, from his earliest days, Clarence seemed to be searching for an authentic way to live—"to be an honest Christian," as he put it, in his interview with P.D. East.[49] In a letter to Howard Johnson, Clarence wrote that the most difficult thing about the Koinonia experiment would not be farming, but living out the commands of Jesus.[50]

In a statement about the crisis, which he gave in Cincinnati, Ohio, Clarence described how he saw the local merchants as having the same problem as the Koinonians. He recounted how he told the merchants, "You are facing the same question as we are." The issue was one of integrity, as Clarence saw it: Can you "be true to your convictions or will you sell out to business?" Will you sell your soul for business profits? The merchants could not see the issue with the same clarity that Clarence had found.[51] Neither could his own brother, Bob. Clarence spoke with him about some of the legal issues. Robert Jordan was a lawyer, later elected to the Georgia Supreme Court. After looking over the legal maneuvers that had been thrown against Clarence, Robert Jordan said, "These charges are trumped up." Clarence asked his brother to take the case for him. Robert said, "I can give you all the advice that you need, but I cannot be your attorney." Then Clarence asked him if he were a Christian and a deacon in the church. Bob said that he was a follower of Jesus, but only up to a point. That point was the cross. In a stark confrontation,

Clarence told his brother, "I think you should go to the church and tell them that I am not going to follow Jesus." Bob's response was, "If we all did that, there would be no one left in the church." Furthermore, Bob said, "If I were to take your case, I would lose my business." Clarence retorted, "Then you could come to Koinonia and join us [and] then we could be true brothers."[52]

Clarence framed yet another episode of the boycott in terms of integrity. The dentist who had treated the Koinonia group for fifteen years suddenly refused to see any of them for treatment. One of the little girls had a toothache. The call was made for an appointment, but the doctor refused. Clarence tried to go see the dentist. He refused to see Jordan. So Clarence wrote him a letter and asked him four questions: First, what does your refusal to see this little girl do to your Hippocratic Oath? Second, what does this refusal to help a sick child do to your Christian commitment? Third, what does this disregard for a sick child do for your ideals of democracy? And, fourth, as a human being, what does this basic disregard for another person do to your soul? Implicit in Jordan's letter to the doctor is his vision of the necessity of integrity as a basis for human life.[53]

Just as attention to Jordan's restatement of the cultural overstatement helps to clarify Clarence Jordan's role as a true spiritual innovator in Southern culture, so does a focus on Jordan's quest for integrity. For the religious genius, like Jordan, the "integrity crisis," which is the last one for most people, is lifelong and chronic. Put differently, this special innovator spends a lifetime looking for a way "to escape corruption in living and how in death to give meaning to life." This chosen one, as Clarence clearly was from early in life, must extend his own search for identity to the borders of the universe, and often act as if history somehow starts over with him.[54] Clarence thought that all the people of the earth would eventually adopt the lifestyle that he had emulated at Koinonia.

Koinonia As a Land of Violence and Persecution:
Clarence Jordan's Ultimate Environment in the 1950s

Clarence Jordan began the 1950s with the energy and vision of his original dream of Koinonia, as a place of individual commitment to the egalitarian ideals and principles that he had hammered out in his time in Kentucky. He came home in search of a "true country" where he could live out those high ideals. And, for almost a decade, he worked with unusual zeal and courage against the odds of the cultural establishment—before the public outcry began. But the Rehoboth incident framed his early adult faith and ushered in an era of pain that began to push Clarence Jordan beyond human faithfulness to a place where he had to begin a search for a deeper resolve—a way not yet known, something like a divine redemptive subversiveness. The Rehoboth incident was, in part, a call to a deeper faith beyond what Clarence had known up to this point—beyond his own tradition and experience. As the Koinonia group began to turn inward and seek to find meaning in a renewed commitment to community life, Clarence heard painful stories claiming that the people with whom he lived and worked did not fully understand or appreciate his faith either. He felt he had to offer to leave the farm he had started in an effort for that testament to continue.

In time, the life of violence and fear that the Koinonia of the 1950s became pushed Clarence to a new way of looking at life—more dialogical, deeper into himself, indeed more Christ-like. In Clarence's reflections on the heartbreak of cultural rejection and complete misunderstanding, one could hear what some have called the "pathos" of God—Clarence Jordan joining in the pain of God, as Koinonia is seemingly being dismantled by the forces of cultural opposition.[55] After being arrested, violently persecuted, and tried in the law courts—and in the court of public opinion—Clarence continues to identify with the rebel Jesus and takes a more communal and cruciform stance as he searches for a place of redemptive subversiveness.[56] In the midst of the violence and the boycott, Clarence, essentially, says that now the community has been enlarged to include those who oppose us, and that we are bound up with them in a covenant that seeks to redeem them, even if it costs us our lives.

Chapter 13

From the Egypt of the Confederacy: Clarence Jordan and the Growth of Prophetic Consciousness

> God placed His seal upon you and set you apart to do his bidding,
> even before you came into the world....
> —Maude Jossey Jordan

What happened to the faith of Clarence Jordan when he became an ex-Baptist, voted out of Rehoboth? What was the impact of the violent boycott years on Clarence's religious pilgrimage? For a time, while he was still a member of Rehoboth, it seems that his faith and witness were somewhat divided by his effort to stay in dialogue with Rehoboth and, by implication, the cultural faith of the South. Yet the misunderstanding ran deep, and the shared consensus was that Clarence was a subversive, a communist. How else could one explain his race-mixing ways? The Grand Jury also linked Clarence to communism, described him as dishonest and untruthful—essentially, guilty of perjury—and accused him of being subversive to the government of the United States. In 1958, there were efforts in the state legislature to make Koinonia illegal. Representative Paul Jones said that he was "ashamed Koinonia existed in the state." The very existence of such a place seems "to weaken our whole stand on segregation. Something ought to be done about it."[1] Jordan's own brother, Robert, an attorney and judge, refused to help and support him publicly.

Yet there is documentation that, throughout this period, there were numbers of people who saw Clarence differently. In 1949, the FBI contacted the Chamber of Commerce in Americus and inquired about Clarence. The response was, "Dr. Jordan is a very highly educated religious man, and his ideas from a social standpoint are very extreme for our part of Georgia....Our information indicates that he is thoroughly sincere, but not very popular."[2] Another informant wrote that Dr. Jordan is "very religious, and that his opposition to the war is based on his religion and that his socializing with Negroes is likewise based on his religion."[3] Many of Jordan's biographers have seen his stance against the cultural consensus of the South to be that of a prophet.[4] How does one understand Jordan as a prophet?

In 1957, when asked why there was an outbreak of violence and such an intense boycott, Jordan responded by saying that some Southerners wanted to preserve the plantation system built on the exploitation of blacks.[5] In doing so, Jordan essentially identified with the metaphorical language of Dubois, who described Southwest Georgia as the "Egypt of the Confederacy." Egypt was an archetype of the oppression of the meek and lowly, and continued in the black church tradition to represent "humiliating oppression, ungodly exploitation, and crushing domination."[6] The struggle of the oppressed in American life against "Pharaohlike" forces was only a later chapter in a continuing story.[7] By the same token, when Clarence raised the specter of slavery, he also made allusion to the biblical narrative about Israelite experience in Egypt, which is the core narration of the Hebrew Bible and the beginning of the prophetic tradition. It is the story of Moses and his call to the Hebrew people to walk to the Promised Land and not to get weary! In one of the articles that came out of the boycott era, internationally known writer Andre Fontaine described Clarence Jordan as an American prophet, and using the description of Dubois, one could add, in the "Egypt of the Confederacy."[8]

The black church proclaimed, and Clarence Jordan affirmed, that the God of the Bible was (and is) aligned with the poor and the powerless over against the "pharaohs." The story of Egypt, known as "Exodus" in the Bible, is not only the heart of biblical faith, but also describes the origin of the Israelite people and the phenomenon of prophecy. In the language of contemporary scholar Walter Brueggemann, this core narration is the description of a paradigmatic event—a story that provides the key to understanding historic and contemporary reality. Exodus is, then, on the part of oppressed Israel in Egypt, the story of the development of an alternative consciousness. Israel learns to think differently from the surrounding culture, which is characterized by the "politics of oppression and exploitation," all stemming from the "royal consciousness" of the pharaoh and a religion seen as "triumphalist."[9]

The Call of the Prophet (Then and Now)

The challenge of the people of faith, seen from this perspective, was and continues to be a call to intentionally form a new social reality—to counter the way of the pharaoh.[10] In its earliest days, ancient Israel could be seen, then, as a radical and revolutionary "counter-community" calling for a counter-consciousness—a different way of thinking and being. The origin of the prophetic movement was the call to "grieve"—to feel deeply about the numbness that permitted one group to dominate and exploit another. The task of the prophet was, therefore, to cut through the numbness and self-deception, and to lead the community by using symbols adequate to the horror of the contemporary exploitation, the public expression of the fears and terrors long denied, and metaphorical language to describe the deathliness active in the culture.[11]

In the foregoing description, Walter Brueggemann moves away from the idea that prophets were simply reporters, predictors, or social analysts. In his mind, they are best understood as "poets" who exercise a liberated imagination, which helps their contemporaries see the life and culture before them. In this way, Moses, the archetypal prophet, provided an "alternative vision" of the freedom of God over against the royal consciousness and slavery of Egypt. In a paradigmatic speech delivered on Mt. Nebo, Moses instructed the people that continued life required care for the neighbor. If not, the vision of justice given coming out of Egypt would be lost and the society would be destroyed by an economy of greed and selfishness.[12]

Jeremiah follows in the footsteps of Moses. The literary logic of Jeremiah is typical of the prophets and demonstrates the poetic imagination illustrated in Brueggemann's definition of the prophet as poet. The literary logic given to Jeremiah by God, and demonstrated in his writings and poetry, is that of shattering, evoking, and enacting. This literary logic also indicates the multifaceted nature of prophecy. It is not only poetic, but also praxis-oriented, which means the prophet holds word and action together and lives out, or "enacts," the vision implied by the words. This means that prophets are a breed apart! As poets who write and proclaim words from God, they are also generative religious personalities who seek to reshape the religious world of the day. In this sense, they are *homines religiosi*, spiritual innovators of the highest order.[13] Often sleepless and grave, and in communion with the divine consciousness, the prophets feel fiercely and take the burden of that relationship to a place deep within their souls before they find a way to enact the vision. In time, the words of the prophets become the voice that God loans to the silent agony of the oppressed. What gave the prophets the courage and strength to demythologize the certain realities of the present, to shatter the shared conventions of the day? They themselves must have been shattered by some excruciating experience in order to so challenge others.[14] Put another way, the prophet as religious genius is that individual whose own conflicts and struggles merge with the group, and who eventually seeks to establish a new and more humane sense of personhood, not only for himself, but also for his generation.[15]

In this reading, Clarence Jordan is a grieving poet-prophet whose task came to be the calling of an entire people to a new South, alternative to the old ways of exploitation and humiliation. How did Clarence Jordan come to this perspective? It is not likely that Jordan came to this stance either gladly or quickly. In fact, it appears that Jordan, a loyal and proud son of the South, came to this perspective only slowly as the years unfolded, and after he had learned to deal with the sacrament of defeat and had been pushed and pulled—perhaps lured—by the exigencies of human history.[16] In the language of Rabbi Heschel, Clarence Jordan came to the vocation of a prophet only after he himself had been shattered. Put another way, for almost the first decade of the Koinonia experience, Jordan attempted to work within the structures of Southern society and to be a loyal member of Rehoboth Baptist Church.[17] It was only when the church forced him out—rejected him and his vision—that he was pushed deeper into himself and, eventually, began to speak as something of a peripheral prophet. Ernest Becker makes a similar analogy when he says the secret of the religious genius is that "he re-centers himself beyond the world, by making the meaning of life dependent on the ultimate source of meaning, not on the worldly one."[18] Ironically, as long as Jordan was in the Rehoboth church, he was hampered by worldly forces and understandings. Once he was excommunicated, he was free to begin a long journey of refocusing beyond the shared consensus of local-ized meaning and shared values that were Rehoboth.

Clarence Jordan As a Jeremiah Figure

How did Clarence Jordan come to prophetic vision? From his earli-est days, Clarence Jordan had taken in a religious vision of life. Maude Jossey Jordan had described Clarence early on in terms of a Jeremiah fig-ure consecrated before birth. What could she have meant by this? Per-haps she meant that she had seen Clarence growing up with the Bible and its models for living, which he first learned on her knee, and that he had drunk in the scriptures, as with mother's milk. But his love for a reli-gious perspective did not stop there. He had spent a lifetime attempting to read and live out the teachings of the book. So intense was Jordan's commitment that his mother told him just before she died, "I am quite sure that God placed his seal upon you and set you apart to do his bid-ding, even before you came into the world, for at a tender age you loved to read the Bible and found for yourself a Savior's redeeming love." In essence, she told Clarence that his life had been "set apart," like Jeremi-ah. Eventually, Jordan's life will unfold in the manner of a modern Jere-miah, or along the path much like his own protagonist in the "Cotton Patch Gospels"—Jesus the Rebel.

Grieving the Grief of Southern Society: The Shattering of Clarence Jordan

In the language of Walter Brueggemann, Jeremiah is the "clearest model for prophetic imagination and ministry." He is a paradigm for those who follow in his footsteps and attempt to address the deathliness and denial of a culture bent on self-deception. Indeed, Jeremiah embod-ies and lives out the "alternative consciousness" of Moses in the face of the pharaoh-like figures of a culture. In so doing, Jeremiah "grieves the grief of Judah because he knows what the king refuses to know." In simi-lar fashion, Clarence Jordan "grieves the grief" of Southern society in the context of Rehoboth and the boycott that followed. Jordan embraces the brokenness of the covenant and turns, eventually, to reestablish a new one. What Jordan knows, and the South of the 1950s refuses to accept, is that the Old South is dying and a new South is being born, and he is playing a part in the unfolding drama.[19]

As it may be gleaned from the words of Maude Jossey Jordan, the parents seem to have a role in the radical religious journey of Clarence Jordan. Erik Erikson saw it clearly in the lives of young men of genius, who sense early on that their parents expect each of them to be something of a "potential redeemer." These young men grow up with an obligation to create a new future.[20] This is part of what one hears in the pronouncements of Maude Jossey Jordan. Since his earliest days, Clarence has been pushed and "called" to create a new world. In time, Jordan called that new world "Koinonia," after the idealized sense of community that he found in the earliest expressions of Christianity. The potential loss of that new creation through rejection, by the very people he was trying to help, would have been devastating—shattering—for Clarence Jordan. Rehoboth, the later boycott, and attacks on the farm were assaults on the project of Jordan as a great man who has a problem other individuals do not have. The project carries the burden of justifying one's life.[21] Jordan must earn his worth as a human being through the ongoing work and worthiness of his new creation—in this case, "Koinonia." Jordan must protect this vision and reality at all costs, the loss of which is the loss of selfhood and worth. Consequently, Rehoboth meant that Jordan must go beyond the conventional way and speak truth at a deeper level. After Rehoboth, Clarence Jordan became increasingly prophetic and courageous, in part because the very meaning of his life was at stake!

Jordan's journey toward prophetic calling begins with his ability to grieve. Michelangelo's painting of the Sistine Chapel is often considered one of the masterpieces of the world's art. He poured himself into this work and its interpretative schemes. His portrait of Jeremiah is seen by many as an especially poignant and psychological portrayal. The anguish and suffering that Michelangelo saw in the biblical narrative of Jeremiah are demonstrative in the portrait of the prophet's downcast body, with its drooping right shoulder and bowed head. Clarence's mother died before his life took a major turn into the suffering and heartache that was Rehoboth and the boycott. Would she have understood what was happening to her son? One reading of Jeremiah is that his portrait in the biblical text is characterized by "questioning reflexion," and that the latter part of his life is a journey further into darkness along a "via dolorosa," where a prophet begins to play a part in divine suffering.[22]

The personal suffering of Clarence Jordan was immense during the 1950s. His brother Frank would later say that Clarence died of a broken heart. His physical problems, apparently, also began in the 1950s.[23] The violence and hostility also took its toll on Clarence Jordan. He wrote to his college friend and seminary roommate, Claude Broach, and said, "Deep in the heart of every man is the desire to be loved, and it is never pleasant whenever one is hated. The real hurt...is for those people who through blindness, ignorance, and prejudice resist God's love."[24] One of the most poignant speeches or sermons that Jordan ever gave was one titled "Incarnating Brotherhood," in which he responds to the question, "Why don't you folks sell out and move away?" In the heart of the boycott, and soon after he had been arrested, Jordan responds, "If we must be hung on a cross to redeem our brothers and sisters in the flesh, so let it be."[25] The anguish and pain resonates in the tenor of his voice. The youthful optimism is gone—that young self shattered. Jordan is now ready to speak from a deeper place in his being, and his journey will now be toward an increasingly prophetic understanding.

A study of Jordan's childhood indicates that the theme of his early life is "abandonment over against community." The narrative of Jordan's early life is a story of a strong sense of neglect and fear of abandonment, and loss of community. The theme of solidarity with the victim emerges in his young adulthood, and his personal quest, now joined with a larger group, is for "koinonia" to offset the neglect and abandonment that he saw for the poorest of the poor. The establishment of Koinonia Farm was Jordan's adult way to answer the central issue of his childhood. With Rehoboth and the boycott that followed, the devastating sense of abandonment Clarence had felt in his childhood returns and pushes him deeper into himself. The early adult vision of life was "shattered." Jordan had to rework how he would carry out his vocation. This poignant movement in Jordan's life requires a reworking of his understanding of what it means to be a person of faith.

Enacting the Faith: Koinonia As a Demonstration Plot

On reflection, it was no accident that Clarence Jordan went to the region Dubois had called the "Egypt of the Confederacy." There was intention in Jordan's action. Like Moses before him, he wanted to call Israel out of Egypt. But, in the beginning, Jordan's concept of ministry was "incarnational evangelism." In later years, Jordan would live out other dimensions of the prophetic life. In the language of the prophets, when he first came to Southwest Georgia, he saw his task as that of "enacting the vision." The task for Koinonia was "to embody an alternative social order shaped by countercultural habits and practices."[26] In short, Jordan saw his task as living out an alternative vision within Southern community. The reason Jordan came back to the Deep South was because he felt compelled to be a witness in the areas of race, wealth, and war. Koinonia as a demonstration plot, as Jordan called it, was essentially a prophetic word in symbolic action. This idea intensified after the Rehoboth incident and, eventually, became "a full-scale assault on Southern Christendom."[27]

By the early sixties, Koinonia had reached a crossroads. The social circumstances for the experiment that was Koinonia were changing. The original vision in the 1940s of an agricultural missionary enterprise was both timely and needed. But, by the 1960s, the mission seemed outdated because people were moving from the farm to the city, and the changing times had made Koinonia's approach ineffective. The idea of living with a common purse was simply not attractive to African Americans. Clarence was beginning to see that he needed a new vision for himself and for the community.[28]

Clarence knew that the status-quo reality of Sumter County and Southwest Georgia was a place where whites wanted to maintain the oppression and old mentality of slavery. His work was, therefore, not unlike that of Moses in Egypt land, or Jesus, the new Moses, each seeking a deliverance from the pharaohs of the then-current order. Clarence also knew that the politics of oppression and exploitation were tied to a religion of static "triumphalism." He came to see that his work in Sumter County was nothing less than an assault on the consciousness of the old-world status quo and, for that reason, was seen as a serious threat by local whites.[29]

Much of the conflict between Clarence and the people of Sumter County had to do with the reading and interpretation of the Bible. Clarence had learned to read the Bible from the standpoint of the prophets, while the status-quo religion of Sumter County was a conventional Southern reading. Clarence's prophetic reading of the Bible had taught him that the God of the Bible was subversive to culture, not allied with conventional strategies of the management of society promoted by a "domesticated" Bible.[30] At the end of the 1950s, Clarence knew he needed to continue his witness to critique the old order, but also find a way to energize a new vision. A part of the problem was that the encounter with "Egypt" and its "royal consciousness" can lead to numbness. Clarence was tired and the new vision was slow in coming.

So Clarence, in the interim, sought for a way to reframe his own life and to find help for Koinonia. He wanted to work on some writing projects that had been on his mind for some time. To do that, he would need help with the farming operation he had directed since 1942. The twenty years he had spent leading Koinonia had left him physically and emotionally exhausted. Clarence began to look for someone to help with the farming operation, but he also explored the possibility of disposing of the farm altogether. The concept of Koinonia as an intentional community had, essentially, come to an end, at least for now. Strangely, however, the farm had taken a new turn—the mail order business was growing, especially pecans and fruitcakes.

Clarence Jordan and Shattering: An Abiding Critique of the Southern White Protestant Church

After the Rehoboth incident, it became clearer to Clarence that the Southern church—called to be the "body of Christ"—embodied "domesticated" religion, and the hoped-for redemption and reconciliation were an even more-distant possibility. In that regard, Koinonia must be an outpost that reflected an alternative community of the faithful. After Rehoboth, Clarence sought for a renewed commitment to brotherhood across all barriers without compromise. Since the church existed as a mirror of the Southern culture, Koinonia was desperately needed as an "alternative social order," which practiced a consciousness counter to the dominant realm. In this way, Koinonia had embodied a prophetic model from the beginning.[31] But in the late 1950s and into the 1960s, Clarence wrestled with the very real possibility that Koinonia, his attempt at prophetic witness, could come to an end. How would Jordan embody the prophetic challenge if that happened?

How had the Southern church become domesticated? In part, by making conversion (*metanoia*) too easy, Southern churches had failed young people "by muting the social scope of salvation." The legacy of the inferior status of African Americans and the supremacy of whites was allowed to continue, while "growing in Christ" was restricted to a form of cultural piety, such as refusing to dance and refraining from the use of curse words. Likewise, the Southern church through its doctrines on the Bible and Christ tended to create an otherworldly form of religion, which, ironically, allowed the believer to escape the demands of the humanity of God. Jordan thought that an overemphasis on the deity of Christ allowed followers to dismiss the demands of the humanity of God, such as, "Love your neighbor." Religion could become so otherworldly that it became divorced from everyday human experience.[32]

This critique of Southern white Protestantism may have been Jordan's most radical challenge. That is, the greatest threat Clarence Jordan posed to the Southern status quo may not have been his egalitarian beliefs on race, but his relentless assessment of the church, which sought to demonstrate that Southern white Protestantism followed an ancient heresy—docetic Gnosticism—which taught that Christ only seemed to have a body, that he was essentially a "spiritual" being.[33] The Docetics saw the physical realm as evil; consequently, God would not have come to dwell in the flesh. Docetic Gnosticism was, therefore, an overemphasis on the divine nature and a rejection of the physical nature of Jesus. Jordan came to believe that this was what had happened in Southern Protestant theology. "When God became man, we didn't know what to do with him," Clarence said. "We created in our minds an image of him as a super-being, and thus safely removed him from our present experience and his insistent demands on us." Jordan understood that, whenever one overemphasizes Jesus as God to the exclusion of the humanity of Jesus, then the product is Gnosticism.[34] For years, Clarence wrestled with this issue and wondered how to address it. He would eventually conclude that a "flesh-and-blood" translation of scripture was a proper antidote.

Chapter 14

Evoking a New Era:
Rewriting the Bible and Culture

The South wanted to preserve the plantation system.... The momentum of slavery is still carried on by men who are...trying to perpetuate the slave mentality.
—Clarence Jordan

Before the crisis began in 1956, there were some sixty residents on the farm. Three years later, when Koinonia had survived what could be called the worst of the crisis, there were only three families and a few guests and newcomers. In the early sixties, Clarence was not traveling and speaking as much as before. The year 1962 was the year of the Albany Movement, which galvanized the young people who were still at the farm. There were no adequate words to describe this period—one had to "feel it." The mood was not explained by rational attempts. The movement was something like a series of "prayers that well up from a lifetime of hurt...with rhythms that are outlets for determination and solidarity, actions that rise out of a new attitude: what is there left to lose?"[1] Koinonia was involved primarily in an advisory capacity. The Koinonia young people strongly identified with the movement.[2]

After the Albany Movement, the focus of the Civil Rights Movement in Georgia became Americus. During 1963, the facilities of Koinonia were made available to SNCC for training sessions and for residence of some of the leaders, until they were arrested and put in the Sumter County Jail. Four of these young people were charged with inciting to insurrection, which is a capital offense in Georgia, and they were held without bail. Three young Koinonian high-school students (Greg and David Wittkamper, and Jan Jordan) were completely ostracized at the high school where they were also objects of vicious name-calling.

The small group of Koinonians who were left on the farm continued to search deeply for a sense of purpose—"as to whether to continue here. Our group is so small now that the burdens carried by the remaining few are very heavy."[3] Though the group continues to pray and search, no clear answer has come. Indeed, the answer would not come with clarity until 1968 and the death of Martin Luther King, Jr. Clarence has finally begun to write down some of his "Cotton Patch" translations. At this point, he has completed Ephesians and Hebrews.[4]

The End of an Era: The Rise of a Post-Colonial Hermeneutic

Though the Koinonians may have thought themselves to be part of the backwater of history, they were, in reality, interwoven with a global movement for social change. In the late 1950s, a young Jewish refugee from Eastern Europe who had seen the worst era of civilization's violence, which shattered his own childhood and his memories of nonviolence, began to write his memoir. In 1960, Elie Wiesel published his now-classic *Night* in English and, in somber tone, gave a poignant description of the end of the modern age—the world as we had known it, characterized by a naïve understanding of human goodness and certain belief in the myth of inevitable progress, was gone. The end of this older age and its way of perceiving human history and culture was seen by many. Gandhi "saw" the end of British colonialism in India and led the indigenous people of that country to invite the British to leave, taking their colonial ways with them. The new era was dubbed as "post-colonial" by some. Martin Luther King, Jr., sitting in his jail cell in Birmingham, Alabama, felt the *zeitgeist,* or spirit of the new age, and wrote that "the nations of Asia and Africa are moving with jet-like speed toward the goal of political independence...." Meanwhile, forces of the status quo in Birmingham were calling upon King to "wait."[5]

Some radical theologians characterized this turbulent era with stunning themes reflecting the immense cataclysmic movement in history. In England, the Anglican clergyman and Bishop of Woolwich, John A.T. Robinson, caused a stir of controversy with his book *Honest to God,* which, in its synthesis of Tillich and Bonhoeffer, called for a reappraisal of the conversation about God, who is not "up there," but is a "ground of being."[6] Radical American theologians in Atlanta and Tallahassee also called for a new appraisal of "god talk" in both Judaism and Christianity. Thomas Altizer wrote that "the radical Christian condemns all forms of faith that are disengaged with the world." And Rabbi Richard Rubenstein taught that "Nazism is the product of a negative reaction to the Judeo-Christian world....The aim of creating a world in which the Judeo-Christian God is dead (or, more precisely, in which the Judeo-Christian God is negated) was at the heart of the Nazi program."[7] By the end of the decade, black theologians had joined the fray with a discussion of the "God of the Oppressed," and the connection between black theology and black power.[8]

Like the Bishop of Woolwich, Clarence Jordan did not want to talk about the God who was "up there" or "out there." Jordan did not speak of the deity of Jesus, salvation in the hereafter, or the resurrection as entrance into immortality. Jordan and John A.T. Robinson also agreed that Gnosticism was a problem of address for the 1960s.[9] Like Robinson, Jordan had a drive to be an "honest Christian," and, like Altizer, Jordan spoke against religion that was disengaged with the world.[10] In a time of the emergence of immense cultural change, including a new emphasis on honesty in theological conversation and the radical dialogue about the death of God and liberation theology, Jordan sought to rewrite the gospel in an idiom of the common folk, which would penetrate human illusion, rewrite cultural myths, and present a new portrayal of the humanity of God.

In concert with Robinson's and Jordan's emphasis on honesty in Christianity, Martin Luther King, Jr., one of the main protagonists in the civil rights era of the 1960s who helped change the South and the nation, surveyed the Southern religious establishment and framed a question central for Clarence Jordan: "What kind of people are white southerners who worship in these beautiful buildings and what is the nature of their God?"[11]

Samuel S. Hill attempted to answer King's question and to demonstrate the place of Southern religion at the beginning of a post-colonial world. The South has two cultures: Evangelical Protestantism and Southernness, Hill wrote. In time, "religion legitimated the (white) Southern Way of Life." Many Southerners came to see their society as "God's most favored." In time, religion came to be a "reinforcing agent" for the values held by Southern whites. The shared consensus of belief or moral worldview came to hold the transcendent place of God. Thus, both religion and regionality were primary frameworks for meaning and value among Southern whites. But in the common life of the folk, regionality, or cultural consensus, became a "god above God."[12] Clarence Jordan knew, like Martin Luther King, Jr., that the country had reached the end of an era and that change was surely on the horizon. Both King and Jordan lived in the hope that "the arc of the moral universe is long but it bends toward justice," and both lived in such a way as to bring about that reality.[13]

Evoking—Writing Toward a Vision:
The Emergence of a Poet-Prophet

Though Jordan lived at a time when the "Death of God" theology developed in the United States, his abiding concern was the demise of the church. For Jordan, the "ordinary reader" was under the powerful sway of a failed institution: the established Southern church. It had failed, he thought, primarily because the gnostic tendencies of the Southern white Protestant church had allowed a split between the religion of the spirit and the everyday functions of life. Clarence chose to rewrite the gospel and confront the folk with the religion of the spirit ruled by Jesus the Rebel. [14]

Jordan's work on the *Cotton Patch Version* can be characterized in several ways. First, it was a renewed effort to overcome the gnostic tendencies of the Southern church and an attempt to restore it to health. Second, it was an effort to reach the "ordinary reader"—the average Southerner—whom the church had failed to reach with the serious implications of the gospel. He seemed to know instinctively that the church in the South operated in imperialistic ways, and he actively sought a genuine "flesh-and-blood" reading from a Southern perspective.[15] That is, over the years, he was intentional about learning the language of the poor and the downtrodden in the South so that he could translate the New Testament in idiomatic ways. Third, it brought focus to Jordan's attempt, in concert with the demonstration plot of Koinonia, to overcome the bifurcation in the Southern soul—to bring Southerners into direct confrontation with the message of Jesus about spiritual matters. Jordan's attempts at translation—from Hebrews in 1963 to Matthew and John in 1969—grew more and more radical.[16] Fourth, Jordan's writing also tended to rewrite the culture, and to rewrite Jordan himself. His work became clearer and clearer as a critique of culture and an effort to provide a new model for society.

Evoking a New Era

Clarence Jordan knew that he had resources of spiritual power at his disposal, such as gifted figures within the Bible who served as models and whose words could penetrate the illusions that humans construct in their quest for control over their environments.[17] The paradigmatic model for this special group of poets was Moses, who, according to tradition, was molded and shaped in the desert surrounding Sinai, just as Clarence Jordan was being formed into a deeper prophetic awareness by the crucible that was Sumter County. Just as Moses, in contrast to the mythological society of Egypt, began to value an alternative vision of the freedom of God over against the "royal consciousness" of the Pharaoh's imperial realm, Clarence Jordan came to see that Koinonia and, now, a flesh-and-blood reading of the Bible could be an alternative vision to the domesticated Bible and plantation mentality of Southern culture—calling for a new humanity, a new way of being. Eventually, Jordan attempted to deconstruct that plantation mentality the same way ancient Israel attempted to demythologize the imperial strategies that sought to continue a politics of control and status quo.[18]

Rewriting the Bible and Culture: From Jew and Gentile to White and Black

Clarence Jordan was a man of the book, and he knew the Bible was the book of the people—more than the "great code" of human civilization, it provided the worldview for an entire society. Therefore, Jordan's issues with Southern culture and with America were matters of interpretation. Since that time when he got down off of his horse and turned in his spurs to his ROTC commander, Jordan knew his developing understanding of the Bible ran counter to the deeply-held values of the culture, and the disputed values, by and large, had to do with very different ways of reading the Bible, seen to be the authoritative word of God from on high. Jordan knew, therefore, that an important part of his effort to change Southern society was to make an impact on the way people read and understood the Bible. He would rewrite the Bible in the hope of rewriting the culture and the important myths of American society.

Just as the ancient gospel writers, like Luke, traced the orderly or organic development of the work of God in the day—from temple to church—so also Jordan moved from the church to Koinonia and the God Movement. Jordan's region had become known for its orthodox theology, world missions, and gracious hospitality. But Jordan understood the Southern church as a failed institution, and that the message of the meek and lowly Jesus competed with some powerful myths. The most fundamental mythic image was that of the American Dream. From the beginning, Americans have understood their history in religious terms. America was a new Israel. The Canaanites of old were represented by Native American Indians. Like the original Canaanites, there was an effort to blot them out.

Slavery was a second component in the dark side of the dream which merged with the planation system. [19] The white Southerner came to believe that God created and endowed them as a special people to live out and protect the only authentic version of human life. Clarence Jordan, therefore, came to see that the Southern church was propped up and controlled by deep-seated cultural myths that were most visible as a "plantation mentality," which acted as a "god above God"—a powerful set of cultural mores and values that mitigated against a true spiritual life and, therefore, gave a perverse understanding to issues of race, wealth and property, and war.[20]

Jordan's reading of the New Testament, through the lens of a "cotton patch" gospel, was juxtaposed to the plantation mentality and meant to subvert it. The demonstration plot as a "koinonia"—a place where all things were shared or held in common—was directly aimed at destroying the plantation system in the lives of ordinary readers. To achieve the sense of desired confrontation in the life of the ordinary Southern reader, Jordan focused on the racial situation in the American South. He translated the words "Jew" and "Pharisee" as "white man," and "gentile" and "sinner" as "black man" or "Negro." The geography of ancient Palestine became the Georgia countryside. Jesus was from "Valdosta" (instead of

Nazareth) and was born in Gainesville (instead of Bethlehem). The "crucifixion" became a "lynching." The centerpiece to Jordan's koinonia theology was the Sermon on the Mount given by "Jesus the Rebel," who was nothing short of an incarnation of the humanity of God and sought to bring a revolution of values concerning race, property and wealth, and issues of war and peace.

Rewriting Jesus and the Humanity of God

Jesus was a problem for Jordan! Though Flannery O'Connor was surely right when she claimed that the South was "Christ-haunted," the temptation for the average reader was to view Jesus as so divine that he became an otherworldly, ethereal, spiritual figure unrelated to everyday life. So Jordan rewrote Jesus and gave him a new image as a rebel prophet—not a Southern rebel, but one who leads a revolution in values.[21] These values, as preached by Jesus, become the basis for a new society. Jordan introduces John the Baptist and the prelude to the portrayal of Jesus as prophet by saying, "...the word of God came to Zack's boy, John, down on the farm. And he went all around in the rural areas preaching and dipping in the water—a symbol of a changed way of life as a basis for getting things straightened out."[22] What does John say to the folks in the "rural areas"? "You sons of snakes, who put the heat on you to run from the fury about to break over your heads? You must give some *proof* that you've had *a change of heart*. And don't start patting one another on the back with that 'we-good-white-people' stuff, because...God...can make white-folks out of...rocks."[23]

After Jesus was "dipped" in the Chattahoochee, he returned "on fire for God." Then he went into the backwoods, where the Confuser took "some cracks at him." Since you are God's man, then "tell this rock to become a pone of bread." After Jesus rejected this first offer, the Confuser made a second: "Look here, all this power and glory has been turned over to me, and to anybody I want to share it with. Now if you'll just let me be boss, I'll put you in charge and turn everything over to you." But Jesus rejected this offer, pointing out that the scripture says only the Lord shall be your boss. Then the Confuser had one final offer. The Confuser took Jesus to Atlanta, to the steeple of the First Church, and said, since you are God's man, "jump down from here, because you know the scripture says, 'He will give orders to his angels to keep close watch on you.'" But Jesus responded with, "It also says, 'Don't make a fool out of the Lord your God.'"[24]

After this, Jesus was "spiritually invigorated" and he returned to South Georgia, where the word about him went throughout the entire area. He went to his hometown of Valdosta and went to church on Sunday, where he was asked to preach. Jesus read from Isaiah: "The Lord's spirit is on me; He has ordained me to break the good news to the poor people. He has sent me to proclaim freedom for the oppressed…." When he finished reading, the eyes of the crowd were focused on him, and he said, "This very day this scripture has become a reality in your presence." Jesus went on to tell them that "no prophet is welcome in his own hometown.…[T]here were a lot of *white* widows during the time of Elijah…but Elijah did not stay with any of *them*. Instead he stayed with a *Negro* woman over in Terrell County. When the congregation heard this, they ran him out of town and tried to kill him, but he escaped."[25]

Rewriting the Sermon on the Mount: Rewriting
the Culture with a Revolution of Values

The reader discovers the revolutionary prophetic nature of Jesus the Rebel in Jordan's translation of the prophet's teaching in the Sermon on the Mount. As Jesus and his disciples were going through a grain field on a Sunday, some church members saw the disciples picking the grain and eating it. The church members said, "How come you all doing what's wrong to do on a Sunday?" Then, on a later Sunday, Jesus went to preach in a church and there was a man there whose "hand was dried up." The deacons and other folk were watching Jesus closely to see if he would heal on Sunday, because they were ready to charge him with violating the religious rules. When Jesus healed the man, the deacons and some others "pitched a fit and started conferring with each other as to what in the world they would do to Jesus."[26]

After a night of prayer on a mountain with his students, they came down and were met with a great crowd of folks from Atlanta, other parts of Georgia, and as far away as Virginia. They came to hear him teach and to be healed by him. With the large crowd all around, Jesus turned to his disciples and began to instruct them concerning the God Movement, especially about race, wealth and possessions, and war and peace. He began by saying, "The poor are God's people, because the God Movement is yours....But it will be hell for you rich, because you've had your fling. It will be hell for you whose bellies are full now, because you'll go hungry."[27]

For Clarence Jordan, the God Movement was characterized by a renunciation of possessions and wealth. Jordan's "demonstration plot" between Plains and Americus was called "Koinonia," which meant the fellowship or community modeled after the "koinonia" of the early church. Jordan translated the key text in this way: "They were all bound together...by the sense of community, the common meal, and the prayers. They were selling their goods and belongings, and dividing them among the group on the basis of one's need." A new way of living had been taken up by this early group—they had adopted the principle of living by needs. In so doing, this group, Jordan thought, became citizens in the God Movement. They took the assets already given by God and used them to care for the needs of others. Thus, in Jordan's mind, "When his kingdom comes, when his will is done on earth, both poverty and riches will go away."[28]

Clarence Jordan understood the blessing of the poor as a mandate for giving up one's possessions before one entered into the God Movement.[29] Before one could become a member of Koinonia, one had to give away one's possessions and be willing to live in common with the community based on one's need. Jordan understood and appreciated Luke's emphasis on the economic and social conditions of the God Movement, and he enacted that vision in his life and the life of Koinonia as a demonstration plot of the true kingdom. For Jordan, the call to the God Movement was a decision to follow an economic principle of living by sharing based on need. Jesus and his followers, in the past and the present, were to choose a life of poverty. Jesus refused to put any value on earthly possessions "because he saw the utter futility of striving for something that was nothing, in the final analysis, but wormwood." Wealth and material goods are perishable and unworthy of ultimate allegiance. Material wealth can also lead to addiction and a distortion of clear vision. Furthermore, such a life can rob one of a proper relationship with God and others.[30]

The Sermon on the Mount is, therefore, the core teaching of the faith, or a manifesto for the God Movement.[31] This text moves from the foundational social and economic issues to include models of the human, relationships with the other (race), and violence and warfare. In this core teaching, the rebel Jesus gives a revolutionary command: "Love your enemies, deal kindly with those who hate you, give your blessings to those who give you their cursing, pray for those insulting you."[32] According to Jordan, this text raises the "most vexing problem" of human history—how to deal maturely with those who want to do one harm.[33]

Historically, human beings have dealt with this issue in a series of ways. The first major method of dealing with violence is "unlimited retaliation." This essentially means that there is no limit to the amount of retaliation one uses to respond to a violent act against oneself, family, community, or nation. A second major approach is "limited retaliation." Here, restraint is brought to one's strength. For example, "an eye for an eye" is an advance beyond unlimited retaliation. A limit is placed on the harm one can bring to an enemy. The third major approach is "limited love." For example, Jordan thought that the Hebrew Bible calls on the nation to "love your neighbor and hate your enemy."[34] Jordan read these texts to mean that, at this point in history, people thought the "proper place to draw the line was with your race." Based on this understanding, people develop a double standard for dealing justly with others. Jordan thought that this happens without variation when the minority group is large, and that this type of prejudice can be seen in both American and German history, for example. Such prejudice is found in the cry for "white supremacy," in the ideology of the Third Reich, and echoed in the various forms of nationalism, such as "America for Americans."[35]

When commenting on this stage of human history represented by "limited love," Jordan exposed and critiqued the cultural mores and myths embedded in the American self-understanding. In a sermon titled "Loving Your Enemies," Jordan tells about an epitaph he read on a tombstone from the frontier days in Mississippi: "Here lies John Henry Simpson. In his lifetime he killed 99 Indians and he lived in the blessed hope of making it 100 until he fell asleep in the arms of Jesus." How can one kill "99 Indians" and then fall "asleep in the arms of Jesus"? This can happen only if the Indians are made into sub-humans and not counted as human beings—for the law of the land was that, if an Indian killed even one white man, he would get the death penalty. By the same logic, Jordan thought, a nation in a time of war could drop a bomb on yellow people and destroy two entire cities, and those involved would be rewarded with the highest military medals. The conventional logic found in these examples is that of "limited love"—love only your neighbor or those of your race or nation.[36]

In the same sermon, "Loving Your Enemies," Jordan told a second story from the Civil Rights era. A small group of students were traveling in Georgia, and they ran out of gas near a small farm. The two white students walked to the farm to ask for gas from the farmer, while the young black student waited in the car. The farmer was gracious and was glad to give them gas. He offered to drive them back to their car so they would not have to walk in the hot Georgia sun. The students initially refused because they knew that might cause a confrontation. The farmer, however, would not take "no" for an answer. So, when the farmer pulled up to the stalled car and saw the young black student, he became indignant. He associated this integrated group of students with the Civil Rights Movement, and he then refused to give them gas. Apparently, said Jordan, as long as he could work out of the context of "limited love," he could be a Southern gentleman, but when confronted with the reality of need beyond his race, he was no longer able to help.[37]

For the Jesus who rebels against cultural mores and traditional myths, it is not enough to limit one's love for one's own group. This Jesus demands a response of love to those outside of the group. For Jordan's rebel Jesus, this means to respond positively to Black Americans, and to all those who are somehow "other" or outside the group. Jordan prophesied that we, as Americans, will learn to take this step of "unlimited love" or we will perish in the folly of "limited love"—or even with the use of "unlimited retaliation," which seems to rule many military departments. But what is the nature of "unlimited love," and what will it mean for Jesus the Rebel and those who follow him?

The Road to Atlanta and the Scandal of Unlimited Love

At the end of chapter 9, Luke begins to describe a long travel narrative that will take Jesus to Jerusalem. Jordan transposes Jerusalem for Atlanta. The question of "unlimited love" remains in the background for the reader/participant. What follows at the end of this road is the story of Jesus' ministry in Jerusalem and the Passion. The story of the Passion is presaged in as much as Luke says at the outset that Jesus "set his face to go to Jerusalem." Jordan put it this way in the *Cotton Patch Version*: "Now when the days for his arrest approached, he set his heart on going to Atlanta."[38] In this long narrative, Luke provides some of the best-known and, perhaps, most characteristic teachings of Jesus, such as the parable of the Good Samaritan and the parable of the Prodigal Son. Both of these well-known stories help the reader understand Jordan's translation and retelling of the narrative.

One day, a Bible class teacher came up to Jesus and tested him with the question, "Doctor, what does one do to be saved?" Jesus answered simply: "Love the Lord with all your heart…and love your neighbor as yourself." Perhaps the simplicity and quickness with which Jesus answered the question brought another question from the Bible teacher: "But…just who is my neighbor?" In order to answer this question, Jesus began to tell a story. While he was on his way from Atlanta down to Albany, a man was attacked by some gangsters. The robbers took the man's wallet and brand new suit, and then drove away in his car. They left the poor man beaten and unconscious on the side of the road. Not long after this incident, a "white preacher" came down the same road. "When he saw the fellow, he stepped on the gas and went scooting by." Soon after this, a "white Gospel song leader" came by and "he, too, stepped on the gas." Then it so happened that a black man was traveling down this road, and when he saw the fellow on the side of the road, he was moved to compassion and tears. Unlike the other two, he stopped and attended to his wounds and drove the man to the hospital in Albany. Then Jesus the Rebel said to the Bible teacher, "Which of these three would you consider to be your neighbor?" After the Bible teacher said, "The one who treated me kindly," Jesus said, "You get going and live like that!"[39]

On another occasion, on the way to Atlanta, controversy arose and became the background for one of Jesus' most famous stories. The black people and those who supported them were gathering around Jesus to hear his words. But "the white church people and Sunday-school teachers were raising Cain, saying, 'This fellow associates with black people and *eats* with them.'" When this happened, Jesus told a series of stories with the common theme of "lost and found." The most famous of these stories has usually been the parable of the Prodigal Son. In this story, a father has two sons. The younger of the two brothers comes to the father one day and says, "Father, give me my share of the business." Soon thereafter, the young man packs his belongings and left for a foreign country, where "he threw his money away living like a fool." His situation became so desperate that he decided to take a job feeding hogs. When the young man realized that his situation was worse than that of his father's hired hands, he decided to go back home and ask for a job as a hired hand. He had decided to tell his father that he had sinned against him and against God and that he was no longer worthy of being called a son. But, when the young man went home, his father ran to him and kissed him. While the young man was trying to get his confession out of his mouth, his father was commanding servants to butcher the stall-fed steer and barbecue it, and to invite the neighbors for a party. "And they began to whoop it up."[40]

The older brother, who had been working in the fields, came in and heard all the music. He asked a young boy what was happening. When he heard that his father was giving a party for his returning brother, "he blew his top, and wouldn't go in." When his father came out to check on him, the older brother said, "Look here, all these years I've slaved for you, and never once went contrary to your orders. And yet, at no time have you ever given me so much as a baby goat with which to pitch a party for my friends. But when this son of yours—who has squandered the business on whores—comes home, you butcher for him the stall-fed steer."[41] The meaning of this text seems to flow from the context where "the white church people...were raising Cain," saying, "This fellow associates with black people and *eats* with them." So this famous story justifies and vindicates the revolutionary action of table fellowship with outcasts.

New Covenant in a New South: Models for the Post-Colonial Era

As Clarence Jordan surveyed the religion and culture of the South, he knew an old era was passing and a new one was dawning. His rewriting of the Bible essentially rejects the old colonial ways, whereby whites claim superiority over blacks, the wealthy hoard resources, and the nation spreads violence through war. The foundational issue, as he saw it, was a bifurcation of the life of the spirit and that of everyday life and practice. Religion and ethics had been separated from the way people lived. How could this be addressed in the life of the church and in the life of the ordinary reader? Jordan seemed to know instinctively that a praxis-oriented translation of the gospel was necessary for the church and for the ordinary reader. Jordan tried to hold together the life of the spirit and the way people lived. With his translation for everyday life, Jordan redirected the teachings of Jesus to the citizens of the region so that they could no longer divorce their religious experience from daily living. In so doing, he redefined the biblical narrative, setting forth a new covenant that brought on a revolution of values. His translation became an exercise in shattering and evoking. Jordan dismantled the old way and sought to evoke a new vision. In so doing, he carried on the prophetic task that he had begun by establishing Koinonia in 1942.

In summary, the ordinary reader had been accustomed to being a spectator. The religious world was bifurcated, and the reader or average church member could use religion to dehumanize and denigrate other persons on the basis of race, gender, wealth, or nationality. By rewriting the gospel in a Southern idiom, Jordan placed the ordinary reader in the midst of the action and flow of the narrative, thereby making the reader a "participant" rather than an observer. In this way, Jordan sought to re-create the Jesus event and help Southerners experience the God Movement as "news" rather than history. A good example of this practice is Jordan's translation of the parable of the Good Samaritan. By replacing the Samaritan with a black man, Jordan recaptures the original setting of the good "outcast," which becomes potentially world-reversing. In so doing, Jordan challenges cultural images and mythic models of the good person. Through the work of Jesus the Rebel, myths are re-described and, thus, rewritten. Now, the good person is the one who lives with unlimited love and can stand against cultural stereotypes that demean and denigrate. Consequently, Jordan's reading of the New Testament through the lens of a "cotton patch gospel" was juxtaposed to the plantation mentality, and meant to subvert it. The demonstration plot as a "koinonia"—a place where all things were shared or held in common—

was directly aimed at destroying the plantation system in the lives of ordinary readers. To achieve the sense of desired confrontation in the life of the ordinary Southern reader, Jordan focused on the racial situation in the American South. He interjected the language of race and put a focus on blacks and whites. The centerpiece to Jordan's koinonia theology was the Sermon on the Mount given by "Jesus the Rebel," who was nothing short of an incarnation of the humanity of God and sought to bring a revolution of values concerning race, property and wealth, and issues of war and peace. The portrayal of divine-human relationship was now transposed to one's relationship with the poor and the outcasts of society. Such a portrayal of Jesus was a direct challenge to a society that tried to privilege one group over another, and became the basis of a new covenant and the vision of a new South.

The teachings of Jesus, now rewritten, challenge and rewrite cultural tradition, especially with regard to race, wealth and property, and war and peace. The teachings of unlimited love to the enemy or outcast undermine the cultural traditions regarding race and tribe in the South, and revise the images of the good citizen. Thus, Jordan shows how the gospel is extended beyond the exclusivity of the church to the poor and vulnerable elements of society to include all people, and how the nature of the church can be transformed through following Jesus the Rebel in the practice of unlimited love. Jordan would add more specificity to the nature of the new covenant when, in the last two years of his life, he began to read the Bible more decisively in economic terms and to call for a redistribution of wealth.

Chapter 15

Rewriting Clarence: Radical Faith in the 1960s

People who knew Clarence early in his work thought that by the late 1960s he had changed.[1] How did Clarence change and what brought on the changes? The answer appears to be a convergence of several factors in Jordan's life: (1) The violence and stress of Rehoboth and the Boycott; (2) His ongoing crisis of integrity over against despair; (3) The changing sociocultural and economic climate of the South; (4)The writing project for a "flesh and blood" translation along with his own personal reading of the scriptures; (5) The death of Martin Luther King, Jr.; (6) Jordan's on-going reading and critique of society and church; (7) Jordan's encounter with Millard Fuller.

In his early years, Clarence was widely acknowledged as one of the denomination's "best and brightest." He was admired and loved by many. Clarence was not rebellious, nor was he antagonistic. In his early ministry, he tried hard to be part of the mainstream of Baptist life. In Louisville, Clarence Jordan had worked tirelessly to identify the principles by which he would live out his Koinonia experiment. He had taken the scriptures very seriously—reading the Sermon on the Mount almost literally. Furthermore, the scriptures for Jordan did not lead to static doctrine alone but to a lived faith. What he learned, he tried to live out in daily practice. Despite his acceptance of a "go slow" approach which was clearly dictated by the denomination, he was eventually branded as a liberal who was guilty of unleashing his brand of Christian egalitarianism in church and community.[2]

The Violence of Rehoboth and the Boycott

Rehoboth and the boycott in Americus brought an end to the kind of self-certainty that Clarence had struggled to find in Louisville.[3] The violence and stress brought on by Rehoboth and the boycott in all of its related machinations undermined Clarence's way of being in the world. It meant a reordering of his way of being a person of faith. The violent rejection by Rehoboth meant that he could not go back to that way of approaching the community with a missionary zeal that sought to win over the people. The community had responded with complete and violent rejection.

The Rehoboth incident made Clarence an ex-Baptist and he would spend years trying to understand what that meant. He would be increasingly dislocated from his native tradition and separated from the culture that gave him birth. The boycott intensified that experience. In the midst of the boycott, Clarence had written to his former roommate and in human terms described the anguish of being hated. The pain and frustration of the 1950s pushed him into a new communal experience of faith away from what he had previously known. In response to Rehoboth and the boycott, Clarence began to develop a new way of being in faith which included something like a "second naiveté" involving a deeper journey where he was forced to look at himself and valued traditions in new ways. He and the other Koinonians were confronted with an ongoing sense of alienation and estrangement. Jordan was forced to see himself and society in new ways. Consequently, Clarence began to learn more about the traditions of other groups such as the Church of the Brethren, the Lutherans, the United Churches of Christ, the Hutterites, the Bruderhoff, the Mennonites, and the American and the National Baptists.

Integrity Versus Despair

In his speaking engagements in the context of the boycott, Jordan would often turn to the issue of integrity. He did so in discussing the problem for the business men of Americus, the role of his brother Robert as a possible defense attorney, and the story of a dentist who refused to accept a child from Koinonia as a patient.[4] A leader like Jordan has problems others do not have. His project must justify his life, and his analysis of the life and project are subject to an ongoing scrutiny in a lifelong integrity crisis. In his last interview, Jordan admitted, "Ours has been a struggle for integrity."[5] Jordan's use of the theme of integrity in the midst of the boycott implies that he himself was reflecting on his own life in the context of that theme. His admission in his last interview suggests, as typical of other spiritual innovators, Jordan's struggle for integrity has been lifelong and chronic.[6] That is, at this point in his life, Jordan, as he notes in his interview, is looking for a way to be obedient and faithful. In the context of Southwest Georgia in the late 1950s and early 1960s, this also tends to push Jordan toward a more radical faith because the options are minimized by the rejection by the surrounding culture.

The Changing Sociocultural and Economic Climate of the South

When Jordan came to Southwest Georgia in 1942, the economy was just coming out of the Depression era. The farms were desolate and the economy essentially wrecked. There were few jobs for the poor. Tenant-farming had broken down. Racism was institutionalized. Jordan's idea was to create a "demonstration plot" where individuals, without regard to race, could pool their resources and live as the early church did and take care of one another. In 1942, most of the population of the region lived on farms. But by 1960 people had begun to move to the city. Further, for an African American to join such a community was a step backwards. They already lived in an economic system of dependency on white Americans. The kind of lifestyle offered at Koinonia had been rendered both ineffective and impractical as an approach to breaking the color barrier.[7]

Writing and Reading a Flesh-and-Blood Translation

In the 1960s, for the second time in his life, writing would play a part in the restructuring of the life of Clarence Jordan. Writing played a part in the decisive move in his college years beyond tribal and cultural ways. In the context of the radical change that was the sixties, for years, Clarence had wanted to write, especially to work on his idea of a translation of a "Cotton Patch" version of the New Testament. When he did sit down to work, several things began to happen. The volumes became increasingly radical and more controversial over time, mirroring the transformation that was occurring within Jordan himself. His writing also pushed him into theological thought which seemingly stimulated theological changes in his mind. The publication of his Cotton Patch volumes brought a renewed popularity with certain religious groups and brought new speaking engagements.

Ironically, Jordan had sought to do a "flesh and blood" translation of the New Testament so as to put the reader in the flow of history—in the flow of the text. It is very likely that during the writing process, Jordan also put himself squarely in the flow of the text, and wound up with something of a greater prophetic awareness. As Walter Ong puts it, "writing restructures consciousness."[8] It is in the writing process that Jordan found the necessary space from which to envision alternative destinies, and from which to begin to remake the world. In this regard, one might say that Jordan's rewriting the Bible stimulated within himself the growth of an even more intense prophetic consciousness. Put differently, in his rewriting of the New Testament, Jordan rewrites himself. He not only writes himself toward a deeper prophetic awareness but this, in turn, promotes an ever intense prophetic-like stance toward society. Theologically, there were two major foci that received increasing significance for Jordan—the concept of the kingdom, and his view of Jesus.

As Jordan continued his study of the New Testament and read the temper of the 1960s, he began to rethink his understanding of the "kingdom of God." Though Jordan used the phrase "kingdom" early in his work, he later came to conclude that while "the word 'kingdom' fit exactly in Jesus' day...it's out of style for modern man." Jordan went on to say, "I doubt if Jesus would have used it if he had been preaching to 20th-century people." Since the spirit of the times of the 1950s and 1960s was about "movements," Jordan coined the phrase the "God Movement" in order to give the concept of the kingdom a more contemporary understanding.[9]

Though contemporary terms were in order, Jordan went much further. He wanted a rewriting of the text that prevented readers from yielding to the historical temptation of the contemporary church—Gnosticism. Clarence thought that modern Christianity had succumbed to the 2nd-century heresy of docetic Gnosticism. The docetics had affirmed the deity of Christ and rejected his humanity. This was a great modern temptation: to deify Christ and in the process reject the humanity of God. This Jordan thought was a modern tactic within churches and became a way of avoiding responsibility in human affairs "by substituting worship for obedience, liturgy for service, contemplation for action, programs for people, piety for compassion, and a futuristic orientation for the reality of the present."[10]

Consequently, in addressing the issues of translation for the contemporary scene, Jordan found himself, as with the prophets of old, reformulating the old traditions in an effort to make them relevant for the contemporary generation. Jordan's rereading of the text in an effort to make it contemporary, ironically, became a rereading of himself. His reflection on the text inevitably gave way to an increasing identity with the subject of the text—Jesus the Rebel. In fact, Jordan's translation work essentially assumed a "rebel-like" stance as he tried to rework the environment for contemporary Christians who had become spectators, as Jordan put it. In a Jesus-like move, Jordan reordered the circumstances to confront readers with the truths of Jesus the Rebel which they had attempted to avoid. So Jordan tried to put flesh on the radical ideas of the God Movement and confront the reader with it by making them participants in the flow of history. That is, the *Cotton Patch Version* put "the idea of reconciliation in Christ squarely in the context of the South's angry struggle against equality. The Gospel idea of brotherhood was where it belonged—in the discomforting here and now, not in the distant and unthreatening then and there."[11]

In retrospect, it seems that Jordan's writing project for the "Cotton Patch" version of the New Testament promoted a new consciousness in himself and in that sense helped to "rewrite" the author. Clarence wrote himself toward a deeper sense of prophetic awareness that helped to rewrite the concept of the kingdom into the idea of a God Movement with an emphasis on Jesus the Rebel. Reflection and writing on those two ideas also promoted an increasing clarification and identification with both. It also promoted reflection and critique on the Civil Rights Movement, along with the contemporary church and local pastors.

The Death of Martin Luther King, Jr.:
  Shame, Guilt, and Recommitment

Rehoboth and the boycott had essentially dismantled the original Koinonia. Throughout the 1960s Jordan struggled with a definition of his work. By early 1968 with only two families on the farm, Clarence was exploring opportunities for himself and his family. He had decided to take a position with Elton Trueblood, temporarily working at Yokefellow Institute in Richmond, Indiana. What had led to this decision? Jordan was unable to redefine the work at Koinonia. He lacked both the will and the energy to do it. He was disillusioned with the Civil Rights Movement and the Vietnam War. Sociocultural changes had made Koinonia almost irrelevant.

Jordan's reflection on the New Testament and his ongoing interest in civil rights prompted him to write an ironic parable published in the Koinonia Newsletter.[12] It was April 1965, shortly after the Selma to Montgomery march. Jordan found it strange that a "man of no violence" had to appeal to a "man of great violence" in order to accomplish the goals of liberation for a people. Meanwhile the "man of great violence" was busy elsewhere oppressing other people. This was a satire about the Civil Rights Movement and Martin Luther King, Jr., who was dependent upon the federal government which was spending large amounts of money to kill people in Vietnam. Jordan was sad that King, in his mind, had lost a sense of the power of spirituality and needed to appeal to a secular power. But Jordan was also angry over what the government was doing in Vietnam.

Though critical of King and the Civil Rights Movement, Jordan was deeply affected by King's assassination on April 4, 1968. Jordan had several opportunities to leave Koinonia in 1968, but he turned them all down and recommitted himself to ministry in the South. A short time later, Jordan wrote that "now, more than ever, we feel the need to be in the South as white people witnessing to the faith of Jesus Christ." He began to call for "a greater and deeper movement than the Civil Rights Movement—the God Movement," which would be a movement of "God's power, God's love, God's mercy, in short, God's spirit."[13]

How can one understand Jordan's complete change, moving from a severe critique of the Civil Rights Movement and its leader to a new commitment in ministry upon hearing of that leader's demise. When he heard of the death of Martin Luther King, Jr., Robert Kennedy gave what became a famous speech in Indianapolis, Indiana. Kennedy surveyed the options in light of King's death and said: "We can move in...[the] direction as a country, in greater polarization....Or we can make an effort, as Martin Luther King did, to understand, and to comprehend, and replace that violence, that stain of bloodshed that has spread across our land, with an effort to understand, compassion, and love." Kennedy went on to tell of the loss of his own brother to violence and how he had come to view Aeschylus, the Greek poet, as his personal favorite. Aeschylus once wrote:

> Even in our sleep, pain which cannot forget
> falls drop by drop upon the heart,
> until, in our own despair,
> against our will,
> comes wisdom
> through the awful grace of God.[14]

Clarence Jordan responds to the death of Martin Luther King, Jr., in the same manner that he did in the midst of the boycott when he was asked why he did not leave. Jordan chose Kennedy's alternative that included "an effort to understand, compassion, and love." During the earlier season of the boycott, Jordan had written to his former roommate about the pain that Aeschylus says falls drop by drop upon the heart. And Jordan said that "the real hurt...is for those people who through blindness, ignorance, and prejudice resist God's love."[15] The hurt that Clarence expresses in the context of the boycott is a mixture of shame and guilt for the exposure of an entire culture and region. As Jordan says, the hurt for others can be the greatest.[16] The pain that fell drop by drop upon Jordan's heart pushed him to stay at Koinonia and to look for a new way to heal the brokenness of his land.

Reading the American Church and Society

The journey to more radical vision and faith in Jordan's last years is nowhere more evident than in his critique of the contemporary white church. Clarence had concluded that Jesus was the leader of a revolutionary movement, and that Jesus was serious when he called upon his disciples to follow him in that revolutionary life. That is, for Jordan, the God Movement was a revolutionary new life and his followers were to invite others to join. The marching orders for that revolutionary movement were to be found in the Sermon on the Mount. In his last years, Clarence put aside the charm he often exhibited in his youth, and went on the attack calling for the well-to-do church people to share their wealth and move forward in the struggle for peace and harmony in the nation. "You ought to spend at least as much trying to help house your poor brothers [and sisters] whom you have seen as you do trying to house God whom you have never seen," Jordan often said.[17]

Perhaps, above all others, the one symptom of the cultural Christianity that raised the prophetic ire of Clarence Jordan was the refusal of white churches to open their doors to blacks. He gave a scathing critique of the First Baptist Church of Atlanta when they refused to seat Ashton Jones and three black friends. He wrote an open letter to the church and told them that at the very least they should be honest and say that they were not a church of Jesus Christ and that they should repent.[18]

While Clarence had lived his adult life refusing to create unnecessary confrontations outside of normal activities—and had once lectured his daughter on the topic—by late 1965 he was so exasperated with fellow pastors and churches that he thought the time might be right to join in an effort to integrate a white church. Carol Henry's father was speaking at an associational meeting at a Baptist church in Americus. So a large group from Koinonia went to town to attend the meeting and hear Carol's father. Collins McGee, a young black man currently living at Koinonia, was in the group. The group walked in and began to sit down. When an usher realized what had happened, he came down the aisle and asked them to leave. The congregation had just sung "Gloria in Excelsis Deo." Four years later, Clarence would try again with another integrated group at the First Methodist Church of Americus.[19]

In his last years, Jordan grew increasingly frustrated with not only churches but also with pastors who refused to speak clearly on the issues. Many would say to Clarence that they could not be too outspoken or they would lose their influence. Clarence later responded by saying what they were afraid of losing was "affluence." Whenever Clarence had the opportunity, he would lobby for a redistribution of wealth. He often critiqued churches who tried to show off their love for extravagance. Clarence told the story of the Georgia church which spent $25,000 installing a fountain to decorate the church lawn when many in the town did not have running water. When God is God and far removed from the human, Clarence argued, then the church can build a fountain. But if God is seen as a man, then the church has to give a cup of water to the thirsty. In the same manner, Clarence saw the crosses on church steeples not as testimony to the humanity and crucifixion of Jesus but to the deification of Christ and the avoidance of responsibility to care for the human needs of others. To the pastor who bragged to Clarence that we just spent $10,000 for the cross on the top of our steeple, Clarence responded sarcastically that he had been cheated. "Time was when Christians could get those for free."[20]

Encounter with Millard Fuller: The Radical New Thing

In December 1965, Jordan met Millard Fuller. It was, as Dallas Lee described, a "magnificent collision."[21] They met at a time when both men were in the process of change. Millard was a very successful businessman who was looking for spiritual direction, while Clarence was a "religious genius" who needed someone who could respond to an idea and then make it happen.[22] Together, they created a daring new conception that came to be known as Koinonia Partners, which included the original brainstorm of what would become "Habitat for Humanity."

By 1968, Jordan had given up on the idea of a Christian commune. By spring, Clarence seemed to have a sense of "growing despair over the lack of direction for his life." He also had an urgent need to move in a new direction. On April 4, Martin Luther King, Jr., was shot down in Memphis. Jordan grieved over this tragic event but resolved to stay in the South to try to make things better. In May that year, he called Millard Fuller and they agreed to meet at Oakhurst Baptist Church in Atlanta for conversation. After further conversation with a larger group of trusted advisors, "Koinonia Partners" was born. There would be a focus on communication, instruction, and application. The first part meant public speaking events as well as tapes, films, books—all about the radical ideas of the Gospel. Second, there would be intensive workshops with small groups for people willing to join in a more active journey of faith. The third part of application meant a "Fund for Humanity" with an emphasis on partnership industries, farming, and housing. "The fund would provide an inheritance for the disinherited and offer a means through which the possessed could share with and invest in the dispossessed."[23]

A New Covenant with America: Clarence Jordan's Larger Vision

In October 1968, Clarence sent out a newsletter to the "Friends of Koinonia" in which he outlined the new strategy. He began by saying that it had been clear for a number of years that Koinonia was at the end of an era. The goals and methods that were used in the 1940s and 1950s were no longer adequate for the "vast and rapid changes" of the 1960s. Clarence indicated that the changes in the farming industry had made Koinonia, as it was set up, irrelevant. "An integrated, Christian community was a practical vehicle through which to bear witness to a segregated society a decade ago," Jordan wrote in 1968. "But now it is too slow, too weak, not aggressive enough." He outlined how he and Millard Fuller had a shared sense of the "leading of God's spirit." Clarence wrote that now "we want to throw every ounce of our weight into helping men to radically restructure their lives so as to be in partnership with God." Then he summarized the three "prongs" of the new "Koinonia Partners": Communication, Instruction, and the Fund for Humanity.[24]

Clarence now had a larger vision and he was thinking big—in revolutionary terms. Jordan wanted an encounter with the nation. It would be an encounter that might "rock the foundations of the American way." The objective for the new movement was to bring the radical demands of the gospel into clear focus and unleash "a whole new spirit." He was looking for a forum in which he could say that humans must stop all the competition—stop the stereotypical behavior: black, white, rich, poor. "We must be people together, partners under God." He was looking for a way to wage a war on wealth, to create land reform. He was calling on those who had a surplus to share with those who needed it. Jordan was now reading the Bible in economic terms. He was essentially saying that if one had a surplus, or has too much, one "should set a reasonable living standard for your family and restore the 'stolen goods' to humanity through some suitable means."[25]

Jordan had come to think that the "the present structure of capitalism" was wrong, especially with regard to land tenure. He wanted to go back to the ancient Hebrew idea that the earth belonged to God. Clarence wanted to buy a million acres which would be held in trust for families to farm in partnership or to use for rural industries. His "Fund for

Humanity" would be a legal means for restoring the land to the poor. This would be a way of announcing the coming of the new order and the new spirit which Jesus had proclaimed in his sermon in Nazareth: "The Spirit of the Lord is upon me because he has anointed me to bring good news to the poor. He has sent me to proclaim release to the captives and recovery of sight to the blind, to let the oppressed go free, to proclaim the year of the Lord's favor."[26] Jordan read this text as the permanent arrival of the spirit of the Year of Jubilee. Every fifty years slaves were to be set free, land would be returned to those who had owned it previously, and debt would be forgiven. Jordan thought that this was the original spirit of the early church and hence the basis for holding everything in common. The permanent Year of Jubilee, Jordan thought, was needed in 1968 to correct the injustices that had been created by American society.[27]

Rewriting Clarence Jordan:
Charting the Journey to Radical Faith

Clarence Jordan's journey to radical faith began to be visible when he was excommunicated from Rehoboth Baptist Church. He was pushed beyond tribe and cultural religion. His lifelong integrity crisis and his battle with despair helped to push Jordan toward faithfulness to his vision of radical faith. The changing sociocultural and economic background of the region pulled Jordan out of a form of ministry that had grown ineffective and impractical. The writing of his flesh and blood translation had a profound impact on the author. The writing project promoted a new consciousness in him, and helped to rewrite the author. During the writing project, Jordan wrote himself toward a deeper sense of prophetic awareness. Jordan responded to the death of Martin Luther King, Jr., with renewed and deeper commitment. His prophetic vision began to find focus in a critique of American Evangelical Christianity. The journey to radical faith culminated for Jordan in the establishment of Koinonia Partners and a more economic reading of the Bible which called for a redistribution of wealth and the building of partnership houses for the poor. This was essentially Jordan's new covenant idea, no longer simply with the South but with humanity.

The type of faith pilgrimage that Jordan demonstrates is exceedingly rare. Jordan's journey takes him far beyond the accepted cultural consensus of his region and country and places him with others recognized as being "great souls." This type of pilgrimage has been described by James Fowler as that of "Universalizing faith." There are several characteristics of this style of faith which help to understand the journey of Clarence Jordan. (1) Persons with this form of faith defy the usual criteria for normalcy. They have an "enlarged vision" of human community which discloses the partial nature of cultural visions of tribal boundaries. Jordan's inclusion of the poor and disadvantaged threatened the cultural consensus of his region so much so that they tried to drive him from the area. (2) Persons who have this form of faith typically make real and tangible "the imperatives of absolute love and justice." They can be described as an "activist incarnation" of the truths of their vision.[28] It is in this sense that many described Clarence Jordan as the most Christian person they had ever known.

A Land of Activist Incarnation:
Koinonia Partners as Ultimate Environment

During the last years of his life, Clarence established a new landscape of faith. It was more daring and dangerous than previous conceptions. It incorporated a larger vision that eventually became known as Koinonia Partners. It was a land where Jordan's growing identity with Jesus the Rebel seemed more clear and can thereby be labeled, metaphorically as the "land of activist incarnation."[29] Yet it was a place where his vision became extraordinarily simple—a kind of "simplicity beyond complexity," one might say. Dallas Lee, who knew Clarence during that era, said that "what was so intimidating to some and so challenging to [others]...was how...simple he made it....Feed the hungry, clothe the naked....He kept pounding away at the simplicity of it with an intellectual force that made it hard to deny." The central premise for Jordan was the humanity of Jesus. Once that was accepted then the other steps begin to fall in line. It was fundamental and basic.[30]

Clarence identified with and embodied a sense of Jesus as a strong individual. He believed that Jesus could walk through an angry crowd "because he looked like somebody you didn't mess with...." Jordan thought that Jesus had a strength, an inner strength about [himself]...that made you not want to deal with him head-on." Clarence Jordan was that kind of person—"the kind of guy you would think twice about before you went and jumped on him."[31] In his last years, Clarence came to be a powerful presence, a very magnetic individual, in part because of the clarity of his vision and his own inner strength which embodied this vision of Jesus the Rebel. The theme of the incarnation of the divine was so strong in his life—in word and deed—that some were frightened by it. Al Henry, who was at Koinonia for a time, said that "if he stayed in his presence too long, he feared he would become one of his disciples." Clarence was such a powerful presence that one could feel that one was sitting at the feet of Jesus, that he "almost manifest the embodiment of Jesus incarnate."[32]

This land of activist incarnation was based on a new concept of the kingdom of God—a God Movement located in the discomforting here and now. It was shaped by the prophetic critique of the contemporary church and its ministry. The model for the new community was Jesus the Rebel. This land was a place where one could proclaim the freedom of God who played no favorites, but was in fact subversive to the American way. This new land was a place where wealth could be redistributed. There would be an opportunity for the rich to share from their wealth and for the poor to receive the goods necessary for life. There would be a fund for humanity with partnership farms, houses, and industries. A new spirit would grip the land which was international in scope because the inhabitants were partners with God who was free, unrestrained by culture or religion. Such was the faith of Clarence Jordan in late 1968 and exemplified by his new covenant, embodied in Koinonia Partners and the Fund for Humanity.

Chapter 16

An Interlude in Africa

I think we would probably have been asked to leave, but we were
not staying there that long.

—Florence Jordan

Out of Africa: The Gospel of the Freedom of God

In spring 1969, Florence and Clarence Jordan went to Africa. They left
on February 24 and returned on April 10. Clarence spoke many times to
college groups, churches, groups of pastors, and at conferences in Central
and South Africa. Their oldest son, Jim, was getting married to a South
African. Clarence was reluctant to spend the money for such a trip, but
Millard Fuller encouraged him to go, and arranged for sponsorship from
the American Baptist Convention and other groups with missions in Africa. In return, Clarence would visit the missions. They traveled for two
months on an itinerary arranged by Beyers Naude. It was "an itinerary
which could get us in trouble," Florence remembered almost twenty years
later.[1] Like Clarence, Naude's religious journey had been radical. He had
been the youngest member of the Broederbond, a secret Afrikaner Cal-
vinist organization that advocated apartheid. But, after the Sharpeville
massacre in 1960, during which sixty-nine black demonstrators were
killed for demonstrating against restrictions, Naude cut himself off from
his church's political teachings and effectively turned against Dutch Re-
formed support for apartheid. From 1962 to 1977, Naude gave himself
to the African liberation movement. He became friends with Desmond
Tutu, Mamphela Ramphele, and Stephen Biko, who became the "hero
of rising expectations" and whose brutal death brought the status of a
martyr.[2] Naude would later, like Stephen Biko and many others, be
banned by the South African government. Clarence had met Naude in
Winston-Salem at the home of G. McLeod Bryan.[3]

The year was 1969. It was just a bit more than twenty years after Alan Paton had written the novel *Cry the Beloved Country*, a story of social protest describing the kind of society that would later give rise to apartheid. But, even before Paton's story of the 1940s, in Johannesburg and the rural Natal, Mohandus K. Gandhi had an epiphany about the social structures of the country in the Natal at Pietermaritzburg. It was also in the Natal that Gandhi had his awakening in the context of the Bambata Rebellion, and would later go on to develop his ideas about *satyagraha*, or "grasping the truth," which was the basis for his movement to free India from colonial rule by the British, and which was very influential on the life and thought of Martin Luther King, Jr., and the American Civil Rights Movement.

Bambata was a Zulu chief who ruled more than 5,000 indigenous South Africans, who resisted a British tax levied to encourage the Zulus to go into the labor market. The Zulu resistance led to the imposition of martial law in the Natal and, in reprisal, guerrilla attacks from Bambata. Gandhi, surprisingly, at this early point in his life in 1906, thought that the Indians in South Africa could gain from standing with the British. So he actively recruited Indians in South Africa to join in serving as part of a regiment of stretcher-bearers. As a passionate patriot, Gandhi set out at the beginning of the Bambata Rebellion to serve the empire as the leader of a corps of combat medics. But what he saw roused his soul as nothing before—the horrors of war, up close and personal. He learned quickly that this was not so much war as a man hunt—that the British soldiers enjoyed stalking and killing the Zulus, as a hunter pursued wild game. The spears and leather shields of the Zulus were no match for the British Gatling guns. What Gandhi saw pushed him to a personal transformation. As Nelson Mandela put it, "The sight of the wounded and whipped Zulus, mercilessly abandoned by their British persecutors, so appalled him that he turned full circle from his admiration of all things British to celebrating the indigenous and ethnic." His pursuit of a life of transformation pushed him in the direction of the Hindu vow of celibacy, *brahmacharya*. Gandhi's rejection of British nationalism allowed him to see the need for eliminating all violence and serving humanity instead of a colonial nation state. He would eventually go on to advocate *satyagraha*—grasping for truth—which includes a nonviolent lifestyle.[4]

Jordan's trip to Africa took six weeks with visits in four countries: Ghana, Zaire, South Africa, and Kenya. It was an "eye-opening" trip.[5] Jordan found among the whites of South Africa a view very similar to that of the American South—a very religious people who were "cursed by the yoke of white racism."[6] Clarence also thought that many of the missionaries were "living very high," and were separated from the people they were trying to help by their living arrangements. One Mennonite couple in Ghana was an exception. He also found that the poverty in Africa was astounding.[7] While in a village in Ghana, Clarence met an African man who was saving money from his subsistence living in order to buy a mill to grind grain in the village. There was no mill for hundreds of miles, and the villagers had to grind the grain by hand. Though he had saved faithfully, inflation had prevented him from establishing the mill. Clarence advanced him the money necessary and became a partner with him in the venture.[8]

Jordan's most famous disciple would come back in 1973 to Zaire, the former Belgian Congo, and extend the work for "partnership housing" that began on Koinonia Farm under the auspices of the "Fund for Humanity." Consequently, the initiative in Zaire was an extension of the work begun by Jordan and Fuller at Koinonia, and was an effort to share the wealth of those who had with those who did not. Fuller described the history of the region as "one of cruelty, exploitation, and suffering." The effort to help relieve the inadequate housing of this extremely impoverished region was the beginning of the international effort that, in time, became known as Habitat for Humanity. One hundred houses were planned and built.[9]

The Gospel of the Freedom of God

After visiting in Ghana and Zaire, Jordan came to visit with Beyers Naude at the Christian Institute in Johannesburg. Naude had established an itinerary for Clarence to see his country—the beauty of the land, and the people who were struggling to be free. Clarence and Florence went to the Kruger National Park, which was an 8,000-square mile expanse reserved for animals native to the region. There Jordan saw "giraffes, elephants, lions, zebras, impalas, and other wild animals" in what he labeled as a virtual "Garden of Eden."[10] Naude also made arrangements for Clarence to speak at several places, including the Federal Theological Seminary of South Africa at Alice in the Eastern Cape, and the University College at Ft. Hare, which was nearby.[11] The seminary at Alice was, for decades, the main place for training black candidates for the ministry. Because it was multiracial in character and linked with the black-consciousness movement started by Stephen Biko, the seminary became a problem for the South African apartheid regime. When Clarence spoke there in spring 1969, he spoke out of his own sense that the culture of South Africa was much like that of the American South. His message would have been consistent with the ideals of Biko's black-consciousness movement, which sought to critique the status quo and energize and empower black South Africans.

Clarence likely shared the fact that the status-quo reality of the American South was also a place where whites wanted to maintain the oppression and old mentality of slavery, and that this was very similar to what he saw in South Africa. Jordan would have told the young ministers that God was a God of freedom who did not play favorites, and that they were free also. He would have told them to take up the work of the God Movement with utter abandon, that there was a spiritual power in their work. Jordan could have said that their work was, therefore, not unlike that of Moses in Egypt land, or Jesus the Rebel (a new Moses), both seeking a deliverance from the pharaohs of the then-current order. Clarence also knew that the politics of oppression and exploitation were tied to a religion of static "triumphalism"—that religious groups often supported the oppression of minorities, as Beyers Naude had done in his youth. So he knew that a part of the spiritual power of the God Movement was nothing less than an assault on the consciousness of the old-world status quo and, for that reason, would be seen as a serious threat by local whites. So, when Clarence called these young ministers to take up the work of the God Movement with utter abandon, he was calling them to take up a cross and be willing to suffer for the faith, as did Jesus the Rebel.

On his way over to speak at Ft. Hare, one of the professors who went with him told Clarence, "You really caused some disturbance over there this morning." But Clarence continued to speak freely. The University College at Ft. Hare was an elite black institution, where Nelson

Mandela had studied at the same time Clarence was studying in Louisville. It was one of the oldest universities in the country and one of the first Western-style universities to be open to students of color. Desmond Tutu served as chaplain in 1960. Clarence's session at Ft. Hare was a type of question-and-answer time. Again, Clarence spoke forthrightly, as was his custom. The young black students asked important questions and, as Florence said, "Clarence gave them the answers."[12]

When Clarence and Florence returned to Johannesburg, there was an item in the paper indicating that four students from Ft. Hare had been forced out because of "behavior unbecoming to students." Clarence was fairly certain these four were part of the student group to which he spoke. But the students knew the price they might pay for finding the answers to the culture in which they lived. They knew they could be punished by an oppressive regime—that they were going against the rules just to ask questions. "But they were anxious enough to hear, and they did."[13]

In South Africa, Clarence appeared ready to speak to young ministers—to answer the questions they had. He did so seemingly without fear, though the dangers were apparent. When Florence Jordan reminisced about what she saw there, one could sense that there were memories of uneasiness and some element of fear—fear of what could have happened.[14] The story of Clarence Jordan in Africa has never been told before. The little evidence that remains suggests that Jordan spoke with courage and, as he did in the American South, challenged the status-quo apartheid regime in South Africa with his understanding of the gospel of the freedom of God, and Jesus the Rebel. And it came across with spiritual power and energized the students to the point that four of them were arrested. There were likely government informants at the places where Clarence spoke in South Africa. Florence thought that, after Clarence had spoken at several places, word got back to the apartheid regime, and she said that, if they would have had plans for a longer stay, "I think we would probably have been asked to leave."[15]

Clarence left Africa with a confirmation of his new direction. He had seen the stark poverty that existed in Africa. He knew now, more than ever before, that, if one had a surplus, then one had an obligation to share with the poor. He also saw again, as he had in the American South and elsewhere in the United States, that whites in South Africa were abusing blacks with oppressive policies, and that to speak out on such issues was dangerous. Yet the "activist incarnation" that Clarence's life had become was made real in Africa, as he spoke in a manner heedless to his own safety. The realities of segregation that he came to know in America were on vivid display in the apartheid policies of South Africa. Clarence left South Africa with an increased awareness of the need for a new spirit of koinonia around the world. Clarence sealed his commitment to Africa and the new spirit of koinonia by instituting a "Partnership enterprise" grant to a group in northern Ghana. The monetary grant was for $500, and was for a grinding mill in a remote area of Ghana. The money was to be repaid to a "Ghanaian Fund for Humanity," which could then be used for other needs in the area. When he returned to the United States, Clarence continued attempting to evoke the new spirit that he had outlined in the new Koinonia Partners and Fund for Humanity.[16]

Chapter 17

Evoking the New Spirit

When Clarence returned from Africa in spring 1969, he began to travel to various speaking engagements, attempting to evoke the spirit of his new covenant embodied in Koinonia Partners and the Fund for Humanity. He went to New York City to speak at the "discipleship school" at Union Theological Seminary, where he called on young ministers to be "radicals for Christ."[1] At Furman University, Clarence spoke in chapel on the subject, "Things Needed for Our Peace."[2] The death of Martin Luther King, Jr., had sparked the greatest wave of social unrest the country had known since the Civil War. Clarence Jordan continued to be burdened by the inequities deeply embedded in the social order of the country, and by the "language of the unheard."[3]

Evoking the Spirit: What Is Needed for Peace

Jordan began his chapel address by reading from the story of the last week in the life of Jesus (Luke 12 and 13), and by quoting Jesus: "I came to set fire throughout the land. Do you think I came to bring peace?…O Jerusalem, O America, you who kill the prophets and hurl smears at those who tell you the truth.…How many times would I have gathered you?" Eventually, Jesus says that "not one brick will be left on top of another."[4] Destruction was at hand, but the citizens of Jerusalem did not know what time it was. They did not know what was necessary for peace. It was hidden from their eyes. Jordan raises the rhetorical question, what is necessary for peace today? First, what was necessary then was a sense of national and racial humility. The people of Judah in the day of Jesus, Jordan thought, had an exaggerated sense of who they were. They saw themselves as the very chosen of God, and this understanding led to a sense of national and racial arrogance. Such arrogance will invite destruction anywhere in the world that it is found. What is needed is a sense of national and racial humility. Second, Jordan affirmed that a realistic understanding of the nature of violence was necessary. He disagreed with Martin Luther King, Jr., on nonviolence. Jordan thought that Jesus went further. Jordan argued that one must respond with love. That is what makes one a son of God, and truly human. When that happens, one learns to share, and a new spirit, a new attitude toward life comes. Old values go away. We become poor through the identification with the lowly. Jordan closed his address by challenging the Furman students to "have a spirit of servanthood."[5] He had evoked the spirit of his new order, his new vision of how the world should be.

Critique and Challenge to the Church

In May 1969, Jordan went to Seattle to address the American Baptist Convention. He spoke of the contemporary problems facing the church: militarism, violence, poverty, and wealth. In an effort to face these issues, the church must see clearly. To emphasize the urgency of the challenge for the contemporary church, Jordan said, "God is not in his heaven and all's well on the earth. He is on this earth and all hell's broke loose." He spoke of the church as the mother of the children of God. "The job of the Church," Clarence said, was "to be the womb through which God can bring his children into this world." The early church, Jordan thundered, did its job and became pregnant. But, Jordan said, "I think the trouble with God's bride today is that she either has passed the menopause or she is on the pill." At that reference, the audience roared with laughter. Then Jordan came with his attack: "Or perhaps even worse, the Church has gone awhoring."[6] By this, Jordan was referring to the churches that had become so secular, they had lost distinctiveness and calling. The church was a "whore" because it had fallen in love with the world. In some of his last sermons, Jordan wondered if the church was capable of helping to bring about the God Movement. Jordan's call to the church, as well as to young seminarians, was to give themselves with utter abandon to the God Movement.[7]

The Churches of Americus Welcome You?

Koinonia's fall newsletter had two pictures: one of an advertisement, apparently from the ministerial association of Americus, which declared that "All the Churches of Americus Welcome You"; and then one with a caption—"You are not welcome"—of the First Methodist Church on August 24, when Clarence and an integrated group from Koinonia attempted to join the worship service.[8]

Jordan's address to the American Baptist Convention in Seattle made it clear that he wanted to continue to challenge the contemporary church to fulfill its calling. The need for the fulfillment of the high calling of the church was seen, by Clarence, as nowhere more evident than in changing the practices of exclusivism in worship. In July 1969, the issue arose once again for Clarence and Koinonia. A group of students had come to the farm to work on the playground equipment for the new housing development. One of the students was a young man named Don Chappell, the son of Methodist missionaries to the Congo. He was on his way to begin his freshman year of college in California. On the way, he had decided to stop at Koinonia to help with the project. During his time at Koinonia, he decided to go into Americus to visit with local Methodists. The date was July 6, 1969. This idealistic young man, who had been part of a noble missionary effort to central Africa by United Methodists, thought that customs would be the same as what he had grown up with on the mission field. So he went into Americus to seek fellowship with local Methodists. But, from the perspective of the Methodists in Americus, he made a mistake. He brought with him a Puerto Rican friend and a young black man. They were met by the "hospitality" committee and told that they were not welcome. Don Chappell was understandably upset. "Since the Methodists had sent his folks to tell blacks in Africa about Christ, he didn't understand why the church in *his own country* wouldn't want to tell blacks about Christ."[9]

A memo of this event was sent to the Director of the FBI, as well as to a series of other government agencies in the region, under the title, "Koinonia Farms Racially Integrated Group Attending Church Services in Americus, Georgia, July, 1969—Racial Matters." The FBI alerted not only its own agents, but also the U.S. Secret Service, Atlanta; the III Military Intelligence Group, Ft. McPherson, Georgia; the Police Department, Americus, Georgia; the Georgia Bureau of Investigation; the U.S. Attorney, Macon, Georgia; the Naval Investigative Office, Charleston, South Carolina; and the Office of Special Investigation, Robins Air

Force Base, Georgia.[10] In another unfortunate event, Millard and Linda Fuller were arrested in the nearby town of Unadilla for violating a city ordinance prohibiting whites from visiting in the homes of blacks.[11]

Apparently, the refusal of the First Methodist Church in Americus to admit people from Koinonia to their worship services raised the prophetic ire of Clarence Jordan. He and two blacks went back to the Methodist Church in Americus on August 24, 1969. Once again, they were refused entry. The group remained outside the church during services and attempted to talk to members of the church as they were leaving. There was a photographer present for this occasion who took pictures of the event. They were turned away again. This time, "Clarence was virtually mute with disappointment and anger."[12] Once again, information on the church-attendance activities of the Koinonians was sent to J. Edgar Hoover and the various security sections in the region.[13] Almost fifty years after such an event, one wonders why there was such interest in people going to church. It seems clear that, in the months after the death of Martin Luther King, Jr., and the violence that rang out in regions all over the nation, the FBI was extremely sensitive to any kind of event that might bring more violence. G. McLeod Bryan wrote of this event, "This carefully documented and thoroughly cross-witnessed FBI surveillance report is probably the last public record of Clarence Jordan before he died. It is a tribute to a life lived unafraid of the consequences of opposing his culture in order to practice universal brotherhood."[14] The pictures of this event were some of the last that were taken of Clarence Jordan, and became part of his legacy.

Toward a Human Universal: Establishing
*   Koinonia Partners and the Fund for Humanity*

In October 1969, Jordan was busy writing a second report to the Friends of Koinonia and giving the details of the first year for Koinonia Partners. The vision is "slowly becoming reality," Clarence wrote. The old charter for the farm was amended in 1969 to reflect the new work. The administration of the new organization was turned over to Millard Fuller. Clarence was now more able to travel, speak, and write. The greatest concern during the first year was, according to Clarence, "whether or not the idea would strike fire in the hearts of people throughout the world....Did it make sense to a searching generation? Or would a mere handful dance in its light?" While these questions were not fully answered during 1969, Clarence reported that sincere people "from California to the Carolinas, from Africa to Australia have joined the circle of partnership." Many have sent prayers and goodwill; others have given generous gifts or free-interest loans; and still others have given time to the new enterprise. "A few have answered the call to radical discipleship by drastically altering their lifestyles to align with the teachings of Jesus." Clarence noted an immediate need for people to help with the funding of "Partnership farming, industries, and houses." He noted that $100,000 had been raised for interest-free capital for these enterprises, but more was needed. He hoped, in the coming year, to build twenty partnership homes on the north side of the Koinonia property. This would cost $130,000 to $140,000. These homes would be built for displaced rural families at a cost of $6,500. They would be "modern, attractive, 3- and 4-bedroom concrete houses" for which the family would pay $25 a month, interest-free. Two houses were already built and a third was under construction. Clarence hoped to purchase another 5,000 acres "to emancipate it from the evils of speculation and to make it available for the free use of disinherited people." This would cost approximately one million dollars.[15]

In October, Clarence also met with Walden Howard to do an interview for publication in *Faith At Work*. They met at 6:00 in the morning before the day's work. Clarence gave a review of his life's work. He said he had often wondered how much good he had done "by letting those people ride by here and shoot at us." Then he went on to say, "Ours has been a struggle for integrity. What will come of it? I hope we can say, 'We've been obedient.'"[16]

Clarence had rarely been sick. He had lived under tremendous stress for a long period of time—a time when he did not get adequate medical care. Apparently, he did have some serious heart trouble, perhaps a heart attack in 1965 and some trouble in 1955. The last year of his life had been exhilarating. True, he was looking tired, but he had new vision and he was rushing ahead with momentum, almost as if he knew there were important things to be done and the day was late. In a service at Oakhurst Baptist Church in Atlanta in summer 1969, Clarence somehow got distracted and started talking about death, almost as if he were thinking out loud. He had a smile on his face and he was speculating about what death would mean. Some of the people there were shocked, but, apparently, it was a subject on his mind.[17]

In October, a few weeks later, Clarence got sick and was ill for several days. On the night of October 28, he spoke with P.D. East, who was planning a visit for the following weekend. October 29 was a cool, crisp day in South Georgia, and Clarence was feeling better. After lunch, he left his apartment and headed for his writing shack. Toby the big, red English Shepherd spotted Clarence and took off trotting behind him. Clarence was working on the translation of the Gospel of John. He had finished eight chapters. It would be a good day to work in the shack, because it was cool outside. Lena Hofer, one of the young people who had recently come to Koinonia, stopped by for a copy of Clarence's new book on Luke–Acts. As she was leaving, Clarence slumped over in his chair with a massive heart attack.[18]

Clarence died as he had lived: the iconoclastic writer-prophet translating scripture to challenge his region, but dressed in an old, green sweater and bright-orange cap—the clothes of a working man. He was also treated in death the way he had been in life. The county coroner refused to come to the farm. Millard Fuller had to take Clarence's body into Americus. The autopsy at the local hospital revealed the cause of death to be heart failure and an incidence of pneumonia. Men from the community dug a grave on the back side of the farm known as Picnic Hill. At 3:30P.M. on October 30, Clarence was laid to rest in the red Georgia soil that he had loved so much. Millard Fuller read selections from Clarence's "Cotton Patch New Testament." Clarence was buried in an unmarked grave on Picnic Hill, in his work clothes in a cedar crate that Millard had found in Americus. He was 57.

Chapter 18

A Dangerous Memory:
The Legend and Legacy of Clarence Leonard Jordan

> The radicality of God's nonviolence constantly challenges the normalcy of civilization's violence....
>
> —John Dominic Crossan

Clarence Jordan was a Baptist dissident and a radical Christian who thought the church had become a slave to culture and an enclave of racism. He taught and preached the concept of the kingdom of God on earth. For Jordan, the constant emphasis on the divinity of Jesus and the elevation of the Bible to support the ethereal Christ were both part of the denial of the humanity of God which, in Jordan's mind, led to a bifurcation between professed faith and daily practice, and to a form of modernday heresy. In marked contrast, Jordan attempted to hold faith and practice together. Against the status-quo segregated South, Jordan took a stand for egalitarian relationships for all people. In contrast to the rampant materialism of the country, Jordan emphasized the conservation and sharing of resources. Over against the nation's militarism, Jordan stood for the peaceful resolution to war.[1] He thought that when one began to truly follow Jesus, then racial reconciliation, economic sharing, and true humility would begin to take place. But as long as churches mirrored the dominant culture, there would be a need for demonstration plots like Koinonia to be an alternative vision against domesticated religion.[2]

After the death of Clarence Jordan, the memory of his radical pilgrimage continued to be in dialogue with the culture, albeit as a minority witness against the larger dominant American ethos. That is, the celebrated memory of the life of Clarence Jordan in the hands of some progressive church groups began to be elevated to the status of a moral exemplar, and in time as a "saint"—a model for contemporary living. A close reading of the legend of Clarence Jordan as a saint, and the nature of the time period since his death implies that the narrative about Jordan in the collective memory developed as a countercultural model and alternative vision to the dominant ethos in America. The legend of Jordan as a moral exemplar continues to critique the contemporary church and the nation, and embodies a rejection of racism, militarism and violence, and consumerism. The dominant ethos was exemplified by figures like W. A. Criswell and his followers.

Jordan and Cultural Christianity: Exemplary Models and the Question of Address

After his death, Jordan's voice and memory has continued to be alive in American culture from 1969 to the present through the work of Koinonia, Habitat for Humanity, and his writings. Yet the dialogue has established only a witness to an alternative vision. The dominant ethos has been very different from the spirit of this minority group of churches and has been very powerful. From the beginning, however, religion has functioned with a pragmatic purpose in the larger culture.[3] One such purpose has been the creation of exemplary models from which the faithful can gain insight and understanding on how to deal with the questions and crises of the day.[4] One of the major issues of address for these exemplary leaders has been historically how to deal with violence especially as seen in the specific areas of racism, poverty, and war.[5] Different groups within a given society choose different figures for emulation—figures who characteristically see the issues in a manner that resonates with their particular societal group.

Two historically important figures who, in time, came to represent different groups in the American South in the twentieth-century were W.A. Criswell and Clarence Jordan. Though they were both described as "saints" by members of their respective following, Criswell tended to endorse the "status quo" while Jordan tended to be "change-oriented."[6] Whereas Criswell tended to endorse the dominant culture in American society, Jordan was a dissident and tended to support minority causes. The larger question of society and violence was an element of "address" for each. Criswell tended to see the issues of the day in terms of strong leadership whereas Jordan sought a voice for the disenfranchised.

Criswell and Jordan shared a heritage as Southern Baptists and both became icons and exemplary leaders in American society. Criswell's story helps to give perspective to Jordan's life and legacy. The lives of Criswell and Jordan were so similar that they graduated from the same institution, at approximately the same time, with an identical degree—the Ph.D. in New Testament Greek from The Southern Baptist Seminary in Louisville.

One of the major issues of address for Criswell and Jordan was how religion functions in society. Criswell tended to see the task of religion and religious leaders in terms of maintaining the shared consensus. Strong leadership was the proper mode for leaders who would function as the moral guardians of orthodox society. Here, there was little or no room for questioning norms and assumptions. The welfare of society was at stake. Jordan, however, saw things differently. As opposed to Criswell's orthodoxy, Jordan looked at society through the eyes of orthopraxy—faith is not simply a matter of orthodox belief, but involves correct practice of belief. This perspective lead Jordan to a dissident stance when it came to the cultural and religious matters of racism, poverty, and war.

The Dominant Ethos: Materialism and Consumerism

The dominant and sociologically orthodox approach to life in America has been "consumerism." The ideology of this lifestyle, Walter Brueggemann argues, has been "that the whole world and all its resources are available to us without regard to the neighbor...[and] assumes more is better." The logic of this script is that this is the way to happiness, and that it is the responsibility of the American government and the military to protect these shared values, this American freedom.[7] The minority critique of this shared consensus is that this set of guiding beliefs for the dominant culture has been "scripted"—Americans have been given a certain ideology essentially through nationalism and greed. This dominant American script which is "consumerist" calls upon "strong" leadership and a dominant role for the military to "protect" American values and freedoms, which essentially means that the military, with proper government oversight controls markets and resources. Yet, as the critique argues, such a system pushes people to be afraid, to see others as competitors, rivals and threats as opposed to the building of an ethic that views the world as a neighborhood.[8] Military consumerism fails as a transcendent ideology and leads to a horrific misuse of national resources with a resultant tragic loss of life and destruction of civilization and culture.

John Dominic Crossan sets forth a similar philosophy of human history. The central dynamic of human history has always been a tension between "the normalcy of civilization" with its emphasis on violence over against the element of nonviolence in the "radicality of God." Jordan's life, however, was witness to another dynamic where, to use Crossan's words, "the radicality of God's nonviolence constantly challenges the normalcy of civilization's violence." The progressive church groups, who have proclaimed Jordan as a moral exemplar, have seen and believed, as did Jordan, that "[b]eyond all doubt, [the] most vexing problem, from prehistoric time to the present, has been learning how to respond maturely to those who oppose [us]. We have learned how to respond to our friends, but to respond to our enemies—that is the problem."[9] Jordan's answer, affirmed by some minority church groups after his death, was an emphasis on the unlimited love of God. Hence the legend of Clarence Jordan picks up where his life left off—giving witness to the radicality of the love of God for all.

After the death of Clarence Jordan, Southern Baptists continued their perceived role as moral guardians of Southern culture through the Conservative Resurgence and linkage with the Republican Party. W.A. Criswell came to symbolize the Baptist church in America, and to embody the form of cultural Christianity that became the focus of Jordan's prophetic ire.[10] As pastor of the First Baptist Church of Dallas, which was "arguably the most powerful Protestant church in America," Criswell became a larger-than-life and legendary figure.[11] The church had 29,000 members and when he became president of the Southern Baptist Convention, he presided over a 15,000,000 member denomination. Criswell's views on race, religion, and politics were typical of many Americans and he would participate in the "Southernization" of American religion and politics. That is, in some essential way, America became "Southernized," as John Egerton has argued in his book.[12] The South and the rest of the nation have, since the end of the civil rights era, become more and more alike. Unfortunately, the two entities have shared "sins" more often than not—"sharing and spreading the worst in each other."[13]

In the year that Clarence Jordan died, W.A. Criswell was President of the Southern Baptist Convention and he published a small but influential book, *Why I Preach The Bible as Literally True.* The book with its narrow emphasis on doctrine—along with Criswell's lifestyle—promoted the kind of "spectator" mentality and spiritual schizophrenia which, in Jordan's opinion, allowed for a bifurcation between faith and practice. The fact that Criswell was a model and hero for thousands of Baptist pastors made this even more serious. For Jordan, an extreme emphasis on the divine historically led to an exclusion of the humanity of God, hence a form of spiritual schizophrenia. With the ecclesial divide between the divine and the human, the reader became free to be a spectator, uninvolved in the ethical issues of the day. Jordan's emphasis on orthopraxy— the holding together of doctrine and practice—led him to severely critique the church which became so "orthodox" that it forgot the human element of relationships.[14]

So, while Criswell was writing a book on the authority of the Bible, Jordan was finishing up his project on the *Cotton Patch Version,* which was meant to overcome the kind of cultural situation the Dallas pastor was helping to create. As Criswell's Baptist brand became more national, it suffered from cultural accommodation. That is, some distinctive spiritual values were cast aside.[15]

While Jordan wrote in his small and humble "writing shack" on the edge of the cotton field, Criswell had three lavish offices from which he exercised control over his religious empire which comprised five blocks in downtown Dallas and included a high school academy, a college, a shelter for the homeless, a radio station, and thirty mission congregations. Criswell also had a study in his million-dollar home in East Dallas and membership in the country club. Jordan lived in an apartment in a remodeled farm house typical of poor farmers in Southwest Georgia. Criswell presided over his empire in the "Big D" which had become known as the capital of materialism in that region of the western hemisphere. According to a first-hand observer, "Dallas understands two things: money and power. You are valued according to how much you possess of one or both. If the gods of materialism blessed you with both, you are virtually worshipped." The location of Criswell's empire then was situated where "the way of the cross meets the American Dream—Via Dolorosa at Wall Street."[16] Criswell himself admitted the possibility of the problem: "I am an affluent preacher," he said. "I often wonder how it would be if I didn't have these things. I like the life I live. I like the car, the house, the place in the community. I like the prestige....Sometimes I wonder if I am as worldly as the materialistic people in the city." From Jordan's perspective, it was clear that whenever the Via Dolorosa met Wall Street that the banking crowd had the upper hand. In his mind, if one had a surplus, then one should seek to find a way to give it to the poor.

Religion and Race

W.A. Criswell continued to promote a cultural view of religion and race throughout much of his life.[17] In a speech to the South Carolina evangelism conference in 1956, Criswell called on ministers to be true preachers of the gospel. True preachers, he said, resist with passion the mandated desegregation order which he decried to be "foolishness" and "idiocy." His rhetoric portrayed the Southern Baptist Convention as the established religion of the South and gave ministers the right to speak for all white Southerners. Within a few weeks of this speech in early spring 1956, Clarence Jordan would begin to endure an unimaginable level of violence and suffering from the culture that Criswell was beginning to incite. The supporters of civil rights, Criswell said, "are all a bunch of infidels, dying from the neck up." Then Criswell called on Baptist ministers and church people to stop those "good-for-nothing fellows who are trying to upset all of the things that we love as good old Southern Baptists."[18] Criswell continued to give racist interpretations of scripture as late as 1979.[19]

Yet Criswell was very discerning in terms of the social and political climate of the day. When he was elected to be President of the Southern Baptist Convention in 1968, Criswell confessed that he had been wrong on race, and he led his church to have an open door policy. Despite Criswell's public stand, racism continued to be a problem for Southern Baptists. He also perceived that the emerging political conservatism in the nation would be a natural ally for the New Religious Right. In this regard, "he would later be hailed as both the godfather of the Conservative Resurgence of the Southern Baptist Convention and a spiritual advisor in the Southern strategy of the Republican revolution."[20] While Criswell came to see that his anti-desegregation stance would marginalize him and his church, he found new avenues of involvement in guarding the cultural consensus through participation in the Conservative Resurgence and the Republican Party.[21] Like George Wallace before him, he continued to preach exclusivism and stirred anger in the larger cultural milieu, attempting to spread a Criswellian soul to the entire country and to remake the nation in his image.

War, Violence, and Protecting American Values

In his quest to guard the social order through strong leadership, Criswell set aside the long-held Baptist distinctive of the separation of church and state and involved himself directly in the campaigns for the presidency. In 1976, despite some differences with Gerald Ford, he publicly supported the Republican over fellow Baptist and Sunday-school teacher Jimmy Carter. In the years that followed Criswell would endorse and actively support Ronald Reagan, and the Bush family.

In fall 1979, as W.A. Criswell prepared to help launch the Conservative Resurgence, an effort to take over denominational control of the Southern Baptist Convention, Jimmy Carter became embroiled in the Iran Hostage Crisis, and *Sojourners*, a monthly magazine promoting Christian social justice, dedicated its December issue to "The Legacy of Clarence Jordan." The magazine commemorated the 10th anniversary of Clarence Jordan's death "by celebrating his life and the enduring evidence of his vision." Jordan was remembered as one who "taught…the meaning of the incarnation" which for him was the major motivating factor in his work. He was described as having lived in such a way that his spirit endures in the life of Koinonia and in the lives of the people who loved him. Jordan became an example of one who was willing to embrace the suffering of Christ and thereby able to accept others who suffer. The basic events of his extraordinary life are rehearsed, and the growth of his "reputation as a powerful, uncompromising preacher" is noted. But there is no mention of what comes a few years later—the idea of Clarence Jordan as a contemporary saint—an exemplary model for the current age offered by some progressive church groups.[22]

Ironically the same language used by Joyce Hollyday to describe Jordan—"powerful, uncompromising preacher" could be used for Criswell. Beginning with the election of Ronald Reagan in 1980, there was a new effort to use religion to attract voters and to solidify political power. Criswell publicly welcomed Reagan to a Roundtable meeting in Dallas, and later described him from his Dallas pulpit as "the best president we ever had."[23] With the political support of many evangelicals, Ronald Reagan tripled the national debt largely because of huge increases in the defense budget. Based on a review of a large number of government documents *The Washington Post* reported that the Reagan administration also arranged for the sale of chemical weapons such as anthrax and bubonic plague to Iraq.[24] According to the report, this U.S. aid came after Iran, an unchecked fundamentalist regime, had gained the upper hand in the Iraq-Iran war and appeared to threaten Persian Gulf states who were "key suppliers of oil to the United States."[25] Reagan initially escalated the cold war with the Soviet Union, sent troops to Lebanon and to Grenada in 1983, and backed repressive regimes in Latin America. Because of his use of the military, some critics accused Reagan of warmongering and being overly aggressive and imperialistic. In that same year, an article appeared in *The Baptist Peacemaker* titled "A Reconciler from 'Dixie': Clarence Jordan." Robert Parham detailed the basic elements of the Jordan story and emphasized his "peacemaking." Then he announced that "Jordan is now recognized as a 'Southern Saint' wearing denim britches...."[26]

In 1988, Criswell publicly endorsed George H. W. Bush for President. Criswell placed Bush's picture in the church newsletter. Bush continued the Reagan administration policy on chemical weapons to Iraq.[27] In January 1991, George H.W. Bush sent troops to the Middle East to liberate Kuwait. In retrospect, it has been described as an elective war. The next year, Henlee Barnette, a distinguished Baptist scholar who had known Jordan since his Louisville days, put together a small but important volume that included his own estimate of the work of Clarence Jordan and the memories and assessments of many who had known him. Barnette made a striking comment about Jordan at the end of a short chapter on Jordan's theological vision: "Clarence was a man who embodied both kinds of sainthood in one life. His lifestyle of compassion for the poor and defenseless, and his courage in the face of evil, provides a model for us all."[28]

There were many military events during the presidency of Bill Clinton: the Battle of Mogadishu in Somalia in 1993; the bombing of Bosnian Serb targets in 1995; a bombing campaign in Yugoslavia in 1999. Clinton had warned of a possible quest for nuclear weapons by Saddam Hussein, and there were 166 aircraft attacks in Iraq in 1999. In the same year, James C. Howell published a volume titled: *Servants, Misfits, and Martyrs: Saints and their Stories*. In this volume Howell describes the typical array of Jordan stories and then lists Clarence Jordan as a saint among a great cloud of witnesses.[29]

George W. Bush, like his father, used the military for elective warfare.[30] In the post-9/11 presidency of George W. Bush there was, arguably, an increased use of religious rhetoric and a commitment to a type of political fundamentalism that challenged both the history and nature of American politics.[31] David Domke has argued that in the aftermath of 9/11, the Bush administration "converged a religious fundamentalist worldview with a political language to create a *political fundamentalism* that offered familiarity, comfort, and a palatable moral vision to the American public...."[32] But this strategy did more. By controlling public discourse, the rhetoric of the president and administration denied an opportunity for national self-examination and a hearing of diverse viewpoints.[33] On March 20, 2003, American forces invaded Iraq. By May 1, President Bush, feeling the success of his campaign, declared an early victory. But the war and heavy fighting continued. In 2004, the scandal of Abu Ghraib emerged with horrific stories of human rights abuses. The Iraqi insurgency began in 2004 and casualties in the hundreds of thousands began to be reported. Though the Bush administration had begun the war on the rationale that Iraq possessed weapons of mass destruction, no substantial evidence was found to prove the claim. The misrepresentations began to draw heavy criticism from within the US and abroad.

By 2005, despite all of the use of religious rhetoric emanating from the White House, there seems to have emerged a sense of imminent disaster in the country. Peggy Noonan, a prominent Republican journalist, wrote an essay for *The Wall Street Journal* in which she described "an un-spoken subtext in our national political culture...a subtext to our society." That subtext is, Noonan wrote, the idea that "in some deep and funda-mental way things have broken down and can't be fixed."[34] The basic question, as John Dominic Crossan reads the issue, is "How is it possible to be a faithful Christian in an American Empire facilitated by a violent Christian Bible?" For Crossan, the story of struggle implicit in the later years of the twentieth-century and the early years of the 21st century is the tension between the "normalcy of civilization's violence" and the "radicality of God's nonviolence." The dominant political history of the day has been the normalcy of civilization negating the radicality of God's justice incarnate in Jesus.[35]

Noonan read the struggle in 2005 as being so intense that she de-scribed the cultural sense of imminent disaster with the image of the "wheels...coming off the trolley." For John Dominic Crossan this central image of Noonan's article was a metaphor for the decline of an empire, something of an allegory of the role of empires in civilization.[36] The hor-rific narrative of the Iraq war was soon followed by the international hor-ror story of the worst economic disaster since the Great Depression. This devastating financial crisis which came in the later years of the first dec-ade in the 21st century emerged as a result of the loss of values which allows for abuse of the powerless.[37] Ironically, many American churches had participated in a "conservative resurgence" and witnessed a "South-ernization of American religion," but said little when this debacle moti-vated by greed and criminal behavior spread across the world as the world banking system was pushed to the brink.

Just a couple of months before Noonan wrote her article, Jill Ogles-by Evans preached a sermon at the Emory Presbyterian Church in At-lanta titled: "Yours in Faith and Expectation—Clarence Jordan." Evans rehearsed some of the basic episodes in Jordan's biography with an em-phasis on Koinonia and went on to describe Jordan as being among the saints of Christian tradition. She included a number of quotes from Jor-dan as he interacted with the people of the region, and she described the connection between Jordan and Habitat for Humanity. Evans also gave emphasis to the theme of radical discipleship. She closed by admitting that Clarence would have laughed at the idea of being a saint.[38]

Reading a Legend: Autobiography and Parabolic Event

The legend of Clarence Jordan is essentially a collection of stories that over time gains currency for understanding Jordan's life as a hero worthy of imitation. Jordan's legend is based, in part, on auto/biographical narrative and the embellishment of those who passed the tradition on. There are a series of stories that were "selected" by collective memory, which means they were popular with the people who heard them, in part, because of the witty aspects or unique features and partly because they imply a distinctive truth about Jordan. Clarence participated in the process of telling, which indicates that autobiographical narrative is at the base of the legend. That is, Clarence, either in public speaking or in response to questions, often narrated his own story. Essentially, autobiography is about the mystery of human selfhood unfolded through metaphoric process. Autobiography illumines the unknown mystery through metaphor. Some of the events in autobiographical telling can be understood as "parabolic events." The self of autobiography is incarnated through concrete events, and these aspects of one's life become parabolic when as complex images they embody a part of the secret of the individual's life.[39]

A composite model for the Jordan legend operating among progressive groups includes episodes such as his childhood encounter with racism and violence at the Talbot County Jail; the ROTC episode when he was a college senior; the incident in Louisville when angry blacks are going to kill a white man; the saga of Rehoboth Church when Clarence is voted out; the Koinonia story; the connection with Habitat for Humanity; and the anecdotal tradition: a miscellaneous collection of sayings attributed to Jordan. These incidents and stories all involve Jordan in the work of autobiography and consequently give the reader/listener basic aspects of the "metaphoric unfolding" of the life, and in this sense the larger meaning of the legend.[40]

Perhaps the foundation of Jordan's legend is an event that goes back to his early adolescence. Just before he died, Jordan was asked how he got started on his radical pilgrimage. He told the interviewer that he would have to go back to his childhood. Then he unfolds the autobiographical telling of the incident at the county jail. This narrative is known by all

241

followers of Clarence Jordan. It is a story about the mystery of a young white person growing up in Georgia in the early twentieth-century discovering the contradictions between church and culture—the stark and painful reality of the color bar, especially the brutality and dehumanization of the Georgia chain gang. This story is made for retelling among progressive groups who want to right the wrongs of an unjust past. As a 12-year-old, Clarence sees the contradictions and the hypocrisy of the church. As a parabolic event, this story tells part of the secret of Clarence Jordan—he sees truth beyond his culture to envision a different world. Yet, as a metaphoric event, this narrative points beyond itself—backward to that complex set of experiences which portray Jordan as a genuine *homo religious*, and forward in time when the intuitions of a 12-year-old can be grounded in mature critique of church and society, and an affirmation of the worth and dignity of all persons.

The second major element in the legend of Clarence Jordan is the well-known ROTC incident. Clarence had come into his senior year at the University of Georgia with his sense of vocation unresolved. He had been in the ROTC for four years and just after graduation in his final ROTC camp, he has to demonstrate cavalry skills as he rode through the forest. Having recently memorized the Sermon on the Mount, he found himself as a young cavalry officer in training confronting straw men who become more than targets. In this narrative Clarence's growing and developing faith once again clashed with the surrounding culture—the military as an instrument of death was in conflict with the teachings of Jesus. As a parabolic event, the experiences told in this narrative became foundational for Jordan's rejection of militarism and violence as a way of handling human disputes on any level.[41]

The third element in the legend of Clarence Jordan can be called the Haymarket/Sunshine Center event. In the Haymarket area of Louisville, a young black woman was raped by a white man. A group of blacks, meeting in the Sunshine Center, were making plans to kill a white man in response. Clarence Jordan stepped forward and volunteered to be the victim. The story was repeated as a story of courage and radical faithfulness. Seventy-five years later it can be traced to four different narrations.[42] This story pushes the legend in a specific religious direction— Clarence Jordan and his increasing identity with the one he refers to as

Jesus the Rebel. In his sermon by the title of "Jesus the Rebel," he radicalizes the concept of love as the antithesis of violence. Jordan said that "Jesus the Rebel did not seek to escape the guilt of a society that could produce a Ku Klux Klan." This element in the legend portrays Jordan as one willing to take upon himself the guilt of society in order to create a new sense of community, and thereby pushes the narrative of Jordan further in the direction of saintliness and an identity with Jesus the Rebel. This story—however one is to read it—gives the reader the impression that here is a young man with a radical sense of identification with the life and teachings of Jesus. Because of that sense of identification, he was free to lay his head down on the table in the presence of the racial animosity and invite the group to take revenge upon him. According to this element in the legend, the life of Clarence Jordan is beginning to take a cruciform shape—the shape of a cross. Because of this story and others like it, many people who heard it began to say that Jordan was the most Christ-like person they had known.

The establishment of a "koinonia" in Southwest Georgia thirteen years before the beginning of the Civil Rights Movement is a fourth element in the Jordan legend. This was the vision of his life, and, as one writer put it, "Jordan's most brilliant translation of the New Testament...."[43] It did not appear in print but in the indelible script of human history in Sumter County, Georgia. Koinonia Farm was Jordan's testament to the message of his life—that God is no respecter of persons but loves all with a sustaining grace that reorders human division. The Koinonia story of Jordan's legacy is prophetic deed—an enacting, or living out of a word from God. "Koinonia," was in time a testament to Jordan's authentic faith, and an illustration of his religious genius. Consequently, the meaning of this testament can be read: as partners with God, human beings should live in reordered community sharing goods and responsibilities for the liberation of all.

A fifth element in the Jordan legend is the incident at Rehoboth Baptist Church. The stunning aspect of this story is that this "most Christ-like" man is voted out of his church to which he had been very faithful for almost ten years. In essence, Jordan was voted out because of radical faithfulness to the egalitarian vision of Jesus—"red and yellow, black and white, they are precious in his sight. Jesus loves the little children"—all the children, all people. On one level, this element in the legend affirms Jordan as an exemplar of authentic faith doing battle with cultural accommodation—embracing the worth and dignity of all God's children. But on a deeper level, this narrative portrays Jordan as the persecuted and suffering one, suffering at the hands of those he is trying to help. But as a parabolic event, this is a story of religion over against regionality—a story more than 100 years old, involving the souls of two entire peoples. As a parable, the narrative reads the reader and one chooses between two frameworks of meaning: the unhindered love of God for all, or the traditions and values of culture. This element in the legend portrays Jordan as not only a saint, a model of others to follow, but also a pioneer on a new frontier of sociocultural change.

A sixth aspect of the Jordan legend is the "partnership" program that he, with Millard Fuller, initiated just before he died. Chief among the partnership programs celebrated by the followers of Jordan is the Partnership Housing which set about to create affordable homes for the poor who had been living in substandard houses. There were sixty-two of these houses built on Koinonia land. Eventually, after Jordan's death, Millard Fuller extended this program in partnership housing to become a worldwide ministry. This aspect of Jordan's legend and legacy demonstrates how he visibly changed Sumter County, improved the economic plight of the poor in the region, and eventually around the world.[44]

A final element in the legend of Clarence Jordan can be called the anecdotal tradition—short witty comments by Jordan that embody a central aspect of his thought. These brief stories tend to be told again and again in reference to Jordan. One of the most prominent is the story of the Southern woman who came up to Jordan after one of his sermons and proceeded to tell him that her grandfather had fought in the Civil War and that she would never believe a word that Jordan said. Jordan smiled and said: "Ma'am, your choice seems quite clear. It is whether you will follow your granddaddy or Jesus Christ." Such an anecdote drives home quickly the conflict between religion and regionality that plagued the South, but also portrays Jordan as an authentic person of faith who sees the issues of the region. Another short narrative is about the pastor who wanted to give his janitor a raise but his deacons would not approve it. Jordan simply asked the man how many children he had. The answer was four. How many children does your janitor have? The answer was eight. Jordan said, the solution is simple, just swap salaries with the janitor. This anecdote within the larger legend deftly denounces materialism, and embraces the concept that the sharing of wealth is basic to the kingdom. Another popular anecdote is the brief narrative about Jordan being shown a new church building, and the pastor points to the steeple and brags that the cross on top of the steeple costs $10,000. Jordan replied quickly: "You got robbed—Time was when Christians could get those for free." With witty simplicity, Jordan rejects materialism. The anecdotal tradition allows for repetition of metaphoric and parabolic truth in small, memorable narratives, but it also makes the implicit explicit. Jordan's greatest challenge to the American experiment is the ongoing critique that there is a temptation to something false at the center of the American religious and political process—an overemphasis on the divine creates a neglect of the human and instills an unexamined representation in both the religious and political context.[45]

Hero in the Folk Consciousness:
The Making of a Saint and the Growth of a Legend

How did Clarence Jordan come to be known as a saint or a person worthy of being described as a model for others? Clarence grew up with a "saintly" mother and learned the teachings of Jesus sitting on her knees. Put differently, the teachings of Jesus first came to him through the voice of his mother which was tantamount to the voice of God. The love ethic of Jesus was personal from his earliest days. He would grow up with an overactive sense of conscience and an extreme sense of guilt which made him unusually sensitive to the moral issues of the day. Later, Frank Stagg would describe Jordan as having an "enlightened conscience." He became aware of the issues of race and poverty early in his life. His sensitivity to the plight of others pushed him to search for solutions to the problems of society early in his life. By the time he left the University of Georgia he had already thought through the question of war and violence as it related to the teachings of Jesus and the Sermon on the Mount. In Louisville, Jordan learned to read the Bible in dialogue with culture. When he began this practice, he rediscovered his earlier quest to answer questions on race, poverty, and violence. This reading also pushed him to find the earliest and most authentic form of Christianity.

In the Book of Acts, Jordan found the first Koinonia where followers of Christ pooled their resources and shared according to need. Reading for the doctoral degree involved reading the Greek New Testament—immersing himself in the text. What Clarence discovered while reading was "more than forms and syntax; he found the example and teaching of Jesus."[46] And Clarence heard the voice of Jesus say that losing the life was the way to find true life—the greatest love and commitment was to lay down one's life for others. Clarence took the words of Jesus very seriously, and he was formed by those words in such a manner that stories were remembered about his lived interpretation. Jordan's life, already in Louisville, began to take on a "Jesus-like" quality. He sought to live out the teachings of the New Testament as much as humanly possible.

The Haymarket/Sunshine Center incident can be read in this light. Jordan was attempting to follow what he understood as radical discipleship—the greatest love and commitment was a willingness to lay down one's life for another. Fellow students who knew Jordan during Louisville spoke, almost universally, with an extremely high regard for him. One of those students from that day was H. Cornell Goerner who said of Jordan, he "was the most completely dedicated Christian I have ever known." Goerner went on to say, "With childlike simplicity he took the Sermon on the Mount seriously and tried to follow the teachings of Jesus literally and absolutely. His life was to me personally a rebuke and a challenge."[47]

Clarence Jordan took this vision of radical discipleship to Sumter County, Georgia where his goal was to establish a modern "Koinonia" as a "demonstration plot." The truths that were learned in the crucible that was Louisville and the Haymarket would be lived out in Southwest Georgia. In the midst of these struggles in Sumter County, Clarence was seen as a communist and traitor by many and a prophetic figure by others. He became a hero in the folk consciousness of progressive groups and was an exemplary model for many by the early 1950s. His status was enhanced as he began to publish the "Cotton Patch" translations in the 1960s and as he continued to travel and speak widely. His death came in

1969 and had the effect of sanitizing any impurities in the collective memory of Jordan.

Several aspects help to build the legend further. The changing cultural mores in the South to a tacit commitment to racial equality provide the background for Clarence to be seen more widely as a prophet and a pioneer of a new authentic form of Christianity. The production of an off-Broadway play, "The Cotton Patch Gospel," written by Tom Key with the lyrics by Harry Chapin, spread the news of Jordan and his work. The fidelity of Florence Jordan and other members of the Koinonia community in telling the story continued to promote the legacy and legend of Clarence Jordan. The success of Habitat for Humanity under Millard Fuller recast the initial struggle. Millard Fuller told the story of Clarence Jordan in a more positive way than Jordan would have told it himself. And finally, the renewed interest in Jordan and the experiment at Koinonia resulted in a series of dissertations and new books on Jordan which have continued to spread the legend to an ever-widening audience.

Why has Clarence Jordan been remembered as a saint? The answer to this part of the question appears simple at first. Groups have a need for models for living in the present.[48] At first glance, this elevation of Clarence Jordan in the collective consciousness of some Americans seems to note not only the extraordinary nature of his life but also the need in the contemporary era for bold and daring new models by which to live in the late twentieth and early part of the 21st century. Storytelling began and continues with a pragmatic purpose.[49] Hence these events in the life of Clarence Jordan are being remembered and retold at a specific time to fulfill some need. It seems plausible that the honoring of Clarence Jordan with legendary status in the latter part of the 20th and the early years of the 21st century is an attempt by progressive church groups to answer Crossan's question: "How is it possible to be a faithful Christian in an American Empire facilitated by a violent Christian Bible?" Remembering Clarence Jordan in this manner both challenges and critiques the American culture, nation, and religious establishment. For the American church, it offers an alternative vision. In dialogue with the nation, the legend of Clarence Jordan rejects racism, military consumerism, and violence as the way to wholeness and happiness. If the legend of Clarence Jordan is more vital today than in earlier years it may be because the legend of Jordan's life fits almost perfectly as an antithesis to contemporary American culture.

The celebration of Jordan as a modern day saint indicates that many have come to see Clarence Jordan as an appropriate model for living in contemporary times.[50] The growth of the legend in the early years of the 21st century indicates that progressive church groups are looking for an alternative to what Brueggemann calls "military consumerism"—a consumer society that promotes that idea that human happiness can be found through materialism and incessant consumerism all protected by a violent approach to the protection of wealth and privilege. The legend of Clarence Jordan as a saint not only rejects war, and materialism, but also the division of the human family into the privileged and non-privileged.

The Legend and Legacy:
Clarence Jordan as a Dangerous Memory

Ironically, this latter day celebration of Clarence Jordan comes at a time when the conservative resurgence seems to have achieved its goals. With the election of George W. Bush, it seemed that the joining of religion and politics and the goals of the Southern conservative resurgence were complete. Yet the legend of Clarence Jordan continued and seemed to grow stronger with a model of living and being antithetical to religious nationalism and a militaristic consuming society. The appeal to the memory of Clarence Jordan more than forty-five years after his death seems to indicate the need for new models of living in a time when politics have seemingly given way to excessive greed and corruption, and the growth of an underclass that will no longer tolerate such triumphalism.

Why was Clarence Jordan "selected" as a contemporary saint? There is no one aspect of his legend that explains his place in collected memory. Rather, it is a combination of all the elements under the rubric of authentic faith without cultural accommodation. Jordan became known as an exemplar because people saw in him a profound commitment to live out the teachings of Jesus. It was his life as a radical disciple that led people to so remember him—the fact that he went beyond literalism to see the teachings of Jesus as personal and that for him the only decent theology was a "lived" one. If John Dominic Crossan is correct that the story of struggle implicit in American culture in recent years has been the tension between the "normalcy of civilization's violence" and the "radicality of God's nonviolence," then one can see the appropriateness of the progressive appeal to Jordan's legend and legacy. For Jordan clearly challenged the normalcy of civilization's violence in all of its forms: race, poverty, and war. But civilization struck back. When his life took on a cruciform pattern, people began to see an entire lifetime of service and compassion for the poor and underprivileged, and that he exhibited unusual courage lived out in the face of unrelenting evil which came as a result of his commitment to the downcast.

Yet, in truth, Jordan's legend is remembered only by a minority, and such groups tend to remember and retain traditions from their past in subversive forms of "dangerous memories."[51] The legend of Clarence Jordan is, therefore, told in the manner of a subversive pattern, over against the triumphalism of church, state, and society. Jordan's legend operates mostly among progressive church groups who have sympathy for his goals. Yet, among these groups, Jordan's memory tends to remain strong in large measure because the dominant culture continues in much the same way it did while Jordan was alive. In this way, the legend of Clarence Jordan still seeks to be in dialogue with the culture more than 100 years after his birth, and the dialogue continues to be about the radicality of God's love over against the violence of those processes called civilization. In those religious groups that continue to share Jordan's ideals, there is a need for exemplars who can be an alternative model of authentic faith. In that sense, Clarence Jordan is still alive and with God on earth! He continues to stretch the human imagination of those who hear his story and to give a voice that beckons to an alternative world.

A dangerous memory makes demands and tends to be subversive. Such memories break through to the center of one's life and reveal "new and dangerous insights for the present." Dangerous memories bring illumination, if only briefly, especially about the questionable nature of the reality with which one lives. "They break through the canon of the prevailing structures of plausibility and have certain subversive features."[52] Cornell Goerner wrote about Clarence Jordan in this manner. While Goerner had come to terms with Jordan as a "starry-eyed idealist, at most out of touch with the real world," he had in the recesses of his mind another thought. He wrote, "I can never quite get away from the gnawing suspicion that, if enough of us would agree to create and live consistently with a true New Testament Koinonia, we could make it work, and it would change the world!"[53] Clarence Jordan continues as a "dangerous memory" that military consumerism is a failed and corrupt enterprise, and that the radicality of God's justice and love made incarnate in Jesus of Nazareth is the true authoritative narrative.

Conclusion

The moral journey of Clarence Leonard Jordan was a long pilgrimage in search of a "true" country where he could be an honest and faithful disciple of the one he came to call "Jesus the Rebel." The narrative of this journey involved high drama in the fields of the Lord, including the proclamation of the need for a new understanding of salvation, forgiveness, and costly discipleship. Clarence Jordan was a Southern dissident who waged a peaceful campaign for the soul of his region through the liberation of blacks and whites, rich and poor. On one level, the study of Clarence Jordan is about the making of a contemporary prophet. Yet his story was not just a simple telling of a man's quest, but an enlarged narrative about his religion and the culture that gave him life. What pushed, pulled, and lured Clarence Jordan to take up such a perilous pilgrimage, which evoked an incredibly violent reaction from the very culture he sought to help?

In this study, I have maintained that Clarence Jordan was a pioneer on the frontier of a new South who sought the liberation of both the oppressed and the oppressor. In terms of religious personality, Jordan was a *homo religiosus*, like Gandhi and Martin Luther King, Jr. He was a religious genius, a cultural innovator whose own search for faithfulness and human wholeness was interwoven with the quest to redeem his region. In a more specific sense, Jordan was a poet-prophet calling for a new view of humanity and an alternative portrayal of God and the Bible at a historically crucial time. There were two distinctive poles to the prophetic nature of his personality: one that sought to critique and dismantle the status quo, and another that attempted to evoke a new way of being. Jordan's critique of church and society was profound and increasingly radical. Indeed, the impact of Clarence Jordan on his culture was so strong that, forty-five years after his death, his legend as a "modern saint" lingers as a dangerous memory in American society, still seeking to demythologize cultural views of religion that promote materialism, militarism, and racism.

The study of Clarence Jordan demonstrates the age-old truism given life by Wordsworth that the "child is the father of the man." This has been recently exemplified by David Mariniss in his studies of Bill Clinton and Barack Obama—that which shapes the life comes early. In this regard, the most important documents for the study of Clarence Jordan are found in the previously unstudied corpus of remarkable letters that he shared with his mother. In that collection, one finds that Maude Jossey Jordan was the major religious influence in Clarence Jordan's life. In these letters, Maude Jossey Jordan narrates the life of her favored son and tells him that he had been set apart by God before he was born. Like Will Campbell, Clarence Jordan heard his mother give a religious interpretation of his life, saying that he will be like Jeremiah and Jesus, consecrated for a special calling from the earliest age. If one follows Maude Jossey Jordan's assessment of Clarence Jordan's life, then one must look for the beginning of his pilgrimage early in life.

That journey of faith, then, can be seen as beginning in his first dialogue of mutuality with his "saintly" mother, and rooted in the dialectic of trust over against the experiences that taught him to mistrust. This foundational dialectic, for Clarence, was the basis on which his childhood prehistoric core of community over against abandonment emerged. Put differently, the pilgrimage toward a religious view of life, for Clarence Jordan, was directly related to his own "saintly" mother and the mutuality they shared, the devastating loss of which, due to her own illness, brought a foundation for a childhood understanding of abandonment reinforced by Clarence's experiences of separation from his family during his bout with scarlet fever. This is the beginning of the "Grump" syndrome so well documented from his earliest years, as well as the childhood foundation for his later ability to analyze, critique, and demythologize an entire culture. By the same token, Clarence's role as a magnetic personality and as an entertainer/clown emerged in his earliest years as he imitated the coping skills of his mother. Living through a near-death experience instilled a further sense of destiny and purpose, as well as an emerging sense of courage, if only in embryo.

But there were other things that drove Clarence Jordan. As an adult, Clarence saw himself as coming back to the Deep South to pay a debt to black people. He understood that his father had underpaid workers in order to pay for his education. This was an adult illustration of a severe sense of conscience and guilt that, for Clarence, began very early in life as a precocious sense of guilt. As Clarence indicated himself, he spent a lifetime trying to atone for something like an existential indebtedness. Clarence was driven in some manner to live his life as one of service because of the obligations he felt he had accumulated. Likely, that accumulation of debt began rather early for Clarence. His mother dreamed that he would be a great man in the church. The favoritism she gave him and the sense of expectation that he would succeed left Clarence with a burden and obligation. This burden was increased by the fact that Jim Jordan was an absent father, allowing Clarence to look to his maternal grandfather as a role model. Yet going beyond his father in this manner only increased Clarence's sense of guilt. Clarence attempted to resolve that sense of added guilt by assuming responsibility for the pain of those around him. Clarence's sense of obligation, grounded in a profound feeling of guilt, pushes him to accept an entire group of people as the object of his rescue. The disturbing question, for Clarence, was how to do this. Indeed, Clarence grew up wondering how he could reorder the land that he loved. The answer did not come with clarity until his spiritual awakening in the ghetto of the Haymarket in Louisville. That answer would be revised and become even more radical in the last years of his life.

The well-known story of Clarence Jordan joining the Baptist church and encountering the horrors of the punishment of Ed Russell in the chain-gang camp behind his house plays an important role in the narration of Jordan's pilgrimage. It documents his growing sensitivity, but it also notes his resentment toward the church and God. It is a narrative about the moral education of a young man on the edge of his culture. But it is not the root of Jordan's radical journey, as often perceived in the literature about him. It is, as a dramatic scene, the repository for the burden of memories and expectation that, in actuality, refers to earlier days. This story marks the end of Jordan's childhood faith and the inauguration of his adolescent faith, which will involve a sense of moratorium as well as the beginning of a quest for a vocation by which he could bring a sense of justice to the world he had discovered.

Jordan's adolescent years involved a conventional landscape of faith that included his entrance into the University of Georgia, where, for a time, he danced to every tune. Clarence's religious life in Athens took on an emerging sense of vitality, but without the ability for critical reflection. Several factors eventually pushed him toward a more reflective and individualized faith at the end of his college years: his travels, student meetings in North Carolina, his writing for a college newspaper, his coursework, and his ongoing dialogue and relationship with his mother. But perhaps the most important factor was contained in the episode that marked an end to his conventional faith—the often-repeated story of his study of the Sermon on the Mount in the context of his final ROTC course at the University of Georgia. Clarence began to see a conflict between the words of Jesus and his involvement in the culturally sanctioned ROTC. On that day, he dismounted his steed and went to his commander and turned in his equipment. This narrative also marked the beginning of his reflective faith.

Jordan spent the next decade in Louisville developing his understanding of what it meant to be an honest person of faith. His work in the Haymarket area was a time of spiritual awakening. He rejected the cultural interpretation of ministry and moved in the direction of a more radical reading of the New Testament. Under the influence of Edward McDowell, Jordan learned to read the Bible in dialogue with the culture. This approach, along with his work in the inner city, opened his life to a search for the root meaning of Christianity. The application of the insights that he learned in Louisville took Jordan in a radical direction. To be an "honest" Christian, Jordan learned that he would have to go against the accepted traditions of his region and, eventually, his church. In Louisville, Jordan developed his ideology of a "koinonia" and his initial ideas concerning materialism, militarism, and racism. In conjunction with his work in the Haymarket, he began to hear a "call" to return to the Deep South to establish an interracial farm. Louisville allowed Jordan the opportunity to integrate the lessons of race and injustice that had lain fallow in his heart with a new contemporary reading, which emerged as a radical ideology of communal life, pacifism, and egalitarian race relations.

Clarence Jordan came back to Southwest Georgia when he was 30 years old. His faith was reflective and iconoclastic but he was, at that point, attempting to work within the structure of the church. He established Koinonia Farm, which, for him, was an ideal years in the making.

It was the statement of his life, not simply an intellectual endeavor but, rather, the embodiment of a human struggle that extended backward in time to his early childhood. It was, in that sense, also a personal struggle toward human wholeness that matched the struggle of an entire region— black and white, rich and poor. It was the restatement of 100 years of history and an effort to rework the religious, social, and economic identity of two groups of people who had long lived at odds. Yet it was an exceedingly dangerous conception that would, in time, erupt in violence and bring untold suffering and heartache for Jordan personally, and human struggle for his family and members of Koinonia.

Rehoboth was the place of the first eruption of violence against Jordan. But Rehoboth was not just the name of the church; it was a symbol for Southern culture and represented something like the struggle for a Southern soul. It was descriptive of the distance between the societal status quo and a young man's dreams and idealism. Rehoboth came to mean the end of Jordan's youthful, reflective faith, which had begun when he got down off of his horse near Athens and turned in his sword and spurs to his military commander in 1933. The pain and public rejection at Rehoboth in 1950 would stay with him the rest of his life. He had spent years challenging and demythologizing ideas, and developing his own understanding of what it meant to be a person of faith. He had come to be seen by many as an emerging leader on the forefront of change regarding the most important issues of the day. Indeed, he was a Christian pioneer, but he was now *persona non grata* with many of the people and institutions he wanted to help. The pain and rejection inherent in Rehoboth pushed Jordan toward a deeper and more communal faith. Rehoboth was, then, a before-and-after event. Jordan was now a member of the church universal and an ex-Baptist. But, unfortunately, Rehoboth as a violent overreaction from the community would presage the most turbulent episode in his life.

The Rehoboth incident framed Jordan's early adult faith and ushered in an era of pain that began to push him toward a more communal and paradoxical understanding of life and faith, which included a form of redemptive subversiveness for those who opposed him. He began to question himself and his own religious tradition, and he had to find a new way of being religious. Koinonia, as Jordan had originally conceived it, was dismantled by the church and society in Southwest Georgia. Jordan himself was arrested, violently persecuted, and tried in the law courts—and in the court of public opinion. The violence by Klan-like elements in Sumter County and the participation of local merchants in a sustained boycott left Koinonia as a shadow of its former self. By the early 1960s, with only a couple of families left on the farm, Jordan was immobilized and depressed. He had a vision of the need for a larger ministry, but he did not know how to accomplish it. He turned to the writing project that had been on his mind for years.

For much of the 1960s, Clarence Jordan was unable to act on his developing vision. He lived between a transforming vision and an untransformed world. Yet, ironically, as he rewrote the gospels in a Southern idiom, Jordan also began to rewrite himself. He developed an increasingly prophetic consciousness. Like the texts that he wrote, he became increasingly radical as he seemed to develop a closer identification with Jesus the Rebel. Jordan seemed to know instinctively that a praxis-oriented translation of the gospel was necessary for the church and for the ordinary reader. So, in his writing, he tried to hold together the life of the spirit and the way people lived. The ordinary reader had been accustomed to being a spectator. The religious world of the South was, consequently, bifurcated, allowing church members to use religion to dehumanize and denigrate other persons on the basis of race, gender, wealth, and nationality. By rewriting the gospel in a Southern idiom, Jordan placed the ordinary reader in the midst of the action and flow of the narrative, making the reader a participant rather than an observer. In a Jesus-like move, Jordan had confronted readers with the truths about Jesus the Rebel, and put reconciliation and redemption in the context of the struggle for human equality. Readers were thereby confronted with the revolution of values required by Jesus the Rebel. Ironically, Jordan's writing project promoted a new consciousness in Jordan himself and helped to rewrite the author.

Consequently, Jordan's last years—from 1965 to 1969—were his most daring and radical as he moved toward a type of activist incarnation of the image of Jesus the Rebel that he was writing about in his texts. In spring 1965, Jordan publicly critiqued Martin Luther King, Jr., and, in time, began to call for a "greater and deeper movement than the Civil

Rights Movement." In late 1965, Jordan did what he had never done before. He participated in an effort to integrate a church in Americus. His critique of the contemporary church became so strong that he essentially said the church had become so secular that it had lost its calling. In Seattle in 1969, he wondered aloud to a church convention whether or not "the Church has gone awhoring."

By 1968, Jordan had created "Koinonia Partners" and had begun to read the Bible in economic terms. He called for a whole new spirit in the country, which essentially sought to bypass the American capitalist system by searching for a way to redistribute land and wealth to the poor and dispossessed. He was reading Jesus' sermon in Nazareth to mean the permanent arrival of the spirit of the Year of Jubilee, which called for the release of captives and the overcoming of oppression. Jordan set in place the machinery to build homes for the poor at cost and at no interest, and envisioned the buying of large tracts of land for partnership farming and for rural industries for jobs for the poor. He created a "Fund for Humanity," which, in his mind, was a way of restoring land and redistributing wealth. At the end of his life, Clarence was seeking to be faithful to his reworked image of Jesus the Rebel, which was nothing short of an activist incarnation.

Though Clarence Jordan died early, his memory and legacy did not. The memories of his life and work still linger in legendary form many years after his death, attempting an ongoing dialogue with American culture. His sayings were like those of Jesus the Rebel. They were often hard and made people uncomfortable. Jordan's prophetic voice was a corrective to a church that attempted to make the incarnation more divine than human. His life was a rebuke to Christian churches that had lost a sense of mission and failed to see the humanity of God. The legacy of his work was a sharp focus on the radical demands of the Christian gospel as it relates to materialism, militarism, and racism. As a great soul, a *homo religiosus*, the aim of his life was not success, but faithfulness. Integrity was a lifelong issue for Jordan. He saw faith as a life lived in scorn of the consequences. He tried to restate a cultural overstatement that had brought pain, suffering, and degradation to an entire group of people, and a false sense of identity and pride, as well as oppressor status, to another. Though Clarence Jordan grew up in a society where the color of one's skin brought either privilege or denigration, he spent a lifetime trying to create a true country, where the color of one's skin did not matter. Clarence Jordan had an abiding sensitivity to the plight of the poor and dispossessed. His "Fund for Humanity" lives on in Habitat for Humanity and, through this work, continues to change the world.

If Clarence Jordan's story is that of the making of a prophet, then, in theological perspective, his narrative is something like the plaintiff cry of the human spirit, something like what Rabbi Abraham Heschel called the "pathos of God"—a crossing point of God and the human. And, in that sense, the story of Clarence Jordan can be understood as something like a "scream" in a dark night while others of us have been asleep—the "voice that God has lent to the silent agony" of the "plundered poor." But Jordan's story is also that of one who overcame against all odds, a parable of an entire land seeking redemption, which can reread the reader. An encounter with Clarence Jordan can deform old stories and send one searching for the soul of his country, as the legend of Clarence Jordan as modern saint continues to do. He lived his life in scorn of the consequences, and when he came to die, there was a celebration of that life at Koinonia, but not mourning. Harry Chapin captured the sense of appropriate lyrical celebration for such a life as Clarence Jordan's in his last song for the "Cotton Patch Gospel" when he wrote:

"Now if a man tried to take his time on Earth
And prove before he died
What one man's life could be worth
Well, I wonder what would happen to this world."

Bibliography

Interviews by the Author

Downing, Frederick L. Interview with Henlee Barnette. Louisville, Kentucky: 2 July 1987.

_____. Interview with Mary D. Bowman. Pineville, Louisiana: 17 October 1987.

_____. Interview with Ray Brewster. Macon, Georgia: 26 May 1987.

_____. Interview with Carol A. Brink. Boston, Massachusetts: 27 December 2011.

_____. Interview with Corneila Jordan Callier. Atlanta, Georgia: 30 June 1987.

_____. Interview with Andrew Hamilton. Americus, Georgia: 9 November 1986.

_____. Interview with Joe Hendrix. Macon, Georgia: 26 May 1987.

_____. Interview with Florence Jordan. Koinonia Farm, Americus, Georgia: 8-9 November 1986.

_____. Interview with Frank Jordan. Talbotton, Georgia: 13 April, 1987; 25 May 1987.

_____. Interview with George Jordan. Talbotton, Georgia: 25 May 1987.

_____. Interview with Robert Jordan. Talbotton, Georgia: 13 April 1987.

_____. Interview with Dallas Lee. Atlanta, Georgia: 30 June 1987.

_____. Interview with Frank Stagg. Diamond Head, Mississippi: 12 October 1987.

_____. Interview with Margaret Whitkamper. Koinonia Farm, Americus, Georgia: 8 November 1987.

Other Interviews

East, P.D. Interview with Clarence Jordan. Koinonia Farm, 1958. P. D. East Collection, Howard Gotlieb Archival Research Center, Boston University, Boston, MA, 1958.

_____. Interview with Con Browne. Howard Gotlieb Archival Research Center, Boston University, 1958.

Howard, Walden. Interview with Clarence Jordan. "The Legacy of Clarence Jordan," *Faith at Work*. April 1970.

Morrison, Scott. Interview with Clarence Jordan. Mutual News. New York: 26 February 1968. Also as *The Clarence Jordan Interviews*. Americus, GA: Koinonia Partners Inc., 2003.

Stricklin, David. Interview with Mabel and Martin England. *Oral Memoirs of Jasper Martin England and Mabel Orr England: A Series of Interviews Conducted July –September 1984*. Waco, TX: Baylor University Institute for Oral History, 1996.

Publications by Clarence Jordan

Jordan, Clarence. "Clarence Jordan tells the Koinonia Story." Fellowship House, Cincinatti, Ohio, 10 November 1956. Koinonia Partners, 2003.

_____. "Incarnating Brotherhood." An audio cassette. Americus, GA: Koinonia Records, n. d.

_____. "Jesus and Possessions." an audio cassette. Americus, GA: Koinonia Records, n.d.

_____. "Jesus the Rebel." an audio cassette. Americus, GA : Koinonia Records, n.d..

_____. "Judas." an audio cassette. Americus, GA : Koinonia Records, n.d..

_____. "Loving Your Enemies." an audio cassette. Americus, GA: Koinonia Records, n.d.

_____. "Loving Your Enemies." an audio cassette. Americus, GA: Koinonia Records, n.d.

_____. *Sermon on the Mount*. Valley Forge, PA: Judson Press, 1952.

_____. *The Cotton Patch Version of Hebrews and the General Epistles* . Piscataway, N.J.: New Century Publishers, 1973.

_____. *The Cotton Patch Version of Luke and Acts: Jesus' Doings and the Happenings*. New York: Association Press, 1969.

_____. *The Cotton Patch Version of Matthew and John*: Chicago: Association Press, 1970.

_____. *The Substance of Faith and other Cotton Patch Sermons*. New York: Association Press, 1972.

_____. *The Cotton Patch Version of Paul's Epistles* (New York: Association Press, 1968).

_____. *Sermon on the Mount*. Valley Forge, PA: Judson Press, 1952.

_____. "The Meaning of *Thanatos* and *Nekros* in the Epistles of Paul." Unpublished Ph.D. dissertation. The Southern Baptist Theological Seminary, 1938.

Clarence Jordan Papers
Hargrett Rare Book and Manuscript Library University of Georgia
Jordan, Buddie. "A Letter to Clarence." 4 Feb 1927. MS 756: B1 F1.

_____. "A Letter to Clarence." 11 February 1927. MS 756: B1, F1.

Jordan, Cornelia. "A Letter to Clarence." 22 March 1927. MS 756, B1, F1.

Jordan, Maude Jossey. "A Letter to Clarence." 10 August 1927. MS 756: B1 F1.

Jordan, Clarence. "Tenth Grade Composition Notebook." MS 756: B1, F3.

_____. "A card to mother." MS 756: B1 F3.

Jordan, Cornelia. "A Letter to Clarence." 16 September 1929. MS 756: B1 F3.

Jordan, Clarence. "Clarence to Mama." 16 September 1929. MS 756: B 1, F 3.

Jordan, Maude Jossey. "A Letter to Clarence." 31 May 1929. MS 756: B 1 F3.

Jordan, Clarence. "Clarence to Mama." 16 September 1929. MS 756: B1, F 1.

_____. "Clarence to Mama." 17 March 1930. MS 756: B 1, F 4.

_____. "Clarence Jordan to Mama." 11 May 1931. MS 756: B 1 F 5.

_____. "Clarence to Fellows." 14 August 1931. MS 756: B 1, F 5.

_____. "Clarence to Mama." January 1932. MS 756: B 1, F 6.

_____. "Clarence to Mama." 9 May 1932. MS 756: B 1, F 6.

_____. "Clarence to Mama." 3 July 1932. MS 756: B 1, F 6.

Jordan, George. "George to Mama." 21 September 1932. MS 756: B 1, F 6.

_____. "Clarence to Mama." 4 March 1933." MS 756: B 1, F 7.

_____. "Clarence to Mama." 10 March 1933. MS 756: B 1, F 7.

_____. "Clarence to Mama." 14 March 1933. MS 756: B 1, F 7.

_____. "Clarence to Mama." 22 March 1933. MS 756: B 1, F 7.

_____. "Clarence to Mama." 1 April 1933. MS 756, B 1, F 7.

_____. "Clarence to Mama." 14 April 1933. MS 756: B 1, F 7.

_____. "Clarence to Mama." 1 June 1933. MS 756: B 1, F 7.

_____. "My Call to the Ministry," 13 August 1933, Jordan Papers, Ms. 756, B1, F7.

Jordan, Maude Jossey. "Mama to Clarence." 16 September 1933. MS 756: B 1, F 7.

Jordan, Clarence. "Clarence to Mama." 24 September 1933. MS 756: B 1, F 7.

_____. "Clarence to Mama." n. d. MS 756: B 1, F 8.

_____. "Clarence to Mama." October 1933. MS 756: B 1, F 7.

_____. "Clarence to Mama" 26 March 1934. MS 756: B1 F 8.

_____. "Clarence to Mama." June 1934. MS 756: B 1, F 8.

_____. "Clarence to Mama." 9 July 1934. MS 756: B 1, F 8.

_____. "Clarence to Mama." 24 July 1934. MS 756: B 1, F 8.

Jordan, Maude Jossey. "Mama to Clarence Jordan." 26 July 1934. MS 756: B1, F 8.

Jordan, James. "James Jordan to Clarence." 8 October 1934. MS 756: B 1, F 8.

Jordan, Clarence. "Clarence to Mama." 12 December 1934. MS 756: B 1, F 8.

_____. "Clarence to Mama." 25 December 1934. MS 756: B 1, F 8.

Jordan, James. "Dad to Clarence." 19 January 1935. MS 756: B1, F9.

Broach, Mrs. "Mrs. Broach to Clarence." 6 February 1935. MS 756: B 1, F 9.

Jordan, Jim. "Jim Jordan to Clarence." 19 May 1936. MS 756: B 1, F 10

Jordan, Clarence. "Sermon Notes: The Mother of Jesus." Mt. Carmel Baptist Church, January 1937. The Clarence Jordan Papers, MS 756: B 1, F 11.

_____. "Definitions of Koinonia." MS 756: B 16, F 2.

Leavell, Frank H. "Frank H. Leavell to Clarence Jordan" 6 March, 1942. MS 756: B 2, F 2.

Taylor, Elizabeth. "Elizabeth Taylor to Clarence Jordan." 4 May 1941. MS 756: B 1, F 12.

Jones, Thomas H. "Thomas H. Jones to Clarence Jordan." 6 May 1941. MS 756: B 1, F 12.

Ward, Wayne E. "Wayne E. Ward to Clarence Jordan." 9 May 1941, MS 756: B 1, F 12.

Moore, Marjorie, "Marjorie Moore to Clarence Jordan." 31 May 1941. MS 756: B 1, F 12.

Leavell, Frank H. "Frank H. Leavell to Clarence Jordan." 22 May 1942. MS 756: B 2, F 2.

Jordan, Clarence. "Clarence Jordan to Frank H. Leavell." 26 May 1942. MS 756: B 2, F 2.

_____. "Clarence to Elizabeth Hartsfield." 1 June 1942. MS 756: B 2, F 2.

Colvin, W.A. "W.A. Colvin to C.L Jordan." 3 June 1942. MS 756: B 2, F 2.

Jordan, Clarence. "Clarence Jordan to W.A Colvin." 4 June 1942. MS 756: B 2, F 2.

_____. "Clarence to Buddie" 1 July 1942. MS 756: B 2, F 2.

_____. "Clarence Jordan to Mack Goss." 18 July 1942. MS 756: B 2, F 2.

_____. "Clarence to Mack Goss." 7 August 1942. MS 756: B 2, F 3;

_____. "Clarence to Liston Pope." 3 August 1942. MS 756: B 2, F 3.

_____. "Clarence to the Rev. Glenn T. Settle." 29 August 1942. MS 756: B 2, F 3.

England, Martin, et al. "Martin and Mabel; Clarence and Florence to Friends." 23 September 1942. MS 756: B 2, F 3.

Jordan, Clarence. "Diary." 13 November 1942. MS 756: B 18, F 3.

_____. "Clarence Jordan to Friends." December 1942. MS 756: B 2, F 3.

_____. "Clarence Jordan to Mrs. R.P. Halleck." 21 December 1942. MS. 756: B 2, F 3

_____. "Clarence Jordan to Howard Johnson." 7 January 1943. MS 756: B 2, F 4.

Nicholson, D.B. "Brother Nick to J.W. Jordan." 24 July 1944. MS 756: B 2, F 5.

Jordan, Clarence. "Clarence Jordan to Claude Broach." 7 March 1957. MS 756: B 4, F 14.

_____. "An Open Letter to the First Baptist Church of Atlanta." 24 September 1963. MS 756: B 6, F 1.

_____. "Clarence Jordan to Roy O. McClain." 28 September 1963. MS 756: B 6, F 1.

_____. "Clarence Jordan to Edward A. McDowell, Jr." 29 May 1964. MS 756: B6, F9.

_____. "Clarence Jordan to Ann Morris." 26 April 1968. MS 756: B 7, F 5.

_____. An unpublished manuscript titled "The Kingdom," 5, The Clarence Jordan Papers, MS 756 B 14.

_____. "Clarence Jordan at the Ministers Conference, Union Theological Seminary, New York City." July 1969. MS 2340: B 7.

Student Publications at the University of Georgia: Jordan, Clarence. "Should College Graduates Return to the Farm?" *The Georgia Agriculturalist* 9 (March 1931): 12.

_____. "What Price Should We Pay For A College Education?" *The Georgia Agriculturalist*

9 (November 1931): 5

_____. "When Night Meets Day." *The Georgia Agriculturalist* . MS 756: B 29, F 13.

_____. "A Stroll With Mother Nature." *The Georgia Agriculturalist.* MS 756: B 29, F 13.

_____. "Dan's Death: A True Story of a Georgia Dog's Devotion to His Master," *The Georgia Agriculturalist* 11 (October 1932): 6, 14.

McLeod Bryan Papers,
MS 364, Z. Smith Reynolds Library
Special Collections and Archives,
Wake Forest University

The FBI File of Clarence Jordan, 105-10699-44. McLeod Bryan Papers MS 364, Box 12, Folder 7. Z. Smith Reynolds Library Special Collections and Archives, Wake Forest University, Winston-Salem, N.C.

The Attorney General to Dr. Clarence L. Jordan. The FBI File of Clarence Jordan, 105-14859-19. 28 February 1957.

Letter from the Chamber of Commerce, Americus, Georgia to the FBI. The FBI File of Clarence Jordan, 100-4223-8. 24 October 1949.

Special Collections and Archives, Furman University

Jordan, Clarence. "Things Needed for Our Peace," A Chapel Address, Furman University. (Spring 1969) Special Collections and Archives, Furman University.

Koinonia Archives

Owen, Sara M. "Buying A Mule." Koinonia Partners, Inc. Published on the web at http://www.koinoniapartners.org/History/remembered/s__owen.html. Accessed 19 September 2011.

Jordan, Clarence to Mrs. C.L. Jordan, 14 November 1942. Koinonia Archive.

Jordan, Clarence to Mrs. C.L. Jordan, 15 November 1942, Koinonia Archive.

Jordan, Clarence to Mrs. C. L. Jordan, 18 November 1942, Koinonia Archives.

Jordan, Clarence to Mrs C.L. Jordan, 7 December 1942, Koinonia Archives.

"The Baptists Are Close to Southern Realities," *The Louisville Courier Journal* (April 17, 1949), Koinonia Archives.

Cosby, Paul E. "Perceptions in Contrast." Koinonia Partners. Published online at http://www.koinoniapartners.org/History/remembered/cosby.html. Accessed 19 September 2011.

The Kononia Farm Newsletter 1952 issue. Koinonia Archives.

The Koinonia Farm Newsletter # 13. 24 April 1957. Koinonia Archives.

The Koinonia Farm Newsletter # 26. 1 April 1962. Koinonia Archives.

The Kononia Farm Newsletter # 28. September 1963. Koinonia Archives.

The Koinonia Farm Newsletter. April 1965.

The Koinonia Farm Newsletter. October 1968.

The Koinonia Farm Newsletter, October 1969.

Jordan, Florence. "The Witness Was What Counted." *Catholic Worker Magazine.* (1983).

Jordan, Clarence. "A Personal Letter From Clarence Jordan To Friends of Koinonia," Americus Georgia: 27 October 1969.

Films and Videos

Brueggemann, Walter. "Imagination: New Approaches to the Bible." (A Video of the 23d National Conference of the Trinity Institute, Trinity Church. New York City, 1992.

Fuller, Faith, et al. *Briars in the Cottonpatch: The Story of Koinonia Farm* . Cotton Patch Productions.

Key, Tom, et al. *The Cotton Patch Gospel: The Greatest Story Ever Retold* . Bridgestone Studios, 1988.

Moyers, Bill and Pellett, Gail. "God and Politics: The Battle for the Bible." Public Affairs Television, Inc, 1988.

Stekler, Paul and McCabe, Dan. "George Wallace: Settin' the Woods on Fire," A PBS Film, "American Experience" Program, 2004).

Theses & Dissertations

Chancey, Andrew S. "Race, Religion, and Reform: Koinonia's Challenge to Southern Society" (Ph.D. Dissertation, University of Florida, 1998).

Chancey, Andrew S. "Restructuring Southern Society: The Radical Vision of Koinonia Farm." M.A. Thesis, University of Georgia, 1990.

Glisson, Susan M. "Life in Scorn of the Consequences: Clarence Jordan the Roots of Radicalism in the Southern Baptist Convention," (M.A. Thesis, University of Mississippi, 1994).

O'Connor, Charles S. "A Rural Georgia Tragedy: Koinonia Farm in the 1950s" (M.A Thesis, University of Georgia, 2003),

Westmoreland-White, Michael Lynsey. "Incarnational Discipleship: The Ethics of Clarence Jordan, Martin Luther King, Jr., and Dorothy Day." Ph.D. dissertation, The Southern Baptist Theological Seminary, 1995.

General Works: Articles

Alston, Wallace M. and Flynt, Wayne. "Religion in the Land of Cotton," in *You Can't Eat Magnolias* edited by H. Brandt Ayers and Thomas H. Naylor. New York: McGraw-Hill Book Company, 1972.

Buie, Jim. "Praise the Lord and Pass the Ammunition." *Church and State*. 37 (October 1984): 6.

Brueggemann, Walter. "Counterscript: Living with the Elusive God." *Christian Century* 122: 24 (November 29, 2005): 22-28.

Byron, Dora. "Courage in Action: Koinonia Revisited." *Nation* 184 (March 16, 1957): 226-228.

Campbell, Will D. "Remembering Clarence." in Clarence Jordan, *Clarence Jordan's Cotton Patch Gospel: Paul's Epistles*. Macon, GA: Smyth & Helwys Publishers, Inc. 2004.

Campbell, Will. "Where There's So Much Smoke: Thirty-Caliber Violence at Koinonia." *Sojourners* 8:12 (December 1979).

Donald Capps, "Psychohistory and Historical Genres: The Plight and Promise of Eriksonian Biography," in Peter Homans, ed., *Childhood and Selfhood* .Lewisburg: Bucknell University Press, 1978.

Capps, Donald. "John Henry Newman: A Study of Vocational Identity." *Journal for the Scientific Study of Religion* 9 (Spring 1970) : 33- 51.

Capps, Donald E. "The Parabolic Event in Religious Autobiography." *The Princeton Seminary*

Bulletin 4 (83).

Carey, Greg. "Clarence Jordan as a (White) Interpreter of the Bible." in Kirk Lyman-Barner and

Cori Lyman-Barner, eds., *Roots in the Cotton Patch*, Volume 1(Eugene, Oregon: Cascade Books, 2014).

Chambliss, Sam. "A Matter of the Mind: 10 Persons, Negroes and Whites Live Together in Americus Plan." *Albany Herald* (1 August 1948) : 4 A.

Criswell, W.A. "An Address To the South Carolina Joint Assembly." (22 February 1956). Duke University Library, Special Collections.

Downing, Frederick L. "Ascent of the Mountain: The Spiritual Awakening of Clarence Jordan," *Perspectives in Religious Studies* 41/4 (Winter 2014): 401-405.

Downing, Frederick L. The Dangerous Journey Home: Charting the Religious Pilgrimage in

Druin, Toby and Wingfield, Mark. "Literal Legend: W. A. Criswell Remembered." *The Baptist Standard* (January 14, 2002): 1.

Evans, Jill Oglesby. "Yours in Faith and Expectation–Clarence Jordan," A Sermon. Emory Presbyterian Church. (7 August 2005).

Fey, Harold E. "Report from Koinonia: Creative Church in Georgia." *The Christian Century* 74 (March 6, 1957): 285-287.

Fine, Ellen. "Search For Identity: Post Holocaust French Literature." Yehuda Bauer, ed. *Remembering for the Future: The Impact of the Holocaust on the Contemporary World.* Oxford: Pergamon Press, 1989.

Fontaine, Andre. "The Conflict of a Southern Town." *Redbook* 109 (October 1957).

Fowler and Peck." *Perspectives in Religious Studies* 25:3 (Fall 1998): 249-265.

Freeman, Curtis W. "'Never Had I been So Blind': W.A. Criswell's 'Change' on Racial Segregation." *The Journal of Southern Religion* X (2007): 1-12.

Gailey, Phil. "Koinonia Founder C.L. Jordan Dies." *The Atlanta Constitution* (31 October 1969): 19A.

Gandhi, Arun. "Gandhi:--Weaving A Universal Thread," M. K. Gandhi Institute. Found online at http://www.jpcarter.com/Spirituality/PDF/AshramArt.Pdf. Accessed 15 September 2015.

Gandhi, Mohandus K. "My Spiritual Message," A Speech at Kingsley Hall, London, England (October 1931). Old. Harrappa. com 2000-2006. Found online at http://www.ndtv.com/article/india/mahatma-gandhi-s-famous-speech-at-kingsley-hall-in-1931-138262. Accessed 15 September 2015.

Hayes, Rudy. "A T-R Reader Speaks His Mind." *Americus Times Recorder* (28 July 1956): 2.

_____. "Incident Here Wrong Approach." *Americus Times-Recorder* (25 July 1956): 4.

Hollyday, Joyce. "The Dream That Has Endured: Clarence Jordan and Koinonia," *Sojourners* 8 (December 1979).

Hollyday, Joyce. "A Scandalous Life of Faith." *Sojourners* 8:12 (December 1979): 3-5.

Howell, James C. A Blog. "Heroes Found Faithful: Clarence Jordan," Myers Park UMC, Charlotte, NC. 1 November 2010, located at http://heroesfoundfaithful.blogspot.com/2010/11/true-saints-never-dwell-in-splendid.html. Accessed 13 November 2015.

Kennedy, Robert F. "Remarks on the Assassination of Martin Luther King, Jr.," Speech, Indianapolis, IN, 4 April 1968. American Rhetoric Speech Bank. Located at http://www.americanrhetoric.com/speeches/rfkonmlkdeath.html. Accessed 17 March

2017.

Kessler, Glenn. "History Lesson: When the United States looked the other way on chemical weapons." *The Washington Post*, (4 September 2013). Located at: http://www.washingtonpost.com/blogs/fact-checker/post/history-lesson-when-the-united-states-looked-the-other-way-on-chemical-weapons/2013/09/04/0ec828d6-1549-11e3-961c-f22d3aaf19ab_blog.html. Accessed 13 November 2015.

King, Jr., Martin Luther. "An Autobiography of Religious Development." King Papers, Boston University Library. (n.d.).

King, Jr., Martin Luther. "Letter from Birmingham Jail." An Open Letter. 16 April 1963. *Christian Century* 80 (12 June 1963): 767-773.

"Klansmen Meet In City; Motorcade Goes to Koinonia," *The Americus Times-Recorder* (25 February 1957).

Kliever, Lonnie D. *The Shattered Spectrum: A Survey of Contemporary Theology*. Atlanta: John Knox Press, 1981.

Lawrence, Linda. "P T Conversation: James Fowler," *Psychology Today* (November 1983): 59-60.

Lee, Dallas. "Clarence Jordan: Modern Disciple." *Messenger* (8 May 1969): 8-10.

Lee, Dallas. "In Scorn of the Consequences." in Kirk Lyman-Barner, et al.. *Roots in the Cotton Patch: The Clarence Jordan Symposium 2012, Volume 1*. Eugene, Oregon: Cascade Books, 2014.

Mandela, Nelson. "Mandela on Gandhi: The Sacred Warrior." *Time* (December 31, 1999).

Maraniss, David. *Barack Obama: The Story*. New York: Simon & Schuster, 2012.

_____. *First in His Class: The Biography of Bill Clinton*. New York: Simon & Schuster, 1995.

McCloud, Linda. A Blog. "Sunrise on the Marsh: Saints: Clarence Jordan," The Episcopal Church of Our Savior at Honey Creek," July 11, 2007, located at http://oursaviorhoneycreek.blogspot.com/2007/07saints-clarence-jordan.html;" Accessed 13 November 2015.

McDowell, Jr., Edward A. "Introduction," in Clarence Jordan, *The Cotton Patch Version of Hebrews and The General Epistles*. Piscataway, New Jersey: New Century Publishers, 1973.

Moore, Charles. "Bi-racial Farm Probe Due for Action Today." *The Atlanta Constitution* (29 January 1958).

Morgan, Sr., S.L. "The Full Rehoboth Story." *The Christian Century* (October 11, 1950): 1204.

"Negro Lynched at Talbotton." *Atlanta Constitution* (24 June 1909): 1.

Nicholson, D.B. "Ridgecrest." *The Christian Index* (July 2, 1942): 20.

Noonan, Peggy. "A Separate Peace: America is in trouble—and our elites are merely resigned." *The Wall Street Journal* (27 October 2005) located at http://www.wsj.com/articles/SB122487970866167655. Accessed 13 November 2015.

Parham, Robert. "A Reconciler from Dixie: Clarence Jordan." *The Baptist Peacemaker* (July 1983): 6.

Pittman, Bill. "About Koinonia." *Americus Times-Recorder* (10 August 1956): 4.

Rappaport, Ernest A. "The Grandparent Syndrone." *The Psychoanalytic Quarterly* 27 (1958): 518-37.

"Rev. Clarence L. Jordan Dead; Led Interracial Farm Project." *New York Times* (31 October 1969).

Sanders, James A. "Adaptable for Life: The Nature and Function of Canon." in *Magnalia Dei:*

The Mighty Acts of God. Frank M. Cross, Werner E. Lemke, and Patrick D. Miller, Jr., eds. Garden City, New York: Doubleday, 1976: 53.

Sengupta, Somini. "Carter Sadly Turns Back On National Baptist Body." *New York Times* (21 October 2000).

Sibley, Celestine. "New Bill Aimed at Koinonia." *The Atlanta Constitution* (13 February 1958).

Sitikoff, Harvard. "The Postwar Impact of Vietnam," in John Whiteclay Chambers, ed., *The Oxford Companion to American Military History* (New York: Oxford University Press, 1999).

Smylie, James H. "On Jesus, Pharaohs, and the Chosen People: Martin Luther King as Biblical Interpreter and Humanist." *Interpretation* (January 1970).

"Store Dynamited Here Last Night." *Americus Time-Recorder* (24 July 1956): 1.

Stricklin, David. "Clarence Jordan (1912-1969), Jasper Martin England (1901-1989), and Millard Fuller (1935–) Koinonia Farm: Epicenter for Social Change." in Larry L. McSwain, Ed., *Twentieth-Century Shapers of Baptist Social Ethics.* Macon, GA: Mercer University Press, 2008.

Valentine, Foy. "The Signed Blank Check." *Christian Ethics Today* 12: 4 (1997): 2.

Wilder, Amos. "Story and Story-World" *Interpretation* 37/4 (October 1983): 353-364.

General Works: Books
Altizer, Thomas J. J. *The Gospel of Christian Atheism.* Philadelphia: The Westminster Press, 1966.

Armstrong, Karen. *The Battle for God.* New York: Alfred A. Knopf, 2000.

Barnette, Henlee, H. *Clarence Jordan: Turning Dreams into Deeds.* Macon: Smyth & Helwys, 1992.

Barthes, Roland. *The Pleasure of the Text.* New York: Hill and Wang, 1975.

Becker, Ernest. *Angel in Armor: A Post-Freudian Perspective on the Nature of Man.* New York: George Braziller, 1969.

Becker, Ernest. *The Denial of Death.* New York: The Free Press, 1973.

Blackmon, Douglas A. *Slavery by Another Name: The Re-Enslavement of Black Americans from the Civil War to World War II.* New York: Doubleday, 2008.

Boney, F. N. *A Walking Tour of the University of Georgia* . Athens, GA: Univeristy of Georgia Press, 1989.

Bonhoeffer, Dietrich. *The Cost of Discipleship.* New York: The MacMillan Company, 1937, 1959.

Brueggemann, Walter. *The Prophetic Imagination.* 2nd ed.; Philadelphia: Fortress Press, 2001.

Bryan, G. McLeod. *These Few Also Paid A Price: Southern Whites Who Fought For Civil Rights* Macon: Mercer University Press, 2001.

Bryan, G. McLeod. *Voices in the Wilderness: Twentieth-Century Prophets Speak to the New Millennium.* Macon, GA: Mercer University Press, 1999, 68.

Campbell, Joseph. *The Hero With A Thousand Faces.* Princeton: Princeton University Press, 1949.

Campbell, Will D. *Brother to a Dragonfly.* New York: The Seabury Press, 1977.

Capps, Donald. *Life Cycle Theory and Pastoral Care.* Philadelphia: Fortress Press, 1983.

Capps, Donald. *Pastoral Care: A Thematic Approach.* Philadelphia: The Westminster Press, 1979.

Carter, Dan T. *The Politics of Rage: George Wallace, The Origins of the New Conservatism, and the*

Transformation of American Politics . Baton Rouge: Louisiana State University Press, 1995, 2000.

Carter, Jimmy. *Our Endangered Values: America's Moral Crisis*. New York: Simon & Schuster, 2005.

Cassirer, Ernst. *An Essay On Man*. Garden City, New York: Doubleday & Company, Inc., 1944.

Coble, Ann Louise. *Cotton Patch for the Kingdom*. Scottdale, PA: 2002.

Cone, James H. *Black Theology and Black Power*. New York: The Seabury Press, 1969.

Criswell, W.A. *Why I Preach That The Bible Is Literally True* . Nashville: Broadman Press, 1969.

Crossan, John Dominic. *God's Empire: Jesus Against Rome, Then and Now* . San Francisco: Harper Collins, 2007.

Davidson, William H. *A Rockaway in Talbot: Travels in an Old Georgia County, Vol I*. West Point, Georgia, 1983.

de Paola, Tomie. *The Clown of God*. New York: Harcourt Brace Jovanovich, 1978.

Dodd, C.H. *The Authority of the Bible* . London: Nisbet and Company, 1929, revised edition, 1960.

Domke, David S. *God Willing: Political Fundamentalism in the White House*. Ann Arbor, Michigan: Pluto Press, 2004.

Domke, David S. *The God Strategy: How Religion Became A Political Weapon In America*. New York: Oxford University Press, 2008, 2010.

Downing, Frederick L. *Elie Wiesel: A Religious Biography*. Macon: Mercer University Press, 2008.

Downing, Frederick L. *To See The Promised Land: The Faith Pilgrimage of Martin Luther King, Jr*. Macon: Mercer University Press, 1986.

Dubois, W.E. B. *The Souls of Black Folk* . New York: Barnes and Noble Books, 1903, 2003.

Easwaran, Eknath. Translator. *The Bhagavad Gita*. Tomales, CA: Nilgiri Press, 1985.

Egerton, John. *The Americanization of Dixie: The Southerization of America*. New York: Harper's Magazine Press, 1974.

Einstein, Albert. *Ideas and Opinions*. New York: Crown Publishers, Inc., 1954.

Eliade, Mircea. *Myths, Dreams, and Mysteries: The Encounter between Contemporary Faiths and Archaic Realities*. London: Harvill Press, 1959, 1975.

Erikson, Erik H. *Childhood and Society*. New York: W.W. Norton and Company, Inc., 1963.

Erikson, Erik H. *Gandhi's Truth: On the Origins of Militant Nonviolence* . New York: W.W. Norton & Company, Inc., 1969.

Erikson, Erik H. *Identity: Youth and Crisis*. New York: W. W. Norton & Company, Inc., 1968.

Erikson, Erik. *Insight and Responsibility*. New York: W.W. Norton & Company, 1964.

Erikson, Erik H. *Life History and the Historical Moment*. New York: W.W. Norton & Company, Inc., 1975.

Erikson, Erik. *Toys and Reasons: Stages in the Ritualization of Experience*. New York: W.W. Norton & Company, 1977.

Erikson, Erik. *Young Man Luther: A Study in Psychoanalysis and History*. New York: W.W. Norton & Company, 1958.

Ferguson, Charles, H. *The Predator Nation: Corporate Criminal, Political Corruption, and the Hijacking of America*. New York: Random House, 2012.

Fowler, James. *Stages of Faith: The Psychology of Human Development and the Quest for Meaning*. San Francisco, Harper and Row Publishers, 1981.

Fowler, James W. and Lovin, Robin W., et. al. *Trajectories in Faith: Five Life Stories* Nashville: Abingdon Press, 1980.

Freud, Sigmund. *The Interpretation of Dreams.* trans. and ed. James Strachey. New York: Basic Books, 1955.

Fuller, Millard. *Bokotola.* New York: Association Press, 1977.

Gandhi, M.K. *An Autobiography or The Story of My Experiments with Truth.* Ahmedabad: Navajivan Publish House, 1927.

Gregory, Joel C. *Too Great a Temptation: The Seductive Power of America's Super Church* Fort Worth, Texas: The Summit Group, 1994.

Hamilton, Edith. *The Greek Way.* New York: W. W. Norton & Company, Inc., 1930, 1942.

_____. *Three Greek Plays: Prometheus Bound, Agamemnon, The Trojan Women.* New York: W. W. Norton & Company, Inc., 1937.

Heschel, Abraham Joshua. *The Prophets, Volumes 1 & II.* New York: Harper & Row, 1962.

Hill, Samuel S., ed. *Religion and the Solid South.* New York: Abingdon Press, 1972.

Howell, James C. *Servants, Misfits, and Martyrs: Saints and Their Stories.* Nashville: Upper Room Books, 1999.

Isikoff, Michael, and Corn, David. *Hubris: The Inside Story of Spin, Scandal, and the Selling of the Iraq War.* New York: Random House, 2006.

Jordan, Hamilton. *No Such Thing As A Bad Day.* Marietta, GA: Longstreet Press, 2000.

Jordan, Robert H. *There Was A Land: A History of Talbot County, Georgia.* Columbus, Georgia: Columbus Office Supply, 1971.

Keniston, Kenneth. *Young Radicals: Notes on Committed Youth* . New York: Harcourt Brace Jovanovich, Inc., 1968.

Tracy Elaine K'Meyer, *Interracialism and Christian Community in the Postwar South: The Story of Koinonia Farm* . Charlottesville: The University of Virginia Press, 1997.

King, Jr., Martin Luther. *Strength to Love.* Cleveland: William Collins, 1963.

King, Sr., Martin Luther. *Daddy King: An Autobiography.* New York: William Morrow, 1980.

Lee, Dallas. *The Cotton Patch Evidence: The Story of Clarence Jordan and the Koinonia Farm Experiment (1942-1970)* . Americus, Georgia: Koinonia Partners, Inc., 1971.

Lindbloom, J. *Prophecy in Ancient Israel* . Philadelphia: Fortress Press, 1962.

Lynd, Helen Merrell. *On Shame and the Search for Identity.* New York: Harcourt, Brace, 1958.

Marsh, Charles. *Strange Glory: A Life of Dietrich Bonhoeffer.* New York: Alfred A. Knopf, 2014.

Marsh, Charles. *The Beloved Community: How Faith Shapes Social Justice, From the Civil Rights Movement to Today.* New York: Basic Books, 2005.

McClendon, Jr., James Wm. *Biography As Theology: How Life Stories Can Remake Today's Theology.* Nashville, Abingdon Press, 1974.

Metaxas, Eric. *Bonhoeffer: Pastor, Martyr, Prophet, Spy A Righteous Gentile VS. The Third Reich.* Nashville: Thoms Nelson, 2010.

Metz, Johann Baptist. *Faith in History and Society: Toward a Practical Fundamental Theology* . New York: The Seabury Press, 1980.

Niebuhr, H. Richard. *Christ and Culture.* New York: Harper and Row, Publishers, 1951.

Novak, Michael. *Ascent of the Mountain, Flight of the Dove: An Invitation to Religious Studies.* New York: Harper & Row, Publishers, 1971.

Ong, Walter. *Orality and Literacy.* New York: Methuen & Co., 1982.

Otto, Rudolf. *The Idea of the Holy.* Oxford: Oxford University Press, 1931.

Parker, Theodore. *Ten Sermons of Religion*. Boston: Crosby, Nichols, and Company, 1853.

Parks, Sharon. *The Critical Years: Young Adults & The Search For Meaning, Faith & Commitment*. San Francisco: Harper & Row, 1986.

Peck, M. Scott. *The Different Drum: Community Making and Peace*. New York: Simon and Schuster, 1987.

Peck, Scott M. *The Road Less Traveled: A New Psychology of Love, Traditional Values and Spiritual Growth*. New York: Simon and Schuster, 1978.

Phillips, Kevin. *American Theocracy*. New York: Viking, 2006.

Ricoeur, Paul. *The Symbolism of Evil*. Boston: Beacon, 1967.

Rizzuto, Ana-Maria. *The Birth of the Living God: A Psychoanalytic Study*. Chicago: The University of Chicago Press, 1979.

Robinson, John A. T. *Honest to God*. Philadelphia: Westminster Press, 1963.

Rubenstein, Richard L. *After Auschwitz:Radical Theology and Contemporary Judaism*. New York: The Bobbs-Merrill Company, Inc., 1966.

Sagan, Eli. *Freud, Women, and Morality: The Psychology of Good and Evil*. New York: Basic Books, Inc., Publishers, 1988.

Segovia, Fernando F. and Tolbert, Mary Ann., eds. *Reading from this Place: Social Location and Biblical Interpretation in the United States* I. Minneapolis: Fortress Press, 1995.

Spence, Donald P. *Narrative Truth and Historical Truth: Meaning and Interpretation in Psychoanalysis*. New York: W. W. Norton & Company, 1982.

Stricklin, David. *A Genealogy of Dissent: Southern Baptist Protest in the Twentieth Century* Lexington: The University Press of Kentucky, 1999.

Sulloway, Frank J. *Freud, Biologist of the Mind: Beyond the Psycholanalytic Legend*. New York: Basic Books, 1983.

von Rad, Gerhard *Old Testament Theology II* . New York: Harper and Row, Publishers, 1965.

Acknowledgments

My indebtedness for this project is large. There have been a great number of people with whom I have spoken who knew Clarence Jordan personally. To a person, they were eager to speak about their memories of Jordan. Some of the information gathered during those interviews appears nowhere else. Frank Jordan was especially kind and generous with his time. He had significant memories of Clarence's childhood and the family. Frank Jordan also arranged for a dinner in the Jordan home where Clarence lived as a teenager, and where I ate with the extended family. I also spoke with George Jordan and Robert Jordan both of whom had important things to add about their brother. Corneila Jordan Callier, Clarence's sister, gave me indispensable information during her interview, and may have been the most important conversation partner for Jordan's early years. I am indebted to James Fowler for making the suggestion that I speak with her.

Likewise, my conversation over the course of two days at Koinonia with Florence Jordan was crucial for this study. Her memory of Clarence's adult years was foundational for this writing and the information that she gave about their interlude in South Africa can be found nowhere else. Margaret Whitkamper also gave an invaluable perspective on Clarence and the shared history of Koinonia. Engaging conversations with Ray Brewster and Joe Hendrix in Macon gave an important perspective on Clarence during the days of conflict from the 1950s and later in the 1960s, and on how Clarence was understood in the community especially at Mercer University. The dialogue with Dallas Lee in Atlanta was engaging and seminal. Henlee Barnette and Frank Stagg gave memories of Clarence from college and seminary days, as did Mary D. Bowman.

On a hot summer day in Louisville, I listened with rapt attention to Henlee Barnette as he recounted his time with Clarence Jordan in the inner-city ministry that they had shared in downtown Louisville. At the end of that conversation, Henlee Barnette stressed that the story of Clarence Jordan was yet untold and that the center of that story was the narrative of his radical journey and the central theme of the narrative was always "koinonia"-community. Professor Barnette also remembered Clarence Jordan's unusual capacity for human sensitivity and that one should take note of this aspect of his character in the study.

A large group of individuals helped with the gathering of information. Amanda Moore and Bren Dubay at Koinonia Farm were instrumental in my gaining access to articles and pictures from the Koinonia Archives. Bren Dubay provided permission to read the FBI file on Koinonia Farm. Peter Roberts at Georgia State University helped with an article on Joe Hendricks and Talbot County. Julia Cowart at Furman University provided access to a stirring chapel address that Clarence Jordan made there in 1969, and Furman gave permission to use one of the last pictures of Jordan taken in public during his visit to the university in the spring of 1969. Rebecca Petersen May arranged for me to read the FBI file on Clarence Jordan that is housed in the Special Collections and Archives of Wake Forest University. Amy Purcell sent historic photographs of the Haymarket district in downtown Louisville and the permission to use them. Likewise, Adam Winters of Southern Baptist Seminary gave permission for the use of a photograph of Mullins Hall. The staff of the Hargrett Rare Book and Manuscript Library at the University of Georgia provided access to the important collection of materials in the Clarence Jordan Papers. Adam J. Dixon at Boston University helped to locate an interview that P.D. East did with Clarence Jordan.

The work of two former professors, Donald Capps and James Fowler, remain foundational for the writing of this project. I have drawn heavily on Capps' idea of "religious biography" and on other theories of psychology and religion that I learned from him. I have not only drawn much from the writing of James Fowler, as this volume indicates, but I also have a vivid memory of his support for the Jordan project. Of course, neither Capps nor Fowler are responsible for my shortcomings in the appropriation of their work. I have also continued to draw heavily on the work of Walter Brueggemann, especially his concept of the "poet-prophet" as well as his insightful analysis of American culture. Brueggemann's work has been utilized to portray the prophetic dimensions of Jordan's life and teaching.

I am also indebted to Linda Downing and Jonathan Downing for their reading and extended conversation about the manuscript. Linda was especially helpful in her comments on Clarence's childhood. Jonathan also took photographs at Koinonia and in Talbotton, and worked on the cover art. Last of all, I am indebted to Marc Jolley and the staff at Mercer University Press for their editorial work in putting this volume together.

NOTES

Introduction
[1] See Henlee H. Barnette, *Clarence Jordan: Turning Dreams into Deeds* (Macon GA: Smyth & Helwys, 1992) 6.

[2] W.E.B. Dubois, *The Souls of Black Folk* (New York: Barnes and Nobles Books, 1903, 2003) 82–97.

[3] Douglas A. Blackmon, *Slavery by Another Name: The Re-Enslavement of Black Americans from the Civil War to World War II* (New York: Doubleday, 2008) 1–10, 58–83.

[4] P.D. East, interview by Clarence Jordan, n.d., Howard Gotlieb Archival Research Center, Boston University. Jordan describes the jail as being behind his house and on his way to and from school. There was an "old-time Georgian chain gang" there. Jordan went on to say that he spent a lot of time over there beginning when he was about 8 or 9 years old. It was a place of "terrible brutality" (see p. 16). For the imagery of Georgia as "frontier," see Harold E. Fey, "Report from Koinonia: Creative Church in Georgia," *The Christian Century* 74 (6 March 1957) 285-287.

[5] Dan T. Carter, *The Politics of Rage: George Wallace, the Origins of the New Conservatism, and the Transformation of American Politics* (Baton Rouge: Louisiana State University Press, 1995, 2000) 68–109. The actual vow that Wallace takes is: "No son-of-a bitch will ever out-nigger me again" (96). See also, the compelling film titled *George Wallace: Settin' the Woods on Fire* (Steve Fayer, writer; and Paul Stekler and Dan McCabe, producers—A PBS "American Experience" Program, 2004). In the beginning Wallace was a liberal—seen as one of the most liberal judges in the state of Alabama and a moderate on racial issues. Later, his political gospel of rage and alienation preached across the South and into Northern cities during his presidential campaigns helped to transform American politics and set the stage for a new Republican strategy, beginning with Richard Nixon. After being shot down in an attempted assassination, Wallace would live out his remaining years searching for some form of redemption for the division he helped create and forgiveness for the people he had maligned and oppressed.

[6] Dan T. Carter, *The Politics of Rage*, 370.

[7] Ibid., 8.

[8] Mary D. Bowman interview by author, Pineville, Louisiana, 17 October 1987. Her father was Roland Q. Leavell, a prominent Baptist pastor in the Southern Baptist Convention and, later, President of New Orleans Baptist Seminary. While Jordan was at the University of Georgia, Leavell was pastor of the First Baptist church in Gainesville, Georgia. "Leavell regarded him [Jordan] as a failure because he had strayed from the path of soul-winning to minister to people other than 'our kind.' Leavell frequently shook his head when Clarence Jordan was mentioned and said, 'What a waste. I had such high hopes for him. What a waste of that scholarly mind and superior personality. I had no idea he would turn out to be an offbeat fanatic.'"

[9] See Dan Carter's chapter 11 titled "Richard Nixon, George Wallace, and the Southernization of American Politics," in Carter, *The Politics of Rage*, 324–70.

[10] To date, some 500,000 homes have been built around the world, affecting the lives of some 2 million people. In 1968, Jordan and Millard Fuller proposed a revolutionary idea—a "Fund for Humanity"—which would be a way of restoring land to the poor, and an appropriate way for the affluent members of society to share with the less fortunate. As a prelude to "Habitat," Jordan and Fuller established forty-two home sites on the northern boundary of the farm. The houses would be built for cost, and sold for the same price. The money was to be loaned interest-free from the Fund for Humanity. Since these first homes were built, the project has been an effort to help eliminate poverty and inadequate housing among the poor. See Jordan's last interview, by Walden Howard, "The Legacy of Clarence Jordan," *Faith at Work* (April 1970): 17.

[11] This issue can be confusing to some readers of Clarence Jordan. He seemed to describe himself as a fundamentalist. Will Campbell, who knew Jordan well, described Jordan as an "authentic fundamentalist," and went on to say that "Clarence was just a poor, befuddled bastard who believed the New Testament." See Susan M. Glisson, "Life in Scorn of the Consequences: Clarence Jordan and the Roots of Radicalism in the Southern Baptist Convention" (M.A. thesis, University of Mississippi, 1994) 118–19. See also, Charles Marsh, *The Beloved Community: How Faith Shapes Social Justice, from the Civil Rights Movement to Today* (New York: Basic Books, 2005) 83. Marsh writes that "Jordan read scripture with the passion of an old-school fundamentalist...." The most helpful classification of Jordan's theology within the spectrum that was the Southern Baptist Convention is that of David Stricklin, *A Genealogy of Dissent: Southern Baptist Protest in the Twentieth Century* (Lexington: The University Press of Kentucky, 1999) 23–47. Stricklin places Jordan in the context of a group of progressive dissidents, all of whom eventually achieve the status of *persona non grata* in the Southern Baptist Convention, which was largely composed of fundamentalists.

[12] For an introduction to Criswell's view of the Bible, see especially, W.A. Criswell, *Why I Preach That the Bible Is Literally True* (Nashville: Broadman Press, 1969) 119–25.

[13] See James C. Howell, *Servants, Misfits, and Martyrs: Saints and Their Stories* (Nashville: Upper Room Books, 1999) 30.

[14] Clarence Jordan, interview by P.D. East, Koinonia Farm, Americus, Georgia, 1957.

[15] See Bill Moyers and Gail Pellett, "God and Politics: The Battle for the Bible" (Public Affairs Television, Inc., 1988). For an additional insider perspective to Criswell and the nature of corporate Southern Baptist life, see Joel C. Gregory, *Too Great a Temptation: The Seductive Power of America's Super Church* (Fort Worth TX: The Summit Group, 1994) 37–69.

[16] See Curtis W. Freeman, "'Never Had I Been So Blind': W.A. Criswell's 'Change' on Racial Segregation," *The Journal of Southern Religion* 10 (2007): 1–12.

[17] Gregory, *Too Great a Temptation*, 1. Gregory begins his first chapter by describing the church: "The First Baptist Church of Dallas sits at the intersection where the Way of the Cross intersects the American Dream—via Dolorosa at Wall Street. Such an intersection has no stoplights, not even a yield sign. Where the road to the cross and the road to success meet, there can be a head-on collision between a man's ambition and his desire to serve God."

[18] Cited in Michael Lynsey Westmoreland-White, "Incarnational Discipleship: The Ethics of Clarence Jordan, Martin Luther King, Jr., and Dorothy Day" (Ph.D. diss., The Southern Baptist Theological Seminary, 1995) 72. For Niebuhr's typology, see H. Richard Niebuhr, *Christ and Culture* (New York: Harper & Row, Publishers, 1951) 230–56.

[19] Carter was a moderate on the issues that were crucial to Criswell, and it is likely that Criswell saw Carter as a liberal, which meant that, despite being a Baptist, Carter was not in Criswell's camp.

[20] Criswell kept a list of those who disagreed with him or used historical criticism in reading the Bible. He published the list early in his career. He called for the expulsion of those who refused to read the Bible literally. They should leave the ministry or go to another school, he said. For the view that these stories were never intended to be read literally, see Karen Armstrong, *The Battle for God* (New York: Alfred A. Knopf, 2000) xi–xv. Ironically, Armstrong notes that fundamentalist movements, like Criswell's, have a "symbiotic relationship with modernity." By rejecting the original intention of the great stories, the fundamentalists create a void of spirituality at the center of their movement and begin to mimic the models available to them in the contemporary culture. The conservative resurgence mimics the "hostile-takeover" and "raw-power" politics of the secular business world of the 20th-century West. The "takeover" of the Southern Baptist Convention in the 1980s is strangely reminiscent of Nietzsche's "will to power." See especially, Dan Vestal's poignant rebuke and rejection of this fundamentalist tactic in the PBS series by Moyers and Pellett, "God and Politics," 1988.

[21] The Southern Baptist fundamentalists did successfully take control of the Southern Baptist Convention through the political processes associated with the so-called "conservative resurgence." All of the seminaries and agencies of the convention took on a fundamentalist character, and dramatically altered the nature of Southern Baptist life. See especially, Kevin Phillips, *American Theocracy* (New York: Viking, 2006) x, 99–217. See also, David S. Domke, *The God Strategy: How Religion Became a Political Weapon in America* (New York: Oxford University Press, 2008, 2010) 3–70; and David S. Domke, *God Willing: Political Fundamentalism in the White House* (Ann Arbor MI: Pluto Press, 2004) 2. Domke shows that, beginning with the election of Ronald Reagan in 1980, there was a new effort to use religion to attract voters and solidify political power. Beginning with the post-9/11 presidency of George W. Bush, there is the unprecedented use of religious rhetoric and a commitment to a type of "political fundamentalism" that challenges the history and nature of American politics.

[22] See Glisson, "Life in Scorn of the Consequences," 88.

[23] Jordan's FBI file is ironically very large. See G. McLeod Bryan, *These Few Also Paid a Price: Southern Whites Who Fought for Civil Rights* (Macon GA: Mercer University Press, 2001) 49–51.

[24] For an introduction to Bonhoeffer, see Dietrich Bonhoeffer, *The Cost of Discipleship* (New York: The MacMillan Company, 1937, 1959) 9–83. See also, Eric Metaxas, *Bonhoeffer: Pastor, Martyr, Prophet, Spy; A Righteous Gentile Versus the Third Reich* (Nashville: Thomas Nelson, 2010) 1–4.

[25] Arun Gandhi, "Gandhi—Weaving a Universal Thread," M. K. Gandhi Institute, http://www.jpcarter.com/Spirituality/PDF/AshramArt.Pdf (15 September 2015).

[26] Marsh, *The Beloved Community*, 53–54.

[27] Martin Luther King, Jr., quoted in Hamilton Jordan, *No Such Thing as a Bad Day* (Marietta GA: Longstreet Press, 2000) 122–23.

[28] Ibid.

[29] Mary D. Bowman remembered Clarence Jordan speaking about Gandhi in fall 1948, when Jordan led a study session at a Baptist Student Union conference at Northwestern State University in Natchitoches, Louisiana. See interview with Mary D. Bowman, Pineville, Louisiana, 17 October 1987.

[30] Mohandas K. Gandhi, "My Spiritual Message," Kingsley Hall, London, England (17 October 1931), Old. Harappa.com 2000-2006, http://www.ndtv.com/article/india/mahatma-gandhi-s-famous-speech-at-kingsley-hall-in-1931-138262 (15 September 2015).

[31] Clarence Jordan in Dallas Lee, ed., *The Substance of Faith and Other Cotton Patch Sermons* (New York: Association Press, 1972) 94–95.

[32] See Erik Erikson, *Gandhi: On the Origins of Militant Nonviolence* (New York: W.W. Norton & Company, Inc., 1969) 118–33.

[33] Joe Hendrix, interview by author (Fredrick L. Downing), Macon, Georgia, 26 May 1987. Many students were bored by the churches but thought that Koinonia was the real thing—an authentic expression of Christianity.

[34] Interview with Ray Brewster, Macon, Georgia, 26 May 1987.

[35] See especially, Robert Parham, "A Reconciler from 'Dixie': Clarence Jordan," *Baptist Peacemaker* (July 1983): 6.

[36] Greg Carey, "Clarence Jordan as a (White) Interpreter of the Bible," in Kirk Lyman-Barner and Cori Lyman-Barner, eds., *Roots in the Cotton Patch: The Clarence Jordan Symposium 2012, Volume 1* (Eugene OR: Cascade Books, 2014) 38.

[37] Interview with Joe Hendrix, Macon, Georgia, 26 May 1987.

[38] Interview with Dallas Lee, Atlanta, Georgia, 30 June 1987.

[39] It is in the stories of the Hebrew Bible that one first learns of the "poet-prophet," the gifted figure whose words penetrate the illusions that humans construct in their quest for power and control over their environments. The paradigmatic model for this special group of Hebrew poets is Moses, who, according to tradition, was molded and shaped in the desert surrounding Sinai. In contrast to the mythological society of Egypt, Moses began to value an alternative vision of the freedom of God over against the "royal consciousness" of the pharaoh's imperial realm. Under the leadership of Moses, Israel begins to learn how to demythologize the imperial strategies that seek to continue a politics of control and status quo. This original core narrative of the great poet-prophet who challenged the ways of the pharaoh and the politics of oppression was told by the writers of the Bible who themselves held to a vision characterized by a decoding or demythologizing "sacred discontent." In contrast to the surrounding cultures, this first Yahwistic vision allowed its adherents to confront the ancient world with a new mode of thought—a demythologizing consciousness that was turned against culture itself. These first writers then resisted the common forms of mythological thought that surrounded them, and went on to overturn the routine assumptions of their time. This probing skepticism that was turned against the surrounding cultures eventually became an enduring gift to Western civilization by way of the literary tradition and the tradition of self-criticism. Put

another way, after these first writers of the Bible ceased giving their messages, the theme of "sacred discontent" had to take different forms. The writers of the New Testament also saw the significance of Moses as poet-prophet and proclaimed that Jesus stood in that tradition. In fact, he was a new Moses, according to Matthew, who gave a new sermon from the mount and for the new border crossing. Jesus, like John the Baptist, called that generation to an alternative future—alternative to the ways of the Herods. The poet-prophet, then, is one who sees God at work in social processes in subversive ways for judgment and redemption—to generate new social possibilities, and entertain new narratives alternative to the old ways. The age will be blown open for new possibilities. This, then, is a form of the primal core of biblical faith—a call to practice an ethic of care for the neighbor, especially the oppressed and the powerless. See especially, Walter Brueggemann, *The Prophetic Imagination,* 2nd ed. (Philadelphia: Fortress Press, 2001) 1–37. See also, Frederick L. Downing, *Elie Wiesel: A Religious Biography* (Macon GA: Mercer University Press, 2008) 15–20. Brueggemann argues that the "alternative consciousness of Moses" was a radical break with Egyptian culture. Moses replaces the "static triumphalism" of Egypt with the freedom of God, and he counters the "politics of oppression and exploitation" with the "politics of justice and compassion."

[40] How does one chart the spiritual periods or the stages of Jordan's life? One begins with the understanding that is a human universal—that is, all persons have some form of faith. This is essentially a way of composing meaning. The human being is like a cosmologer in that he or she creates a cosmos, and this picture of the world is an inherently human construction dependent upon the individual for its unique shape and configuration. Ernst Cassirer puts it this way in his book, *An Essay on Man*: "In language, in religion, in art, in science, man can do no more than to build up his own universe—a symbolic universe that enables him to understand and interpret, to articulate and organize, to synthesize and universalize his human experience." Albert Einstein wrote something very similar in his book, *Ideas and Opinions*. He noted that the human tries to make for oneself "a simplified and intelligible picture of the world," which is then substituted for one's present world of experience. In this way, says Einstein, one tries to "overcome" the chaos of one's world and, by making this new cosmos the center of one's emotional life, seeks "to find…the peace and security he cannot find in the narrow whirlpool of personal experience." Put in more religious terms, faith is trust or devotion that becomes a basic stance of the person or self. That is, religious faith presupposes a type of theological world construction. The way one sees the world is directly related to one's faith as a basic stance toward existence. Therefore, Clarence Jordan's life story and the artifacts of his life reveal a series of basic stances of faith across a lifetime, which then comprise the religious or spiritual pilgrimage.

[41] The faith development theory of James Fowler utilized in this biographical study of Jordan follows a similar pattern. See my (Frederick L. Downing's) essay titled "The Dangerous Journey Home: Charting the Religious Pilgrimage," in James Fowler and Scott Peck," *Perspectives in Religious Studies* 25/3 (Fall 1998): 249–65; and also Joseph Campbell, *The Hero with a Thousand Faces* (Princeton: Princeton University Press, 1949) 30.

[42] For the role of "disciplined subjectivity" in such studies, see Erik Erikson, *Insight and Responsibility* (New York: W.W. Norton & Company, 1964) 53. Erikson also writes

that in the study of a life, one must be able "to recognize major trends even where the facts are not all available...must be able to make meaningful predictions as to what will prove to have happened." See Erik Erikson, *Young Man Luther: A Study in Psychoanalysis and History* (New York: W.W. Norton & Company, 1958) 50.

Chapter 1

[1] This story is told by Robert H. Jordan, Clarence Jordan's brother, in his book, *There Was a Land: A History of Talbot County, Georgia* (Columbus GA: Columbus Office Supply, 1971) 180–81.

[2] Ibid., 181.

[3] Ibid.

[4] Ibid., 182.

[5] Ibid. See also, "Negro Lynched at Talbotton," *The Atlanta Constitution,* 24 June 1909, 1.

[6] W.E.B. Dubois, *The Souls of Black Folk* (New York: Barnes and Noble Books, 1903, 2003) 90.

[7] Ibid., 79.

[8] Frank Jordan, interview by author (Frederick L. Downing), Talbotton, Georgia, 13 April 1987.

[9] (Robert H.) Jordan, *There Was A Land*, 182.

[10] This description and verification of the lineage comes from (Robert H.) Jordan, *There Was a Land*, 181, 344–45.

[11] Clarence Jordan, interview by P.D. East, Koinonia Farm, 1958, P.D. East collection, Howard Gotlieb Archival Research Center, Boston University. The manuscript is filed under "Koinonia-Jordan" by P.D. East, Tape 1.

[12] William H. Davidson, *A Rockaway in Talbot: Travels in an Old Georgia County, Volume I* (West Point GA: 1983) 126.

[13] Frank Jordan, interview by author (Frederick L. Downing), Talbotton, Georgia, 13 April 1987.

[14] George Jordan, interview by author (Fredrick L. Downing), Talbotton, Georgia, 25 May 1987.

[15] Cornelia Callier, interview by author (Fredrick L. Downing), Atlanta, Georgia, 30 June 1987.

[16] See Clarence Jordan, "Sermon Notes: The Mother of Jesus," Mt. Carmel Baptist Church (January 1937) in the Clarence Jordan Papers, UGA, MS756: B1, F11.

[17] Ibid. See also, a sermon titled "The Mother of Jesus," 9 May 1937.

[18] Davidson, *A Rockaway in Talbot*, 127.

[19] Ibid., 125.

[20] James Weaver Jordan was born in Taylor County in 1878. His father was Green Henry Jordan, born in 1834, and his mother was Cornelia Weaver Jordan, born in 1850.

[21] Interview with Frank Jordan, Talbotton, Georgia, 13 April 1987; and Clarence Jordan, interview by P.D. East, Koinonia Farm, Americus, Georgia, 1957.

[22] See especially, the letter from Jim Jordan to Clarence, 19 May 1936.

[23] Davidson, *A Rockaway in Talbot*, 125. Also see interview with Frank Jordan, Talbotton, Georgia, 13 April 1987.

[24] Davidson, *A Rockaway in Talbot*, 126.

[25] Interview with Frank Jordan, Talbotton, Georgia, 13 April 1987.

[26] Clarence Jordan, interview by P.D. East, Koinonia Farm, Americus, Georgia, 1957.

[27] Ibid.

[28] Clarence Jordan in Dallas Lee, ed., *The Substance of Faith and Other Cotton Patch Sermons* (New York: Association Press, 1972) 144.

[29] Letter from brother Budde to Clarence, 11 February 1927, the Clarence Jordan Papers, UGA, B1, F1.

[30] Davidson, *A Rockaway in Talbot*, 125.

[31] Clarence Jordan, interview by P.D. East, Koinonia Farm, Americus, Georgia, 1957.

[32] Ibid.

[33] Ibid.

[34] Clarence Jordan, interview by Walden Howard, "The Legacy of Clarence Jordan," *Faith At Work* (April 1970): 15–16.

[35] Ibid., 16.

[36] Tracy Elaine K'Meyer, *Interracialism and Christian Community in the Postwar South: The Story of Koinonia Farm* (Charlottesville: The University of Virginia Press, 1997) 27.

Chapter 2

[1] Will D. Campbell, *Brother to a Dragonfly* (New York: The Seabury Press, 1977) 43–46.

[2] Frank Jordan, interview by author (Frederick L. Downing), Talbotton, Georgia, 13 April 1987.

[3] In a letter dated 22 March 1927, Cornelia writes to Clarence from Shorter College, and she begins by writing, "'Grump' ole dear..." (MS 756, B1, F1, 1927).

[4] Frank Jordan, interview by author (Downing), Talbotton, Georgia, 13 April 1987.

[5] Cornelia Jordan, interview by author (Downing), Callier, Atlanta, Georgia, 30 June 1987.

[6] Interview with Frank Jordan, Talbotton, Georgia, 13 April 1987. Frank Jordan said, "It was perfectly alright with us and we weren't envious." The whole family seemed to know that Clarence was their mother's favorite, but to a one they said that it was not an issue.

[7] Letter from Mother to Clarence Jordan, 26 July 1934, MS 756, B1, F8.

[8] Erik H. Erikson, *Toys and Reasons: Stages in the Ritualization of Experience* (New York: W.W. Norton & Company, 1977) 85–91.

[9] Fowler calls this form of faith "Intuitive-Projective." It is typical in children ages 2–6 or 7. The term "intuitive" suggests the way the child envisions faith as a map of reality, and the term "projective" implies an imitative projection of this reality. See especially, James W. Fowler, *Stages of Faith: The Psychology of Human Development and the Quest for Meaning* (New York: Harper Collins Publishers, 1981) 119-134. Ana-Maria Rizzuto,

The Birth of the Living God: A Psychoanalytic Study (Chicago: The University of Chicago Press, 1979) 206–208; Eli Sagan, *Freud, Women, and Morality: The Psychology of Good and Evil* (New York: Basic Books, Inc., Publishers, 1988) 27, 159–82; and Scott Peck, *The Road Less Traveled: A New Psychology of Love, Traditional Values, and Spiritual Growth* (New York: Simon and Schuster, 1978) 190–91.

[10] Letter from Clarence Jordan to Mama, 11 May 1931, MS 756, B1, F5.

[11] Letter from Clarence Jordan to Mama, 10 March 1933, MS 756, B1, F7.

[12] Rizzuto, *The Birth of the Living God*, 7.

[13] Interview with Henlee Barnette, Louisville, Kentucky, 2 July 1987.

[14] Donald Capps, *Pastoral Care: A Thematic Approach* (Philadelphia: The Westminster Press, 1979) 47.

[15] See Campbell, *Brother to a Dragonfly*, 43. The vicarious nature of the call would explain Clarence Jordan's willingness to present himself to the black community in Louisville as an object of punishment/sacrifice. See the story rehearsed on page 1 above.

[16] Erikson, *Toys and Reasons*, 85–91; Donald Capps, *Life Cycle Theory and Pastoral Care* (Philadelphia: Fortress Press, 1983) 24, 58–60.

[17] Interview with Frank Jordan, Talbotton, Georgia, 13 April 1987.

[18] Ibid.

[19] Ibid.

[20] Ibid.

[21] Interview with Cornelia Callier, Atlanta, Georgia, 30 June 1987.

[22] See Donald Capps, *Men, Religion, Melancholia: James, Otto, Jung, and Erikson* (New Haven: Yale University Press, 1997) 4, 205.

[23] See Capps, *Life Cycle Theory and Pastoral Care*, 25.

[24] See Peck, *The Road Less Traveled*, 25.

[25] Erik H. Erikson, *Young Man Luther: A Study in Psychoanalysis and History* (New York: W.W. Norton & Company, 1958) 124.

[26] Erik H. Erikson, *Life History and the Historical Moment* (New York: W.W. Norton & Company, Inc., 1975) 165.

Chapter 3

[1] Interview with Frank Jordan, Talbotton, Georgia, 13 April 1987; and interview with Cornelia Callier, Atlanta, Georgia, 30 June 1987.

[2] There is a picture of this building in (Robert H.) Jordan, *There Was a Land: A History of Talbot County, Georgia* (Columbus GA: Columbus Office Supply, 1971) 105.

[3] Interview with George Jordan, Talbotton, Georgia, 25 May 1987.

[4] Interview with Frank Jordan, Talbotton, Georgia, 25 May 1987.

[5] Interview with George Jordan, Talbotton, Georgia, 25 May 1987.

[6] Interview with Frank Stagg, Diamond Head, Mississippi, 12 October 1987.

[7] Interview with Dallas Lee, Atlanta, Georgia, 30 June 1987.

[8] Interview with George Jordan, Talbotton, Georgia, 25 May 1987.

[9] Interview with Cornelia Callier, Atlanta, Georgia, 30 June 1987.

[10] A contemporary retelling of this ancient French and Italian legend can be found in Tomie de Paola, *The Clown of God* (New York: Harcourt Brace Jovanovich, 1978).

[11] See the comments on the clown in Donald Capps, *Life Cycle Theory and Pastoral Care* (Philadelphia: Fortress Press, 1983) 112–13.

[12] Interview with Cornelia Callier, Atlanta, Georgia, 30 June 1987.

[13] Ibid.

[14] Letter from Clarence Jordan to Mother, 10 March 1933, MS 756, B1, F6.

[15] Erik H. Erikson, *Gandhi's Truth: On the Origins of Militant Nonviolence* (New York: W.W. Norton & Company, Inc., 1969) 132.

[16] Interview with Cornelia Callier, Atlanta, Georgia, 30 June 1987.

[17] Erik Erikson, *Childhood and Society* (New York: W.W. Norton & Company, Inc., 1963) 314.

[18] Erik Erikson, *Insight and Responsibility* (New York: W.W. Norton & Company, Inc., 1964) 66.

[19] See Donald Capps, "John Henry Newman: A Study of Vocational Identity," *Journal for the Scientific Study of Religion* 9 (Spring 1970): 33–51; and Ernest A. Rappaport, "The Grandparent Syndrome," *The Psychoanalytic Quarterly* 27 (1958): 518–37.

[20] Interview with George Jordan, Talbotton, Georgia, 25 May 1987.

[21] Ibid.

[22] This stage of faith is described by Fowler as "Mythic-Literal." Typically, the child in this stage is between 7 and 12 or 13 years of age. The child's social world has expanded beyond the family and includes teachers and leaders in community organizations. See James W. Fowler, *Stages of Faith: The Psychology of Human Development and the Human Quest for Meaning* (New York: Harper Collins Publishers, 1981) 135-150.

[23] See M. Scott Peck, *The Different Drum: Community Making and Peace* (New York: Simon and Schuster, 1987) 190.

[24] Clarence Jordan, "Jesus the Rebel," an audio cassette (Americus GA: Koinonia Records, n.d.).

[25] See Amos Wilder, "Story and Story-World," *Interpretation* 37/4 (October 1983): 353–64.

[26] See Erik H. Erikson, *Identity: Youth and Crisis* (New York: W.W. Norton & Company, Inc., 1968) 298–99.This temptation seems to be part of human psychosocial evolution, in which an individual or tribe becomes rooted in the conviction that some "all-wise deity" created and endowed this special people to live out and protect the only authentic version of human life.

[27] See Erikson, *Gandhi's Truth*, 118. See also, Erik Erikson, *Young Man Luther: A Study in Psychoanalysis and History* (New York: W.W. Norton & Company, 1958) 103.

[28] See Michael Novak, *Ascent of the Mountain, Flight of the Dove: An Invitation to Religious Studies* (New York: Harper & Row, Publishers, 1971) 104–108; Paul Ricoeur, *The Symbolism of Evil* (Boston: Beacon, 1967) 350–52; James A. Sanders, "Adaptable for Life: The Nature and Function of Canon," in *Magnalia Dei: The Mighty Acts of God*, ed. Frank M. Cross, Werner E. Lemke, and Patrick D. Miller, Jr. (Garden City NY: Doubleday, 1976) 53.

Chapter 4

[1] In Jordan's last interview, by Walden Howard, Clarence says, "I heard one of the prisoners on the chain gang being whipped." In the book by Dallas Lee, Clarence is

quoted as saying, "Ed Russell was in the stretcher. I knew not only who was in the stretcher but who was pulling the rope."

[2] Interview with George Jordan, Talbotton, Georgia, 25 May 1987.

[3] Clarence Jordan, interview by Walden Howard, "The Legacy of Clarence Jordan: *Faith At Work* (April 1970): 16.

[4] Dallas Lee, *The Cotton Patch Evidence: The Story of Clarence Jordan and the Koinonia Farm Experiment (1942–1970)* (Americus GA: Koinonia Partners, Inc., 1971) 8.

[5] Interview with Cornelia Callier, Atlanta, Georgia, 30 June 1987.

[6] For this language, see W.E.B. Dubois, *The Souls of Black Folk* (New York: Barnes and Noble Books, 1903, 2003) 90.

[7] See Lee, *The Cotton Patch Evidence*, 8–9.

[8] Ibid., 9.

[9] Clarence Jordan, interview by P.D. East, Koinonia Farm, Americus, Georgia, n.d.

[10] Clarence Jordan to the Rev. Glenn T. Settle, Cleveland, Ohio, 29 August 1942, MS 756, B2, F2. In this letter, Clarence mentions his "debt" in relation to Warren Trice, the black porter in his father's hardware store. "Because Warren Trice, his wife, and eight children were willing to go hungry, I went to college. I owe them a debt." Again, Erikson notes that no one episode (or person) can be the cause or focus of the debt, which is, in fact, a pervasive childhood conflict. See Erikson, *Gandhi's Truth*, 128.

[11] The concept of the "curse" comes from Erik Erikson: "The curse in the lives of spiritual innovators with a similarly precocious and relentless conscience…is indicative of an aspect of childhood or youth which comes to represent an account that can never be settled and remains an existential debt for a lifetime" (*Gandhi's Truth*, 128).

[12] Ibid.

[13] Ibid., 128–32.

[14] Clarence Jordan, quoted in Lee, *The Cotton Patch Evidence*, 9.

[15] Clarence Jordan, quoted by Howard, "The Legacy of Clarence Jordan," 16.

[16] Ibid.

[17] See Rev. Martin Luther King, Sr., *Daddy King: An Autobiography* (New York: William Morrow, 1980) 109; Martin Luther King, Jr., "An Autobiography of Religious Development" (n.p.: circa 1950) 10–11; the Martin Luther King, Jr. Papers, 1950-1968, Boston University, Boston, MA, B106, F22. Frederick L. Downing, *To See the Promised Land: The Faith Pilgrimage of Martin Luther King, Jr.* (Macon GA: Mercer University Press, 1986) 99–102. See also, James Fowler, interview by Linda Lawrence, "PT Conversation: James Fowler," *Psychology Today* (November 1983): 59–60.

[18] James W. Fowler, *Stages of Faith: The Psychology of Human Development and the Quest for Meaning* (New York: Harper Collins Publishers, 1981) 119-134 and Sharon Parks, *The Critical Years: Young Adults & the Search for Meaning, Faith, & Commitment* (San Francisco: Harper & Row Publishers, 1986) 76. Fowler describes the form of faith exhibited here as "Synthetic-Conventional." The term "synthetic" implies the drawing together of one's faith into a synthesis, and the term "conventional" signifies that the beliefs and values are drawn from one's friends or significant others. This stage, typical of adolescents, is a "conformist" style of faith and reflects a time characterized by the power exhibited by the expectations and judgments of others. Values and beliefs, at this point,

remain tacit or unexamined by critical thought. Clarence will remain in this era of faith for approximately ten years.

[19] Interview with Robert H. Jordan, Talbotton, Georgia, 13 April 1987.

[20] Interview with Margaret Whitkamper, Koinonia Farm, 8 November 1986. See also, the interview with Joe Hendrix, Macon Georgia, 26 May 1987. This educational climate for blacks in Talbot County continued to be the same through the 1940s, 1950s, and likely into the 1960s.

[21] Interview with George Jordan, Talbotton, Georgia, 25 May 1987.

[22] Ibid.

[23] Interview by Robert H. Jordan, Talbotton, Georgia, 13 May 1987.

[24] William H. Davidson, *A Rockaway in Talbot: Travels in an Old Georgia County, Volume I* (West Point GA: 1983) 126.

[25] Ibid.

[26] Maude Jossey Jordan to Clarence, 10 August 1927, the Clarence Jordan Papers, UGA, MS 756, B1, F1. Maude Jossey underlines the word "risks." Apparently, this had become an issue with Clarence's mother.

[27] Interview by Frank Jordan, Talbotton, Georgia, 13 May 1987.

[28] Clarence Jordan, tenth-grade composition notebook, UGA, MS 756, B1, F3.

[29] Card from Clarence Jordan to mother, UGA, MS 756, B1, F3.

[30] Letter from Cornelia Jordan to Clarence, 16 September 1929, B1, F3.

[31] Letter from Buddie Jordan to Clarence, 4 February 1927, the Clarence Jordan Papers, MS 756, B1, F1.

[32] Letter from Buddie Jordan to Clarence, 11 February 1927, the Clarence Jordan Papers, MS 756, B1, F1.

[33] The word "Grump" actually looks like "Gump." "Grump" is used here because that appears to be the nickname his brothers and sisters gave him, and "Gump" was the name given by classmates at school.

[34] The term "go-fetcher" is difficult to interpret. Does this imply that Clarence is at a difficult point in his life? Both his brother and his sister are writing letters of encouragement.

[35] Clarence Jordan, interview by P.D. East, Koinonia Farm, Americus, Georgia, 1956.

[36] Ibid.

[37] Clarence Jordan, quoted by Howard, "The Legacy of Clarence Jordan," 16.

[38] Ibid.

[39] Clarence Jordan, interview by P.D. East, Koinonia Farm, n.d.

[40] Lee, *The Cotton Patch Evidence*, 10.

[41] Martin England, as quoted in interview by David Stricklin, *Oral Memoirs of Jasper Martin England and Mabel Orr England: A Series of Interviews Conducted July–September 1984* (Greenville, SC: Baylor University Institute for Oral History, 1996) 37.

[42] See, for example, Clarence Jordan, interview by P.D. East, Koinonia Farm, n.d.; during which Clarence is very modest in his conversation with East.

[43] Letter from Maude Jossey Jordan to Clarence, Rome, Georgia, 31 May 1929, the Clarence Jordan Papers, MS 756, B1, F3.

[44] Apparently Maude Jossey did not recognize the element in Clarence's temperament that allowed them to call him "Grump."

[45] Letter from Maude Jossey Jordan to Clarence, Rome, Georgia, 31 May 1929, the Clarence Jordan Papers, MS 756, B1, F3.

Chapter 5

[1] Interview with Frank Jordan, Talbotton, Georgia, 25 May 1987. See also, James Wm. McClendon, Jr., *Biography as Theology: How Life Stories Can Remake Today's Theology* (Nashville: Abingdon Press, 1974) 115.

[2] Letter from Clarence to Mama, Athens, Georgia, 16 September 1929, the Clarence Jordan Papers, MS 756, B1, F1.

[3] Clarence often uses the word "shame" or "ashamed" in his letters to his mother. See especially, his letters to Mama dated 16 September 1929, 3 July 1932, and 23 February 1933 (located in the Clarence Jordan Papers, MS 756, B1, F3; B1, F6; and B1, F7, respectively).

[4] Letter from Clarence to Mama, 17 March 1930, MS 756, B1, F4.

[5] Interview with P.D. East, Koinonia Farm, Americus, Georgia, n.d.

[6] Letter from George to Mama, 21 September 1932, MS 756, B1, F6.

[7] Letter from Clarence to Mama, 9 May 1932, MS 756, B1, F6.

[8] Frank Jordan, interview with author (Downing), Talbotton, Georgia, 25 May 1987.

[9] George Jordan, interview with author (Downing), Talbotton, Georgia, 25 May 1987. See also, interview with P.D. East, Koinonia Farm, n.d.

[10] Martin England, the founding partner with Clarence Jordan at Koinonia Farm, credited Clarence's mother with a major influence in his ultimate choice of vocation and lived faith. See England's interview by David Stricklin, *Oral Memoirs of Jasper Martin England and Mabel Orr England: A Series of Interviews Conducted July–September 1984* (Waco, TX: Baylor Institute for Oral History, 1996) 37.

[11] See James W. Fowler, *Stages of Faith: The Psychology of Human Development and the Quest for Meaning* (New York: Harper Collins Publishers, 1981) 172–73; and Sharon Parks, *The Critical Years: Young Adults & the Search for Meaning, Faith, & Commitment* (San Francisco: Harper & Row Publishers, 1986) 76.

[12] See the comments of McClendon, *Biography as Theology*, 115–16.

[13] For a move beyond the "tyranny of 'they,'" James Fowler writes, "there must be an interruption of reliance on external sources of authority." Then there must be a "relocation of authority within the self." The two essential elements necessary for the emergence of a reflective faith are: a critical distancing from one's previous value system, and the emergence of an executive ego (see Fowler, *The Stages of Faith*, 179).

[14] Interview with P.D. East, Koinonia Farm, Americus, Georgia, n.d.

[15] Letter from Clarence to Mama, January 1932, MS 756, B1, F6.

[16] Letter from Clarence to Fellows, 14 August 1931, MS 756, B1, F5.

[17] Letter from Clarence to Mama, 3 July 1932, MS 756, B1, F6.

[18] See Rudolf Otto, *The Idea of the Holy* (Oxford: Oxford University Press, 1931) 10. On the subjective side of this experience is "creature feeling," or "the emotion of a creature, abased and overwhelmed by its own nothingness in contrast to that which is

supreme above all creatures." This is Otto's substitute for Schleiermacher's "feeling of absolute dependence." On the objective side, this numinous feeling is the experience of a *mysterium* that is both *tremendum* and *fascinans*. Each of these words indicates significant aspects of the experience. At the center of this experience is the mental reaction that indicates the numen as "wholly other."

[19] For example, sacred mountains are central in Judaism, Christianity, Islam, and Daoism. See especially, Ronald E. Clements, *God and Temple* (Philadelphia: Fortress Press, 1965).

[20] See interview with Frank Stagg, Diamond Head, Mississippi, 12 October 1987; and also, England, quoted in Stricklin, *Oral Memoirs of Jasper Martin England and Mabel Orr England*, 42. After his days at Athens, Clarence continued that relationship and was invited to speak at conferences across the South and, eventually, at major Southern Baptist universities.

[21] Interview with Frank Stagg, Diamond Head, Mississippi, 12 October 1987.

[22] Interview with Mary D. Bowman, Pineville, Louisiana, 17 October 1987. Mary D. Bowman was the daughter of Roland Q. Leavell.

[23] Ibid.

Chapter 6

[1] These letters can be found in the Clarence Jordan Papers, MS 756, B1, F1, F9; at the Hargrett Rare Book and Manuscript Library, University of Georgia, Athens, Georgia.

[2] Sigmund Freud, *The Interpretation of Dreams*, Trans. and ed. James Strachey (New York: Basic Books, 1955) 5. See also, Frank J. Sulloway, *Freud, Biologist of the Mind: Beyond the Psychoanalytic Legend* (New York: Basic Books, 1983) 477.

[3] Letter from Clarence to Mama, 11 May 1931, MS 756, B1, F5.

[4] Letter from Clarence to Mama, 10 March 1933, MS 756, B1, F7.

[5] Kenneth Keniston, *Young Radicals: Notes on Committed Youth* (New York: Harcourt Brace Jovanovich, Inc., 1968) 20–55.

[6] Letter from Clarence to Mama, 14 April 1933, MS 756, B1, F7. See also, letter from Clarence to Mama, 16 September 1929, MS 756, B1, F3. In this letter, Clarence writes, "I was certainly glad to get your letters. …They are an inspiration to me to make good."

[7] Roland Barthes, *The Pleasure of the Text* (New York: Hill and Wang, 1975) 10, 47. For a full statement of the thesis, see chapter 1.

[8] Raczymow, quoted in Ellen Fine, "Search for Identity: Post Holocaust French Literature," in Yehuda Bauer, ed., *Remembering for the Future: The Impact of the Holocaust on the Contemporary World* (Oxford: Pergamon Press, 1989) 1474.

[9] Ibid., 114–19.

[10] Walter Ong, *Orality and Literacy* (New York: Methuen & Co., 1982) 78.

[11] Ibid., 105.

[12] Clarence Jordan, "Should College Graduates Return to the Farm?" *The Georgia Agriculturalist* 9 (March 1931): 12.

[13] Clarence Jordan, "What Price Should We Pay for a College Education?" *The Georgia Agriculturalist* 9 (November 1931): 5.

[14] Clarence Jordan, "When Night Meets Day," *The Georgia Agriculturalist*, found in the Clarence Jordan Papers, MS 756, B29, F13.

[15] Clarence Jordan, "A Stroll with Mother Nature," *The Georgia Agriculturalist*, found in the Clarence Jordan Papers, MS 756, B29, F13.

[16] Clarence Jordan, "Dan's Death: A True Story of a Georgia Dog's Devotion to His Master," *The Georgia Agriculturalist* 11 (October 1932): 6, 14.

[17] Tracy Elaine K'Meyer dates Jordan's "call" to a "Baptist student retreat at Ridgecrest." See K'Meyer, *Interracialism and Christian Community in the Postwar South: The Story of Koinonia Farm* (Charlottesville: University of Virginia Press, 1997) 29. But the announcement of the acceptance of the call does not come until spring 1933. It is likely that his "call experience" was something of a protracted personal struggle from summer 1932 until spring 1933.

[18] George Jordan, interview by author (Fredrick L. Downing), Talbotton, Georgia, 25 May 1987.

[19] Martin England recalled from his conversations with Jordan that Clarence's struggle was, in part, a battle within his own life over the ideas of his father and his mother, and that finally his mother won. See England's interview by David Stricklin, *Oral Memoirs of Jasper Martin England and Mabel Orr England: A Series of Interviews Conducted July–September 1984* (Waco, TX: Baylor University Institute for Oral History, 1996) 37.

[20] Ibid.

[21] Clarence Jordan, interview by Walden Howard, "The Legacy of Clarence Jordan," *Faith At Work* (April 1970): 16.

[22] Letter from Clarence to Mama, 4 March 1933, MS 756, B1, F7.

[23] Clarence Jordan, "My Call to the Ministry," 13 August 1933, the Clarence Jordan Papers, MS 756, B1, F7.

[24] Letter from Clarence to Mama, 14 March 1933, MS 756, B1, F7.

[25] Letter from Clarence to Mama, 22 March 1933, MS 756, B1, F7.

[26] "Compartmentalizing" is a typical conventional way for people of adolescent/young-adult faith to affirm conflicts in values.

[27] Letter from Clarence to Mama, 1 June 1933, MS 756, B1, F7.

[28] Letter from Clarence to Mama, 10 March 1933, MS 756, B1, F7.

[29] Letter from Clarence to Mama, 1 April 1933, MS 756, B1, F7.

[30] Letter from Clarence to Mama, 1 June 1933, MS 756, B1, F7.

[31] Clarence Jordan, interview by P.D. East, Koinonia Farm, n.d.

[32] Ibid.

Chapter 7

[1] See Dallas Lee, *The Cotton Patch Evidence: The Story of Clarence Jordan and the Koinonia Farm Experiment (1942–1970)* (Americus GA: Koinonia Partners, Inc., 1971) 15.

---

[2] The type of critical reflection and the claiming of responsibility for one's own beliefs, necessary to make the decision about the military, show Clarence to be moving into a realm of "individuative-reflective" faith. See Fowler, *The Stages of Faith*, 174–83.

[3] Clarence Jordan, interview by Walden Howard, "The Legacy of Clarence Jordan," *Faith At Work* (April 1970): 16.

[4] Letter from Mama to Clarence, 16 September 1933, MS 756, B1, F7.

[5] Letter from Clarence to Mama, 24 September 1933, MS 756, B1, F7.

[6] Letter from Clarence to Mama, n.d.; dated by the special collections at the University of Georgia to 1934. But the context of the letter indicates that this is the first letter he writes home and, thus, around the time of mid-September 1933, likely about 17 September, MS 756, B1, F8.

[7] Robertson died in spring 1934.

[8] Edward A. McDowell, Jr., "Introduction," in Clarence Jordan, *The Cotton Patch Version of Hebrews and The General Epistles* (Piscataway NJ: New Century Publishers, 1973) 9–10.

[9] Letter from Clarence to Mama, 26 March 1934, MS 756, B1, F8.

[10] Ibid.

[11] Clarence to Mama, June 1934, MS 756, B1, F8.

[12] See Jordan's note about his schedule for preaching in his letter to Mama, 9 July 1934, MS 756, B1, F8.

[13] Ibid.

[14] Dale Moody, quoted in Henlee H. Barnette, *Clarence Jordan: Turning Dreams into Deeds* (Macon GA: Smyth & Helwys, 1992) 98.

[15] There is some discrepancy in the names of these churches in the biographies on Jordan. Dallas Lee identifies the first church as "Knob Creek," while Joel Snider identifies it as "Knob Hill." Snider also adds the Vine Hill Church not listed in Lee's book.

[16] Dale Moody, in Barnette, *Clarence Jordan: Turning Dreams into Deeds*, 98.

[17] Letter from Clarence to Mama, 24 July 1934, MS 756, B1, F8. Clarence added that "nearly all…were moved to tears. It must be a divine word that can so touch men's hearts."

[18] Ibid.

[19] Ibid.

[20] Letter from James Jordan to Clarence, 8 October 1934, MS 756, B1, F8.

[21] There are two letters for December 1934, one from Christmas day: Clarence to Mama, 12 December 1934; and Clarence to Mama, 25 December 1934, MS 756, B1, F8.

[22] Letter from Dad to Clarence, 19 January 1935, MS 756, B1, F9.

[23] Interview with Frank Jordan, Talbotton, Georgia, 13 April 1987.

[24] Letter from Clarence to Mama, 11 May 1931, MS 756, B1, F5.

[25] Ann Louise Coble, *Cotton Patch for the Kingdom: Clarence Jordan's Demonstration Plot at Koinonia Farm.* (Scottdale, PA: Herald Press, 2002), 42.

[26] Letter from Mrs. Broach to Clarence, 6 February 1935, MS 756, B1, F9.

[27] See MS 756, B1, F11.

[28] Clarence Jordan, "Jesus the Rebel," an audio cassette (Americus GA: Koinonia Records, n.d.).

[29] See Erik Erikson, *Young Man Luther: A Study in Psychoanalysis and History* (New York: W.W. Norton & Company, 1958) 208. Erikson notes that Luther concluded that "a lecturer should feed his audience as a mother suckles her child." Erikson goes on to say, "I think that in the Bible Luther at last found a mother whom he could acknowledge: he could attribute to the Bible a generosity to which he could open himself, and pass on to others, at last a mother's son."

[30] Interview with Florence Jordan, Koinonia Farm, 8 November 1986.

[31] Ibid.

[32] Ibid.

[33] James Wm. McClendon, *Biography as Theology: How Life Stories Can Remake Today's Theology* (Nashville: Abingdon Press, 1974) 117–18.

[34] Letter from Dad to Clarence, 19 May 1936, MS 756, B1, F10.

Chapter 8

[1] Letter from Clarence Jordan to Edward A. McDowell, Jr., 29 May 1964, MS 756, B6, F9.

[2] See Tracy Elaine K'Meyer, *Interracialism and Christian Community in the Postwar South: The Story of Koinonia Farm* (Charlottesville: University of Virginia Press, 1997) 30.

[3] Clarence Jordan, interview by Walden Howard, "The Legacy of Clarence Jordan," *Faith At Work* (April 1970): 16.

[4] Henlee H. Barnette, *Clarence Jordan: Turning Dreams into Deeds* (Macon GA: Smyth & Helwys, 1992) 3.

[5] Ibid., 4.

[6] Clarence, quoted by Howard, "The Legacy of Clarence Jordan," 16.

[7] Letter from Clarence to Mama, October 1933, MS 756, B1, F7.

[8] Letter from Clarence to Mama, 9 July 1934, MS 756, B1, F8. See also, the interview with Henlee H. Barnette, Louisville, Kentucky, 2 July 1987.

[9] Letter from Clarence to Mama, 26 March 1934, MS 756, B1, F8.

[10] Ibid.

[11] Bob Herndon, quoted in Barnette, *Clarence Jordan: Turning Dreams into Deeds*, 98–99.

[12] Barnette, *Clarence Jordan: Turning Dreams into Deeds*, 5–6.

[13] Ibid., 6.

[14] Ibid., 6, 106; D.B. Nicholson, "Ridgecrest," *The Christian Index* (2 July 1942): 20.

[15] Donald E. Capps, "The Parabolic Event in Religious Autobiography," *The Princeton Seminary Bulletin* 4 (1983): 27.

[16] Frank Stagg, quoted in Barnette, *Clarence Jordan: Turning Dreams into Deeds*, 103.

[17] H. Cornell Goerner, quoted in Barnette, *Clarence Jordan: Turning Dreams into Deeds*, 91.

[18] Clarence Jordan to Edward A. McDowell, Jr., 29 May 1964, MS 756, B6, F9.

[19] See Erik H. Erikson, *Gandhi's Truth: On the Origins of Militant Nonviolence* (New York: W.W. Norton & Company, Inc., 1969) 118.

[20] Acts 2:44–45.

[21] Clarence Jordan, "Definitions of Koinonia," MS 756, B16, F2.

[22] David Stricklin, *A Genealogy of Dissent: Southern Baptist Protest in the Twentieth Century* (Lexington: The University Press of Kentucky, 1999) 39; and Martin England, in Barnette, *Clarence Jordan: Turning Dreams into Deeds*, 89–90.

[23] K'Meyer, *Interracialism and Christian Community in the Postwar South*, 34; and Coble, *Cotton Patch for the Kingdom: Clarence Jordan's [MARC: there's a word written here I can't understand. Maybe Demonstration? I checked the bibliography, but the full title is not given there] Plot at Koinonia Farm*. (Scottdale, PA: Herald Press, 2002),

[24] Letter from Marjorie Moore to Clarence Jordan, 31 May 1941, MS 756, B1, F12.

[25] Letter from Frank H. Leavell to Clarence Jordan, 22 May 1942, MS 756, B2, F2.

[26] Letter from Clarence Jordan to Frank H. Leavell, 26 May 1942, MS 756, B2, F2.

[27] Letter from Wayne E. Ward to Clarence Jordan, 9 May 1941, MS 756, B1, F12.

[28] Letter from Thomas H. Jones to Clarence Jordan, 6 May 1941, MS 756, B1, F12.

[29] Letter from Frank H. Leavell to Clarence Jordan, 6 March 1942, MS 756, B2, F2.

[30] Letter from Elizabeth Taylor to Clarence Jordan, 4 May 1941, MS 756, B1, F12.

[31] Letter from W.A. Colvin to C.L. Jordan, 3 June 1942, MS 756, B2, F2.

[32] Letter from Clarence Jordan to W.A. Colvin, 4 June 1942, MS 756, B2, F2.

[33] Letter from Edward A. McDowell to Mrs. Mittlebeeler, 19 October 1942, MS 756, B2, F3.

[34] Letter from C.L. Jordan to T. Howard Johnson, Jr., 14 August 1942, MS 756, B2, F3.

[35] Letter from Clarence Jordan to T. Howard Johnson, 17 December 1942, MS 756, B2, F3. See also, the form letter from Martin and Mabel England and Clarence and Florence Jordan to Friend[s], December 1942, MS 756, B2, F3.

Chapter 9
[1] Letter from Clarence to Buddie, 1 July 1942, MS 756, B2, F2.

[2] Letter from Clarence to Mack Goss, 7 August 1942, MS 756, B2, F3; and letter from Clarence to Liston Pope, 3 August 1942, MS 756, B2, F3. There were some large donors to Koinonia, one of which was a Louisville contractor, H.J. Steilberg, who made money as a government contractor building for the Army. See Dallas Lee, *The Cotton Patch Evidence: The Story of Clarence Jordan and the Koinonia Farm Experiment (1942–1970)* (Americus GA: Koinonia Partners, Inc., 1971) 31.

[3] Letter from Clarence to Elizabeth Hartsfield, 1 June 1942, MS 756, B2, F2; Sara M. Owen, "Buying a Mule," Koinonia Partners, Inc., http://www.koinoniapartners.org/History/remembered/s__owen.html (19 September 2011).

[4] Letter from Martin and Mabel England and Clarence and Florence Jordan to Friends, 23 September 1942, MS 756, B2, F3.

[5] Andrew S. Chancey, "Restructuring Southern Society: The Radical Vision of Koinonia Farm" (M.A. thesis, University of Georgia, 1990) 135–36.

[6] Clarence Jordan, interview by Walden Howard, "The Legacy of Clarence Jordan," *Faith At Work* (April 1970): 16.

[7] Ibid.

[8] Ibid.

[9] Letter from Clarence Jordan to Mack Goss, 18 July 1942, MS 756, B2, F2. See also, the interview with Dallas Lee, Atlanta, Georgia, 30 June 1987.

[10] David Stricklin, "Clarence Jordan (1912–1969), Jasper Martin England (1901–1989), and Millard Fuller (1935–): Koinonia Farm: Epicenter for Social Change," in Larry L. McSwain, ed., *Twentieth-Century Shapers of Baptist Social Ethics* (Macon GA: Mercer University Press, 2008) 166–67. See also, letter from Clarence Jordan to Glen T. Settle, 29 August 1942, MS 756, B2, F3.

[11] Joe Hendrix, interview by author (Downing), Macon, Georgia, 26 May 1987.

[12] See Erik Erikson, *Young Man Luther: A Study in Psychoanalysis and History* (New York: W.W. Norton & Company, Inc., l958) 103.

[13] See Erik Erikson, *Gandhi's Truth: On the Origins of Militant Nonviolence* (New York: W.W. Norton & Company, Inc., 1969) 129–32.

[14] At least two scholars who have written on Jordan understand that his religious development is more complex than Clarence's memory allows. See especially, James Wm. McClendon, Jr., *Biography as Theology: How Life Stories Can Remake Today's Theology* (Nashville: Abingdon Press, 1974) 115. McClendon describes the ROTC incident as "melodramatic." See also, Tracy Elaine K'Meyer, *Interracialism and Christian Community in the Postwar South: The Story of Koinonia Farm* (Charlottesville: University of Virginia Press, 1997) 27. K'Meyer writes that the "stories about Jordan's childhood are glimpses of his character seen in retrospect through the lens of his later work."

[15] See Jordan's interview by Walden Howard, "The Legacy of Clarence Jordan," 16.

[16] Clarence Jordan, *The Cotton Patch Version of Luke and Acts: Jesus' Doings and the Happenings* (New York: Association Press, 1969) 46–47.

[17] See David Stricklin, *A Genealogy of Dissent: Southern Baptist Protest in the Twentieth Century* (Lexington: The University Press of Kentucky, 1999) 55–56.

[18] See Erik Erikson, *Childhood and Society* (New York: W.W. Norton & Company, Inc., 1963) 314; and Erik Erikson, *Insight and Responsibility* (New York: W.W. Norton & Company, Inc., 1964) 66.

[19] Stricklin, *A Genealogy of Dissent*, 59. Stricklin also points out that the England story about the grandfather illustrates the distinction between "narrative truth" and "historical truth." See also, Donald P. Spence, *Narrative Truth and Historical Truth: Meaning and Interpretation in Psychoanalysis* (New York: W.W. Norton & Company, 1982) 31–33.

Chapter 10

[1] Clarence Jordan, diary, 13 November 1942, MS 756, B18, F3.

[2] Ibid.

[3] Letter from Clarence Jordan to Mrs. C.L. Jordan, 14 November 1942, Koinonia Archive.

[4] Letter from Clarence Jordan to Mrs. C.L. Jordan, 15 November 1942, Koinonia Archive.

[5] Letter from Clarence Jordan to Mrs. C. L. Jordan, 18 November 1942, Koinonia

Archive

[6] See Dallas Lee, *The Cotton Patch Evidence: The Story of Clarence Jordan and the Koinonia Farm Experiment (1942–1970)* (Americus GA: Koinonia Partners, Inc., 1971) 35. Clarence describes how this situation was resolved in his letter to Mrs. C.L. Jordan, 15 November 1942, Koinonia Archive. The black man's wife told him they were going to have to move "'cause that was too close to live to white folks." Clarence helped the family move, and the man agreed to work for Clarence if needed.

[7] Interview with Florence Jordan, Koinonia Farm, Americus, Georgia, 8 November 1986.

[8] Florence Jordan, quoted in Joyce Hollyday, "The Dream That Has Endured: Clarence Jordan and Koinonia," *Sojourners* 8 (December 1979): 12.

[9] Mabel England, quoted in Lee, *The Cotton Patch Evidence*, 41.

[10] Letter from Clarence Jordan to Mrs. C.L. Jordan, 7 December 1942, Koinonia Archives.

[11] Mabel England, interview by David Stricklin, "16 August 1984, Interview 2," in David Stricklin, ed., et al., *Oral Memoirs of Jasper Martin England and Mabel Orr England* (Waco TX: Baylor University Institute for Oral History, 1984) 149.

[12] Interview with Florence Jordan, Koinonia Farm, Americus, Georgia, 8 November 1986.

[13] Ibid.

[14] Ibid.

[15] Letter from Clarence Jordan to Mrs. C.L. Jordan, 7 December 1942, Koinonia Archives. In this same letter, Clarence talks about his hunting prowess. On the day that the sow was finally captured, he had been hunting and brought back a rabbit, two quail, and a dove.

[16] Letter from Clarence Jordan to Friends, December 1942, MS 756, B2, F3.

[17] See the statement by Florence Jordan in Phil Gailey, "Koinonia Founder C.L. Jordan Dies," *The Atlanta Constitution,* 31 October 1969, 19A.

[18] See "The Baptists Are Close to Southern Realities," *The Louisville Courier Journal,* 17 April 1949, Koinonia Archives.

[19] Letter from Clarence Jordan to Mrs. C.L. Jordan, 7 December 1942, Koinonia Archives.

[20] Letter from Clarence Jordan to Mrs. R.P. Halleck, 21 December 1942, MS 756, B2, F3.

[21] Ibid.

[22] See letter from Clarence Jordan to the Reverend Glenn T. Settle, 29 August 1942, MS 756, B2, F3.

[23] Letter from Clarence Jordan to Howard Johnson, 7 January 1943, MS 756, B2, F4.

[24] This often-told story was apparently first recorded in Lee, *The Cotton Patch Evidence*, 38.

[25] Ibid.

[26] Tracy Elaine K'Meyer, *Interracialism and Christian Community in the Postwar South: The Story of Koinonia Farm* (Charlottesville: University of Virginia Press, 1997) 50–51.

[27] Lee, *The Cotton Patch Evidence*, 43.

[28] Ibid., 42–43. See also, letter from Brother Nick to J.W. Jordan, 24 July 1944, MS 756, B2, F5.

[29] Mabel England, interview by Stricklin, "16 August 1984, Interview 2," 153. At the time of the interview, Mabel England had forgotten the name of the group. It was likely a "home extension" group, part of the University of Georgia Co-operative Extension.

[30] Ibid. See also, Lee, *The Cotton Patch Evidence*, 39.

[31] Mabel England, interview by Stricklin, "16 August 1984, Interview 2," 154.

[32] Mabel England, interview by Stricklin, "16 August 1984, Interview 2," 157.

[33] Foy Valentine, "The Signed Blank Check," *Christian Ethics Today* 12/4 (1997): 2.

[34] Ibid.

[35] Will Campbell, "Remembering Clarence," in Clarence Jordan, *Clarence Jordan's Cotton Patch Gospel: Paul's Epistles* (Macon GA: Smyth & Helwys, 2004) v–vi.

[36] Lee, *The Cotton Patch Evidence*, 53–61.

[37] Ibid., 64.

[38] Ibid.

[39] Fowler, *The Stages of Faith*, 182–83.

[40] Carlyle Marney, quoted in David Stricklin, *A Genealogy of Dissent: Southern Baptist Protest in the Twentieth Century* (Lexington: The University Press of Kentucky, 1999) 80.

[41] See the statement on inevitable conflict and threat between people of different stages of faith in M. Scott Peck, *The Different Drum: Community-Making and Peace* (New York: Simon and Schuster, 1987) 195.

Chapter 11

[1] Interview with Florence Jordan, Koinonia Farm, Americus, Georgia, 8 November 1986. See also, Andrew S. Chancey, "Race, Religion, and Reform: Koinonia's Challenge to Southern Society" (Ph.D. diss., University of Florida, 1998) 54.

[2] Interview with Florence Jordan, Koinonia Farm, Americus, Georgia, 8 November 1986.

[3] Paul E. Cosby, "Perceptions in Contrast," Koinonia Partners, Inc., http://www.koinoniapartners.org/History/remembered/cosby.html (19 September 2011).

[4] Tracy Elaine K'Meyer, *Interracialism and Christian Community in the Postwar South: The Story of Koinonia Farm* (Charlottesville: University of Virginia Press, 1997) 59–61.

[5] Ibid., 59.

[6] Ibid., 44–50. See also, Clarence Jordan, interview by P.D. East, Koinonia Farm, n.d.

[7] Charles S. O'Connor, "A Rural Georgia Tragedy: Koinonia Farm in the 1950s" (M.A. thesis, University of Georgia, 2003) 29.

[8] Ibid., 29–30.

[9] K'Meyer, *Interracialism and Christian Community in the Postwar South*, 60.

[10] See the FBI file of Clarence Jordan, 105-10699-44, the McLeod Bryan Papers, MS 364, B12, F7Z, Smith Reynolds Library Special Collections and Archives, Wake Forest University, Winston-Salem, North Carolina.

[11] See the FBI file of Clarence Jordan, most readily available in the G. McLeod (Mac) Bryan Papers, MS 364, B12, F7, Z, Smith Reynolds Library Special Collections and Archives, Wake Forest University, Winston-Salem, North Carolina.

[12] Ibid., MS 364, B12, F7.

[13] See the FBI file of Clarence Jordan 100-4223, page 21, Koinonia Archives. The deacons were D.C. Shephard, B. Tom Finch, Claude Harvey, and Urben Bowen.

[14] The FBI file of Clarence Jordan, 100-4223, Koinonia Archives. Jack Singletary was arrested on 29 September 1948. See also, the article in the *Macon Telegraph*, 31 August 1948, about Singletary's refusal to register.

[15] The FBI file of Clarence Jordan, 105-10699, the McLeod Bryan Papers, MS 364, B12, F7.

[16] See Eknath Easwaran, trans., *The Bhagavad Gita* (Tomales CA: Nilgiri Press, 1985) 7.

[17] Dallas Lee, *The Cotton Patch Evidence: The Story of Clarence Jordan and the Koinonia Farm Experiment (1942–1970)* (Americus GA: Koinonia Partners, Inc., 1971) 75.

[18] Ibid., 76–78.

[19] See Clarence Jordan, "10 November 1956," in "*Clarence Jordan Tells the Koinonia Story*" (Cincinnati OH: Fellowship House, Koinonia Partners, 2003).

[20] Ibid., 77–80.

[21] Clarence Jordan, quoted in Lee, *The Cotton Patch Evidence*, 80.

[22] Florence Jordan, interview by author (Downing) Koinonia Farm, Americus, Georgia, 8 November 1986. See also, Clarence Jordan, "10 November 1956."

[23] Florence Jordan, interview by author (Downing) Koinonia Farm, Americus, Georgia, 8 November 1986.

[24] Ibid.

[25] Letter from Martin Luther King, Jr., an open letter later published in *Christian Century* 80 (12 June 1963): 767-773, "Letter from Birmingham Jail," 16 April 1963.

[26] See Wallace M. Alston, Jr., and Wayne Flynt, "Religion in the Land of Cotton," in *You Can't Eat Magnolias*, ed. H. Brandt Ayers and Thomas H. Naylor (New York: McGraw-Hill Book Company, 1972) 99–123; and Samuel S. Hill, *Religion and the Solid South* (New York: Abingdon Press, 1972) 61.

[27] See Hill, *Religion and the Solid South*, 43–50.

[28] See Charles Marsh, *The Beloved Community: How Faith Shapes Social Justice, from the Civil Rights Movement to Today* (New York: Basic Books, 2005) 83, 242–43. There were two contemporary reports on the Rehoboth incident. See Clarence Jordan, "News from Georgia," *The Christian Century* (6 September 1950): 1053; and S.L. Morgan, Sr., "The Full Rehoboth Story," *The Christian Century* (11 October 1950): 1204. Jordan's attack on the Southern church establishment was that it was "gnostic"—ancient heresy— when it "emphasized the deity of Jesus to the exclusion of the humanity of Jesus…pure Gnosticism." See Clarence Jordan in Dallas Lee, ed., *The Substance of Faith and Other Cotton Patch Sermons by Clarence Jordan* (New York: Association Press, 1972) 120–21.

[29] Clarence Jordan in Lee, ed., *The Substance of Faith*, 126–27.

[30] Clarence Jordan, in a speech given to the American Baptist Convention, Seattle, Washington, May 1969. See also, Lee, *The Cotton Patch Evidence*, 225; and G. McLeod Bryan, *Voices in the Wilderness: Twentieth-Century Prophets Speak to the New Millennium* (Macon GA: Mercer University Press, 1999) 68.

[31] James Fowler describes the hallmarks of the young adult faith that he calls "individuative-reflective" as a demythologizing process concerning one's values and identity formation, which creates a "critical distancing from one's previous assumptive value system and the emergence of an executive ego." See Fowler, *The Stages of Faith*, 179.

[32] See ibid., 182–83. Fowler notes that the "dangers" of individuative-reflective faith "inhere in its strengths: an excessive confidence in the conscious mind and in critical thought…in which…[a] reflective self over-assimilates 'reality' and the perspectives of others."

Chapter 12

[1] G. McLeod Bryan, *These Few Also Paid a Price* (Macon GA: Mercer University Press, 2001) 48.

[2] Florence Jordan, interview by author (Downing), Koinonia Farm, Americus, Georgia, 8 November 1986.

[3] Ibid.

[4] This is a weakness of what James Fowler has described as "individuative-reflective" faith. See Fowler, *The Stages of Faith*, 182–83.

[5] See Tracy Elaine K'Meyer, *Interracialism and Christian Community in the Postwar South: The Story of Koinonia Farm* (Charlottesville: University of Virginia Press, 1997) 61.

[6] The Koinonia Farm newsletter, January 1951, Koinonia Archives.

[7] Ibid.

[8] Clarence Jordan, quoted in Dallas Lee, *The Cotton Patch Evidence: The Story of Clarence Jordan and the Koinonia Farm Experiment (1942–1970)* (Americus GA: Koinonia Partners, Inc., 1971) 82.

[9] Ibid.

[10] The Koinonia Farm newsletter, 1952. The 1952 issue of the newsletter listed some of Clarence's travels. Jordan had spent a month on a speaking trip to Wisconsin and South Dakota schools. In past years, he had been the Bible teacher or speaker for several Baptist conventions at Green Lake, Wisconsin. Other events in 1952 included: a religious emphasis week at Earlham College, a conference of the American Baptist Convention at the University of Pittsburgh, and the Kansas Baptist Youth Fellowship.

[11] Ibid., 83.

[12] Ibid., 84. Those who left included the Singletary's, the Sanfords, Willie and C.Z. Ballard, and the Atkinsons, who would eventually return. See K'Meyer, *Interracialism and Christian Community in the Postwar South*, 71.

[13] The FBI file of Clarence Jordan, 100-4223-23. McLeod Bryan Papers MS 364, B12, F7.

[14] Ibid.

[15] Erik Erikson, *Identity: Youth and Crisis* (New York: W.W. Norton & Company, 1968) 298.

[16] Ibid.

---

[17] See K'Meyer, *Interracialism and Christian Community in the Postwar South*, 81; and the interview with Florence Jordan, Koinonia Farm, Americus, Georgia, 8 November 1986.

[18] K'Meyer, *Interracialism and Christian Community in the Postwar South*, 82–83.

[19] Ibid., 84.

[20] Clarence Jordan, interview by P.D. East, Koinonia Farm, Americus, Georgia, n.d.

[21] Clarence Jordan,"10 November 1956," in *Clarence Jordan Tells the Koinonia Story* (Cincinnati OH: Fellowship House, Koinonia Partners, 2003)

[22] Lee, *The Cotton Patch Evidence*, 106.

[23] *Americus Times Recorder*, 24 March 1956. See also, Con Browne, interview by P.D. East, Koinonia Farm, Americus, Georgia, 1957.

[24] K'Meyer, *Interracialism and Christian Community in the Postwar South*, 85.

[25] Clarence Jordan, "10 November 1956."

[26] Margaret Whitkamper, interview by author (Downing), Koinonia Farm, Americus, Georgia, 8 November 1986.

[27] Clarence Jordan, interview by P.D. East, Koinonia Farm, Americus, Georgia, 1957. See also, Con Browne, interview by P.D. East, Koinonia Farm, Americus, Georgia, 1957.

[28] The Koinonia Farm newsletter #13, Koinonia Archives.

[29] Clarence Jordan, "10 November 1956."

[30] See the FBI file of Clarence Jordan, 100-4223. McLeod Bryan Papers MS 364, B12, F7.

[31] Will Campbell, "Where There's So Much Smoke: Thirty-Caliber Violence at Koinonia," *Sojourners* 8/12 (December 1979).

[32] Sam Chambliss, "A Matter of the Mind: 10 Persons, Negroes and Whites Live Together in Americus Plan," *Albany Herald* (August 1, 1948) 4A, and quoted in Lee, *The Cotton Patch Evidence*, 112.

[33] Lee, *The Cotton Patch Evidence*, 114–17.

[34] Letter from Clarence L. Jordan to President Dwight Eisenhower, 22 January 1957, Koinonia Archives.

[35] The Attorney General to Dr. Clarence L. Jordan, 28 February 1957, the FBI file of Clarence Jordan, 105-14859-19, the McLeod Bryan Papers, MS 364, B12, F6.

[36] The Grand Jury report was sent to the FBI where it became part of Clarence Jordan's file, 105-14859, McLeod Bryan Papers MS 394, B12, F7. See Clarence Jordan's response to the Grand Jury investigation in the interview by P.D. East, Koinonia Farm, Americus, Georgia, 1957. See also, the detailed report of this episode in Lee, *The Cotton Patch Evidence*, 131–32.

[37] The FBI file of Clarence Jordan, 100-4223-85, found in the McLeod Bryan Papers, B22, F4. The serious nature of this further scrutiny by the FBI is found in a memo in which J. Edgar Hoover writes to the Assistant Attorney General, William F. Tompkins, and directs him to get a copy of the Grand Jury presentment, because Koinonia "may be an appropriate subject for review pursuant to the provisions of the Subversive Activities Control Act of 1950." See the FBI file of Clarence Jordan, 105-14857,

McLeod Bryan Papers MS 394, B12, F7. Letter from the Director to William F. Tompkins, 15 April 1957, Koinonia Archives.

[38] This event was covered by the local paper. See "Klansmen Meet in City; Motorcade Goes to Koinonia," *The Americus Times-Recorder,* 25 February 1957. There were pictures of the Klan in Americus, in the motorcade, and at Koinonia.

[39] See Lee, *The Cotton Patch Evidence,* 123–25.

[40] Harold E. Fey, "Report from Koinonia—Creative Church in Georgia," *The Christian Century* 74/10 (6 March 1957): 285–87; Dora Byron, "Courage in Action: Koinonia Revisited," *Nation* 184 (16 March 1957): 226–28; Andre Fontaine, "The Conflict of a Southern Town," *Redbook* 109 (October 1957): 50.

[41] Lee, *The Cotton Patch Evidence,* 148.

[42] Clarence Jordan, "Incarnating Brotherhood," Koinonia Records, Americus, Georgia.

[43] Ibid.

[44] Clarence Jordan, interview by P.D. East, Koinonia Farm, Americus, Georgia, 1957.

[45] Erik H. Erikson, *Young Man Luther: A Study in Psychoanalysis and History* (New York: W.W. Norton & Company, Inc., 1958) 218.

[46] "Store Dynamited Here Last Night," *Americus Times-Recorder,* (24 July 1956) 1.

[47] The editor was James R. Blair and the main reporter was Rudy Hayes.

[48] See Rudy Hayes "Incident Here Wrong Approach" *Americus Times Recorder* (25 July 1956): 5. and Rudy Hayes, "A T R Reader Speaks His Mind," *Americus Times Recorder,* (28 July 1956): 2. See also Bull Pittman, "About Koinonia," *Americus Times Recorder* (10 August 1956): 4. See also, Charles S. O'Connor, "A Rural Georgia Tragedy: Koinonia Farm in the 1950s" (M.A. thesis, University of Georgia, 2003) 41–42.

[49] Clarence Jordan, interview by P.D. East, Koinonia Farm, Americus, Georgia, 1957.

[50] Letter from Clarence Jordan to Howard Johnson, 7 January 1943, MS 756, B2, F4.

[51] Clarence Jordan, "10 November 1956."

[52] Ibid.

[53] Ibid.

[54] Erikson, *Young Man Luther,* 259–62.

[55] For the term "pathos of God," see Abraham Joshua Heschel, *The Prophets, Volume II* (New York: Harper & Row, Publishers, 1962, 1971) 1–47.

[56] The ironic communal faith exhibited by Jordan beginning in the early 1950s after the Rehoboth incident can be characterized by what James Fowler calls "conjunctive," or "paradoxical consolidative" faith, with an emphasis on a deeper faith characterized by dialogical knowing, the union of opposites, the rise of the second naiveté, and the ironic imagination. See Fowler, *The Stages of Faith,* 197–98. See also, M. Scott Peck, *The Different Drum: Community Making and Peace* (New York: Simon and Schuster, 1987) 192–93. Peck refers to this stage as "mystic, communal," with an emphasis on the "underlying connectedness between things."

Chapter 13

[1] Charles Moore, "Bi-racial Farm Probe Due for Action Today," *The Atlanta Constitution*, 29 January 1958. See also, Celestine Sibley, "New Bill Aimed at Koinonia," *The Atlanta Constitution*, 13 February 1958. Also found in the FBI file of Clarence Jordan, 100-4223, the McLeod Bryan Papers, MS 364, B22, F4.

[2] Letter from the Chamber of Commerce, Americus, Georgia, 24 October 1949, located in the FBI file of Clarence Jordan, 100-4223-8, 24 October 1949. See also, the McLeod Bryan Papers, MS 364, B22, F3.

[3] The FBI file of Clarence Jordan, 100-4223-8, 24 October 1949. See also, the McLeod Bryan Papers, MS 364, B22, F3.

[4] See, for example, Henlee H. Barnette, *Clarence Jordan: Turning Dreams into Deeds* (Macon GA: Smyth & Helwys, 1992) 1–24.

[5] Clarence Jordan, interview by P.D. East, Koinonia Farm, Americus, Georgia, n.d. See also, Florence Jordan, "The Witness Was What Counted," *Catholic Worker Magazine* (1983). Florence noted, "What we were doing at Koinonia was preaching the end of the world—our neighbors' world…the end of the big plantation owners."

[6] Martin Luther King, Jr., *Strength to Love* (Cleveland: William Collins, 1963) 78.

[7] See James H. Smylie, "On Jesus, Pharaohs, and the Chosen People: Martin Luther King as Biblical Interpreter and Humanist," *Interpretation* (January 1970): 82.

[8] Andre Fontaine, "The Conflict of a Southern Town," *Redbook* 109 (October 1957): 50.

[9] Walter Brueggemann, *The Prophetic Imagination* (Philadelphia: Fortress Press, 1978) 11–43.

[10] Ibid., 49–50. In similar fashion, Dominic Crossan found that the deep structure in human civilization itself is an ongoing struggle between the radicality of God's nonviolence and the normalcy of civilization's violence. See John Dominic Crossan, *God's Empire: Jesus Against Rome, Then and Now* (San Francisco: Harper Collins, 2007) 237–38.

[11] See Brueggemann, *The Prophetic Imagination*, 1–61.

[12] Walter Brueggemann, "Imagination: New Approaches to the Bible," a video of the 23rd National Conference of the Trinity Institute, Trinity Church, New York City, 1992.

[13] See Johannes Lindblom, *Prophecy in Ancient Israel* (Philadelphia: Fortress Press, 1962) 1; and C.H. Dodd, *The Authority of the Bible* (London: Nisbet and Company, 1929, rev. ed., 1960). Dodd argues that the dominant personalities of the Bible are marked by religious genius.

[14] Abraham Joshua Heschel, *The Prophets* (New York: Harper & Row Publishers, 1962) 3–26.

[15] Erik Erikson, *Gandhi's Truth: On the Origins of Militant Nonviolence* (New York: W.W. Norton & Company, Inc., 1969) 129–32.

[16] Here I draw from the language of James W. Fowler in his description of the journey to a more radical faith. See Fowler, *The Stages of Faith*, 202. Though Fowler in this context is describing the pilgrimage to what he calls "universalizing faith," I think his language is applicable for Jordan's movement toward a more radical, prophetic faith. I will describe Jordan's journey to a more "universalizing" perspective in a later chapter.

[17] Dallas Lee, interview by author (Downing), Atlanta, Georgia, 30 June 1987.

[18] Ernest Becker, *Angel in Armor: A Post-Freudian Perspective on the Nature of Man* (New York: George Braziller, 1969) 96–98.

[19] See (Florence) Jordan, "The Witness Was What Counted."

[20] See Erikson, *Gandhi's Truth.*

[21] Ernest Becker, *The Denial of Death* (New York: The Free Press, 1973) 109–10.

[22] Gerhard von Rad, *Old Testament Theology Volume II* (New York: Harper & Row, Publishers, 1965) 205–208.

[23] See Dallas Lee, *The Cotton Patch Evidence: The Story of Clarence Jordan and the Koinonia Farm Experiment (1942–1970)* (Americus GA: Koinonia Publishers, Inc., 1971) 221.

[24] Letter from Clarence Jordan to Claude Broach, 7 March 1957, MS 756, B4, F14.

[25] Clarence Jordan, "Incarnating Brotherhood," Koinonia Records, Americus, Georgia.

[26] Charles Marsh, *The Beloved Community: How Faith Shapes Social Justice, from the Civil Rights Movement to Today* (New York: Basic Books, 2005) 73.

[27] Ibid.

[28] Andrew S. Chancey, "Restructuring Southern Society: The Radical Vision of Koinonia Farm" (M.A. thesis, University of Georgia, 1990) 172–73.

[29] The descriptive language concerning Jordan is influenced by Brueggemann, *The Prophetic Imagination,* 11–27.

[30] Brueggemann, "Imagination: New Approaches to the Bible," 1992.

[31] See Brueggemann, *The Prophetic Imagination,* 11–27.

[32] Marsh, *The Beloved Community,* 73.

[33] Ibid., 242–43.

[34] Clarence Jordan in Dallas Lee, ed., *The Substance of Faith and other Cotton Patch Sermons* (New York: Association Press, 1972) 19, 121–24.

Chapter14

[1] The Koinonia Farm newsletter #26, Americus, Georgia, 1 April 1962.

[2] Ibid.

[3] The Koinonia Farm newsletter #28, Americus, Georgia, September 1963.

[4] Ibid.

[5] Martin Luther King, Jr., "Letter from Birmingham Jail," *Liberation* (June 1963): 10-16, 23.

[6] See John A.T. Robinson, *Honest to God* (Philadelphia: Westminster Press, 1963) 7–63.

[7] Thomas J.J. Altizer, *The Gospel of Christian Atheism* (Philadelphia: The Westminster Press, 1966) 17; Richard L. Rubenstein, *After Auschwitz: Radical Theology and Contemporary Judaism* (New York: The Bobbs-Merrill Company, Inc., 1966) 19–35.

[8] James H. Cone, *Black Theology and Black Power* (New York: The Seabury Press, 1969) 91–115.

[9] See Robinson, *Honest to God,* 65; and Clarence Jordan in Dallas Lee, ed., *The Substance of Faith and other Cotton Patch Sermons* (New York: Association Press, 1972) 120–24.

---

[10] See Clarence Jordan, interview by P.D. East, Koinonia Farm, 1958, P.D. East collection, Howard Gotlieb Archival Research Center, Boston University. The manuscript is filed under "Koinonia-Jordan" by P.D. East, Tape 1.Clarence Jordan in Lee, ed., *The Substance of Faith*, 120–24; and Charles Marsh, *The Beloved Community: How Faith Shapes Social Justice, from the Civil Rights Movement to Today* (New York: Basic Books, 2005) 83–84.

[11] Clarence Jordan also "...understood the deep loyalty of his region to a cluttered pantheon of cultural gods." See Marsh, *The Beloved Community*, 57.

[12] Samuel S. Hill, ed., *Religion and the Solid South* (Nashville: Abingdon Press, 1972) 24–50.

[13] Martin Luther King, Jr., spoke these words at commencement exercises for Wesleyan University in Middletown, Connecticut, on 8 June 1964. King likely drew this thought from Theodore Parker, *Ten Sermons of Religion* (Boston: Crosby, Nichols, and Company, 1853) 84–85.

[14] See especially, Clarence Jordan, *The Cotton Patch Version of Paul's Epistles* (New York: Association Press, 1968) 7–11. Also see, Clarence Jordan, interviewed by Scott Morrison on "Mutual News" (New York: 26 February 1968), currently found in *The Clarence Jordan Interviews* (Americus GA: Koinonia Partners Inc., 2003).

[15] See Fernando F. Segovia, "And They Began to Speak in Other Tongues: Competing Modes of Discourse in Contemporary Biblical Criticism," in *Reading from This Place: Social Location and Biblical Interpretation in the United States Volume I*, ed. Fernando F. Segovia and Mary Ann Tolbert (Minneapolis: Fortress Press, 1995) 28–29.

[16] As early as 1955, Jordan was being asked for his translations, and if he had done the complete New Testament. In 1960, a publisher approached him about "a book on the Greek New Testament translated freely for today." The first of the *Cotton Patch Version* translations was the Letter to the Hebrews in 1963. The Epistle to James was added in 1964. Paul's epistles were finished and published in 1968, and the general epistles were published in 1969, as were Luke and Acts. The manuscript for Matthew and John was on Jordan's desk when he died in October 1969. This volume was published in 1970.

[17] Though Clarence Jordan was linked with Martin Luther King, Jr., in many ways, there were important differences. While Jordan was sometimes seen as a champion for civil rights in the early days, he actually disagreed with some of the tactics of the movement. He was opposed to marches and boycotts as staged, unnatural events that typically alienated whites even further. Jordan did support activism in the natural course of events, such as the effort to get a meal at a lunch counter when one was hungry. In short, for Clarence Jordan, civil rights were theological in character and an offshoot of the true nature of Christian community. Jordan would eventually change his mind and become more direct in terms of activism. But theology—and loyalty to his understanding of Jesus—was the basis of his involvement in civil rights. In time, Jordan would critique King for his failure to use the spiritual power of the Christian tradition. The Civil Rights Movement had not gone far enough for Jordan. Changing the laws of the country did not change the hearts of the citizens. Jordan's critique was essentially that "the Civil Rights Movement had failed to stay the course on redemption and reconciliation in the South." For Jordan, racial reconciliation was one of the fruits of the spirit of being in Christ. See

Marsh, *The Beloved Community*, 69; and Coble, *Cotton Patch for the Kingdom: Clarence Jordan's Plot at Koinonia Farm*. (Scottdale, PA: Herald Press, 2002) 161.

[18] Clarence Jordan knew that the writers of the New Testament understood the nature of spiritual power, and proclaimed that Jesus stood in the tradition of Moses—the great poet-prophet—and that Jesus also went up to the mountain and gave a transforming vision for his society. In fact, Jesus was a "new Moses," according to Matthew, who gave a "new Sermon on the Mount" and for a new border crossing, just as Moses had addressed the crossing into ancient Canann.

[19] See Erik H. Erikson, *Identity: Youth and Crisis* (New York: W.W. Norton & Company, Inc., 1968) 298–99.

[20] For an analysis of the South and the plantation system, see especially, Hill, *Religion and the Solid South*, 24–91.

[21] See Clarence Jordan, "Jesus the Rebel," an audio cassette (Americus GA: Koinonia Records, n.d.).

[22] Clarence Jordan, *The Cotton Patch Version of Luke and Acts: Jesus' Doings and the Happenings* (New York: Association Press, 1969) 21. Compare to Luke 3:2–3.

[23] Ibid., 22. Compare to Luke 3:7–8.

[24] Ibid., 23-24. Compare to Luke 4:1–12. See (Clarence) Jordan, *The Cotton Patch Version of Luke and Acts*, 23–24.

[25] Ibid., 24-25. Compare to Luke 4:13–27. See (Clarence) Jordan, *The Cotton Patch Version of Luke and Acts*, 24–25.

[26] Ibid., 30-32. Compare to Luke 6:17–49. See (Clarence) Jordan, *The Cotton Patch Version of Luke and Acts*, 29–33.

[27] Ibid., 30-31. Compare to Luke 6:17–28. See (Clarence) Jordan, *The Cotton Patch Version of Luke and Acts*, 30–31.

[28] (Clarence) Jordan, *Sermon on the Mount*, (Valley Forge, PA: Judson Press, 1952) 97–98.

[29] See Dallas Lee, *The Cotton Patch Evidence: The Story of Clarence Jordan and the Koinonia Farm Experiment (1942–1970)* (Americus GA: Koinonia Partners, Inc., 1971) 86–87. Perhaps the best-known example of this demand to give away one's possessions is Millard Fuller, who had to dispose of more than a million dollars.

[30] See Clarence Jordan in Lee, ed., *The Substance of Faith*, 78–81. See also, Clarence Jordan, "Jesus and Possessions," an audio cassette (Americus GA: Koinonia Records, n.d.). See also, Jordan's translation of Luke 12:27–34 in (Clarence) Jordan, *The Cotton Patch Version of Luke and Acts*, 54.

[31] See Clarence Jordan in Lee, ed., *The Substance of Faith*, 70. Luke's "Sermon on the Plain" is his version of the Sermon on the Mount.

[32] (Clarence) Jordan, *The Cotton Patch Version of Luke and Acts*, 31. Compare to Luke 6:27.

[33] Ibid.

[34] Leviticus 19:18. See also, Deuteronomy 20:10–20. See Clarence Jordan in Lee, ed., *The Substance of Faith*, 70.

[35] (Clarence) Jordan, *The Sermon on the Mount*, 65–66; and Clarence Jordan in Lee, ed., *The Substance of Faith*, 71–72.

---

[36] Clarence Jordan, "Loving Your Enemies," an audio cassette (Americus GA: Koinonia Records, n.d.). See also, Clarence Jordan in Lee, ed., *The Substance of Faith*, 71.

[37] Ibid.

[38] Luke 9:51. See (Clarence) Jordan, *The Cotton Patch Version of Luke and Acts*, 44. Compare to Luke 9:51.

[39] See (Clarence) Jordan, *The Cotton Patch Version of Luke and Acts*, 46-47. Compare to Luke 10:25-37.

[40] See (Clarence) Jordan, *The Cotton Patch Version of Luke and Acts*, 61–62. Compare to Luke 15: 1-24.

[41] See (Clarence) Jordan, *The Cotton Patch Version of Luke and Acts*, 62–63. Compare to Luke 15:25-32.

Chapter 15

[1] Dallas Lee, *The Cotton Patch Evidence: The Story of Clarence Jordan and the Koinonia Farm Experiment (1942–1970)* (Americus GA: Koinonia Partners, Inc., 1971) 221.

[2] Lee, *The Cotton Patch Evidence*, 222–23.

[3] This represents the closure of Jordan's "individuative-reflective" faith in Fowler's terms, and the beginning of a new era of "conjunctive" faith. See James M. Fowler, *Stages of Faith: The Psychology of Human Development and the Quest for Meaning* (New York: Harper Collins Publishers, 1981) 179-98.

[4] Clarence Jordan, "10 November 1956," in *Clarence Jordan Tells the Koinonia Story* (Cincinnati OH: Fellowship House, Koinonia Partners, 2003).

[5] Clarence Jordan, interview by Walden Howard, "The Legacy of Clarence Jordan," *Faith At Work* (April 1970): 18.

[6] The lifelong, chronic nature of the "integrity crisis" is typical for Erikson's *homo religiosus*. See Erik Erikson, *Young Man Luther: A Study in Psychoanalysis and History* (New York: W.W. Norton & Company, 1958) 261.

[7] Andrew S. Chancey, "Race, Religion, and Reform: Koinonia's Challenge to Southern Society," (Ph.D. diss., University of Florida, 1998) 172; and Dallas Lee, "In Scorn of the Consequences," in Kirk Lyman-Barner, *Roots in the Cotton Patch: The Clarence Jordan Symposium 2012, Volume 1* (Eugene OR: Cascade Books, 2014) 146.

[8] Walter Ong, *Orality and Literacy* (New York: Methuen & Co., 1982) 78.

[9] Clarence Jordan, an unpublished manuscript titled "The Kingdom," page 5, found in the Clarence Jordan Papers, MS 756, B14.

[10] Lee, *The Cotton Patch Evidence*, 185.

[11] Ibid., 188.

[12] The Koinonia Farm newsletter, April 1965.

[13] Letter from Clarence Jordan to Sam Emerick, 17 May 1968; and letter from Clarence Jordan to Ann Morris, 26 April 1968, MS 756, B7, F5.

[14] Robert F. Kennedy, "Remarks on the Assassination of Martin Luther King, Jr., (Speech, Indianapolis, IN, April 4, 1968) American Rhetoric Online Speech Bank. Retrieved March 17, 2017. For the work of Aeschylus, see Edith Hamilton, *Three Greek Plays: Prometheus Bound, Agamemnon, The Trojan Women,* (New York: W. W. Norton & Company, Inc., 1937) 161; 162-239. See also Edith Hamilton, *The Greek Way*, New York: W.W. Norton & Company, Inc. Publishers) 257.

[15] Letter from Clarence Jordan to Claude Broach, 7 March 1957, MS 756, B4, F14.

[16] See Helen Merrell Lynd, *On Shame and the Search for Identity* (New York: Harcourt Brace, 1958) 56. Lynd writes that "the impact of shame for others may reach even deeper than shame for ourselves."

[17] Lee, *The Cotton Patch Evidence*, 222.

[18] Letter from Clarence Jordan to Roy O. McClain, 28 September 1963; and Clarence Jordan, "An Open Letter to the First Baptist Church of Atlanta," 24 September 1963, MS 756, B6.

[19] Lee, *The Cotton Patch Evidence*, 200, 224.

[20] Ibid., 185–86.

[21] Interview with Dallas Lee, Atlanta, Georgia, 30 June 1987.

[22] Ibid.

[23] Lee, *The Cotton Patch Evidence*, 214.

[24] The Koinonia Farm newsletter, October 1968.

[25] Clarence Jordan, quoted in Dallas Lee, "Clarence Jordan: Modern Disciple," *Messenger* (8 May 1969): 8–10.

[26] Luke 4:16–19. Here Jesus quotes Isaiah 61:1–2.

[27] See Lee, "Clarence Jordan: Modern Disciple," 8–10. See also, Lee, *The Cotton Patch Evidence*, 210–11.

[28] Fowler, *Stages of Faith*, 200.

[29] The term "activist incarnation" is taken from James Fowler and implies that Jordan's faith in this era reflects "universalizing" faith. See Fowler, *The Stages of Faith*, 200.

[30] Interview with Dallas Lee, Atlanta, Georgia, 30 June 1987.

[31] Ibid.

[32] Interview with Ray Brewster, Macon, Georgia, 26 May 1987.

Chapter 16
[1] Florence Jordan, interview by author (Fredrick L. Downing), Koinonia Farm, Americus, Georgia, 8 November 1986.

[2] G. McLeod Bryan, *Voices in the Wilderness: Twentieth-Century Prophets Speak to the New Millennium* (Macon GA: Mercer University Press 1999) 40.

[3] Ibid., 69.

[4] M.K. Gandhi, *An Autobiography or the Story of My Experiments with Truth* (Ahmedabad: Navajivan Publishing House, 1927) 287–92; Nelson Mandela, "Mandela on Gandhi: The Sacred Warrior," *Time* (31 December 1999).

[5] Florence Jordan, interview by author (Downing), Koinonia Farm, Americus, Georgia, 8 November 1986.

[6] Bryan, *Voices in the Wilderness*, 69.

[7] Florence Jordan, interview by author (Downing), Koinonia Farm, Americus, Georgia, 8 November 1986.

[8] Clarence Jordan, quoted in Dallas Lee, *The Cotton Patch Evidence: The Story of Clarence Jordan and the Koinonia Farm Experiment (1942–1970)* (Americus GA: Koinonia Partners, Inc., 1971) 219.

[9] Millard Fuller, *Bokotola* (New York: Association Press, 1977) 61–87.

[10] Clarence Jordan in the Koinonia Farm newsletter, October 1969.

[11] Interview with Florence Jordan, Koinonia Farm, Americus, Georgia, 8 November 1986. The details of Jordan's trip to South Africa are very sketchy. It is intriguing to speculate on what the rest of Jordan's itinerary in the country may have been like, given Naude's place in the history of that region. Did Clarence Jordan meet and talk with Stephen Biko? If so, one can only assume that it would have been a very "dancing" conversation.

[12] Ibid.

[13] Ibid.

[14] Ray Brewster had a memory that Jordan either got arrested or, in fact, was run out of South Africa. That is, Clarence did get into trouble of some kind there. See interview with Ray Brewster, Macon, Georgia, 26 May 1987.

[15] Ibid.

[16] The elements of "activist incarnation" and a heedlessness for one's own safety are characteristics of "universalizing" faith. See Fowler, *Stages of Faith*, 200.

Chapter 17

[1] See also, the information on this New York trip in the obituary notice titled "Rev. Clarence L. Jordan Dead; Led Interracial Farm Project," *New York Times*, 31 October 1969.

[2] Clarence Jordan, "Things Needed for Our Peace," a chapel address, Furman University, Spring 1969, Special Collections and Archives, Furman University.

[3] Martin Luther King, Jr., said that "a riot is the language of the unheard." This statement is first recorded in an interview that King gave to Mike Wallace during the 27 September 1966 broadcast of *CBS Reports*. The text of the interview can be found online at http://www.cbsnews.com/news/mlk-a-riot-is-the-language-of-the-unheard/ (21 September 2015).

[4] Jordan was doing a paraphrase of portions of Luke 12–13.

[5] (Clarence) Jordan, "Things Needed for Our Peace," chapel address, Spring 1969.

[6] Clarence Jordan, quoted in Dallas Lee, *The Cotton Patch Evidence: The Story of Clarence Jordan and the Koinonia Farm Experiment (1942–1970)* (Americus GA: Koinonia Partners, Inc., 1971) 226–27; and Clarence Jordan in Dallas Lee, ed., *The Substance of Faith and Other Cotton Patch Sermons* (New York: Association Press, 1972) 12.

[7] Clarence Jordan at the Ministers Conference, Union Theological Seminary, New York City, July 1969, MS 2340, B7.

[8] The Koinonia Farm newsletter, Fall 1969.

[9] Ibid.

[10] Contained in the FBI file of Clarence Jordan 105-14859, 14 July 1969. McLeod Bryan Papers MS 364 B12, F7, Reynolds Leroy, Special Collections Wake Forest University, Wake Forest, NC.

[11] The Koinonia Farm newsletter, Fall 1969.

[12] Lee, *The Cotton Patch Evidence*, 200, 224.

[13] Contained in the FBI file of Clarence Jordan 157-3857-13, 25 August 1969. McLeod Bryan Papers MS 364 B12, F7, Reynolds Leroy, Special Collections Wake Forest University, Wake Forest, NC.

[14] G. McLeod Bryan, *These Few Also Paid A Price* (Macon GA: Mercer University Press, 2001) 51.

[15] Clarence Jordan, "A Personal Letter from Clarence Jordan to Friends of Koinonia," Americus, Georgia, 27 October 1969. This letter was also reprinted by P.D. East in *The Petal Paper* 17/2 (December 1969): 1–2.

[16] Clarence Jordan, interview by Walden Howard, "The Legacy of Clarence Jordan," *Faith At Work* (April 1970): 15–18.

[17] Interview with Dallas Lee, Atlanta, Georgia, 30 June 1987.

[18] Lee, *The Cotton Patch Evidence*, 230–31. See also, Clarence Jordan in East, "A Personal Letter from Clarence Jordan to Friends of Koinonia," (Americus, GA: 27 Octoer, 1979) Koinonia Farm Archives.

Chapter18
[1] See Dallas Lee, "In Scorn of the Consequences," in Kirk Lyman-Barner, *Roots in the Cotton Patch: The Clarence Jordan Symposium 2012, Volume 1* (Eugene OR: Cascade Books, 2014) 145.

[2] Charles Marsh, *The Beloved Community: How Faith Shapes Social Justice, from the Civil Rights Movement to Today* (New York: Basic Books, 2005) 72–84.

[3] Amos N. Wilder, "Story and Story-World," *Interpretation* 37/4 (October 1983): 359.

[4] See Mircea Eliade, *Myths, Dreams, and Mysteries: The Encounter Between Contemporary Faiths and Archaic Realities* (London: Harvill Press, 1975) 32–33.

[5] See Clarence Jordan in Dallas Lee, ed., *The Substance of Faith and Other Cotton Patch Sermons* (New York: Association Press, 1972) 70.

[6] It is evident from the biographies of both Criswell and Jordan that they were moral exemplars for separate constituencies. Criswell was, like Jordan, at times listed among the "saints." See Toby Druin and Mark Wingfield, "Literal Legend: W.A. Criswell Remembered," *The Baptist Standard* (14 January 2002): 1.

[7] Walter Brueggemann, "Counterscript: Living with the Elusive God," *Christian Century* 122/24 (29 November 2005): 22–28.

[8] Ibid. There seems to be a symbiotic relationship between military consumerism and religious fundamentalism, which is also based on fear. See Karen Armstrong, *The Battle for God* (New York: Alfred A. Knopf, 2000) 368–71.

[9] Clarence Jordan in Lee, ed., *The Substance of Faith*, 70.

[10] Gregory, *Too Great a Temptation*, 1–29.

[11] Ibid., 1.

[12] John Egerton, *The Americanization of Dixie: The Southernization of America* (New York: Harper's Magazine Press, 1974) xx, 213.

[13] Ibid., xx.

[14] See Clarence Jordan in Lee, ed., *The Substance of Faith*, 120–24.

[15] In her important book *The Battle for God*, Karen Armstrong shows that, through literal interpretation, fundamentalists around the world—in Judaism, Islam, and Christianity—turned their mythologies into ideologies and, thereby, cut themselves off from the deeper spiritual truths of the tradition. See especially, page 355. Jimmy Carter eventually severed his relationship with the Southern Baptist Convention over this issue. Two his-

toric Baptist positions—the "separation of church and state" and the "priesthood of the believer"—were part of Carter's critique. See Somini Sengupta, "Carter Sadly Turns Back on National Baptist Body," *New York Times* (21 October 2000): [P. #?]. See also, Jimmy Carter, *Our Endangered Values: America's Moral Crisis* (New York: Simon & Schuster, 2005) 33–101.

[16] See especially, Gregory, *Too Great a Temptation*, 1–29.

[17] See Curtis W. Freeman, "'Never Had I Been So Blind': W.A. Criswell's 'Change' on Racial Segregation," *The Journal of Southern Religion* 10 (2007): 1.

[18] "An Address by Dr. W.A. Criswell, Pastor, First Baptist Church, Dallas, Texas, to the Joint Assembly," Wednesday, 22 February 1956, Duke University Library, Special Collections. Criswell gave the same speech to the evangelism conference the day before.

[19] Freeman, "'Never Had I Been So Blind,'" 11.

[20] Ibid., 12.

[21] Ibid.

[22] Joyce Hollyday, "A Scandalous Life of Faith," *Sojourners* 8/12 (December 1979): 3–5; and Joyce Hollyday, "The Dream That Has Endured: Clarence Jordan and Koinonia," *Sojourners* 8/12 (December 1979): 12–18. One of the first to note that Jordan was being described as a "saint" was Robert Parham, in his article "A Reconciler from 'Dixie': Clarence Jordan," *Baptist Peacemaker* (July 1983): 6. See also, Howell, *Servants, Misfits, and Martyrs,* 30. Progressive ministers who have referred to Jordan as a modern-day saint are: Jill Oglesby Evans, in a sermon titled "Yours in Faith and Expectation—Clarence Jordan," Emory Presbyterian Church, 7 August 2005; Linda McCloud, in a blog: "Sunrise on the Marsh: Saints: Clarence Jordan," the Episcopal Church of Our Savior at Honey Creek, 11 July 2007, http://oursaviorhoneycreek.blogspot.com/2007/07saints-clarence-jordan.html (13 November 2015); and James C. Howell, in a blog: "Heroes Found Faithful: Clarence Jordan," Myers Park UMC, Charlotte, North Carolina, 1 November 2010, http://heroesfoundfaithful.blogspot.com/2010/11/true-saints-never-dwell-in-splendid.html (13 November 2015).

[23] Jim Buie, "Praise the Lord and Pass the Ammunition," *Church and State* 37 (October 1984): 6. Criswell was also on the program of the Republican National Convention (held in Dallas, 20–23 August 1980) and closed one of the sessions in prayer.

[24] On Reagan's sale of chemical weapons to Iraq, see Glenn Kessler, "History Lesson: When the United States Looked the Other Way on Chemical Weapons," *The Washington Post*, 4 September 2013, located at http://www.washingtonpost.com/blogs/fact-checker/post/history-lesson-when-the-united-states-looked-the-other-way-on-chemical-weapons/2013/09/04/0ec828d6-1549-11e3-961c-f22d3aaf19ab_blog.html (13 November 2015).

[25] Ibid.

[26] Parham, "A Reconciler from 'Dixie': Clarence Jordan," 6.

[27] See Kessler, "History Lesson," 4 September 2013.

[28] Henlee H. Barnette, *Clarence Jordan: Turning Dreams into Deeds* (Macon GA: Smyth & Helwys, 1992) 24.

[29] Howell, *Servants, Misfits, and Martyrs,* 25–30.

[30] For an analysis of George W. Bush's use of military intelligence leading up to the war against Iraq, see Michael Isikoff and David Corn, *Hubris: The Inside Story of Spin, Scandal, and the Selling of the Iraq War* (New York: Random House, 2006).

[31] See especially, Kevin Phillips, *American Theocracy* (New York: Viking, 2006) x, 99–217. See also, David S. Domke, *The God Strategy: How Religion Became a Political Weapon in America* (New York: Oxford University Press, 2008, 2010) 3–70; and David S. Domke, *God Willing: Political Fundamentalism in the White House, the "War on Terror," and the Echoing Press* (Ann Arbor MI: Pluto Press, 2004) 2.

[32] Domke, *God Willing: Political Fundamentalism in the White House*, 2.

[33] Ibid., 2–6.

[34] Peggy Noonan, "A Separate Peace: America Is in Trouble—and Our Elites Are Merely Resigned," *The Wall Street Journal*, 27 October 2005, located at http://www.wsj.com/articles/SB122487970866167655 (13 November 2015).

[35] John Dominic Crossan, *God's Empire: Jesus Against Rome, Then and Now* (San Francisco: Harper Collins, 2007) 237–38.

[36] Ibid., 239.

[37] See especially, Charles H. Ferguson, *The Predator Nation: Corporate Criminal, Political Corruption, and the Hijacking of America* (New York: Random House, 2012) 1–3. Ferguson provides evidence for widespread fraud and increasing corruption in the financial markets as the cause of the housing bubble leading to economic chaos.

[38] Jill Oglesby Evans, in a sermon titled "Yours in Faith and Expectation—Clarence Jordan," Emory Presbyterian Church, 7 August 2005. Two other ministers who have spoken of Jordan as a saint are: Linda McCloud, in a blog: "Sunrise on the Marsh: Saints: Clarence Jordan," the Episcopal Church of Our Savior at Honey Creek, 11 July 2007, located at http://oursaviorhoneycreek.blogspot.com/2007/07saints-clarence-jordan.html (13 November 2015); and James C. Howell, in a blog: "Heroes Found Faithful: Clarence Jordan," Myers Park UMC, Charlotte, North Carolina, 1 November 2010, located at http://heroesfoundfaithful.blogspot.com/2010/11/true-saints-never-dwell-in-splendid.html (13 November 2015).

[39] Donald E. Capps, "The Parabolic Event in Religious Autobiography," *The Princeton Seminary Bulletin* 4 (1983): 27.

[40] See Lonnie D. Kliever, *The Shattered Spectrum: A Survey of Contemporary Theology* (Atlanta: John Knox Press, 1981) 180. "Legend" is being used as a collection of stories in the life of a notable person.

[41] See especially, Frederick L. Downing, "Ascent of the Mountain: The Spiritual Awakening of Clarence Jordan," *Perspectives in Religious Studies* 41/4 (Winter 2014): 401–405.

[42] See Barnette, *Clarence Jordan: Turning Dreams into Deeds*, 6, 106; and D.B. Nicholson, "Ridgecrest," *The Christian Index* (2 July 1942): 20.

[43] Howell, in blog: "Heroes Found Faithful: Clarence Jordan," 1 November 2010.

[44] Andrew S. Chancey, "Race, Religion, and Reform: Koinonia's Challenge to Southern Society," (Ph.D. diss., University of Florida, 1998) 184.

[45] See Marsh, *The Beloved Community*, 242–43.

[46] Frank Stagg, quoted in Barnette, *Clarence Jordan: Turning Dreams into Deeds*, 103.

---

[47] H. Cornell Goerner, in Barnette, *Clarence Jordan: Turning Dreams into Deeds*, 91.

[48] Mircea Eliade writes that one of the chief characteristics of the stories we collectively value is "the creation of exemplary models for a whole society." In fact, as Eliade continues, this process itself does not appear to be out of the ordinary. It is, rather, "a very general human tendency," which is "to hold up one life-history as a paradigm and turn a historical personage into an archetype." The telling of the story and the efforts to copy the model become ways to transcend the ordinary, mundane existence. See Eliade, *Myths, Dreams, and Mysteries*, 32–33.

[49] Wilder, "Story and Story-World," 359.

[50] See Oglesby Evans, "Yours in Faith and Expectation—Clarence Jordan," 7 August 2005; and Howell, in blog: "Heroes Found Faithful: Clarence Jordan," 1 November 2010.

[51] This concept of "dangerous memory" comes from Johann Baptist Metz, *Faith in History and Society: Toward a Practical Fundamental Theology* (New York: The Seabury Press, 1980) 109–10. Metz notes that there are different types of memory. One is the memory that is a refuge, a paradise-like setting, or the "good old days." Another form is dangerous memory, where memory makes a demand on the person and reveals "new and dangerous insights for the present." Thus, totalitarian efforts seek to erase memory.

[52] Ibid.

[53] H. Cornell Goerner, quoted in Barnette, *Clarence Jordan: Turning Dreams into Deeds*, 93.

Index